Fire Insurance Inspection & Underwriting ... - Primary Source Edition

Charles Carroll Dominge, W O. Lincoln

The Rescue.

FIRE INSURANCE

INSPECTION AND UNDERWRITING

An Encyclopedic Handbook Defining Insurance Terms and Describing Processes and Materials Used in Mercantile and Manufacturing Establishments, and Their Fire Hazards

By

CHARLES C. DOMINGE

Author of First Illustrated Book of Schedule Rating

and

WALTER O. LINCOLN

Members National Fire Protection Association

Price $5.00

THE SPECTATOR COMPANY

CHICAGO OFFICE
INSURANCE EXCHANGE

135 WILLIAM STREET
NEW YORK

PREFACE

Fire insurance literature is surfeited with technical nomenclature, therefore we have tried to follow the advice of Ruskin who said, "The greatest thing any living soul can do is to see something clearly and tell it plainly."

In the last decade there have been more books written on the subject of insurance than at any time since insurance has been looked upon as a scientific problem. Most of the writings have been from the pens of men of long experience who realized the necessity of committing to print their valuable experiences for the benefit of the profession. These works have been in the main of a highly technical character designed for the use of experienced men, or at least for those who have been engaged in the profession for some time and to whom was denied the opportunity of getting the information at first hand. There are numerous admirable text books on any particular subject, but so written that only those who have had some experience in the insurance business can fully comprehend the terms and expressions that are in the writings.

As far as we know, there is no one book which can be called a "primer" for the guidance of those entering our business and who, from their inability to secure the practical elementary books for study, are handicapped at the start of their career, and must needs spend many years of close application before their advancement really begins. It is for the benefit, primarily, of the young student who seeks the rudimentary education, and to save the needless expenditure of time at the start, which has been the lot of most insurance men, that this book is presented. Our aim is to make this volume a "ready reference handbook" for general use of underwriters, inspectors, examiners, map clerks, countermen, storage clerks, schedule men, and others.

In inspection work particularly, the beginner is at a disadvantage in not knowing the names and purposes of the various machines used, or the usual materials or processes of any particular manufacture and is therefore unable to give a "word picture" in his report.

The authors have endeavored to present features which may be overlooked or forgotten by the experienced man, and as far as possible have avoided technicalities. The chemical terms mentioned are merely from a fire insurance standpoint, so as to aid in determining whether or not a certain material is hazardous. The brevity of some of the subjects is due to the desire to cite only the necessary data, with the thought in mind that any reader interested in any particular subject can secure more detailed information from books on the shelves of insurance libraries. At the present time there are very few manufacturing processes about which nothing has been written.

While strictly a fire insurance work, this book is intended also for use of members of fire departments, fire prevention bureaus, warehousemen, fire marshals, factory engineers and others employed in the conservation of life and property.

Grateful acknowledgement is hereby given to all those who have assisted us in writing this volume, especially Messrs. Charles E. Jahne, Sinclair T. Skirrow, William J. Tallamy, Thomas O. Gildersleeve, William Slavik and Walter Bladen.

The authors would appreciate being advised of any needed corrections so that changes may be made in future editions.

C. C. D.
W. O. L.

ILLUSTRATIONS

(Mostly Drawn by the Authors)

"Preventable fire is more than a private misfortune. It is a public dereliction. At a time like this of emergency and of manifest necessity for the conservation of national resources, it is more than ever a matter of deep and pressing consequence that every means should be taken to prevent this evil."

Woodrow Wilson

FIRE INSURANCE
INSPECTION AND UNDERWRITING

A

ABACA is Manila hemp.

ABANDONMENT CLAUSE—The standard policy states that there shall be no abandonment, i. e., instead of the property owner turning over what is left in the way of salvage to the company and demanding a full payment of the policy, he is obliged to take care of all damaged property and protect it from further damage to the best of his ability until an adjustment of the loss has been made.

ABATTOIR OR SLAUGHTERING-HOUSE—Usually a nuisance to neighborhood unless located in outlying district. The majority are large area, frame. Note if coal stove heat in office or lounging room; refrigerating; casing making. Casings for sausage are made from entrails, cooked, cleaned and dried, and require a boiler for steam kettles.

ABRASIVE CUTTING is performed by means of stones, sand, emery dust, glass, carborundum and in some cases by soft, friable iron alone.

ABSORPTION SYSTEMS—See Refrigeration.

ACADEMIES OR COLLEGES—Usually of very large area with unprotected floor openings including well holes, the individual rooms enclosed in lath and plaster partitions with sash doors. Common hazards are those of schools, i. e., heating, lighting, laundries, manual-training class rooms, kitchens, pranks of students, repair shops. The moral hazard is that of private ownership, unprofitableness from poor selection of location, inaccessibility, lack of transit facilities. (See School Hazards.)

ACCESSIBILITY—In reporting out-of-town risks, it is necessary to state whether the property can be easily reached by fire department and the distance to nearest company, the distance to nearest fire hydrant and alarm box, the condition of roads whether dirt, stone or other pavements, grade of road, average hydrant pressure, open bridges or other handicaps which bear on the chances of salvage. See Protected Risks; see Remote Risks.

ACCOMMODATION LINE—A line of insurance taken by a company on a poor risk to accommodate a broker whose volume of business warrants the acceptance of an occasional undesirable risk. This practice has been very much abused. Brokers who have no prestige and very little "good" business, are at times hard pressed or unable to properly cover risks whose insurance they have solicited, and therefore "peddle" the business out to large brokers on a percentage basis. See Underwriting.

ACCRUED CHARGES—This insurance is to recompense the warehouseman for charges which have accrued on goods left in his charge.

ACETATE OF ETHYL—Is a clear, colorless, volatile liquid of fragrant odor used in medicine and flavoring. Very inflammable. Flash point about 40 degrees F.

ACETATE OF METHYL—Is a clear colorless liquid. Highly inflammable. Flash point about 35 degrees F.

ACETATE—A salt formed by the union of acetic acid with a base.

ACETENE—Highly combustible gas.

ACETIC ACID—A colorless liquid obtained from the dry distillation of wood or from the oxidation of alcohol. Used in the manufacture of dye stuffs, coal tar products and various manufacturing processes. Not inflammable.

ACETIC ETHYL—Same as acetate of ethyl.

ACETONE—A colorless liquid consisting of 3 parts carbon, 3 parts hydrogen, 1 part oxygen. Obtained by dry distillation of wood. Used as solvent for nitro-cellulose in production of lacquer, and celluloid cement. Highly inflammable. Flash point about 35 degrees F. (See volatile solvents.)

ACETYL CELLULOSE—Made from cellulose and acetic anhydride. Analagous to nitro-cellulose. Used same as celluloid. Not inflammable.

ACETYLENE—A form of illuminating gas formed by the action of calcium carbide and water, in which action the lime leaves the carbon with the production of considerable heat and becomes slaked lime, while the carbon unites with the hydrogen and becomes acetylene. There is 12 times as much carbon as hydrogen in it. Inflammable. See Calcium Carbide.

ACETYLENE GAS GENERATORS—Should be located outside of insured buildings and not within five feet of any opening thereto, nor should they be opened toward any adjacent building, and must be kept under lock and key. The dimensions of the generator house to be no greater than the apparatus requires to allow convenient room for recharging and inspection of parts. The house to be thoroughly ventilated and any artificial heating necessary to prevent freezing, shall be steam or hot water systems. Generator houses not to be used for the storage of calcium carbide except that contained in the generator.

ACIDS should be kept well apart from other chemicals and in many cases from each other. Fires are best fought with water as organic substances will only feed the fire. Sand and earth are not recommended for extinguishment.

ACID WORKS (Hydrochloric or Muriatic)—Note the construction and arrangement of roasters and furnaces, glauber salts dryers and nitric retorts; arrangement and method of storing nitre and nitre bags; condensers; condition of pyrites burners, glovers tower and Guy-Lusac tower; the stills, mills for grinding nitre cakes, the elevator boot and legs, the shafting, sulphur storage, reclaiming lead pans, sealing and packing of carboys.

ACTORS—Lines on household furniture are not very attractive, unless the applicant is personally known to the broker as reliable and at the "top of the ladder" in his profession. The value is mainly personal effects and wearing apparel which must be constantly renewed "to keep in style." As this becomes out-of-date, the moral hazard becomes pertinent. See Furnished Rooms.

ADJACENT—Near but not adjoining.

ADJOINING—Buildings are adjoining when they are built against each other.

ADJUSTER—Merchandise losses present many angles to the adjuster; they may be partial or total; there may be loss by smoke to cast iron presses, or water damage to a water-pump intended for pumping water out of a mine. Such claims have been made and, unfortunately for the credit of the profession, have been allowed. Claims for smoke damage to cigars in air-tight tin cans covered with wood, because of fire 2 or 3 doors away have also been allowed; claims for smoke damage to various classes of stocks because of fire next door or in the next block are so common that the merchant who does not make a claim for smoke damage when there is a fire anywhere in his neighborhood is looked upon by underwriters as an oasis in the desert. Allowing loss on property that does not show damage, and that is not damaged indicates weakness in the adjuster, sometimes manifested in order to get business, but more times because he has not the backbone to be fair to the insured and to the company, or because he does not take pains to place the so-called damaged property before the insured and insist upon the damage thereon being shown. The adjuster must hail from the state where "Show Me" is the slogan; the adjuster should be ignorant and helpless; ignorant on values until shown, and helpless because he is compelled to follow the contract made by the company and the claimant. Probably not over one loss in fifty on merchandise comes under the heading of a book loss; the other forty-nine are damage or damage-claimed losses, to be closed by examination of the property and agreement on appraisement of the amount of loss thereon. In all cases where the total loss on goods does not exceed, say 10 to 15 per cent of the stock, taking the claimant's verbal statement of the amount of and class of goods in the part of the building where the fire occurred, verifying his story by the debris, agreeing on the amount of loss on the total loss to the stock, and then fixing the loss on the damaged goods by agreement or appraisal, is safer than settling by the books. Where the loss must be adjusted by the books, the inventory should be verified by the previous year's books in order to detect any case of double entry or purchases charged twice, or stuffing the inventory. This applies particularly to branch stores, or to stores doing a losing business, where stuffing the inventory might be necessary to maintain the character of the branch manager or the credit of the concern. The net inventory, the purchases at net invoice, the per cent of freight on net invoice, makes up the total to be accounted for at invoice and freight. The safe cash and credit; the per cent of profit over invoice cost, and all other transactions as noted in the statement of loss should be ascertained and agreed on in writing by the adjuster and the claimant before proceeding to find the net cost. Proofs should not be made up for the total loss if there be any pending unsettled questions, as a claim for total loss can be admitted at any time. The adjuster's certificate on the proof as to the amount of and honesty of the loss should be dispensed with, as it is a bad feature if the claim be contested because of acts or facts ascertained after the adjustment. When the loss to the property is fixed, ownership, names of owners, chattel mortgages, gasoline and other factors that might throw more light on the loss should be inquired into and reported with proof, but in cases where the policy is voided by acts of the insured or others, and admitted by him, the inquiry must stop.—Fireman's Fund Record.

See Valuation of Buildings, also Loss Adjustment; see Proof of Loss.

ADMIRALTY METAL is an alloy of copper, zinc and tin. Used in engine making.

ADVERTISING CONCERNS—Mild hazard, consisting of artist's rooms where designs are drawn or painted, tube colors being generally in use. Storage of plates and cuts (some very expensive), patterns and mailing records. The latter may form considerable of the value, and should be kept in duplicate or in fire-proof cabinet.

ADVERTISING MATTER—Lines should be written cautiously. Stock may be obsolete; very susceptible.

ADVERTISING NOVELTIES consist of cheap jewelry, paper, metal or wood boxes, leather and celluloid goods.

AEROPLANE MANUFACTURING consists of power

woodworking, gluing, metal working, wiring wood parts together, covering planes and rudders with linen, varnishing wood parts and propellers, coating fabrics with lacquer having a cellulose base. Main hazards are storage and use of large quantities of lacquer, woodworking, testing gasoline motors, glue melting. Usually located in old buildings, large open areas subjecting whole plant to one fire, and contents very susceptible. A small amount of heat will render a machine valueless account of removing temper of guy wires, braces and weakening framework and structure.

Dopes for Airplanes—Two classes of "dope" are now in use, and the first class, comprising varnishes, consists essentially of a solution of cellulose nitrate or pyroxylin, the second class comprising the varnishes made by dissolving cellulose acetate. According to a paper presented by Gustavue J. Esselen, Jr., before the Northeast Section of the American Chemical Society.

The great outstanding difference between the coatings given by cellulose acetate and cellulose nitrate dopes is the inflammability of the latter, a difference which will probably be emphasized more and more as the use of airplanes for peaceful purposes increases. Cellulose acetate dopes leave a non-inflammable finish. The relative behavior of the coatings left by the two types of dope is well illustrated by the fact that some gasoline can be poured on the piece of fabric coated with a good cellulose acetate dope and allowed to burn, and the fabric does not ignite. The same test applied to a pyroxlin-coated cloth results in the immediate ignition of the coating, and in the very short space of time there is nothing left of the fabric or coating but a puff of smoke.

AFFIDAVIT RISK—A risk on which the licensed companies have all the insurance they care to write, therefore it is necessary to secure insurance from unlicensed companies, through brokers specially licensed for that purpose.

AFFINITY OF CHEMICALS—The phrase chemical attraction is sometimes used to denote affinity. It signifies a tendency of different kinds of matter to unite with each other.

AFRICAN BLACK WOOD—A species of hard wood extensively used in making clarinets and fifes.

AFTER DAMP (choke damp) mixture is carbon anhydride and nitrogen resulting from explosion of fire damp.

AGAVA—A fibre, native of Mexico, called "patent hair," a substitute for horse hair.

AGENT—The authorized representative of a company with power to commit a company to liability, make endorsements, collect premiums, sign policies and other similar duties. Receives an over-writing commission above the usual brokerage. May solicit insurance as a broker. See Broker.

AGITATOR—A paddle or similar contrivance used to stir or mix material in a kettle or tank while in process of manufacture.

AIR-BRUSH—A sprayer operated under air pressure for spraying liquids.

AIR COMPRESSOR—An air pump worked under power for delivering air under pressure for various purposes.

AIR SPACE—The intervention of an air space preventing direct contact of combustible material with the heated body is essential. This prevents the combustible material attaining a dangerous temperature. One of the best known insulators for either heat or cold.

AISLES—Should be maintained in all warehouses or risks where bulk stock is kept to allow of easy access to all parts of the floor in case of fire, and at windows so that a passer-by could see the interior and so detect fire and also allow firemen to enter building. Aisles should be 2 to 4 feet wide. See Clear Space.

ALARM, AUTOMATIC—A thermostat placed on ceilings, spaced about 10 feet. Heat expands a diaphragm which causes an electrical circuit to send in an alarm to a central station. See Central Stations.

ALARM, THERMOSTATIC—Alarms consist in brief of two plates which are sensitized to heat, or a thermostatic strip between two plates. A rise in temperature forces the plates together, causing an electrical circuit which transmits the alarm. See Fire Alarm System; also Combination Red Fire Alarm Box.

ALARM VALVE—Usually a part of a sprinkler system so designed that when water flows through the sprinkler pipes an alarm is transmitted to a central station or to the engine room in the building. See Variable Pressure Alarm Valve.

ALCOHOL (ethyl or grain)—Distilled from grain. Flash point about 61 degrees F. Denatured alcohol, flash point about 55 degrees F. Methyl alcohol, inflammable, distilled from wood, flash point about 60 degrees F. Wood alcohol distilled from sawdust or wood particles. Flash point about 35 to 50 degrees F. Alcohols of different strengths give off inflammable vapors at different temperatures. Alcohol burns with a pale blue flame because it is very rich in carbon. Can be extinguished with water. See Wood Alcohol.

ALCOHOL DISTILLERIES—Distilling from high wines and juices of fruits or grains. Setting of, and ventilation of furnaces important. Stills to have plenty of ventilation. Storage to be in separate building.

ALCOHOL RECLAIMING—Used alcohol placed in steam heated mixing-tank with agitator, treated with fresh alcohol and other ingredients and then distilled in steam kettles, the alcohol passing through various water-cooled rectifiers and then put in drums. Distilling apparatus should be in well-ventilated buildings.

ALCOHOL (Solidified) is now put up in cube form for cooking and heating. It can be used on a sheet of metal or asbestos without a burner.

ALDEHYDES—Derived from sulphuric acid, alcohol and bichromate of potash. Volatile and inflammable. It is the intermediate product in the oxidation of an alcohol to an acid.

ALIEN—See Enemy Alien Clause.

ALIGNUM FIRE DOORS are a composition of raw ground asbestos mixed with silicate of soda and placed between two sheet metal plates greased with paraffin to prevent adherence. Wood strips about 2 inches square are used to form the shape. Material is then placed in a hydraulic steam press to compress the substance, and the heat drives the moisture out. Wire mesh or screens are sometimes placed in the mixture. Doors may or may not be metal covered. The only woodworking is the occasional cutting and planing of wood strips to size. Class may be likened to a general metal worker but susceptibility not so great. Mild painting hazard. Sometimes use small quantities of zapon for giving a finished surface. Zapon is a highly inflammable lacquer with a cellulose base.

ALKALI—A substance capable of combining with and thereby neutralizing or counteracting acids.

ALKALOIDS are such substances as morphine, cocaine and the like.

ALLOY—When metals are melted and mixed together they form alloys.

ALMOND OIL is used in pharmacy for making emulsions and ointments.

ALMOND PASTE manufacturing. Grinding and crushing almonds, mixing and cooking in steam heated kettles with glucose.

ALMS HOUSES—Correctional institutions and insane asylums have a severe moral hazard due to the defective mentalities and proclivities of the inmates, such as pyromaniacs, which might take a vicious turn and set fire to the building to escape therefrom. Usually of a large area, with open shafts and well holes. Boiler house, kitchen, laundry, paint and carpenter shops, also attics used for storage are important hazards. See Asylums.

ALPHABETICAL LIST—A rating bureau booklet containing charges to be added to the "base rate" for goods in storage stores. See Storage.

ALTERNATING CURRENT—Difference between direct and alternating current: Direct current flows continually in one direction; alternating current flows back and forth, constantly changing direction around the circuit. A direct current of same voltage is considered the more dangerous.

ALTERNATING MOTION—Up or down, or backward and forward, instead of revolving.

ALUM POTASSIUM (aluminum sulphate)—Can be used as good fire-extinguishing agents.

ALUMINATES—Compounds of alumina with potassium or sodium.

ALUMINUM—A white metal which melts about the fusing point of zinc. In powdered form, burns readily. The manufacturing process is very hazardous.

ALUMINUM BRONZE POWDERS are of different degrees of fineness, the finer forms being extremely hazardous on account of the ease with which they may become ignited. Water when applied to the burning powder increases the force of the flames and may create an explosion.

ALUMINUM PAINT—See Bronzing Liquids.

AMALGAM—A combination of any metal with mercury.

AMBER—A fossil resin. Inflammable. Highly electrical when rubbed. Used extensively for pipe stems. Imitation amber, may be celluloid or gum resins.

AMMETER, AMPEREMETER—An instrument for measuring the quantity of electrical current flowing in a circuit.

AMMONIA is a compound of two gases, hydrogen and nitrogen, one atom of nitrogen and three atoms of hydrogen; it is a gas at ordinary temperature and pressure. Chiefly obtained as a by-product in the manufacture of illuminating gas from the distillation of coal, and from the manufacture of coke in by-product coke ovens.

AMMONIA GAS—Not inflammable. In case of fire the heat will cause the gas to expand and cylinders to burst (coils usually have lead joints which expand and prevent rupture). Ammonia gas will kill almost instantly when a fire breaks out where ammonia is used for refrigeration, therefore no one will stay to fight it and the plant burns unless the firemen are equipped with helmets. In cold storage risks, heat has been known to expand the cold air to such an extent as to burst the walls of the building. It is soluble in water, the solution commonly called aqua ammonia. See Refrigeration.

AMMONIA HELMET as manufactured by American-La-France Fire Engine Co., consists simply of a sturdy leather helmet which is pulled over the head, and a tank which is swung from the shoulder. By means of a flexible metallic tube, pure air from the tank is passed to the interior of the helmet, thus affording the wearer an ample supply of pure air; simply opening a valve makes the outfit ready for action.

AMMONIA WATER—See Aqua Ammonia.

AMMONIUM CARBONATE—See Heat Liberation.

AMMONIUM NITRATE—See Heat Liberation.

AMMONIUM HYDROXIDE—See Aqua Ammonia.

AMMONIUM PICRATE—A crystalline powder of yellow color, highly explosive.

AMMONIUM SALTS are volatile.

AMMONIUM SULPHATE—Derived from gas works; principally used in fertilizer plants. Not considered hazardous.

AMMUNITION—Not necessarily the same as munitions, the former applying to explosives and the latter to supplies of war.

AMMUNITION FACTORIES—Blending, dry houses and loading of fuses are the most hazardous. Loading fuses, if properly arranged, is not dangerous. Powder house drying and blending-houses are seldom insured.

AMOLENE—A benzine substitute, classed as kerosene.

AMPERE—The electrical unit for measuring current, as 200 ampere. An ampere is that current which one volt will force through one ohm of resistance.

AMPEREMETER—See Ammeter.

AMYL ALCOHOL—Prepared from the residue of grain alcohol distillation, known also as fusel oil.

AMYL ACETATE—Prepared by treating amyl alcohol with acetate of lime in the presence of sulphuric acid and distilling. A clear, colorless liquid, having an odor like bananas. Used as a solvent for nitrocellulose. Flash point 65 to 70 degrees F. See Banana Oil.

AMYL ACETATE LACQUER (Pear Perfume) contains celluloid in solution.

AMUSEMENT ENTERPRISES—Usually large area, light frame construction in sparsely settled locations; season occupancy only. Fires caused by cigarettes and matches. Bad fire record.

ANÆSTHETICS—Volatile liquids (used to produce anæsthesia), such as ether, chloroform, nitrous oxides.

ANGLE IRON—A bar of iron with cross section shaped like the letter "L" or at an angle of 90 degrees.

ANGOLA is a mixture of cotton and wool.

ANHYDRIDES—Compounds free from water. See Hydrates.

ANHYDROUS AMMONIA, by reason of its ability to liquify under comparatively low pressure, is most generally employed in refrigerating and ice making machines. It is compressed liquid gas, non-combustible.

ANILINE is a product of coal tar produced by distillation. Also prepared by reducing nitro-benzine with iron and hydrochloric acid.

ANILINE DYES—Process consists of cold mixing in wooden tanks, boiling in steel tanks, kettles and retorts (some under pressure), gas or steam heated. The raw materials are aniline oil, napthalene, nitro-benzolé, zinc dust, sodium nitrate, sodium nitrite, nitric acid, fuming and concentrated sulphuric acid, muriatic, hydrochloric and acetic acids, caustic soda, sodium bisulphide, carbolic acid, dimethyl and ethyl aniline, salt-petre, castor oil, barium peroxide, prussiate of potash, bichromate of potash, red oil, hydrogen peroxide, salts, etc. The first process is to make the intermediates (use dimethyl and ethyl aniline and similar substances), or base for dyes, and then to produce and precipitate the colors themselves, followed by drying, grinding and mixing of finished colors. Some of these chemicals are inflammable and carelessness or accident will cause fire or explosion by combining certain chemicals. Large quantities of chemicals, alcohol, acids and oxidizing agents are a source of danger.

In nitrosating, chemicals (usually dimethyl and diethyl aniline), are placed in wood tanks with water, ice and acids, then treated with solution of sodium nitrite and acids, dried in centrifugal extractors.

Autoclaves are used in manufacturing intermediate aniline products such as dimethyl and ethyl aniline (a mixture of aniline oil, alcohol and acids). They are steel retorts, asbestos clad, heated by direct gas heat, under pressure, to about 350 deg. F., and developing and maintaining a pressure of about 500 lbs. for several hours, the resulting product contained therein and thus formed is treated with alkalies, redissolved and washed. Autoclaves should have a relief valve of one-half inch and vent and smoke pipes to outer air.

Color drying and grinding and alcohol reclaiming are severe hazards. When grinding dry colors, fires are so frequent that an employee is usually stationed at the grinder with a hose or fire extinguisher. See Paste Colors. See Color Works.

ANIMAL CHARCOAL (or Bone Black) consists of a charcoal formed by the destructive distillation of bones. Non-inflammable solid. See Charcoal.

ANIMAL OILS are divided into two classes—the first class is prepared from the fat of land animals, while the second class is derived from fish or some of the warm blooded marine animals. They are inflammable and would readily assist a fire in a building, but are practically without the spontaneous combustion hazard. See Vegetable Oils.

ANIMI—A resinous gum used in varnish manufacturing.

ANNATTO—A yellow-red pigment, chiefly used in dyeing silk.

ANNEALING—The heating and gradual cooling of metals, glass, etc., for the purpose of removing brittleness or increasing ductility. High temperatures required and setting of furnaces important.

ANNEALING FURNACES (used in glass works), resemble ordinary bakers' ovens, arranged in series of three or four adjoining, and heated by gas flames. The hot glassware is introduced by hand and removed from one oven to another, each being heated at a reduced temperature to perfect annealing without rupture.

ANTHRACENE—A product of the distillation of coal found in the residual tar. Boiling point about 550 degrees F. Anthracene is separated from the tar distillate by cooling and freezing, and is finally purified by washings in naphtha. This process should only be done in a detached building and there should be no artificial light or heat therein.

ANTIMONY oxidizes when very hot. Its oxide is volatile.

ANTIMONY SULPHIDE, used in match heads, very inflammable and in burning gives off sulphur dioxide.

ANTIQUES—Usually consist of porcelains, furniture, draperies, odds and ends of novelties. The collection of antiques is usually a hobby and in the eyes of the owner, the value increases in the event of a fire. Should not be insured unless inventoried. Dealers in high class goods usually keep the smaller and more valuable articles in a vault. Real antiques cannot be replaced, and, like old wine, the value increases with age. The moral hazard is important. Inspection and mercantile report required by most underwriters. Antiques, so-called, are being made in factories devoted to that purpose. See Art Galleries.

ANVIL MANUFACTURING—Hazards of machine shop, foundry, pattern shop and storage. Large drop hammers are sometimes used, and small fires may so affect them as to warp the beds of the hammers and render them useless, except as old iron.

ANVILS—The combustible floor, 4 feet all around, should be protected against falling red-hot particles.

APARTMENT HOTEL—A hotel in which apartments are rented in suites for a term usually not less than a month, in which there are no kitchens, dining rooms or serving rooms, but a common dining room. See Hotels.

APARTMENT HOUSE—A building occupied by three or more families for dwelling purposes only. The **"New Law"** apartments (of New York City), are much more desirable risks than the old type in that the grade floor, and sometimes the second floor, is of fire-proof construction; i. e., brick, terra cotta, or concrete arches on steel beams, and the hallways and dumb waiter shafts throughout are either brick, terra cotta, or plaster block witth metal-covered (kalameined) doors at openings. The exterior light courts are usually very large.

The **old type** of apartments are of the ordinary joisted floor construction; the floor openings, such as stairways, vent shafts and dumb waiter shafts, are of combustible material. The exterior light courts are usually very small and have ordinary windows facing the windows of adjoining buildings in the row. Many fires have traveled from one building to another through these exterior (or interior) shafts. See Dwellings.

APEX—A point in either chord of a truss where two web members meet.

APOTHECARIES—See Drug Stores.

APPLICATION FOR INSURANCE—Legally, it should

be made out and signed by the applicant. In common practice, an application is made verbally or the facts concerning the proposed insurance are written in by the agent or counterman. It should state the name, location, amount, date of commencement and expiration, property covered, liens and encumbrances. See Binder.

APPRAISALS FOR CO-INSURANCE—When it is desired to insure buildings held by trustees, executors, administrators or others acting in a fiduciary capacity on behalf of minors or incompetents, a certified appraiser may be engaged to fix the amount in advance so that the policies will comply with the provisions of the co-insurance clause. Appraisers' fees are usually as follows: Valuation $10,000 or under, $10; $10,000 to $20,000, $1 per thousand; $20,000 to $100,000, $2 for first $20,000 and 50 cents per $1,000 in excess over $20,000; $100,000 or over, $60 for first $100,000 and 25 cents per $1,000 for the excess of $100,000.

APRON—A covering of timber or metal to protect a surface against the action of water flowing over it. In theatres, it is the portion of the stage floor which projects into the auditorium. Also has many other meanings.

APPROVED—Signifies that the device used has the approval of the Board of Underwriters, and has been tested by the Underwriters Laboratories. Such devices are always labelled.

AQUA AMMONIA—A clear colorless liquid consists of ammonia gas dissolved in water. Non-hazardous.

AQUA FORTIS is the common name for nitric acid.

AQUA REGIA—See Nitro-Hydrochloric Acid.

ARBATINE—A paint thinner, similar to turpentine.

ARBOR—See Journal.

ARC—Made by electricity; is always productive of heat, the intensity of which is dependent upon the voltage and amount of current.

ARC LAMP—An electric lamp in which the light is produced by an electric arc formed by passing a current across the space between two carbons. Open arc lamps should never be used where explosives or inflammable vapors, dust or light flyings are present.

ARCADES—See Shooting Galleries.

ARCH, as used in building construction, is that portion of a floor between beams or girders; or an opening through a wall.

ARCHITECT'S PLANS—Drawings, specifications and blue prints take a higher rate than the office fixtures. Benzine is used for cleaning smudge marks from tracings. The

Before any building is erected, the architect should have a competent insurance engineer review the plans with a double purpose in view: First, to make a building safer. Second, to lower the insurance rate.

wise architect will submit the plans for his proposed building to an insurance rating expert before the work is started so that he may obtain the lowest rate of insurance when the structure is completed. See Plans.

ARCO SPOTZOFF—A cleaning fluid, flashes at ordinary temperatures; classed as volatile, inflammable liquid.

AREA OF A BUILDING includes the thickness of the walls. Floor area is the space inside of the walls excluding partitions. The greater the area, the greater are the possibilities of a fire spreading. Areas in excess of 5,000 feet are usually penalized in rating schedules. Fire stops of brick or concrete walls, 12 inches thick, with approved fire doors, should be provided to decrease the area.

AREAWAYS—Fires are spread to basements by means of poorly protected window openings. Pedestrians drop cigarette butts and mischievous boys make fires in them. Careless tenants use them for rubbish dumps. See Cellar Fires.

ARGOLS—The scrapings from the inside of wine casks, from which cream of tartar is made.

ARMORED—A name sometimes used for reinforced concrete.

ARMORIES—The enormous area and height are the predominating poor features. The height and span of roof require exceptionally heavy walls and supports. Hazards of careless smokers, armorers' shops, ammunition storage, paint shops, stables, mild dance hall hazard and hospital. On January 17, 1917, the Second Regiment Armory at Albany burned causing a nearly total loss. About 2,000,000 rounds of ammunition exploded, impeding the progress of the firemen and rendering fire fighting dangerous and difficult.

ARRIS—The sharp edge or ridge on stone or metal.

ARSENALS usually contain a large amount of explosives. The mixing and blending should be located away from exposed buildings.

ARSENIC ACID—A white crystalline solid material, not inflammable.

ARSENIC TRIOXIDE—See arsenious acid.

ARSENIOUS ACID—A white, solid matter not inflammable.

ARSON—The burning of property, usually spite work or for revenge; malicious burning.

ART GALLERIES—Usually large open areas with open or poorly protected floor openings and numerous well holes. The contents, mainly paintings, bric-a-brac, and other easily damaged articles. As a rule under careful management, but subject to severe loss in case of fire. See Antiques.

ART GOODS—A delicate stock usually consisting of a large proportion of fabrics both modern and old, which usually prove a total loss in case of fire, except pure gold or silver threaded goods, which can be smeltered and the precious metal reclaimed. Pictures and bric-a-brac form a large value.

ARTIFICIAL FLOWERS AND FEATHERS—See Flowers and Feathers.

ASBESTIC—A composition mined in Canada containing a large percentage of asbestos.

ASBESTIC PLASTER is made by mixing lime, putty, freshly slaked lime, and a certain percentage of asbestos.

ASBESTOS—A mineral, both fibrous and crystalline. Can be carded, spun and woven. Not affected by acids. Three general classes, amphibole, antophyllite and serpentine. The first two are much alike and are silicates of lime, magnesia and alumina (hornblend). The serpentine is a hydrated silicate of magnesia.

ASBESTOS BOARDS—Used as lumber; are approximately 80 per cent. portland cement and 20 per cent. asbestos fibre, moulded and pressed into sheets one-eighth inch to one inch thick under hydraulic pressure. Can be worked with machine tools.

ASBESTOS GOODS—Such as paper, textiles, gaskets, washers, curtains, shingles, boards, belt linings and electrical goods. Processes are mixing, grinding, rolling, picking, carding, weaving, spinning, drying with direct heat. Materials used include benzine, japan, mineral oils, asphaltum, graphite, wax, cotton and excelsior. Hazards include carpenter shop, foundry, metal working, paper and textile machinery, printing. In making roof paper use paper and cloth saturated with asphalt, oil solutions, cement, and coated with rubber solution thinned with benzine. In making tape and washers do weaving and winding and treat with rubber cement, then vulcanize. The foundry, mixing house for naphtha, rubber and cement mixtures, the oil house, the benzine vault and japanning room should be outside in separate enclosures. Drying,

Steel Theater Curtain, Lined with Asbestos.

picking, carding, can soldering and vulcanizing are also important hazards.

ASBESTOS INSULATORS—For pipe coverings and boiler casings are composed of about 85 per cent carbonate of magnesia and 15 per cent asbestos fibre. When applied at least 1 inch thick are very effective. Applied same as cement. Besides its economic value, it decreases the degree of heat radiated from a boiler or pipe. See Insulators.

ASBESTOS PAINT—See Fire Resisting Solutions.

ASBESTOS THEATRE CURTAINS—The proscenium curtain shall be composed of asbestos of long, tough, flexible fibre, twisted and wrapped upon substantial brass wire thread and woven into a close, even cloth, 3 feet wide. The strips must be lapped not less than 1 inch and sewed with two lines of asbestos and brass wire stitching. All strips shall be in one continuous length the full height of the curtain. There shall be at least 4 laps of the cloth at the top and at the bottom of the curtain to form pockets for the top and bottom bars, and the curtain shall be lapped on the sides to form a continuous reinforcement for the guide clips.

The curtain shall be at least 36 inches wider than the proscenium masonry opening, and at least 2 feet higher than the highest point of the proscenium arch. It shall have wrought iron or rolled steel top and bottom bars proportioned to size to the width of the curtain, but not less than 1 inch by 2½ inches. The top and bottom bars shall be connected by four steel wire cables $\frac{3}{8}$ inches in diameter to support the weight of the bottom bar.

The curtain must be supported by steel lifting cables, one at each end and intermediate points not over 10 feet apart. It shall be balanced by a counterweight only to such extent that when it is tripped the descent will be made in 15 seconds. The curtain must operate in guides bolted every 2 feet to the proscenium wall. All apparatus connected with the curtain or its operation shall be of metal. All paint used on the curtain must be incombustible. Underwriters' requirements.) See Theatres.

ASBESTOS WOOD is made of short asbestos fibres.

ASCHE BUILDING FIRE (Triangle Waist), March 25,

1911, 23-29 Washington Place, New York City, 10-story fire-proof, steel and cast iron skeleton construction, terra cotta arches, ironwork protected with cement and tile. Fire supposed to have been caused by cigarette or match dropped in basket of clippings. The 145 lives lost due principally to locked exit doors.

ASHES should be kept only in metal receptacles, the bottom of which should be raised above the floor. Numerous fires are caused by hot ashes in wooden or cardboard boxes.

ASHLAR—A wall facing of stone, usually of a granular nature such as granite or marble. Easily damaged by direct or radiated heat from an exposure fire resulting in considerable loss under building insurance policies.

ASPHALINE consists of bran impregnated with chlorate of potash.

ASPHALT—A bituminous substance which probably owes its origin to a vegetable matter which has been subjected to a slow process of decomposition or decay resulting in the production of a bituminous coal, from which, by volcanic agency, the asphalt has been distilled and diffused over neighboring districts.

ASPHALT WORKS—In most plants the asphalt is already refined when received from the previous plant, then placed in coal fired or steam kettles, then roughly mixed with cracked stone and sand from steam heated rotary driers. Usually located in old frame buildings outside of protection. This class is not considered desirable insurance.

ASPHALTUM PAINT OR VARNISH consists of asphaltum solution of benzine or other solvents.

ASSAYERS—Careful class of people. Ores are ground, washed and valuable minerals extracted by dissolving same in acid (heated) baths. The minerals are then reclaimed by electricity and melted in annealing and smelting furnaces. The laboratory and acid sections are the most hazardous.

ASSETS are the funds, stocks, bonds or other resources from which the company obtains funds to carry on the business. See Liability of a Company.

ASSIGNEE—A person assigned by a court to take charge

of the affairs of an insolvent firm, to wind up an estate or similar functions. See Trade Reports.

ASSIGNEE'S SALES STORES—Goods purchased at low figures may be insured for much larger amounts. Should only be written after careful inspection.

ASSURED, OR THE INSURED—The person mentioned in the policy as the legal owner or custodian of property set forth in the form of the policy.

ASTRAL OIL—See Mineral-Burning Oil.

ASTROGAL—A small moulding about semi-circular or semi-elliptic and either plain or ornamented by carving.

ASYLUMS—Hazards of manual-training class rooms, work shops, weaving raffia and dyeing same with aniline or benzine-thinned colors, carpet weaving. See Alms Houses.

"ATE"—Chemical termination applied to certain salts.

ATOM—An indivisible particle. The smallest portion into which an elemental substance can be divided.

ATTICS should be kept clean of rubbish or old furniture, as the dry, unprotected wood is easily ignited and the fire flashes quickly over the surface. In dwellings, usually the dumping place for all kinds of trash. In frame rows, where attics or roof spaces communicate, fires travel quickly from one building to the entire row. See Roof Space, also Frame Rows.

ATTRITION MACHINES are high speed machines, revolving at 1,500 or more revolutions per minute. Consist of two metal discs, separated by a narrow space and turning in opposite directions, between which the material to be ground is passed.

AUCTION STOCKS are of varying description, from diamonds and precious stones to second-hand clothing and furniture. In the latter class, the premises are usually crowded, untidy and have work shops for repairing and refinishing goods. As a class, are not desirable.

AUTHORIZATIONS—Fire insurance companies have underwriters or examiners to make authorizations on the risks which they assume. Authorizations usually read so much on building and so much on contents. Say an authorization is $125,000 on building or $75,000 on contents, or three-fifths as much contents as building being five-thirds as much building as contents. In other words, if the line is $125,000 and a $25,000 policy is written, the company is still open for $100,000 line on building, or three-fifths as much on the contents, $60,000. See Reinsurance.

AUTOCLAVE—See Aniline Dyes.

AUTOGENOUS WELDING—Acetylene gas, blau gas or hydrogen used. Two cylinders of 250 cubic feet of compressed combustible gas or one day's supply permitted. Reserve cylinders of gas should be kept outside of building some distance away. If inside, to be in vault of 8 inches of brickwork or 4 inches of concrete, with approved fire door, and ventilated to outer air. The National Board permits, at one time, five cylinders to be kept, if necessary, in a double-walled metal closet, ventilated, with fire door equivalent to walls of the closet. See Blow Pipes, also Oxy-Acetylene Welding.

AUTOMAT—See Embroideries.

AUTOMATIC DOOR OR WINDOW—One which closes automatically by means of a device operated by heat.

AUTOMATIC FIRE DOOR RELEASE—In the near future it is expected that the N. F. P. A. will require an automatic door release in place of the present fusible links in almost all cases. After exhaustive tests as to the relative efficiency of the fusible links and a fire-door release, the N. F. P. A. says:

"The rate of temperature rise device is very much more sensitive to fire than the fusible link, and under the same fire conditions will operate and release fire-doors far in advance of the fusible link.

"In the tests made, the rate of temperature rise device operated in all cases in sufficient time to permit the doors to close before there was any danger of fire passing through the wall opening, while in only one case was it clear that this was accomplished by a fusible link, and in this case the margin of safety was slight. In two cases the fusible links failed to operate, although the rate of temperature rise device operated in 34 seconds and in 1 minute and 15 seconds, respectively, in these tests.

"In the first and second tests, the rate of temperature rise device operated in approximately one-third of the time required for the most sensitive fusible links, and in about one-fourth of the time required for the least sensitive of the fusible links.

"In the third and fourth tests, the rate of temperature rise device operated and the fusible links failed to operate.

"The tests indicate that under average normal conditions in fairly still air an approved form of rate of temperature rise device will probably operate in less than one minute when exposed to reasonably small freely burning fires several feet distant, and that 1½ minutes is a safe limit of performance under such conditions. The tests also indicate that about double this, or 3 minutes, is a reasonable limitation for fusible links under the conditions mentioned."

The release is an approved device of a pneumatic compensating type, the mechanism consisting of one or more air chambers, a system of levers and a diaphragm mounted in a metal case. The release operates when the rate of temperature increase is abnormal, as in fire conditions, or at the rate of 15 degrees or more a minute. The device will release a fire-door from an incipient fire 25 feet distant.

AUTOMATIC SPRINKLERS—See Sprinklers.

AUTOMOBILE BODY BUILDERS may use converted wagon builders or wheelwright shops. Hazards of wood and metal working include oily floors, varnish and paint hazard, celluloid for windshields, upholstering, picker for hair, gasolene in tanks of cars, gasoline for cleaning grease from parts which are to be painted.

AUTOMOBILE FIRES originating about the engine from back-fires, short circuits of electric wiring, overheated breaks, gasoline on fire in carburettor, etc., are hard to extinguish. A quantity of oil on the engine or in drip pan feeds the fire. Water is of little value. Sand or dirt thrown on is better, but a carbon-tetra chloride (base) extinguisher is best. See Back-fires in Automobiles, also Gasoline Spray for Automobiles and Oxygen Cleaning Process.

AUTOMOBILE TIRES—Many, when shipped from the factory, are wrapped in a paper, the inner side of which has been treated with a water-proof solution. When the paper is wet, the asphaltum composition adheres to the tire. Unless it can be thoroughly removed with benzine, the tires are classed as seconds. All tire stocks should be skidded.

AVERAGE OR CO-INSURANCE CLAUSE—The 80 per cent clause is an "equalizer." It equalizes the payment for indemnity and cost of same among property owners by compelling the insured to become a co-insurer (as an individual insurance company), when he fails to maintain the proper percentage of insurance to value. It does not mean that a company pays only 80 per cent of the amount of loss, but it does mean that where there is a deficiency of insurance, payment is made only in the ratio that the insurance bears to 80 per cent of the actual or cash value of the property covered. The clause is inoperative when: 1—The conditions have been fulfilled; 2—When the insurance exceeds 80 per cent of value; 3—When loss exceeds 80 per cent of value; 4—In case of total loss.

In case of total loss, the insured automatically becomes a co-insurer when his insurance is less than the value of the property. He can collect only the face value of his policies and must stand the balance of the loss himself. When the loss exceeds 80 per cent of value, the company pays policy in full.

The average clause was established for the purpose of forming a uniform basis of value upon which rates could be fixed without unfair discrimination against either the insurance company or the insured. It has been demonstrated that values would not be insured above 50 per cent were it not for the co-insurance clause as the average loss seldom exceeds that figure and the companies would thus be deprived of an equal proportion of premiums. Furthermore, poor risks are usually fully insured and losses on such property are paid from premiums derived from good risks. From the side of the insured, the justice of the average clause may be explained thus: Two building of $10,000 each are erected side by side. One owner decides to insure for $2,500 at the rate of 1 per cent and pays a premium of $25 with no co-insurance required. His neighbor insures for $5,000, at rate of 1 per cent, and pays $50 premium with no co-insurance. Fire occurs and damages each building to the extent of $2,500, which amount each owner collects. The person carrying the larger policy has been discriminated against as his neighbor collects 100 per cent of insurance to his 50 per cent.

The 80 per cent clause is used where the actual or sound value fluctuates; the 100 per cent. clause where the owner always knows the value of the property.

Example, showing inequality of premium income and loss payment, with and without co-insurance:

Value.	Ins. carried.	Rate.	Premium.	Co-insurance.	Ins. required	Loss.	Co. pays.
$10000	$2000	1%	$20.	none	$2000	$2000	$2000
10000	5000	1%	50.	80%	8000	2000	1250

Example—80 per cent. co-insurance clause:

Value of property.	Ins. required.	Ins. carried.	Deficiency	Loss.	Co. pays.
$10000	$8000	$6000	$2000	$4000	$3000 or 6/8ths
			Assured's proportion		1000 or 2/8ths

Example—80 per cent. clause when loss exceeds 80 per cent. of value:

Value of property.	Ins. required.	Ins. carried.	Deficiency	Loss.	Co. pays.
$10000	$8000	$6000	$2000	$8500	$6000

See Appraisals; see Adjustments.

100 Per Cent. Clause—Means that the insured agrees to carry insurance equal to the full value of the property covered. Similar to purchasing commodities, the company allows a reduction of 10 per cent. in the rate where the clause is attached to policies as an incentive to buy more insurance. The benefit to the assured also lies in the fact that he can carry 20 per cent. more insurance with but 12½ per cent. more premium outlay by virtue of the 10 per cent. rate reduction. Thus:

Property value.	Co-insurance.	Ins. required.	Rate.	Premium.
$5000	80%	$4000	1%	$40.00
5000	100%	5000	1% —10	45.00

Example—100 per cent. co-insurance clause:

Value of property.	Ins. required.	Ins. carried.	Deficiency	Loss.	Co. pays.
$10000	$10000	$8000	$2000	$5000	$4000 or 8/10ths
			Assured stands balance or		1000 or 2/10ths

AVERAGE RISK—The basis of all insurance, fire, life, marine, etc., is based on the law of average. In fire underwriting, the "line" is based on the average inherent physical condition and hazards of each class of risk. A risk below average is one wherein the conditions surrounding it inject hazards or conditions not found in the ordinary risk, and is above average when the fire hazard is lessened by the absence of any substance, process, etc., which may be classed as one of the inherent hazards of the class. See Line.

AWNING MANUFACTURING—Cutting, sewing, pipe cutting, threading, and painting are practically the only hazards.

AWNINGS—It is desirable, from a company's standpoint, to leave this item out of the building form, as many fires are caused by cigarettes and matches carelessly thrown from windows onto the awnings. Forms usually limit the amount of coverage to a nominal sum.

AXLE BOX—See Journal Box.

AXLE GREASE—Made from a mixture of heavy mineral oil with soaps made from the saponification of rosin oil, oleic acid, stearic acid with an alkaline metal and carbonate of soda. Cheap grades made of grease graphite and heavy petroleum oils. No boiling is required. Hazards are steam-heated kettles, storage of grease and oily condition of premises.

AZOTINE—A richly nitrogenous product soluble in water, obtained by treating with superheated steam, fabrics containing wool and cotton. Used as a fertilizer.

A1 METAL POLISH is not an approved benzine substitute.

B

BACKING—The rough masonry of a wall faced with finer work.

BACK DRAUGHTS—The phenomena of "back draughts" is the dread of fire fighters, for they never know at what moment they may be caught by one of these outbursts of flame. A "back draught" is really an explosion. When there is not a sufficient supply of air to produce complete combustion, the combustible will give off, in addition to the products of combustion, a gas which is combustible. This gas, when mixed with air, becomes either a combustible or an explosive, according to the mixture. When the adjustment of air and gas is a proper one, the resultant explosion is severe enough to wreck the building. Such a "back draught" is usually accompanied by a burst of flame.

BACK-FIRES IN GASOLENE ENGINES are caused by the improper "timing" of the gasoline engine and by improper adjustment of carburetor. A flame varying in length shoots from the air suction of the carburetor. The distance of the air suction pipe from the floor and from oil and waste depends upon the size of the machine and whether it is of horizontal or vertical type. See Gasoline Engines, also Automobile Fires.

BACK-PLASTERING—An extra coating of rough brown plaster on lath between the outer sheathing and the inner or finish plaster, thus securing two air spaces.

BAD FIRE RISKS—(Fireman's Fund Record.) Nice big **farmhouses** from which the family have moved to town, leaving them as camps for hired men, without watchful wives and mothers to smell smoke and care for stoves, lamps and candles. The hired men are careless, absent most of the time, and fire occurs. See Moral Hazard.

BAFFLE PLATE—A metal shield placed midway between the burners of a gas stove and the stand on which it rests. Baffles are used in some forms of condensers to "baffle" the gas or liquid during a distillation process. There are other similar usages.

BAGASSE BURNER—The furnace in which "bagasse" or waste sugar cane is burned.

BAGGING FACTORIES produce considerable lint, and machinery and fixtures are usually coated with it. Main hazard is fibre weaving. As a class, poor fire risks.

BAKERIES—In order of their hazards—pie, cake, bread, biscuit, cracker, commission. Considerable grease is used in pie and cake bakeries, hence the additional hazard. Commission bakers buy and sell but do no baking. The small bakery is, as a rule, a more serious fire menace than the larger. In large establishments more attention is given to up-keep and care. Brick ovens (wood, coal or gas heated), unless built under sidewalk or under fireproof ceiling, should have plenty of space between top of oven and flooring or roof above, and set on concrete or earth base. Chimney should conform to Underwriters' rules. Setting of confectioner's stove important. Gas plate for heating grease for pans, and wood or metal closet in which is set a gas stove for "proofing" cakes, are also found.

Portable gas heated ovens, as now installed, are usually well arranged, but may be set too near combustible partitions. The floor protection should be the same as for large coal ranges or furnaces. See Matzoth Bakery.

BAKERS' SUPPLY DEALERS—Stock consists of baking soda, lard, spices, sugar, jellies, shortening greases, flour, pie fillings, machinery, pans and moulds used by bakers. Making pie fillings and jellies, using essential oils, cologne spirits, sesame oil, olive oil, bottling of extracts, heating of kettles and bottling cotton-seed oil are usual hazards.

BAKING POWDER—Made of starch, phosphate of soda, and bicarbonate of soda. In manufacture, hazards are sifting, mixing, grinding, drying, paper or wood box-making, dust, and label printing.

BALK, a large beam of lumber.

BALL-COCK—A cistern valve at one end of lever, at the other end of which is a floating ball. The ball rises and falls with the water in the cistern and thus opens and shuts the valve.

BALLOON FRAME—One of the poorest methods of construction. The frame work is of light material, neither mortised or tenoned, continuous spaces between studs from cellar to garret which act as flues for a fire. "In this construction, the studs as well as the corner posts are carried from the sills (i.e., the flat timber which lies along the top of the foundation wall) continuously to the wall plate (usually called plate) at the top of the wall, and the floor beams of the second and third stories are carried by pieces, two by six inches, called "ribbons," spiked securely to the studs. They are stronger if let into the posts or studs. This type of construction costs somewhat less than the braced frame. If well braced with long struts and interties are strong enough for all practical purposes; in fact it forms a rigid structure." (How to Build a Home.) See Braced Frame.

BALSAMS—Are quite inflammable and have low melting points.

BANANA OIL—Prepared by acting upon amyl alcohol with acetate of lime and sulphuric acid, and distilling same.

BANANA RIPENING risks. Usually in low, dark basements with inferior tenants. Hazards consist of an abundance of straw or salt hay, and gas radiators with rubber tubes set among this combustible material.

BANK VAULTS or record vaults. The nature of contents requires massive construction to resist fire, burglary, building collapse or explosion. Ceiling to be 4 inches thicker than walls, which should be built with air space between inner and outer wall. Doors, usually an outer and inner door with a sort of entry between which forms an air space. Doors should be steel, lined with 6 inches of concrete where in pairs, or 16 inches thick where single. All material should be on skids or shelves, and sills raised to prevent water damage. See Vaults.

BARBER SHOPS conducted by natives of southern Europe have shown a surprisingly high loss ratio. The equipment is subjected to considerable wear and tear, and there is considerable incentive to sell old fixtures (especially if upholstered and out of date) to insurance companies. The new enamelled fixtures are usually bought on installments. As attractiveness is a valuable stock in trade, it is best to decline unattractive shops. Few companies care for this class.

BARBER SUPPLIES. Stock consists of perfumes, cosmetics, soaps, brushes, cups. Soap making in a small way, making and bottling perfumes. Use alcohol, essential oils, vegetable oils and compounds of the same. Direct heat may be used in heating oils or emulsions.

BARGE BOARDS—Boards nailed against the outer surface of a wall along the slopes of a gable end of a house to hide the rafters and to make a neat appearing job.

BARIUM CHLORATE—See Chlorate.

BARIUM NITRATE consists of a heavy white crystalline-salt. Classed as not dangerous, but combustible when mixed with carbonaceous bodies.

BARIUM PEROXIDE, barium dioxide. Incombustible alone, but when mixed with organic matter is dangerously inflammable.

BARK, the exterior covering of the trunk and branches of a tree. If piled near tannery or mill the hazard is practically that of the factory. If near railroad, the piles are liable to be set on fire by locomotive sparks.

BARLEY in bags is said to be subject to spontaneous combustion.

BARREL (EMPTY) STOCKS—Underwriters should write this class with caution. There have been more than one fire of unexplained origin on the barrel dealers' premises, as many barrels formerly contained oils, acids, chemicals, etc. Where barrels formerly contained chlorate of potash there is danger from spontaneous combustion on account of the wood being impregnated with this substance.

BARREL STORAGE and re-coopering shops. Barrels, empty or containing a small amount of alcohol, high proof liquors, gasoline or benzine if left in yard where the rays of the sun strike them will vaporize and cause fire if artificial light is brought in contact with the bung hole. The height of piles and spacing are important. Usually frame construction. Barrel heater important hazard. Also painting heads of barrels with benzine-thinned paint. See Cooperages.

BASEMENT SHOPS—Where work is of a manufacturing nature it is not, as a general rule, considered a desirable risk. The lack of floor space brings about untidiness and make-shift heating devices. Swinging gas brackets frequently found. Fires in this class are very numerous.

BATH HOUSES—Those located at seashore resorts usually are of light frame construction and large area. Unsafe gas brackets and temporary heating apparatus may be found. As they are only "season" risks, considerable rubbish is liable to collect in open space under the flooring. Watchmen in winter time liable to force the coal stove ana cause overheating of smoke pipe or stove. Cigarette falling through cracks or space between floor boards is a common occurrence. The fire risk is considered poor.

BATTEN DOORS—See Fire Doors.

BATTENS, pieces of boards or scantling a few inches wide, used to hold several lengths together.

BATTER—The sloping backward of a face of masonry.

BATTERY OF BOILERS—A group of boilers delivering steam into a main pipe.

BATTERIES—Dry cell. Cells filled with salamoniac, chloride of manganese, magnesium. Sealed with parafine, topped with pitch. May have celluloid cells sealed with celluloid cement.

BATTERIES—Semi-dry as used in launches. The body or cell is made of a dark, sandy mixture, finely divided, composed of manganese, peroxide of hydrogen, graphite, retort carbons, sodium, silicates and ores, mixed and pressed in cylindrical forms. This is called "depolarizing" mixture. Forms then put in hollow zinc holder which has been treated with muriatic acid and mercury, and a thin coating of pitch put in bottom of cylinder. Between the depolarizing filling and the zinc shell is a small space filled with "exciting" fluid made of ammonia chloride, zinc and calcium chlorides, calcium oxide, glucose, starch and rye flour. Paraffine coating makes the cell air tight. Two glass tubes are inserted, and remaining space filled with sawdust, then sealed with pitch. The finished battery is dipped in asphaltum or lacquer and paper wrapper glued on. Hazard of pitch and wax heating, excelsior and sawdust storage, dip process lacquering, benzine for thinning asphaltum, glue heating, handling of chemicals, oily floors.

BATTERIES (Storage)—The filling composition may contain ether, amyl acetate, alcohol and chlorates. Celluloid cells and celluloid cement, lead melting furnaces and blow pipe work are chief hazards.

BATTING DROSS consists of fibre and resin formed by filtration of melted resin through raw cotton. Not subject to spontaneous combustion. Not classed as inflammable.

BAY CONSTRUCTION is the term used to denote the absence of the ordinary small-sized beams in floor construction and is the space representing the span between rows of parallel beams or girders. Bays are sometimes panels, sometimes spans. In mill construction a bay is the distance between posts.

BEAM—Iron, wood, or other suitable substance. Usually rests on girders at right angles, or on posts. Used to support floor loads or roof.

BEANS, if wet, and left in bags, will milldew and may be confiscated by Health Department.

BEARING—The points of support of a beam, shaft, axle. The "rest" or the block on which or against which a journal turns.

BEARING WALL—A wall which supports floor or roof beams or girders.

BED MOULDINGS, ornamental mouldings on the lower face of a projecting cornice.

BED PLATE—A large plate of iron laid as a foundation for something to rest on.

BEDSPRING MANUFACTURING — Metal - working hazard with dip process painting, lacquering or bronzing.

BEES-WAX—A solid wax of which the cells of the honey comb are made. Melting point, 143-147 deg. F.

BEET VARNISH—Made from red beets soaked in spirits of wine.

BELL-METAL—Copper and tin melted together. See Bronze.

BELT BOXES, especially in cotton mills should be kept scrupulously clean. Often found filled with dust and flyings of cotton or wool, covering everything not in rapid motion.

BELT HOLES should be boxed, i.e., enclosed at each floor to provide a minimum floor opening. See Boxing.

BELT MANUFACTURING—Many use a water-proof cement composed of acetone and rubber cement with celluloid and carbon bisulphide, or Viscol.

BELTING (COTTON)—Is made of woven cotton, and waterproofed. If the belting is left in water for a few hours the water will dissolve the dressing and render the belting worthless. After being wet, the belt will not run true on pulleys, hence is unsalable.

BENTINE SPIRITS, approved benzine substitute. Flashes at 103 deg. F.

BENZENE, obtained by fractional distillation from coal tar. Colorless, volatile, inflammable. Solvent for fats and gums. Derivatives used in medicines and dyestuffs. See benzole.

BENZIDINE, made from nitro-benzine, alkali solution and zinc dust. Similar to making sulphonic-acid. Used in dye-making.

BENZINE—Obtained by fractional distillation from petroleum. Colorless, inflammable, volatile, consisting of various hydro-carbons. Flash point from about 70-84 deg. F.

BENZINE SUBSTITUTES—See under Trade Names.

BENZOATE OF SODA—Toluol heated in Mott kettle, then mixed with chlorine gas, making benzol chloride, then nitrated. The crystals are then cleaned and dried. The remaining solution is treated with soda ash to complete action.

BENZOLE—Flash point 14 deg. F. Properties same as benzene. Should be stored only in steel drums.

BENZOYL-CHLORIDE consists of a clear colorless liquid. Not combustible, not classed as inflammable.

BENZOL-TRINITRO, high explosive.

BERENCO LACQUER is non-explosive. Alcohol is used as a thinner.

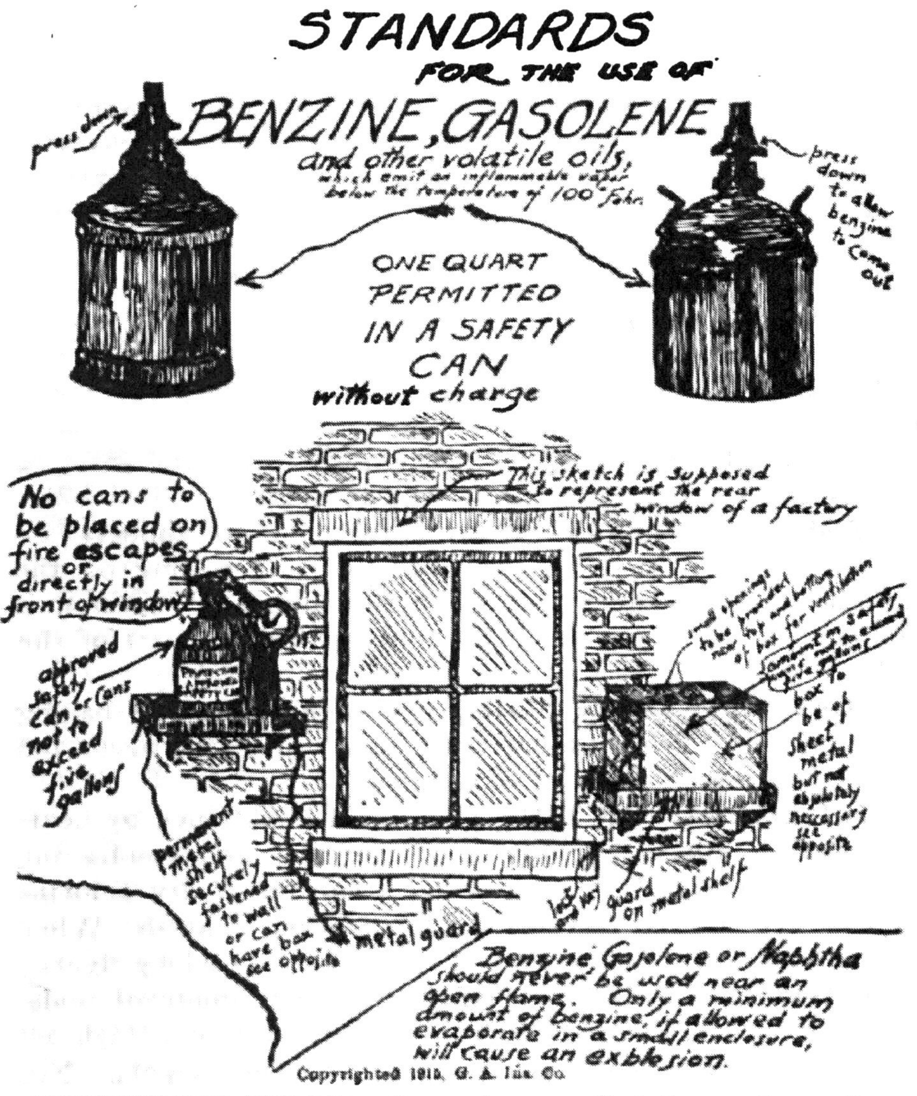

BESSEMER STEEL—Sometimes called Ingot Iron. Produced from cast iron by blowing air through it while in a molten state. This process is repeated until all the carbon is removed. The required degree of carburization is produced by adding a proportion of iron containing a known percentage of carbon and manganese. The Basis Bessemer process, called acid Bessemer process is one where the sulphur and phosphorus cannot be removed except by employing a converter lined with basic material in which other varieties of iron can be used. Bessemer steel can be produced in various degrees of hardness, but it cannot be tempered or hardened subsequently. It has a rather lower tensile strength than other mild steels. A Bessemer converter is a cylindrical iron vessel lined with a refractory material in which molten pig iron is submitted to the oxidizing action of a stream of air.

BETA-NAPHTHA—See Sublime Beta-Naphtha.

BETON, sometimes called artificial stone. Made of hydraulic cement with broken stone, broken bricks, gravel, etc.

BEVEL—The slope formed by trimming away the sharp edge, as of a board.

BEVEL GEAR, cog-wheels with teeth so formed that the wheels can work into each other at an angle.

BEVELLED, or self-releasing, applied to timbers on masonry walls which have the bevelled end resting on the wall in such a manner that when the timber is ruptured it can fall out or release itself without tearing out part of the wall.

BICARBONATE OF SODA, commonly known as baking soda. Composed of one part each of sodium, hydrogen, and carbon and three parts of oxygen.

BICHLORIDE OF TIN—This liquid is obtained by heating metallic tin with chloride of mercury, and condensing the fumes produced, or by passing a current of dry chlorine over melted tin, and condensing the resulting chloride. When mixed with water, great heat is generated. Used by dyers.

BICHROMATE OF POTASH—See Bichromate of Soda.

BICHROMATE OF SODA and bichromate of potash are yellow crystalline salts which act as oxidizing agents. Not considered hazardous in themselves.

BICYCLE AND MOTORCYCLE repair shops. Hand and power shop work. Motorcycles drained or filled in building. Vulcanizing. Gasoline storage. Stock of accessories including celluloid windshields. Have poor fire record. See Motor Cycle.

BINDER—A temporary contract between the insured and the insurer. Issued pending the issuance of a policy. On it is written the name of the insured, the description of property covered, location, mortgage, amount, term for which the policy is to be written, and rate. Issued for fifteen-day period as a rule and is renewable; cancelled in same manner as a policy. See Application for Insurance.

BINITRO-TOLUOL—A yellow crystalline solid (not explosive or dangerously inflammable). Resembles trinitoltol which is highly explosive.

BIRD AND ANIMAL STORES—Live animals and birds easily asphyxiated by smoke. Fixtures, furniture and stock of supplies, however, classed as good risks. Light repair shop work.

BISULPHIDE OF CARBON—See Carbon Bisulphide.

BISULPHIDE OF IRON is iron pyrites.

BLACK DAMP is choke damp.

BLACK DYED GOODS are apt to cause spontaneous combustion.

BLACK JAPAN—A varnish made with tar and alcohol, or lamp-black and resins.

BLACK PAINT—A compound used by tanners. Contains pyroxylin or gun cotton dissolved in amyl acetate. Flash point 35 deg. F.

BLACK POWDER—Explosive, 75 per cent. saltpetre, 10 per cent. sulphur, 15 per cent. charcoal.

BLACKSMITHS—Usually locate in buildings of inferior construction. Note setting of forges and anvils, tire furnaces and painting.

BLANK RATING, when the financial rating of a firm or individual does not appear in any of the mercantile rating books, it is usually a good tip to keep off the line. See Trade Reports; also Mercantile Reports.

BLANK WALL—A wall without openings.

BLANKET FORM—A form covering building, machinery and stock under one item.

BLANKET POLICIES may cover the buildings or contents of one, two or any number of buildings. If communicating, they can be written with the 80 per cent. and distribution clause; if not communicating, the 100 per cent. clause must be used without any allowance for same. These policies must be written cautiously and the liability figured as though the entire amount covered in each building under a blanket form. See Schedule; also Distribution Clause.

BLASTING CAPS consist of small hollow copper cylinders containing fulminate of mercury, or a mixture of fulminate of mercury and potassium chlorate. Very dangerous.

BLASTING GELATINE is a mixture of nitroglycerine and gun cotton. Powerful explosive.

BLAUGAS LIGHTING SYSTEM—This is a gas system for house lighting and heating, using liquified hydrocarbon gas made from petroleum distillate. (Colorless, inflammable, and made by passing mineral oil into highly heated retorts, the oil being decomposed, forming a gaseous product.) The gas is stored under high pressure (900 lbs. per sq. inch) in steel cylinders, and is expanded into the house piping through suitable reducing and regulating valves. The high-pressure cylinders, together with reducing and regulating valves, are contained in a locked and ventilated metal box.

The system is arranged to run automatically with small expansion tanks in this box, or non-automatically with larger expansion tanks which are buried or installed in well ventilated brick or concrete houses when near buildings.

The gas itself, after introduction into the house piping, embodies about the same hazards as ordinary city gas, but under somewhat higher pressure (about 12 inches water column). The apparatus is well constructed and is safeguarded as far as appears to be practicable at the present time. The high pressure apparatus is to be installed outside of buildings, well removed from all openings where escaping gas may enter or accumulate. (Board of Fire Underwriters.)

BLEACH, DYE AND PRINT WORKS—Raw stock includes cotton goods to be worked, acids, chlorate of potash, chlorate of soda, acetate of iron, tin oxalite, sodium sulphate, sumac, chloride of lime, bisulphide of soda, acetate of chrome, caustic soda, starch, aniline and logwood dyes, aniline oils and salts. Process, dyeing, drying, singeing, ageing, calendering, printing, etching and engraving rolls, folding and packing. Poor fire record. Benzine is sometimes used as a mordant in calico printing.

The causes of fire are attributed to lighting, power, singeing, dye mixing, printing, steaming, ageing, napping, and spontaneous ignition of freshly-dyed goods.

BLEACHING POWDER—See chloride of lime. A heavy white powder composed chiefly of calcium hypochloride (known also as chloride of lime). It gives off chlorine gas when heated or mixed with acids. Not classed as inflammable.

BLEACHING ROOMS (sulphur) in hat factories should be constructed entirely of incombustible material as follows: The side walls and ceilings to be wire lath and plaster (preferably on iron supports). If, however, the room is wood enclosed, the same may be lined, including the ceiling, with plaster boards or similar equivalent construction at least ½-inch thick secured by roofing nails, the nail heads to be covered and all joints between the blocks filled in with asbestos cement. The floor to have a course of bricks laid in cement throughout and an additional similar course directly underneath the sulphur pot. When a vent pipe is used, the same is to be constructed of brick or terra cotta with a damper to be controlled from the outside of the room. Metallic substances should not be employed on account of corrosion. See Hats, Straw.

BLENDING—Also known as compounding, is mixing liquor to obtain a desired blend. No material hazard. See Liquors.

BLIND ATTIC—See Attic.

BLISTER STEEL—See Cast Steel.

BLOCK LINES—Are the "lines" which in the aggregate represent the amount of liability which a company has on a city block of buildings. See Line.

BLOCKING PRESS—A gas or steam-heated press under pressure used in shaping hats.

BLOODED LIVESTOCK of fancy value should not be written until the company is in possession of all the facts of physical and moral hazard. Considerable value is wrapped up in a blooded animal. A slight accident will so depreciate an animal's worth that there may be incentive to destroy the animal by fire and collect the insurance. See Lightning.

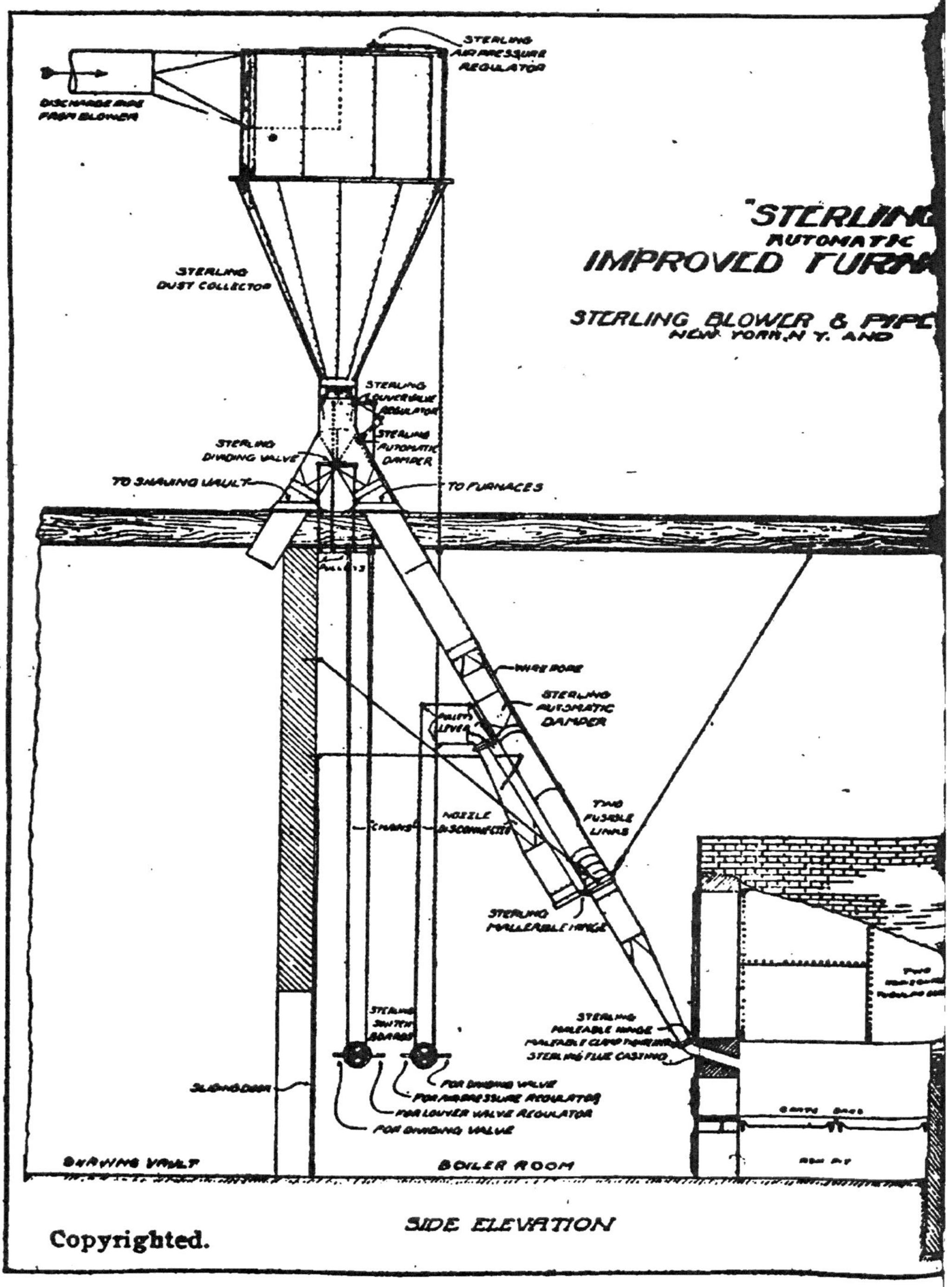

SIDE ELEVATION

FEEDER

COMPANY,
ORD CONN

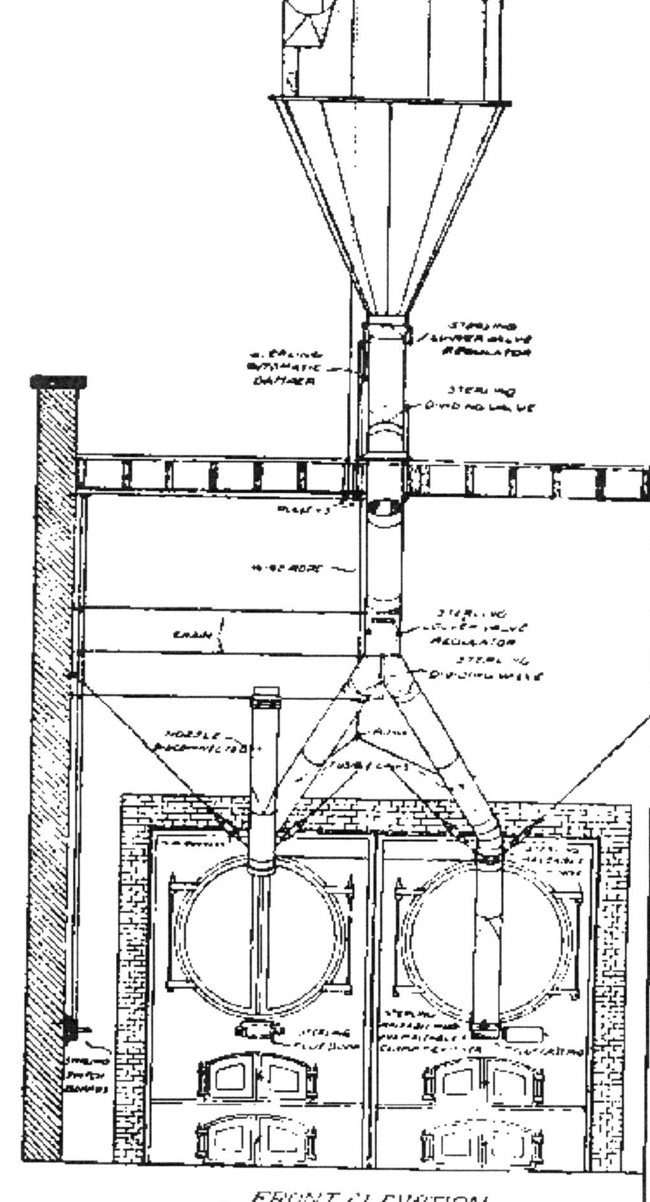

FRONT ELEVATION
"STERLING" IMPROVED AUTOMATIC
FURNACE FEEDER FOR TWO BOILERS

BLOW TORCHES—Should be on incombustible stands. See Brazers.

BLOWER SYSTEMS for heating or ventilating consist of a number of galvanized iron ducts through which air is blown for heat, or from which impure or heated air is sucked for ventilation. In each system, the openings in the ducts are covered with wire screening. Motor-driven fans are usually employed. A clearance of 1 inch from combustible material is recommended, and ducts should not be connected to flues or stacks used for any other purposes; neither should they pierce fire walls unless an automatic drop door is installed where passing through. Where piercing floors, the ducts should be protected by 4-inch tile or its equivalent. The latter two features (piercing walls or floors) reduce the efficiency of the fire wall or floor, as fire, once entering the flue, travels the entire system unless stopped by standard automatic dampers or doors.

BLOWERS FOR REFUSE such as sawdust, shavings or buffing dust from buff wheels operate as noted. The ducts are cylindrical and have a hood which fits quite close to the machinery to allow a larger opening for the refuse to enter the duct or pipe. As these are used in factories, they are liable to breakage and disruption through carelessness or vibration, and therefore should be substantially constructed. The refuse is drawn through a cyclone or separator where the fine dust is allowed to free itself, the heavy material going to a vault or other receptacle. Dust from buff wheels and other light material should pass through a water sprayer or be deposited in a receptacle partly filled with water to keep down the percentage of dust. All blower systems should have suitable clean-out doors, fans and motor bearings easily accessible and be kept clean to prevent clogging and friction. Fires have been caused by exhaust apparatus becoming overheated. See Shavings Vaults; also Buff Wheels and Direct Feed to Boilers.

BLOWN OILS are made by oxidizing rape, cotton seed, linseed and lard oils. Used for lubricating purposes.

BLUE BILLY or pyrites cinder is a residue from burning pyrites in the manufacture of sulphuric acid.

BLUE PRINT making is accomplished by what is known as a printing machine equipped with electric light and gas heat. The paper is received in rolls, passed through a sensitizing solution, then over a roller-frame to a dry room. Use citric and oxalic acids in crystal form, soda ash, aqua ammonia, sulphuric acid, nitric acid. Dry room hazard. Arc lamps.

BLUE VITRIOL is sulphate of copper.

BLUEING—Made from burnt umber, sulphur, soda, clay and a liquid adhesive resembling molasses.

BOARDING-HOUSES where meals are served are considered somewhat better fire risks than furnished room houses. The change of patrons is not so frequent. Inspection should be made before line is written. See Furnished Rooms; also Lodging Houses.

BOILED OIL is made by heating linseed oil. Used in paint, varnish and oilcloth manufacturing.

BOILER EXPLOSION—See Boiler.

BOILERS, brick set, are those which are enclosed in brick-work covering the outside of the boiler, and usually having a concrete or brick top.

An **asbestos-clad boiler** is one which is wrapped in asbestos which is applied as a cement, about 2 to 4 inches in thickness.

Boilers, **portable.** All combustible floors and beams under and not less than 3 feet in front of and 1 foot on side of all portable boilers shall be protected by a brick foundation of two courses of brick. See Battery of Boilers.

For installation of temporary kerosene oil burners, see Kerosene Burners.

BOILER—Does the Boiler or the Water Explode?

Water in an open kettle boils at 212 deg. F. The Fidelity and Casualty Bulletin says that when the surface of boiling water is subject to atmospheric pressure or zero gauge pressure its temperature is 212 deg. F

When the gauge pressure is 150 lbs. per square inch the temperature of the water is 350 deg. F., and if all the inlets and outlets to the boiler be closed, the water will not boil, notwithstanding the fact that its temperature and pressure are many times greater than the temperature and pressure of boiling water.

If, however, a valve be opened, the water immediately begins to boil, even though the furnace heat has been shut off. But when all of the inlets and outlets are closed the highly-heated water in the boiler is in fact nothing more nor less than liquefied steam gas. It remains in the liquid state by reason of the high pressure to which its surface is subjected.

If, however, suddenly there be made a large opening above the water level, as for example when a large steam pipe or header is ruptured, the pressure on the surface of the water being suddenly relieved permits the liquefied steam gas commonly thought of as hot water to violently explode in much the same manner as if it were nitroglycerine.

The result is commonly termed a boiler explosion. It is in fact an explosion of liquefied steam gas. That is to say, it is an explosion of a large body of water at high temperature. It is no wonder, then, that boiler explosions are often as disastrous as dynamite explosions.

BOILER SETTING—A small upright heating boiler has been known to set fire to woodwork under its 8-inch concrete base (laid without air space). All solid materials such as brick, concrete or asbestos have a comparatively high heat conductivity. Porous material such as terra-cotta tile or a liberal air space permitting a circulation of air is a better insulation against heat than solid matter.

BOILER SMOKE PIPE against the under side of an 8-inch concrete floor arch has been known to ignite stock on the floor. Dust and wood chips on top of boilers are ignited by radiated heat.

BOLL WEEVIL—An insect pest whose annual ravages cause a loss of 400,000 bales of cotton in the South. The annual loss in Texas alone as a result of the weevil's depredations is placed at $2,700,000. Thus far the only successful means of control has been the burning of dead cotton stalks in the Fall, thereby destroying in a large measure the hibernating millions that would develop into active parasites during the coming season. These parasites have injected a moral hazard into cotton mills, as the small crop means less work and the corresponding shutting down of the plant.

BOLSTER—A timber or a thick iron plate placed between the ends of a bridge and its seat on an abutment.

BOMBS—Whistling bombs contain potassium picrate.

BONFIRES, especially in open city lots, have caused many losses by flying brands and grass fires.

BOND, the disposing of brick-work or blocks of stone so as to form the whole into a firm structure by the judicious overlapping of each other so as to break joint.

BOND AND CAP STONES, especially if carrying heavy weights should be insulated with concrete, terra cotta or brick 2 to 4 inches in thickness. Heat and the application of cold water under pressure causes the stones to crack and may cause the building to collapse.

BONDED WALL—See Bond.

BONDED WAREHOUSE—See Warehouse.

BONE BLACK—Made from the poorer grade of bones. Subject to combustion in the presence of moisture.

BOOKBINDERS—Process consists of cutting, gluing, embossing, printing and binding paper. Hazards of glue pots, gas-heated embossing presses, paper scraps, printing presses. See Printers.

BOOKBINDERS' BOARD MANUFACTURING—The raw stock consists of paper, rags, wood pulp and fibre. The process is sorting, cutting, shaking and finishing. Machinery used are calenders (steam-heated), paper-making machines, steam dryers, rag cutters, beaters, boiling kettles. Crude oil is used to reduce foam in beaters. Similar to paper-making.

BOOKTILE—Tiling, wide, flat, thin and shaped like a book. Laid so that the convex end of one sets into the concave end of the next. Used in roof construction instead of heavy tile or concrete to lessen the weight.

BOOKS—If new, offer good insurance; if old, the contrary. When piled on shelves, water damages the upper tier as a rule and fire burns the outer edge.

BOOSTING—Dressing stone with a broad chisel called a "booster" and a mallet. The booster gives a smooth surface after the use of the "point," or other narrow chisel.

BOOT AND SHOE FACTORIES—See Shoe Factories.

BOOT DRESSING—See Shoe Factories.

BOOT BLACK AND HAT CLEANERS—Ownership largely a foreign element. Use sulphur for bleaching straw hats, benzine for cleaning hats, gas-heated irons and blocking irons.

BORE—The inner diameter of a hollow cylinder.

BOTTLERS of soft drinks with flavoring extract-making. Work consists of washing, labeling and filling bottles. Making flavoring from fruits and herbs and essential oils, using steam-heated kettles and confectioners' stoves. Boiler. Excelsior for packing bottles for shipment. Sealing bottles with paraffine. See Mineral Waters.

BOTTLE-STOPPERS, called "crowns," are made of sheet metal stamped out and edges crimped, then lined with waxed paper and cork disk. The wax is a mixture of paraffine and rosin, heated by gas or steam. Paper usually waxed on the premises by drawing the paper strip through the melted wax. The machines used are automatic, rotating and gas-heated, and crimp, line and press the crown in one operation. Metal working hazard. Varnishing tops. The cork disks are bought ready-made for use. See Cork.

BOULINIKON, a kind of floor cloth like linoleum. Similar process to linoleum-making, but made from buffalo hide.

BOWLING ALLEYS, if established and run by responsible people, are considered good insurance as practically no stock is carried. Use wax or floor mops for dressing floors. Basement alleys suffer greater damage than those above grade, as water will cause the alleys to warp, necessitating relaying.

BOX-BOARD LINING manufacturing. The process consists of cutting the boards and running them through a press similar in appearance to a cylinder press which has a gravity feed paste-pot attachment which drops the paste into a trough, and a reel of thin paper is automatically pasted on the cardboard. Used in place of paper boxes. Hazards similar to paper box making.

BOX GIRDER—A type of steel or wrought-iron girder having two vertical webs and a flange at top and bottom connecting them.

BOXED STAIRS—See Stairs.

BOXING—Applied to belt openings when same are enclosed at floors to lessen the size of draft opening. Cornices are cut off for same reason.

BRACE-AND-INCLINED BEAM—A bar or strut for sustaining compression.

BRACED FRAME—Girts or beams carry the floor beams of the floors above the first, and are framed into the corner posts (which should extend to the wall plates), those supporting the end of the beams dropped to a secure level with the side girts (for this reason they are called drop girts). On these girts the studs of the outer walls and partitions are framed, so that each story has a separate set of studs. At all angles also there are angle braces tending to strengthen the structure. (How to Build a Home.) See Balloon Frame.

BRACKET CHIMNEY—A chimney which rests on a wall bracket instead of being built up from the ground. An increased danger when bracket is of wood. See also Corbel and Wall Chimney.

BRAID AND DRESS TRIMMING MANUFACTURING—Hazards are storage of raw materials, dyeing, drying, braid and weave machines, winders and spoolers, sewing machines, gas heated straw machines and crimpers, packing and labeling. See also Embroideries.

BRAKE—A long machine used by tinsmiths to bend the sheet metal into proper shape.

BRAMWELL FEED, an automatic attachment for feeding carding machines. It consists of a small pin for holding the stock which is picked up by a slowly moving apron and usually has a hood over the feed. The hoods should be removed or have a sprinkler head placed under the same. Some rating bureaus charge an extra rate for machines equipped with Bramwell feeds. See Carding Machines.

BRANCH OFFICE RISK—Any risk permitted to be written by the Branch Offices, the class consisting of dwellings, stores and dwellings and minimum rated stocks. In other words, this class, owing to the light character, need not be rated except for area or special conditions. Branch offices write only the so-called preferred business, and not manufacturing risks or special hazards. See Risk.

BRANCH STORES—Sometimes goods are removed back and forth from main store to branches. Such stocks should be carefully investigated. Fires have a habit of starting in branch stores which are filled with out-of-season or shop-worn goods shipped from main stores, especially if located in another town. See Mercantile Reports; also Trade Reports.

BRANDY—Made by distilling fermented fruit juices. Whiskey compounds are used as substitutes. See Distilleries.

BRASS—Composed of copper and zinc.

BRAZE—To unite pieces of iron, copper or brass by means of a hard solder called spelter solder. See Weld.

BRAZERS (or blow torches) used in metal-working establishments, consist of stout, flexible tubes, carrying gas from a supply pipe to a nozzle which is attached to another flexible pipe through which the operator directs a stream of compressed air. This stream of air serves the double purpose of intensifying the heat of the gas flame and blowing it with force against the metal surface to be worked. The brazer should rest on a solid iron bed or brick base. Rubber tubes are permitted; but gas shut-off cock should be located at permanent wall connection.

BREAK-JOINT—To so overlap pieces that the joints shall not occur at the same places and thus produce a poor bond.

BREAST-SUMMER—A kind of lintel supporting a wall over a door or other opening.

BREECHING—An iron flue, lined or unlined, or brick or tile, connecting the larger or header flue from the boiler to the stack. See Smoke Pipes.

BREWERIES—Process is steeping or soaking grain in warm water, spreading same on "growing floor" to germinate or sprout the grain; dried in kilns, stored in bins, screened to remove dirt or waste, weighed, crushed in malt mill, mixed with water and other ingredients (and at times adulterants) in mashtub, cooking or brewing with hops in steam kettles (known as wort), the liquor drawn off and filtered or contents dumped into "hop-jack" where spent grain is removed and liquor pumped to coolers, then fermented in wooden vats, and "racked" or drawn off in kegs.

Hazards—In kiln house, the setting of the furnace sup-

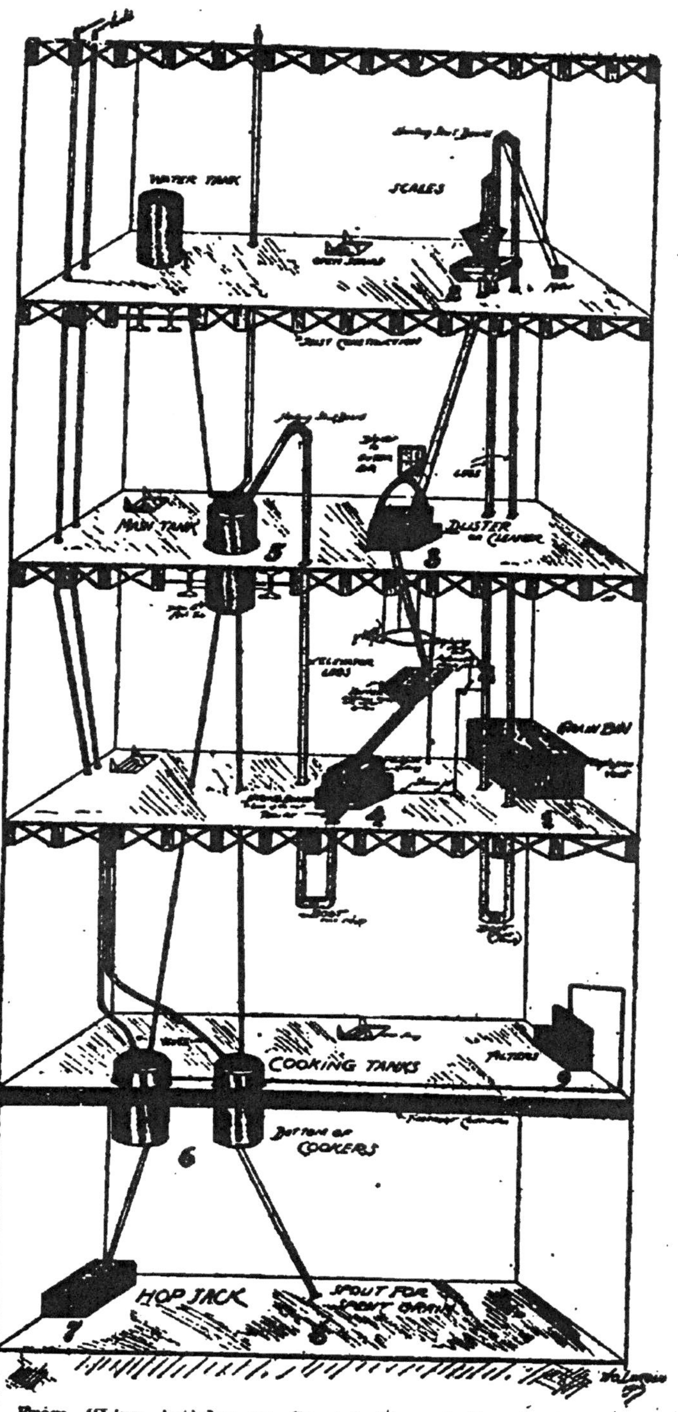

From "Live Articles on Special Hazards," pub. by "Weekly Underwriter."

Brew House.

plying the heat to dry the grain. Where furnace is directly under the drying floors, the grain is apt to fall on the furnace and ignite, therefore the top of furnace should be hooded. Where brick-set furnaces are located in building adjoining, the heated air is blown or forced into the kiln house through brick flues. These buildings should be cut off from balance of the plant. The suction fan over kiln floors at roof collects considerable dust, and fires are caused by friction of machinery and dusty bearings. In "Brew" house, the "lofters" or "legs," which are traveling belts, enclosed in wood boxing, on which buckets are fastened, conveying grain from one floor to another. They should be of metal; whether of wood or metal they should have explosion vents. The latter are small doors kept closed by spring hinges. The force of a dust explosion opens these doors sufficiently to cause a lessening of the force of the explosion. The "strut" board of lofter over which passes the belting should be slanting to prevent the grain from collecting and causing friction fires in bearings. The "boot" or lower part of the lofter should also be slanting and kept clean. Malt mill to be of all metal design with magnets at the rollers where malt is crushed to catch all metallic substances, thus preventing sparks at the rollers. Also springboards under the rollers will keep malt packed against the rollers, preventing an accumulation of dust which in the event of a spark would explode. An automatic steam jet at this point would extinguish fire, resulting from such dust explosions. Screeners should have magnets where grain enters through hoppers, also at grain bins through which pass the lofters.

Incidental hazards are cooper shops with pitch kettle. Pitch kettles are usually heated by direct fires and ought to be outside the buildings under separate cover. Storage of, repairing and varnishing old fixtures. Branding kegs. The branding iron used to impress the name of the brewer on the keg is sometimes heated by an improvised gasoline fuel appliance. Stables with blanket drying room, garages. (C. E. Jahne, "Live Articles on Special Hazards," The Weekly Underwriter.)

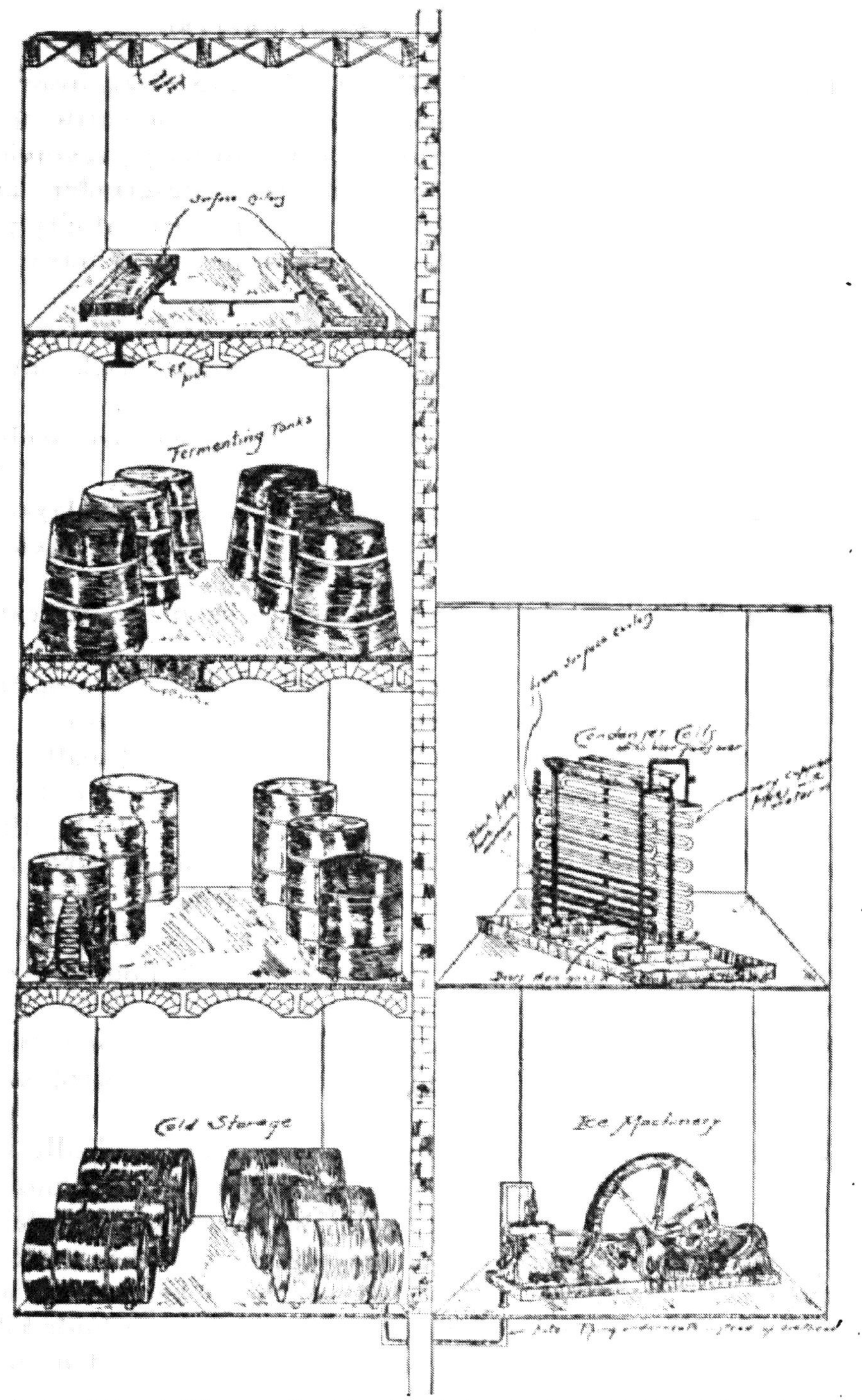

From "Live Articles on Special Hazards," pub. by "Weekly Underwriter."

Cold Storage House.

BREWERY GRAIN DRYERS—Grain is received from the hop-jacks of breweries and used by farmers for cattle feed. The water is pressed out, the grain dried in large, revolving, steam-heated dryers, then ground in knife-grinder and bagged. Usually of frame construction in outskirts of city and "shafty." The floors are pierced by elevator legs, chutes and hoppers. Boiler hazard.

BRICKS should not be laid in freezing weather. Frost expands the water in the mortar and thrusts the brick out of position.

Pale Bricks are those improperly burned and are useless for building material.

Fire Bricks are made from a mixture of several clays, to which has been added a certain amount of ground brick or quartz.

Radial Bricks are perforated radial blocks made of tested clays.

BRICK-ARCHED—An arch of brickwork laid or sprung between "I" beams, as "brick-arched" floor or roof.

BRICK-FILLING or BRICK-LINING—A stud wall filled in with brick. Although classed as frame, they frequently prove to be very valuable in preventing spread of fire. The brick filling should extend to the roof boards when frame buildings are built adjoining. See Frame Rows.

BRICK-NOGGING (used in place of wood-nogging pieces) makes a fire stop between studding at each floor by one thickness of brick set between the studs.

BRICK VENEER—One or two thicknesses of brick used in place of clapboards in frame construction. Classed same as frame buildings.

BRICK WORKS—Bricks are made of clay, principally silicate of alumina with perhaps lime, magnesia and oxide of iron. Made by hand or machinery, air or artificially dried, then burned in kilns. Kilns are permanent, or of knock-down type, built up around the arch of bricks to be burned, and fires built directly under the bricks. Permanently built kilns are the safer. Considered poor fire risks. Physical hazards of boiler location, storage of hay and straw for packing, artificial drying. Moral hazard induced by exhaustion of clay deposits, poor transportation facilities, class of help. Usually large frame areas out of protection. See Tile Works.

BRIDGING JOISTS are those which extend from trimmer joist at flues or fireplace to the opposite wall.

BRIQUETTES—Used in place of coal. Made of ground coal, coal dust and crude oil or other heavy oil. Process is grinding or pulverizing coal, mixing with oil, hydraulic pressing. Oil storage important hazard.

BRISTLES used in brush-making. Prepared from hides which are first softened with unslaked lime and water in a tub, and the hair pulled out by hand, then cleaned with a mixture of peroxide of hydrogen and muriatic acid, and further cleaned with soap and water, wrapped in bundles, dried. For coloring, the small bundles or wads are dipped in boiling permanganate of potash. If white ends are desired, peroxide of hydrogen will bleach the permanganate and leave the ends white. Combed by hand. Dry-room principal hazard.

BRITISH GUM (dextrine)—A stiffening substance extracted from potatoes, wheat or rye. Used by calico printers and for sizing. See Dextrine.

BROKEN-JOINT—An arrangement of material such as brick, laid in courses so that no two joints are immediately over each other. See Bond.

BROKEN PLASTER on wood lath as used for ceilings, etc., must be repaired to prevent fire from readily gaining access to the concealed spaces back of it. See Furring.

BROKER—A business representative of the insured, not of the company. For the commissions received from insurance premiums, he looks after the insurance interests of his clients.

Brokers or agents who agree to procure insurance on terms and conditions as agreed between them and the owner, and then fail to properly protect the owner as agreed, become legally liable for the loss if fire occurs, to the extent of their negligence. See Agent.

BROMATES are bromic acid compounds.

BROMIDES—Compounds of bromine with metals (potassium bromide).

BROMINE is obtained from sea and mineral spring water or seaweed. It is volatile. If united with antimony, arsenic or copper it will burn fiercely. If mixed with potassium it explodes violently, producing potassium bromide. Not inflammable.

BRONZE—Composed of copper and tin.

BRONZE COLORS—Made from metallic bronze, sometimes mixed with such dangerous liquids as collodion and amyl acetate.

BRONZE FOUNDRIES—Use iron, copper or silver nitrate for coloring the bronze castings. The nitrates are diluted, applied by brush, and the castings baked in an oven.

BRONZING LIQUIDS usually contain pyroxylin or soluble cotton dissolved in volatile, inflammable solvents. Classed as inflammable.

BROODERS—See Incubators.

BROOM CORN—See Broom Factories.

BROOM CORN ROOT burns quickly.

BROOM FACTORIES employ power machinery such as seeders, wood-working and metal-working machines. Gluing, varnishing and bleaching. Cheap labor, crowded lofts or buildings. Broom corn liable to spontaneous combustion under some conditions. A poor fire record class.

BRUSH FACTORIES—There are many different kinds of brushes, requiring different methods of manufacture. The bristles and hair are usually received ready to use. Wood-working machinery of various kinds used for backs. Metal-working machines for parts. The wood backs are stained, painted, varnished, enamelled or celluloid covered. In the latter process the wooden backs are slightly warmed on a steam-heated table, a thin sheet of celluloid cemented on, placed in a screw press, then the celluloid edge sandpapered and trimmed. In finishing department, each worker has an individual cup or air brush for touching up with lacquer, shellac or liquid bronze. The metal parts require japanning or enamelling. The bristles are glued, or pitch or rubber-set. Vulcanizing rubber, and use of rubber cement, thinned with naphtha are necessary. The hazards are wood and metal-working, with painting, varnishing, japanning and enamelling, pitch and glue heating, handling of celluloid, use of benzine, dry rooms, vulcanizing rubber. See Bristles.

Twisted wire brushes have no backs, the bristles being twisted in with the wire. The only hazards are the clippers and combers, which are run by individual motors.

BUCK is a small pressing board on top of pressing tables in clothing factories. Steam-heated ones, used without table, but require a small individual gas-heated boiler to generate steam. See Pressing Tables.

BUCKRAM, used for hat frames, is cloth sized with glue, dried on cylindrical or tentering dryer.

BUCKRAM AND LININGS are dyed and sized. In dyeing, aniline colors, muriatic and sulphuric acids, chloride of lime, tannic acid and caustic soda are used. Gums and starches are used for sizing. The gums are sometimes heated by direct fire.

BUCKWHEAT, ground, is said to ignite spontaneously if damp.

BUFFING is polishing by power. Considerable lint made during this process.

BUFFING WAX usually contains emery dust, paraffine, stearic acid, petrolatum, and mineral waxes.

BUFF WHEELS—Pieces of cloth glued and sewed together. To produce a high polish on brass goods without lacquering, the brass part is fixed on a movable iron frame which gradually forces the brass against the buff wheel. Fires have arisen when inexperienced workmen have caused undue friction by applying too much pressure against the buff wheel. This sets fire to the buff wheel, and the flames are sucked into the blower system.

BUILDERS' MATERIAL YARDS—Stock includes brick, lime, cement, lath, tiling, flue pipe. Lime and cement should be skidded and under cover. Unslaked lime will cause fire. Cement if wet will cake and be practically valueless.

BUILDERS' RISK is generally understood to constitute work of a structural nature that requires underpinning or shoring walls, constructing or reconstructing building or additions thereto or enlarging the premises. See Mechanics' Privilege. See Course of Construction.

BUILDINGS SET ON PILES, such as at seashore, should be screened around piling to prevent papers and trash from accumulating under building.

BUILDING SALVAGE—See Salvage.

BULKHEAD—The enclosure of a stair, elevator or other shaft or cornice built above the roof.

BULKHEAD BUILDING—The shore end of a pier. Usually a story higher than the pier proper and used for offices and store-rooms.

BUNKER ROOMS in cold storage plants are sometimes, as in all plants furnishing their own steam, coal storage rooms. This term is applied here usually when plants have expansion coils in refrigeration rooms or congealing tanks. Some plants have a special room for expansion coils or brine pipes only. These rooms are frequently referred to as bunker rooms.

BUNSEN BURNER—A single-flame upright gas jet, set on metal base and usually connected with rubber tubing. Used by jewelers, metal workers, dentists and in laboratories. The gas shut-off to be at permanent wall connection and set on metal covered table with air space under the metal.

BURNETTIZING (fire-proofing) WOOD—The timber is immersed in a solution of zinc chloride, or the fluid may be forced through the pores of the wood by pressure. This tends to harden the wood and renders it partially incombustible.

BURNING POINT of a substance, the temperature at which it will take fire. See Flash Point.

BURNING POINTS OF WOODS—The burning points of wood ranges from 400 to 600 deg. F. By burning point is meant "ignition" point. The all-resinous woods have the lower point of ignition and are also apt to give off an inflammable vapor. Non-resinous hardwoods have perhaps the higher ignition point. It is claimed that California red wood has the highest ignition point. This claim, however, is made by manufacturers who deal in products made of this material.

BURLAP—Said to be subject to spontaneous combustion when oiled or dyed.

BURNISH—To polish by rubbing. Chiefly applies to metals.

BUSINESS BLOCKS IN VILLAGES—Mainly frame buildings built in rows and contain the postoffice, opera house, variety store, paint store. Communicating roof spaces. Bad fire record. See Frame Rows; also Country Stores.

BUSINESS IN WOMAN'S NAME—See Names.

BUSINESS INTERRUPTION INDEMNITY—See Use and Occupancy.

BUTCHER SHOPS—Considered good insurance, as the greater liability is on fixtures rather than stocks. May have an unsafe gas stove in the rear, an unsafe swinging gas bracket at ice box, and a small amount of saltpetre for corning beef. Sawdust is found on the floors of this class. Sausage-making and meat-packing. The fire record is good in even the poorest grade of shops.

BUTTONS, CELLULOID—Celluloid is received in colored sheets. Machinery used are stamping presses, cutters, boring lathes, turning and frazing machines, drop-hammers. Steam and hot water used for moulding; emery, buff and sandpaper wheels, gas or steam-heated die presses, gas blowpipes. Painting with highly inflammable liquids applied by hand or air brush and containing collodion, acetone, amyl acetate and mineral colors. Hazard of dry-rooms with air impregnated with explosive mixtures. See Celluloid.

Cloth-covered Buttons—Cloth scraps cut into shape by hand, fitted over metal form, pressed together. Frayed or rough edges singed with gas flame injected in revolving metal cage or the buttons are lightly covered with alcohol and set on fire in rapidly oscillating or revolving metal screen. Care of scrap cloth, paper linings and cotton padding.

Composition Buttons—Made of rosin, clay, pulverized rock, wheat paste, mineral oils and colors. These are mixed together, heated in steam kettles, rolled into sheets on steam tables, cut into shape, dried.

Glass Buttons—Glass received in bars, reheated in gas furnaces, pressed into shape while hot on gas-heated presses, and gradually cooled in small lehr. Hazards of gas-heated furnaces, lehrs and blow pipes.

Horn, Ivory, Pearl and Bone Buttons—Process similar in all these, including "vegetable" ivory, which is Tanqua nuts from South America. Process is boring, cutting, drilling, smoothing with sand and emery wheels. Hazards of dirty bearings on high-speed machines, dry rooms.

Metal Buttons—General machine shop hazard with metal working, lacquering, buffing, plating, dry rooms.

Pearl Buttons—The pearl used is from clams, oysters, sometimes called mother-of-pearl. High-speed water-cooled saws needed, including special machines for certain kinds of buttons. Pearl cleaned in dilute sulphuric acid, polished with sawdust in tumblers. Aqua ammonia and silver nitrate used for coloring pearl to a darker shade.

Wood Buttons—Involves a wood-working hazard, boring, ing, sandpapering, shellacing and varnishing.

BUTTRESS—A vertical projecting piece of brickwork or masonry built in front of a wall to strengthen it, or a mass of stone or brickwork intended to support a wall or to assist it in sustaining the strain that may be upon it.

C

CABINET FACTORIES—Lumber is brought from yard, dried in kilns, taken to the mill and cut up into various sizes and shapes, the work consisting of cross-cut sawing, dovetailing, rip and resawing, mortising, carving, tenoning. The parts are placed in caul box prior to and after gluing and assembled. A coat of water or oil stain is applied, then varnished, rubbed with pumice, polished and packed. Hazards of wood-workers. See Carpenter Stoves.

CABLES—The best sign of the overloading of a cable (electrically) is given when the cable begins to get hot.

Cables used in deep salt water are made as follows: In the centre there is a core consisting of strands of copper wire. This is covered with several coats of rubber. A coat of jute follows, then a layer of galvanized iron wires, and finally a layer of yarn and compound which forms the outer covering.

CAGE CONSTRUCTION is a term peculiarly descriptive of that type of construction represented by the most advanced and approved practise, a framework of columns and beams, spliced at the joints, riveted at the connections, stiffened by an efficient bracing of rods, portals or gussets that make it independently safe against any external force, leaving the thin and light exterior walls with no duty to perform except that of providing protection and ornamentation to the building.—J. F. Kendall. (See Skeleton Construction.)

CALCINATION—Ores and chemicals are brought to red heat to expel volatile constituents, destroy organic matter and loosen the mass.

CALCIUM CARBIDE is made by the fusion of lime and coke, or quicklime and charcoal in an electric furnace at 3,000 deg. C. See Acetylene.

A substitute for calcium carbide is a disc made of crude

oil, calcium carbide, sulphur, sugar. These are cooked together and pressed into cakes.

CALCIUM CHLORIDE—Reservoirs for use with dry pipe sprinkler equipments in cold storage warehouses. See diagrams issued by New York Fire Insurance Exchange.

CALCIUM LIGHT RISKS—Storage of theatre properties, lighting stands and apparatus, color mixture, asphaltum and alcohol, charging cylinders, air compressors, oxygen reducing devices, hydrogen and oxygen gas outfits for lead burning. Work consists of charging cylinders with illuminating gas using compression of 225 lbs. Reducing pressure on oxygen gas cylinders from 1,800 lbs. to 225 lbs. through a series of valves, the last being set at 225 lbs. This class should be written cautiously.

CALCIUM LIGHT TUBES for lighting are arranged in pairs of steel cylinders, one with oxygen and one with hydrogen. Inflammable.

CALCIUM OXIDE (unslaked lime or quicklime) is a white solid mass obtained by burning limestone (incombustible). If combined with water gives off great heat sufficient to cause ignition. Classed as hazardous.

CALCIUM PHOSPHATE is a reddish or grayish solid mass which decomposes on contact with water, forming hydrogen phosphide, which ignites spontaneously on contact with air. Used in signal fires. Classed as inflammable.

CALENDERING—A process whereby material is finished or glazed by being passed over or under the surfaces of steam-heated cylinders.

CALK OR CAULK—To fill seams with something to prevent leaking. Oakum is usually used.

CALORIZING IRON—No mass of iron, no matter how large, can be heated red in contact with air without rusting. At temperatures above red heat iron rapidly oxidizes and scales away; or, in other words, burns. Calorizing is a process discovered by T. Van Aller, for prolonging the life of iron (or copper) by heating metals in a revolving drum with a mixture containing finely divided aluminum which produces a surface alloy on the metal, thus preventing the metal from burning and providing means of frequent renewals when used in laboratories where high temperature furnaces or retorts are used.

CAMPHENE—A mixture of three parts alcohol and one part turpentine; resembles camphor. Inflammable.

CAMPHENES—Etheral oils destitute of oxygen (oil of turpentine, etc.).

CAMPHOR is obtained by boiling the wood of certain Chinese or Japanese trees. It is inflammable.

CAMPHOR BALLS OR FLAKES—Naphthalene moth camphor is inflammable; melts quickly to a thin liquid and gives off vapors which attack the eyes. The vapors are readily ignited.

CANALS AND FEEDERS—Entering into large bodies of water are usually built for the accommodation of the manufacturing establishments adjacent thereto and act as waterways for boats, supplying water-power, and sometimes as sewers. Surfaces, as a rule, are oily, due to the waste material let into the canal.

CANAUBA WAX—Extracted from the leaves of the Canauba palm. Melting point 185 deg. F. Used as a cement.

CANCELLATION NOTICES are sent by registered mail, personal service or by sheriff or constable. Receipt must be signed by all parties interested as assureds.

CANDELIA—See Vegetable Waxes.

CANDLE FACTORIES—The raw materials used may be of animal, vegetable or mineral origin, such as tallow, spermaceti, paraffine or other waxes. The processes employed are: Tallow in common with mineral fats consist mainly of stearine and olein. It is decomposed into these two constituents by treating it in large copper digestors set over brick furnaces. In these the tallow is treated with superheated steam at a pressure of about 150-160 lbs., equalling a temperature of 365-375 deg. F., the cylinders themselves being heated by direct fire heat. The resulting mixture of the stearic and oleic acids is pressed to remove the former from the latter, which is a liquid. The stearic acid is then melted and run into candles, and the crude oleic acid is barrelled and sold to soap-makers under the name of Red Oil. Hazards: The manufacture of stearine from tallow is not especially hazardous except that occasionally the digestor explodes, in which case the melted fat would be scattered about. The hazard of the raw materials is the large quantities in which they are stored, all of which are combustible. The entire process is generally steam.

CANDLE-POWER is the measure of brilliancy. It is the definite term fixed by American law as the amount of light given by a candle burning 120 grains of wax per hour.

CANDLE STRUCTURE—See Flames.

CANDLES are responsible for many fires during the holiday season in certain congested sections of Greater New York and during religious holidays when used on mantels or Christmas trees. Celluloid candlesticks, under the name of "Composition Ivortur," "Imitation Ivory" and "Domestic Ivory" have been found on sale in department stores. Most of the candlesticks have a cup-shaped metal cap placed in the top and used to receive the candle. The manufacturers claim that this would prevent the candle from igniting the pyroxylin. It was found, however, that such is not the case, for when the candles were lighted and allowed to burn down the candlestick ignited and burned with the customary intensity. They should be prohibited.

CANDLING EGGS—Eggs are held in front of a light before a small aperture which allows the candler to ascertain if there are any blood spots or water spots in the eggs. Dark rooms are required. Carelessness in handling packing material, electric light cords hung on nails, kerosene oil lamps or candles cause many fires. Candling was first done by holding the egg in front of a candle. See Eggs.

CANDY FACTORIES—The materials used are sugar, glucose, chocolate, essential oils, flavoring extracts, syrups, nuts and spices. Starch is used incidentally. The hazards are "batch warmers," which are used to keep stock from setting. They resemble a hood of metal set on a bench with gas burners under same. If direct fire heat is used, they should set on an incombustible base and have a permanent iron gas pipe connection. Candy furnaces are cylindrical iron, fire brick-lined stoves, coke or coal fed with the grate near the bottom and the candy kettles resting directly over the fire. The principal danger is the likelihood of the candy boiling over into the fire, where it might flare up and ignite the ceiling or run over the floor. The furnace should set on proper brick yentilated foundation and have metal hood over. Coaters and Tumblers: Candies with nut centres and sugar-coated are made by tossing and tumbling in spherical copper vessels, steam heated, and have practically no fire hazard. Dipping Pans: These are for dipping unfinished candies, generally in melted chocolate. The pans are usually set in the work table and heated by steam. Kettles: In addition to the kettles used on the furnaces, stationary copper and iron kettles (steam heated) are used for melting sugar, glucose and syrup. Peanut Roasters: These are generally small rotating iron cylinders heated by gas, coke or coal. They should be properly set and guarded from inflammable material. Vacuum Pans, sometimes used for boiling sugar and syrup, present only the hazard of steam pipes. Starch Bucks are employed to coat the candy with starch. These machines are motor-driven with a shaking and shifting motion. Very little dust escapes where these machines are used, although open lights should be removed from the immediate vicinity. Starch Dry Rooms: Candy is moulded in depressions made by patterns pressed upon the flat surface of powdered starch, held in wooden trays, the soft candy being let into the moulds by means of droppers or tin vessels. To facilitate the setting of the candy, the starch trays are placed on racks in dry rooms, which are generally frame and steam heated. Dry rooms should be built of fire-proof material, properly vented and without open lights. See Starch Buck.

CANE AND RATTAN WORKS—As used for chair seats, furniture and baskets. Cleaned and bleached with hydrofluoric acid and chloride of lime, split, shaved and dried. Hazards of dry rooms, soaking tanks, shavers, splitters, gluing, machine shops, weaving cane seats, varnishing, shellacing or painting. Without these latter the hazard is mild.

CANNED GOODS—Generally considered by underwriters to be excellent insurance, as the contents are hermetically sealed. May suffer a severe loss should even a small amount of water remove the labels and thereby destroy the identity of the goods therein. When packed in cases, this is not so apt to occur.

CANNEL COAL—A bituminous variety used by fire departments and in open-hearth grates.

CANTILEVER—A lever fixed at one end and supporting a weight or resisting a force by virtue of its own stiffness and the strength of its attachment to the support.

CAOUTCHOUCINE (or coutchine) is a water-proofing compound and a solvent of resinous substances prepared by vaporization of india-rubber at a temperature of 600 deg. F. Hazardous.

CAP—Post Cap. The top member (flat) of a column or post.

CAPACITY OF WATER TANKS—See Tables.

CAP FACTORY—Cloth caps, largely made from scraps or piece goods; celluloid for visors, cotton batting for stuffing, embossing ornaments, hydraulic presses, dry rooms, sewing machines. Habitually untidy and generally cheap class of help. Unprofitable class.

CAPITAL OF A COMPANY—The money furnished by the stockholders to give stability as required in the organization of a company, thus providing funds from which the policy-holders can draw in case of emergency. It is a liability.

CAP STONE—See Bond and Cap Stones.

CARBIDES—Compounds of carbon and metals. Some are explosive.

CARBINOL-METHYLIC ALCOHOL or wood spirit. Inflammable liquid.

CARBOHYDRATES—Consist of carbon, hydrogen and oxygen. They include all substances bearing names ending in ————ose.

CARBOLIC ACID is derived from coal tar. Melts at 108 deg. F. Not explosive in itself. Manufacturing hazard is mild.

CARBOLINEUM—A wood preserver, chemical fluid. Base is heavy coal-tar product mixed with chlorine gas. Flash about 280 deg. F. Free from combustion.

CARBOLIZING—Consists of extracting the sap and water from the timber and driving carbolic or tar acids through.

CARBON—This element is distributed in nature in the free condition, in organic and inorganic substances. It appears in various forms, the most common being that of charcoal, and the various kinds of coal, which are chiefly carbon.

CARBONATES—Are carbonic acid compounds.

CARBON-BISULPHIDE—Produced by passing the vapor of burning sulphur over charcoal kept red hot. Highly inflammable. Vapor mixed with air takes fire at 300 deg. F. A solvent for fats, oils, india-rubber, phosphorus, bromine, iodine, camphor. Also used in cheap grade paints. When stored in steel drums, the hazard is not severe.

CARBON-BLACK (Lamp Black)—Consists of light and finely divided carbon. It is obtained by burning oil or gas with a smoky flame. Will ignite spontaneously. Classed as inflammable solid. Fires are caused by the sparks remaining from the manufacturing processes.

CARBON BRUSHES, used on motors, are made of carbon and graphite.

CARBON-DISULPHIDE—See Carbon-bisulphide.

CARBON OIL—See Hydrocarbon.

CARBON PAPER AND TYPEWRITER RIBBONS—Use mineral waxes, beeswax, Japanese wax, canauber wax, carbon black, lamp black, castor oil, olive oil, neatsfoot oil, lard oils, vaseline, turpentine, alcohol, paraffine. Hazards of mixing and grinding colors and ingredients, heating waxes and oils, applying mixture to paper and fabrics (a cold process), glue-heaters, storage of materials. See Typewriter Inks.

CARBON TETRA-CHLORIDE—Used as a basis for contents of fire extinguishers and for cleaning fluids in place of benzine. Made by passing chlorine gas over heated carbon-bisulphide, the product condensed in a cooler. A mixture of carbon tetra-chloride and sulphur is thus obtained. By introducing caustic soda or potash the sulphur dichloride is decomposed and dissolved, precipitating the purified carbon tetra-chloride. It is non-hazardous and non-inflammable.

CARBONA—Carbon tetra-chloride and gasoline mixed. Non-inflammable.

CARBONACEOUS SUBSTANCES—Many have no nitrogen in them, and carbon is their most important element. Sugar, starch, oils and fats are carbonaceous substances.

CARBONATE OF AMMONIA is made by heating in closed iron vessels bones, hartshorn or other animal matters and then purifying them by sublimation.

CARBONATE OF LIME is marble which contains lime and carbonic acid.

CARBONATE OF POTASH is obtained from the ashes of plants, potash and carbonic acid.

CARBONATE OF SODA is made from common salt. It is soda and carbonic acid.

CARBONIC ACID—A gaseous compound of carbon and oxygen. It is produced by the process of combustion and respiration, and hence is always present in the air.

CARBONIC ACID GAS OR CARBON DIOXIDE—Calcium magnasite is heated in ovens to about 1,400 deg. F. by fuel oil or gas. The heat breaks up the magnasite into carbonic acid gas and calcide magnasite. Gas is filtered through charcoal purifiers to compressors. At high pressure carbonic acid gas liquefies. Non-inflammable. Cylinders containing same should not be exposed to heat. It extinguishes fire because it eliminates oxygen, which is necessary to combustion. Liquid carbonic acid gas is manufactured from marble dust mixed with water, pumped to generators, mixed with sulphuric acid, charged with carbonic acid gas. From coke-fed retorts, passed through scrubbers, drawn by suction to gas absorbers, boiled, purified in iron tanks, compressed, separated, cooled. Hazards are boilers, coke fuel, clearance of steam conveyor pipes which become hot, acid storage.

CARBONIZING means charring a substance. This process is accomplished by direct fire heat, as a rule. See Embroideries.

CARBORUNDUM—Composed of sand, carbon and a little salt melted electrically, forming silicon carbide, the crystals of which are hard as diamonds and are used for abrasive purposes.

CARBOY—A large glass bottle or demijohn enclosed in a wooden crate and generally packed with straw to prevent breakage. Usually used for corrosive acids.

CARBURETOR is a device to atomize gasoline or other light hydro-carbons, and then mix it with air to make the combination highly combustible.

CARBURETS—Same as carbides.

CARBURETTED HYDROGEN is carbon or charcoal united with hydrogen.

CARDING MACHINES—Lay the fibre straight and form it into a loose roving preparatory to spinning.

In woolen mills fires are caused by sparks igniting the lint or flyings where cotton forms part of the goods. Sparks usually at the first or "licker-in" roll. Machines are fed automatically from a Bramwell feeder. Hazards depend upon the amount of cotton used (wool not readily ignited). Mills using the long, first-grade fibre-wool the least hazardous. Cheap knitting mills and horse blanket factories use cheap grade cotton and wool which contains considerable foreign matter. See Bramwell Feed.

CARDING ROOMS are more preferable if detached or cut off by fire doors.

CAROUSEL MANUFACTURING—A woodworking and machine shop hazard usually located in light, high, one-story frame buildings in sparsely settled locations. Not attractive fire risks. Cheap grade labor as a rule; benzine-thinned paints. Where animals are made, the seats are apt to be upholstered with excelsior.

CARPENTERS' STOVES are three to four feet long, fifteen to eighteen inches wide, set on legs. Usually burn wood or shop refuse. See Cabinet Factories.

CARPET AND RUG MANUFACTURING—Imported wool received in bales, then fed into the washing machines and then into the picking machine, then to the dry room, where the heat from steam coils is forced through it by means of blowers. The wool then passes to the sorting room, where the blends are carefully made before it goes to the machine which tears the wool fibres apart and gets them in shape for the carding and combing processes. The wool is then blown into a spinning mill, after which it is ready to be converted into yarn. It passes through a picking machine, which blends the different grades of the raw material. It is then refined and purified. Through tubes, the wool is forced to the carding room by means of air pressure. It is then taken to the combing machines, which separate the long from the short fibres. The strands of wool are thinned out and given sufficient strength to stand the weaving process. The yarn next appears in rows of spindles in the "mule" room, where the yarn is twisted and brought to its final stage. The yarn next goes to the dyehouse to be boiled, bleached and colored, then to the drying house, and through a steaming process to set the colors, and next to the weave shop, where great skill is required in the assembling of the yarn and the matching of the colors. The skeins of yarn are wound on spools, which are put in sets at back of the looms, each color or set representing one frame of color on the rug. After the weave is completed, the rug comes out rough. It is passed through a finishing machine to remove the roughness on the surface of the rug or carpet.

CARPET CLEANING employs, as a rule, revolving drum-beaters enclosed in wood partitions, equipped with suction to carry off dirt and dust. Also electrical vacuum apparatus, which sucks the dirt out of the material. Dust hazard. No open lights permitted in cleaning rooms; good ventilation required. Hazards of dirty bearings, washing in soap and water, dyeing, recoloring faded spots with aniline colors, dry rooms, pressing irons, sewing machines. Benzine is often used for cleaning. Poor fire record.

In some households, the carpet which is tacked to the floor is cleaned by naphtha without removing it from the floor. The flooring becomes soaked with the naphtha. An open flame may ignite the vapor arising.

CARPET SLIPPER MANUFACTURING—Cut, sew and tack the materials, using pasteboard insoles glued or pasted in. Untidy shops and cheap class labor as a rule. A poor fire record class.

CARRON OIL—A mixture of linseed oil and lime water. A good remedy for burns. Should be kept in every factory and home.

CARTON—A box or container made of pasteboard or corrugated paper.

CARTRIDGE FUSE—A cartridge-shaped shell enclosing an electrical fuse. Used to prevent the molten fuse from igniting inflammable material.

CARVERS—There are two types used in woodworking—duplicating and spindle. Spindle carver is a machine wherein a milling cutter is rotated very rapidly at the end of a horizontal spindle. Duplicating carver, one with a blank tool and small cutters, which are made to pass simultaneously over the outlines and surfaces of a pattern and the pieces to be carved.

CASE—A box for packing goods.

CASE HARDEN—To convert the outer surface of wrought iron into steel by heating to white heat in contact with charcoal.

CASED GOODS—Goods unopened and in cases or original containers.

CASEIN OR LACTEIN—Made from skimmed milk. Used in manufacturing buttons, combs and for surfacing fine printing paper in preference to glue, as it is not subject to moisture. Skimmed milk is heated to about 135 deg. F., sulphuric acid (dilute) added to precipitate the casein, and the whey drained off. The curd (casein) is drained, washed in water to remove the acid, dried, ground into powder. There is about 3½ per cent. of casein in skimmed milk. Hazards, boilers, acid storage, dry rooms, stone grinders.

CASEMENT—Applied to a window which is hung upon hinges in place of cord and sash weight.

CASINGS—See Abattoir.

CAST IRON is very brittle, of granular nature and cannot be welded. When heated and suddenly cooled by water it flies into fragments. All iron work in buildings should be protected (insulated) with at least two inches of fire-proofing material.

CAST-IRON COLUMNS—On account of the heavy, irregular masses of metal forming the flanges, the beams, webs and brackets set up internal strains and stresses which are apt to cause invisible cracks which under any unusual conditions of loading or shock might cause serious calamity. Recommend fabricated steel columns properly protected by either terra-cotta or concrete.

CASTING—Pouring molten metal into moulds. Ordinary iron and brass castings are made in sand moulds. Iron moulds are used for "chilled iron castings."

CASTOR OIL is obtained from the castor bean, the seed of a plant indigenous to Southern Asia. The bean contains from 48 to 60 per cent. of oil. The process of extraction is as follows: After cleaning to remove sand, trash, etc., the beans are crushed, packed in press cylinders and subjected to hydraulic pressure. The oil thus expressed is, after settling and clarifying, known as "cold pressed," or medicinal, and is in color from a water white to pale yellow, depending on the quality of the seed. The remaining 10 per cent. of the oil content of the meat, after cold pressing, is heated or cooked and subjected while still hot to hydraulic pressure in box presses, the resulting oil being known as "hot pressed," or technical oil, and is in color from a pale straw to a brown tint. Approximately 5 per cent of oil still remains in the meat after the above process. In order to reclaim this an extraction plant is necessary. See Extracting Plants.

CATERERS—Combined hazards of bakers, confectioners and restaurants.

CAUL BOX—A long, oblong box with steam coils, used for drying lumber of small dimensions. Should be lined with lock-jointed tin and have wire screen over steam coils. Apt to become untidy with sawdust or shavings. Formerly these were heated by a smoke pipe of a stove passing through the box.

CAUSTIC LIME—See Lime.

CAUSTIC POTASH—Obtained from carbonate of potash or pearl ash solution, contained in an iron pot by mixing it with slaked lime in small quantities at a time, the whole being kept at the boiling point. Insoluble carbonate of lime is formed and potassium hydrate remains in solution. Not inflammable. There is no fire hazard to speak of.

CAUSTIC SODA is prepared by causticizing sodium carbonate with lime. Not inflammable. Practically no fire hazard.

CEDAR OIL MOPS—Liable to ignite spontaneously. Used extensively in dwellings. Should be in well-ventilated room or a metal can with cover. They are the cause of many fires. Proper name is O'Cedar.

CELESTROM EBONITE, BLACK LACQUER—Flash point 290 deg. F. Classed as non-volatile.

CELESTROM GLOSSY BLACK LACQUER—Flash point 290 deg. F. Classed as non-volatile.

CELESTROM THINNER—Flash point 290 deg. F. Classed as non-volatile.

CELESTROM TRANSPARENT LACQUER — Flash point 290 deg. F. Classed as non-volatile.

CELLAR—A room or enclosed space partly or wholly below ground. It is usually under a building.

CELLAR FIRES are usually hard to fight on account of the dense smoke. Generally when the fire department arrives they immediately start to ventilate the place by cutting holes in the floor or sidewalk lights. A special nozzle is used on the hose when access to the cellar cannot be gained. See Areaways.

CELLIT—A substitute for celluloid; does not burn very readily. Cinematograph films are approved by the British Fire Prevention Commission as non-flaming.

CELLULOID—Can be worked with tools while cold or moulded like plaster when heated with steam. The basic element is known as cellulose, such as cotton or fine tissue paper. When cotton is used it is first washed in alkalies to remove dirt and oil, washed in water and dried, cut into small lengths, placed in earthen jars with nitric and sulphuric acids, 1 to 3 parts. This is called nitrating. It is next washed in water, dried in centrifugal extractors, and resembles snow when chopped very fine; then mixed with camphor. Pressed in slabs in hydraulic press. At this point the

material is not very inflammable. The slabs are broken up, moistened with alcohol, and colored with aniline tints, then castor oil added. The product is then passed through steam-heated rolls, pressed in steam-heated presses in sheet form, dried and polished between thin sheets of polished steel. Worked in plastic state at 150-250 deg. F.; if heated to 300 deg. F. will decompose and burn without heavy flame, and may explode if confined. Little ether now used in its manufacture, which makes the process less dangerous.

Celluloid is used as substitute for horn, ivory, shell, pearl, wood veneers. Used in manufacture of harness rings, billiard balls, combs and hair ornaments, picture films, shaving brushes, brush and knife handles, collars, cuffs and buttons, jewelry backings, decorations, emblems, piano keys, ladies' collar supports, eye-shades, wind-shields.

Celluloid burns fiercely, frequently accompanied by explosions. Most of the explosions are caused by the generating of gaseous fumes, due to storing of the material in poorly ventilated places.

Scrap Celluloid in heaps will ignite spontaneously and should be kept free from all other forms of refuse, in metal receptacles with self-closing covers. Scrap from button, comb and other similar risks is sometimes used in horn and fertilizer factories. Before being worked, scraps should be run over a magnet to remove all metallic substances. Ground scrap is used for making harness rings. Grinding and sandpapering produce dust and machines should have blower system with separator and metal receptacle partly filled with water in which is deposited the celluloid dust.

Comb Risks usually employ cheap labor. The work consists of shaping blanks and inserting stones. Blanks are warmed on sheets of metal over gas flame or steam pipe, placed in hand moulds. The stones inserted by use of a cement composed of celluloid and glacial acetic acid.

Button Manufacturing requires the use of stamping presses, blow-pipes for making rims and holders, gas-heated calenders, cold or heated foot-power die presses. Occasionally photo work for taking pictures.

Toys require similar machinery to buttons. Hot water is used to soften and steam tables to mould sheet stock, saws and small boring lathes to work it. Steam tables are apt to become unduly hot and temperature should not exceed 225 deg. F. In working on celluloid, the danger from sparks is always imminent, especially at circular saws if foreign substances find their way into the stock. In boring holes, the spindle is usually cooled with water, as are many of the saws. Dipping (coloring) involves the use of inflammable liquids and should be in a separate fireproof building. An acetone thinned cement is used for cementing the different parts. Sheet stock, scraps, finished goods, all should be in separate compartments or buildings.

Piano keys of celluloid present a fire hazard on account of lighted cigar or cigarette butts being carelessly laid on them.

Imitation Leathers are made of cotton cloths and covered with nitro-cellulose in jelly form and polished with celluloid solutions. See Imitation Leather.

Trade names are Viscoloid, Pyroline, Fiberloid, Gallilith, Pyroxolin.

CEMENT—Natural cements are made by burning impure limestone at a low temperature (insufficient to vitrify). They do not slake with water, but require to be ground in order to convert them into hydraulic cement.

Portland cement is made by heating to incipient vitrification an intimate mixture of argillaceous and calcareous substances, which product does not slake with water, but upon grinding forms an energetic hydraulic cement.

CEMENT BLOCKS—Under-fire tests, show that the usual thin webs crack under the application of very intense heat. Webs should be of sufficient thickness to withstand the stresses due to rapid expansion when heated. A building of cement blocks is classed as frame construction by most rating bureaus.

CEMENT PLANTS AND PLASTER MILLS—There are two processes, the wet and the dry. Raw stock in the dry process is cement, rock, limestone and clay. In the wet process, marble and clay. Process consists of rock crushing drying through slowly rotating iron cylinders heated by coal, and burning in kilns heated to 2,500 to 2,800 deg. F. The hazards are those usual to heat-producing devices, and should be located a safe distance from woodwork. Dryers should be in separate buildings.

CEMENTATION—The process of converting wrought iron into steel by heating it in contact with charcoal.

CENTERING—The supports of an arch while being built.

CENTRAL STATION—A central location where fire alarms are received and immediately transmitted to the fire department. They are superior to local or private alarm systems.

CENTRIFUGAL PUMP—A type of pump in which water is set in rapid rotation by revolving vanes. The water has a centrifugal tendency imparted to it which causes it to rise through a pipe whose mouth faces tangentially the direction of rotation. See Fire Pumps.

CENTRIFUGAL SEPARATOR OR EXTRACTOR—A machine used for separating the lighter from the denser liquids, or liquids from solids. The machine rotates very rapidly on the principle that all liquids fly from the centre of rotation. Used in laundries, dry cleaning establishments, etc., for separating liquids from the cloth. Sometimes called "whizzers."

CEREAL MILLS—See Flour Mills.

CERESINE—A natural mineral wax, same as Ozerite.

CERESINAL—A mineral wax.

CHANDELIER MANUFACTURING—Gas fixtures are manufactured from tubing and gas piping, then cleaned with soap or other compound, plated and lacquered either by dipping or air-spraying, using Egyptian or amyl acetate lacquer. Generally employ cheap labor and occupy crowded lofts. The hazards are the use of volatiles and lacquer in rooms with open lights. Considerable packing material is used. Fire record poor.

CHANDLERS—See Ship's Chandlers.

CHAR is animal charcoal produced by heating bones to a fire heat in closed receptacles and then reducing to a fineness.

CHARCOAL is wood partly burned. Made by burning wood in heaps covered with turf and dirt. Small openings are left above and below so that a little air can circulate through the wood, thus continuing a smothered burning. In powdered form is said to be liable to spontaneous combustion. See Animal Charcoal.

CHAR-HOUSE—See Sugar Refineries.

CHARRING is the heating of organic matter out of contact with air.

CHASERS—Sometimes called edge-runners, consist of a heavy wheel mounted on a horizontal axis which travels slowly around a circular bed, giving a crushing and mixing effect to the material placed in its path. Used in paint or chocolate factories. No hazard.

CHATTEL MORTGAGE—A lien upon personal property, stock, fixtures or machinery for money loaned. To the insurance man it is indicative of financial straits, because the insured is forced to borrow on his movable property.

CHECK VALVE—See Flap-check Valve.

CHEMICALS—Colored fire in any form, flashlight powders, liquid acetylene, acetylide of copper, fulminate of mercury, fulminating gold or silver, gun cotton, nitroglycerine (except U. S. P. solution), chloride of nitrogen, amide or amine explosives, cymogen, volatile coal tar products having a boiling point below 60 deg. F., chlorate of potash in admixtures of organic matter or with phosphorus or sulphur, zinc dust, phosphorus, quicklime, phosphides, calcium carbide, metallic sodium and potassium, should only be allowed to be stored according to municipal requirements. Dangerous chemicals should be isolated in underground vaults. Metallic sodium and potassium in contact with water reacts, releasing hydrogen, and flames result. These latter chemicals should be stored in oil. See Drugs and Chemicals.

CHEMICAL EXTINGUISHERS—Hand chemicals of acid type, consist of a metal cylinder in which is placed a quantity of water, a glass bottle of sulphuric acid, and some bicarbonate of soda. By bringing the acid and soda in contact, a gas is formed which forces the water out through a nozzle. This type will destroy nickel and somewhat corrode brass.

Should be recharged every year. See Dry Powder Extinguishers.

CHEMICAL FIBRE OR FIBREBOARD—It is a board-like substance ⅛ to 3/16 inch in thickness, and will not burn readily. It is especially adaptable for covering and lining trunks.

Fibreboard is made from various waste materials, such as leather clippings, flax, hemp, old rope, tow, rags, paper, wood pulp and in fact, almost any fibrous substance. These materials are chopped or cut up into very small pieces in a cutting machine, then cooked in an agitated steam-heated boiler, in solution with lime, soda ash and an alkali, for several hours, mixed and ground in a "beater" similar in principle and action to that found in paper mills, fitted with revolving knives and agitators, and rosin, soap, coloring matter and other ingredients are added.

From the beater the stock is run into storage tanks or stuff chests, which supply the board-making machine known as the wet machine, where it is allowed to collect uniformly on the surface of a cylinder until it is of the proper thickness. It is then removed and placed on racks to dry, either in steam-heated dry rooms or on roofs in the open. See Fibreboard.

CHEMICAL FIRE ENGINES—Are used by fire departments, railroads, hospitals and factories. Consist of a 40-45 gallon chemical tank mounted on wheels with a length of hose (similar to hand extinguishers). Pressure, 75-160 lbs. or higher. Tested hose especially built for this particular purpose. To operate only necessary (in some types) to turn the operating wheel at rear, which revolves the tanks. The loose lead stopper drops from the acid jar, allowing the acid to flow into the soda or other alkali forming the pressure. In some types, the bottle containing the acid breaks, thereby allowing the acid to mix with the soda.

CHEMICAL LABORATORIES—In congested districts especially where doing experimental work, constitute severe exposures as a rule. In war times, experimenting, or manufacturing of explosives and dangerous gases predominate.

CHEMICAL RISKS—Should be written cautiously. Inspect for furnaces, ovens and chimneys. Liable to be a nuisance on account of obnoxious fumes. The action of acids and corrosives on fire doors and sprinkler heads makes these devices short-lived.

CHEMICAL WAREHOUSES—Buildings where the assured agrees to store separately from all other merchandise, a given list of chemicals, maintaining such separation, each from the other, by a substantial brick wall not less than 12 inches thick, extending through roof without doors or windows.

CHEMISTRY—A knowledge of chemistry is a great asset to an insurance inspector, as it enables him to determine fire hazards due to combination of materials which might be passed by either the assured or a less qualified inspector.

CHEWING GUM MANUFACTURING—Raw stock consists of chicle, which is usually received ready to be made up, essential oils, flour, flavoring extracts and glucose. Work consists of cooking in steam kettles, mixing the ingredients in power mixers, rolling the gum into thin sheets by steam rollers, cutting into strips, powdering and wrapping. The gum is first wrapped in waxed paper. After wrapping, the package is sealed by heating the waxed paper ends on a steam or gas-heated table, then pressing the ends together.

CHICLE comes in various forms, some hard and some soft, depending on locality in which it is produced. It is refined and blended for use as chewing gum. Process consists of breaking it into small bits in a "cracker," grinding in an iron grinder, mixing in steam-heated kettles, filtering in presses. A steam process.

CHILE SALTPETRE (sodium nitrate)—See Saltpetre.

CHILLING—Giving great hardness to the outside of cast iron by pouring it into a mould made of iron instead of wood.

CHIMNEYS are made tall in order to maintain a large hot fire. The hot air and gases ascend the chimney at the rate of 50 to 60 feet a second, and the velocity of the ascending current is based practically on the square root of the height of the stack.

Terra-cotta tile, sewer pipe or hollow bricks are not sufficient protection by themselves. All single thickness chimneys should be lined. Wall brackets are a source of danger due to collapse or rupture, unless it be very substantial brick

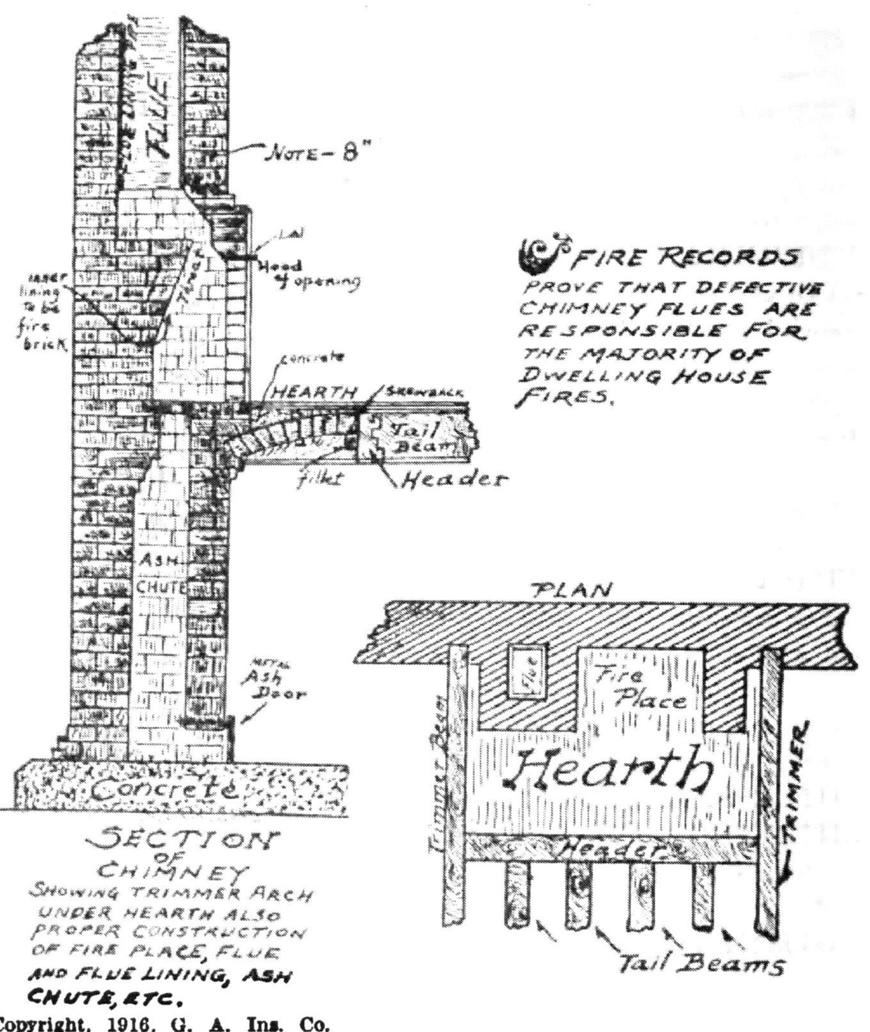

corbelling. Woodwork should not enter any part of a chimney or cover the surface. Smokepipes should enter chimneys horizontally. Chimneys should be cleaned once a year.

The main cause of chimney fires is the accumulation of soot. Soot is nearly pure carbon and is easily fired by sparks from a wood fire. If damp, will smoulder for hours and is liable to ignite spontaneously. Fires are sometimes caused by the house settling, and the weight of the wall resting on the chimney causes the bricks to loosen, leaving cracks which afford a means of sparks communicating to woodwork. See Bracket Chimney; also Wall Chimney.

CHIMNEY ON FIRE—When soot has been ignited by a fire it can be extinguished by shutting all the doors of the room, so as to prevent any current of air and then throwing a few handfuls of common salt upon the fire in the grate or in the stove. In burning the salt, muriatic acid gas is evolved, which is a prompt extinguisher of fire.

CHIMNEY OF RADIAL BRICK—Built of perforated radial bricks, varying in size, and made from refractory clay of great heat resistive quality and crushing strength. Are specially baked or burned and have a series of holes in them to permit even burning. Laid up in cement mortar. The walls are reinforced with steel bands. When built, their perforations form a dead air space which prevents radiation. Better workmanship and material is required to build a radial brick chimney which adds to the safety of a plant.

CHINA DECORATING OR DECALCAMANIE—China is first sized with a varnish, part resin and part turps, by hand brush. Design is then pasted on, pressed and washed by hand with same material, then baked in kiln. Designs are on paper with transfer paper called decalcomanie. See Crockery.

CHINA OIL SILK—As a stock is very inflammable and susceptible. Used for raincoats. Apparently use paraffine for impregnating fabric.

CHINATOWN DWELLINGS—Fires are caused and spread by swinging gas brackets igniting walls covered with Chinese decorations, such as festooned paper, knick-knacks, ornamental wood objects and prints, also unsafe stoves.

CHINESE OIL—Used by varnishers on woodwork, obtained from Chinese nut or berry. Inflammable. Subject to spontaneous combustion.

CHINESE RESTAURANTS are seldom insured on account of their fire record. They are cleaner than the general run of restaurants. Very little frying is done, which reduces the grease fire hazard.

CHINESE WAX—A solid wax deposited by insects on the Chinese ash tree. Melting point about 180 deg. F.

CHINESE WOOD OIL (tung oil)—Prepared from the nut of a Chinese tree. Substitute for linseed oil.

CHIROPODISTS—Usually occupy small places on an upper floor. May have unsafe gas stove. Alcohol is used extensively. Salves may be made on premises and heated by direct heat.

CHLORATES, NITRATES, PEROXIDES—These are all hazardous, owing to the quantity of oxygen which they evolve when heated. Most of them can be detonated or exploded when in contact with starch, sugar, gum, sweepings or dust, or other organic matter, or sulphur and its compounds. Are apt to cause explosion by friction, concussion or high temperature, and should be kept away from mineral acids, carriers of oxygen, organic substances and sulphur. (W. D. Grier in Crosby-Fiske Handbook of Fire Protection.)

CHLORATE OF ZINC—See Zinc Chlorate.

CHLORATE TABLETS contain potassium chlorate. Same hazard as other chlorates in bulk.

CHLOR-BENZOL—Flash point about 90 deg. F.

CHLORIDE OF CALCIUM is muriate of lime.

CHLORIDE OF LIME is made by passing chlorine gas into boxes of lead in which a quantity of slaked lime is laid on shelves. Called bleaching powder.

CHLORIDE OF PHOSPHORUS, phosphorus trichloride, is a fuming colorless liquid. Acts strongly on organic matter containing great heat.

CHLORIDE OF POTASH LOZENGES are highly dangerous if accidentally brought into contact with an unlighted phosphorus match.

CHLORIDE OF SILICON is a colorless liquid fuming strongly in air. Mixed with water it is decomposed, forming hydrochloric acid.

CHLORIDE OF SODA—See Chloride of Lime.

CHLORIDE OF SODIUM is common salt.

CHLORIDE OF SULPHUR, sulphur chloride, is a corrosive fuming liquid used as solvent for rubber in vulcanizing.

CHLORIDES—All the compounds of the gas chlorine are called chlorides.

CHLORINE—A heavy, greenish, poisonous gas given off in some processes of manufacture and by bleaching powder and chloride of lime, especially in the presence of strong acids. It is not inflammable, but may cause fire or explosion if in contact with ammonia, turpentine or finely powdered metal. Good ventilation necessary where gas is generated. Used as a bleaching acid, supports combustion, has a strong affinity for hydrogen, but little for carbon, burns quickly giving off a white smoke. Can be made with two parts dilute sulphuric acid and a trifle more of chloride of lime or bleaching powder.

CHLORITES are chlorous acid compounds.

CHLOROFORM may be obtained by heating chloral with potassium nitrate, or by distillating a mixture of alcohol, water and bleaching powder. Burns with a greenish flame.

CHOCOLATE is made by roasting and then removing the outer shell of the cocoa bean and grinding the entire bean. The ground substance is put through a process to reduce it to a pulp.

CHORDS IN TRUSSES—The top member and the main horizontal tie are often called chords.

CHROMATE OF ZINC is obtained by precipitating a solution of sulphate of zinc with bichromate of potassium. Used in pigment printing. Chromates are of themselves harmless. When treated with sulphuric acid, they will ignite organic matter.

CHROMATES—Compounds of chromic oxide with metals.

CHROMES—Vandyke browns, artificially made from pigments, sometimes contain lamp black.

Chrome Green or Brunswick Green—Made of prussian blue and chrome yellow. Somewhat combustible from causes such as a rise in temperature in a dryer or friction in grinder.

Chrome Yellow—Made from solution of potassium chromate mixed with lead acetate, the chrome yellow being the precipitate (called lead chromate). Sometimes acids are used.

Chromic Acid—A dye used in calico printing.

CHURCHES—Of ordinary construction, have a very bad fire record. The trouble probably lies in the fact that they remain idle and without heat the greater part of the week and then the fires are forced to their capacity so as to get ready for services. Furring and concealed spaces play a large part in spreading fires. To make the interior attractive, the walls, recesses and pipe channels are furred out to make a smooth interior, leaving in some places a concealed space of over a foot in depth. This, and the numerous hot air or ventilating pipes cause the fire to spread and soon reach the attic over the hanging ceiling and burn off the roof, which in collapsing tears down the walls and wrecks the interior. Vestments, altars and statuary are very expensive. Fixed marble work and stained glass windows are insured with the building and may form considerable of the building value. Fires have been caused from upsetting candles, defective wiring and other common causes.

CHURCH OIL is rape oil or a combination of rape and mineral oils. Used in church rituals.

CHURN DRILL—A long iron bar with a cutting end of steel. Much used in quarrying.

CHUTE—An inclined slide, open or enclosed, used for conveying material from one level or floor to another floor level.

CIGARETTE MAKING—Inventions and improvements in modern machinery render this process principally a mechanical operation. An up-to-date plant has automatic cigarette machine with hopper holding the tobacco and attachments which grasp the required amount of tobacco, roll it, paste it, clip the ends, count it. The paste used is cold, although some makes of machines have a small gas flame which dries the wrapper before it leaves the machine. The cork tip machine rolls a piece of cork around the cigarette and pastes it, no heat used. Tobacco is blended in a revolving drum, enclosed in a wood frame, moistened and dried in separate revolving cylinders. The cylinder is on an inclined axis and delivers the tobacco to the cigarette machine. "Textile" dryers, as used in woolen mills, are used for drying leaf tobacco. It consists of a very long traveling belt on which is placed the tobacco, heated by steam coils and hot air blown across steam coils, all enclosed in a wooden frame. Hazards here are steam pipes and dust collecting on fans. The tobacco is ground in an all-iron machine with knife grinder and should have magnet to catch metal particles. Cigarettes spoiled in the making, are macerated in a mill, the tobacco screened out and used again. Storage of tobacco should be in a room with even temperature, so that it will not deteriorate. Paper box making and printing, making flour paste in steam kettles, cleaning and dusting tobacco-drying rooms, and use of bisulphide of carbon for exterminating vermin. See Tobacco.

CINDER CONCRETE—See Concrete.

CIRCUIT BREAKER—An electrical device, manual or automatic for interrupting completely the flow of current in a circuit.

CIRCULAR SAW—A woodworking machine with the saw in the center of a flat table or stand.

CITY LOTS—There are seventeen city lots, 25 by 100, in an acre.

CITY MAIN OR RESERVOIR should be sufficient to give twenty-five pounds pressure at a building. A pump connected to city main should be capable of providing twenty-five pounds pressure at top line of sprinklers. See Fire Pumps.

CLAPBOARDS—Thin boards, thicker on one edge. Used for covering the walls of houses.

CLARIFYING—See Liquors.

CLAROLIN—A benzine substitute, classed as non-volatile.

CLAY is derived from a certain kind of rock called feldspar. When feldspar is exposed to the action of the elements it crumbles slowly at the surface and the little particles combine with a certain amount of water-forming clay.

CLAY OR LOAM—If in fine state, will, if suspended in water, put out a fire quicker than pure water.

CLEANING COMPOUNDS—Usually contain gasoline or other inflammable solvents. Use same care in handling as with gasoline.

CLEANING ESTABLISHMENTS—See Dry Cleaning.

CLEANING MACHINERY FOR GRAIN—Should either be vented to the outer air, or else provided with a standard dust collecting system. Machines should be provided with magnets to catch metallic substances.

CLEARANCE—The clear space or uninterrupted distance between any heating apparatus or device to fixed woodwork or other combustible material. Temporary obstructions are not included.

CLEAR SPACE—Stock should not be placed nearer than 2 feet from the ceiling. If placed directly under the ceiling it shuts off the possibility of hose streams reaching the goods behind the same. In the case of sprinklered risks it obstructs the proper distribution of water. See Aisles.

CLIPPINGS—Cotton or woolen, if clean, are usually classed as desirable insurance, but inspection should always be made to determine if dirty rags or paper are received along with the clean clippings. If sorting is done, the number of hands should be noted, also whether metal receptacles are used under the screens for waste material. No gas lights should be permitted over sorting tables. Clippings in tailor shops should be kept in metal containers. See Rags.

CLOAKS AND SUITS—Busiest season, February, March and April, and June to October. (See clothing manufacturing.)

CLOSED VESSELS that have been standing in a fire should be left unopened until cool inside because vapors may have been generated or contents undergone partial carbonization and by admitting air an explosion may take place or spontaneous ignition follow.

CLOSETS IN SPRINKLERED RISKS should have open, wire mesh or paper-covered tops so that in case of fire, the water can easily wet down the contents. Closets for storage of janitors' or porters' rags and supplies should be metal-lined or fire-proof. Oily waste and rags, as usually found, are likely to cause spontaneous combustion.

CLOTHEL REFRIGERATING MACHINE—Direct expansion system using ethyl chloride for refrigerant. The latter is highly inflammable. Used in small units and at low pressure.

CLOTH SPONGING—Use high temperature live steam rolls for shrinking and steaming. The goods are examined by natural light, the cloth in bolts passing over drums or frames. This class is usually found in congested districts of the garment trade.

CLOTHING MANUFACTURING—See Garment Manufacturing. Poor fire record. See Sewing Tables.

CLOTHING ON FIRE—See Fire in Person's Clothing; also Fireproofing Children's Clothing.

CLOTHING PRESSING—Many small shops now do considerable power pressing by contract. Use small, but high temperature, gas boiler for heating power-pressing machines. These gas-heated boilers are usually poorly set and near woodwork. An unattractive class. See Pressing Tables.

CLUSTER GAS LAMPS IN FACTORIES—Should have springs to take up vibrations so that lamp will not break or become weakened. The main stem is broken with a flexible connection, made at right angles and the projecting piece supported by a spring which takes up the weight and jar. The distance from a combustible ceiling should not be less than 48 inches, unless protected with metal and asbestos shields.

COAL—Anthracite is hard coal. Bituminous is soft. Lignite and peat are forms of coal in transition state.

COAL GAS—Used for heating or illuminating; is made by the destructive distillation of bituminous (or sometimes hard) coal, in externally heated retorts, usually coke fuel is used. The gas from the retorts passes through a standpipe, the temperature being reduced by passing the gas through a water or weak ammonia liquor seal into which is dipped the standpipe. Condensed around cold water pipes. The tar and ammonia is extracted, passing through a series of screens under water pressure. It is then scrubbed to separate the remaining ammonia and napthalene by passing the gas through coke tower or through a horizontal scrubber in which are shafts to which are fastened sticks of wood which revolve in an ammonia solution. After oxide purification, it is stored in gas holders. It is lighter than air and ascends rapidly.

COAL GAS PRODUCERS—Pressure Systems—All pressure systems must be located in a special building or buildings approved by inspection department having jurisdiction for the purpose, at such distance from other buildings as not to constitute an exposure thereto, except that approved pressure systems without gasometer having a maximum capacity not exceeding 250 horse-power and pressure in generator not exceeding two pounds, may be located in the building, provided that the generator and all apparatus connected therewith be located in a separate fireproof room, well-ventilated to the outside of the building; every communication, if any, to be protected by an approved fire door. In all other respects the apparatus must comply with the requirements for suction systems.

Suction Systems—Approved suction gas-producers may be located inside the building, provided the apparatus for producing and preparing the gas is installed in a well-ventilated room. At no time shall the internal pressure of the producer be in excess of atmospheric pressure.

The smoke and vent pipe shall, where practicable, be carried above the roof of the building in which the apparatus is contained, and above adjoining buildings. When buildings are too high to make this practicable the pipe shall end at least 10 feet from any wall opening.

No smoke nor vent pipe shall be within 9 inches of any woodwork or any wooden lath and plaster partition or ceiling.

Where smoke and vent pipes pass through combustible partitions they shall be guarded by galvanized iron ventilated thimbles at least 12 inches larger in diameter than the pipes, or by galvanized iron thimbles built in at least 8 inches of brickwork or other incombustible material. They shall not under any circumstances be connected into chimneys or flues, except that the pipe may pass up in flues used for no other purpose. No smoke pipe shall pass through any floor nor through a roof having wooden framework or covering.

While the plant is not in operation the connection between the generator and scrubber must be closed and the connection between the producer and vent pipe opened, so that the products of combustion can pass into the open air. This must be accomplished by means of a mechanical arrangement which will prevent one operation without the other.

If illuminating or other pressure gas is used as an alternative supply, the connections must be so arranged as to make the mixture of the two gases or the use of both at the same time impossible.

If illuminating or other pressure gas is used as a supplementary supply, mixing of the two gases may be permitted if a suitable device is provided to prevent the supplemental gas from entering any part of the producer gas equipment, including the scrubber or purifier.

The opening for admitting fuel shall be provided with some charging device so that no considerable quantity of air can be admitted, or gas escape, while charging.

(Extracts from N. F. P. A. recommendations.)

COAL, ICE AND WOOD DEALERS usually occupy basements or cellars of tenements, the dealers being largely a foreign element. Unsafe coal stoves, salamanders, kerosene oil lamps, swinging gas brackets and rubbish constitute the features of this class.

COAL OIL—See Kerosene.

COAL POCKETS—Motors for conveyors usually become dusty, and sometimes sparks set explosive fires in coal dust. Steam engines and boilers should be in separate buildings. Garage and stable hazard. These buildings are usually high, shafty and open to all winds.

COAL, POWDERED—Used in Portland cement rotary

kilns, in boilers and brick kilns. Injected under air pressure into a flame or fire and produces intense heat. Eliminates the ash hazard as almost perfect combustion takes place.

COAL SHORTAGE—A nation-wide coal famine, such as experienced during the winter of 1917-18 greatly increases the fire hazard. In all classes of risks, dwellings, mercantile or manufacturing, tenants endeavor to relieve the situation by using improvised and often unsafe heating apparatus. Wood often replaces coal, but as it is more inflammable and produces a more intense heat, overheated smoke pipes and stoves result. Even salamanders with coal fuel are used in loft buildings and kerosene oil stoves in garages. Sprinkler equipments are rendered inoperative through freezing. In such intense weather street cleaning departments are at a standstill. The conveyances for carting refuse become frozen with wet material and cannot be used, barges become frozen and ice-bound and cannot be towed out to sea and dumped, and men will not work. This condition results in accumulations of refuse and rubbish and ashes in cellars. Fire departments are handicapped by frozen hydrants, icy and slippery streets or roads and physical discomforts.

COAL, SOFT—Storage should be kept, if possible, well away from the main buildings of the plant. Under no circumstances should it be piled up against a frame building.

If outside space will permit, the piles should be made low and flat without cone effect (not higher than 12 feet) and of large area, rather than of small area and piled high.

If wet coal is received, it should be dumped around the edges of the pile, or in some location where the air can get to it freely, and where large quantities of other coal will not be packed on top of it.

COAL STOVES should set on metal which should extend 12 inches in front of stove. Where stock is apt to come in contact, a metal shield enclosure should be provided. For installation of temporary kerosene oil burners, see Kerosene Burners. See Pot Stoves.

COAL SUPPLY—See Fuel.

COAL TAR—Obtained during the distillation of coal in

the manufacture of coal gas. Distillates are benzine yielded at temperature of 85 deg. C., toluene at 111 deg. C., phenol, cresol, napthalene and benzole between 150 and 210 deg. C.

COAL TAR DERIVATIVES—Coal tar, made directly from coal or from crude mineral oil, can first be turned into kerosene, benzine, naphtha, gasoline, refined tar or pitch. From these oils are distilled toluol, phenol (carbolic acid), pyridine, eresol, anthracene and other crude products for use as dyes, explosives, disinfectants and medicines. By-product ovens are now used in the manufacture of coal tar derivatives, instead of the old "beehive" coke ovens of the steel plants, which permitted the gas and tar from coal to go to waste. The distilling process is hazardous.

COAMING—The raised curbing surrounding a floor opening to prevent water from overflowing to a lower level. Also called curbing.

COAT PAD MANUFACTURING—Use ordinary sewing machines and power-cutting knives. Care and storage of cotton padding important. Usually have considerable lint around sewing machines and on floors. Not classed as desirable insurance risks.

COBALT—A hard metal.

COBBLER'S WAX, lamp-black, negrosine, beeswax.

COCA-BOLA—A tropical hardwood used in making clarinets, fifes and other similar instruments as a substitute for African black wood.

COCAINE is a white, bitter alkaloid made from cocoa leaves.

COCK—A kind of valve for the discharge of liquids, air, steam.

COCK LOFTS and roof spaces. See Frame Rows.

COCOA is made by roasting and then removing the shell from the chocolate bean, grinding and pressing, which forces all fat out of the bean, leaving a dry substance. The fat that is pressed out of the bean is called cocoa butter.

Cocoa is sometimes used in candy to replace liquid chocolate. The practice of each candy manufacturer making his own cocoa and chocolate, is gradually being discontinued, owing to the skilled labor required to obtain the desired results and because the manufacturers are able to obtain cocoa and chocolate from large factories, practically as cheap as they can make it themselves. In this way they also eliminate the chance they have previously taken in not making the chocolate the right consistency.

COCOA BUTTER—When the oil from cocoa seeds is separated from the seed itself it is turned into cocoa butter. Used in making cosmetics.

COCOA-MATTING—Made from fibre which is "laid" in rope walk, balled by twisting on hand-turned balling machines, braided into strands on ordinary braiding machines, worked into matting on looms. The upper side combed and the uneven edges cut evenly with shears. Shears are iron rolls on which are sharp edges which, rapidly revolving, shear off the edges. These and the combers should have blowers to carry off the fine-cut pieces and dust. The edges of the mats are sewed on ordinary sewing machines. The mats are bleached in chloride of lime, dyed in aniline colors, then dried. Storage of large quantities of fibre, dyeing, bleaching, drying, shearing and combing are the principal hazards. (Avoid this class if possible.)

COCOANUT SHREDDING consist of separating the meat from the shell by machinery, shredding in attrition mills and drying the flake in "textile" dryers. Flake may be dried on steam tables or in large cylinders with wire mesh top and bottom. (Always inspect this class.)

COEFFICIENT, or a constant friction, safety or strength, etc., may usually be taken to be a number which shows the proportion (or rather ratio) which friction, safety, tensile strength, etc., bear to a certain something else which is not generally expressed at the time, but which is well understood.

COFFEE—A bean, the preparation of which for market involves serious hazards, namely, shelling, cleaning, and polishing by power machinery; also roasting by direct fire heat. Coffee in the bean is considered good insurance.

COFFEE AND TEA STORES—Note whether the bulk of stock is in metal containers well covered, also the setting of the small coffee roaster and how the packing material is kept.

COFFEE ROASTING processes consist of shelling, cleaning, roasting, polishing, cooling and bagging. Inspectors should carefully examine construction of roasters and also describe the setting, whether fireproof or non-fireproof floor and kind of ceiling over the roaster.

The blowers attached to the cooling pans should be vented to the outer air.

COFFEE WAREHOUSE—At a recent fire in a paint and oil risk adjoining a coffee warehouse, pungent fumes from the burning paint and oil poured into the coffee warehouse. Although no fire or water entered the warehouse, a large loss was paid on coffee. See Exposures.

COFFER-DAM—An enclosure built in the water and then pumped dry so as to permit masonry or other work to be carried on inside of it.

COFFINS—Manufacturing; carpenter shop hazard, cotton and excelsior for stuffing, gluing, sewing machines, painting and varnishing, metal working. Fires in this class usually very severe, owing to the highly varnished stock of a combustible nature.

COIR—A sort of yarn derived from the husks of cocoanuts.

COKE is the solid material left after evaporating the volatile ingredients of coal by means of the destructive distillation of coal in closed retorts. Used in the manufacture of iron and steel.

COLD AIR BOXES of furnaces should be metal rather than of wood. If metal for a distance of 4 feet from the furnace, the wood is not a very serious feature.

COLD STORAGE—An atmosphere maintained below freezing for the preservation of meat, etc., which are apt to putrefy. See Bunker Rooms.

COLD STORAGE FIRES require tons of water, that is, enough to thoroughly drench the entire mass. A small amount really assists the fire.

In New York City a firm recently converted the fireproof cold storage building of a brewery into fur cold storage, estimating that as much as ten millions of dollars worth of furs could be stored therein. The owners of the furs preferred that the building be not sprinklered, because the water damage would ruin the stock. Fires have been known to expand the cold air pipes to such an extent as to burst the walls of the building. See Ammonia Gas. See Consequential Loss.

COLLAR BEAM—A horizontal beam below the apex of the roof, stretching between every alternate pair of rafters which meet at the top.

COLLAR, CUFF AND SHIRT FACTORIES—Hazard that of white goods manufacturing, such as cutting, shrinking and sewing. Clothing shrunk in steam rooms. Laundering. Small press for printing maker's name on goods. Dry rooms. Collar-shaping machines, and other machinery, same as used in collar and cuff laundries. Incidental hazards are paper box making, wood box making, machine repair shop. See Laundries.

COLLAR SUPPORTERS—Used by women for supporting lace collars. Made of wire, cut and crimped, immersed in dilute muriatic acid and water, washed in water, dipped in solution of cyanide of potassium and water as a galvanic process. Dipped into paint, dried, coated (dip process) with celluloid. Hazards of dip process, painting, coating with celluloid. Turpentine used as thinner for paint, acetone for celluloid. Scrap celluloid, gas-heated drying ovens, open lights near liquid celluloid.

COLLEGES—See Academies.

COLLODION—Gun cotton dissolved in alcohol and ether. Used in photo-engraving. Very inflammable. Vapor is explosive when mixed with air. Open flames or lights prohibited. Flash point 40 deg. F.

COLOGNE SPIRITS—See Grain Alcohol.

COLONIAL WALL BOARDS—A product of calcined gypsum, fibred with wood and containing small percentage of Portland cement and hydrated lime formed into 32 or 36 inch slabs or sheets.

COLOR PRINTING—Lithographing hazard.

COLOR WORKS—Colors made by precipitation. Materials such as sulphuric, muriatic and fortis acid, mineral salts, copperas, zinc white, cyanide potassium, chloride of potash, bi-chromate of lime, nitrate of soda, and soda ash are placed in dissolving vats, drained to settling tanks where water is pumped out. Liquid colors are pumped to filters, placed on trays and dried in dry rooms. They are ground in mills and pulverized, sifted and packed. See Aniline Colors.

COLORED FIRE or tableau usually contains chlorate and often sulphur. Highly inflammable.

COLUMBIAN SPIRITS—See Wood Alcohol. Flash point 44 deg. F.

COLZA OIL is rape oil.

COLUMN—Sometimes called a post. A pillar, built up of steel members.

COMBINATION RED FIRE ALARM BOX—Used for watchman to record his hourly rounds. If watchman fails to record a certain round, a man from the central station is despatched to ascertain the cause of delay. The same box is used for sending in a fire alarm.

COMBS—See Celluloid.

COMBUSTION—What we usually call combustion attends the union of oxygen with some other substance, either solid or gaseous, as with carbon and hydrogen. We generally only use the term combustion when it is accompanied by heat and light, and yet the union of oxygen with other things often takes place without producing any light. This is when the union takes place slowly—thus iron rusts, the oxygen of the air unites with it, but so slowly that no light is given out—there is heat, but so little of it that it cannot be felt because the union is so slow. It is very slow fire. When a man paints his iron fence to keep it from rusting, he really keeps it from getting burned. In this same manner, water puts out fire. It shuts out the oxygen of the air from the burning substance. It acts much as the paint acts on the iron. (Hooker's Chemistry.) See How Water Puts Out Fire.

COMBUSTION ENGINES—See Gas, Gasoline, Kerosene and Fuel Oil Engines.

COMMERCIAL PHOTOGRAPHY—Use collodion in wet

plate photography, which is occasionally mixed on the premises.

COMMERCIAL REPORTS—Reports from bureaus as to the financial standing of individuals or firms. See Trade Reports.

COMMISSION CLAUSE—Covers the property of the insured and his interest in the property of others, such as advances and storage charges. The words "held in trust" have in some cases been given a very liberal interpretation by the courts.

COMMISSION MERCHANT—One who sells merchandise on a commission basis.

COMMISSIONS AND/OR PROFITS insurance indemnifies for loss of prospective profit or commission on merchandise or manufactured goods. There are two kinds of forms (per diem and percentage). See Profit Insurance.

COMMON CARRIERS INSURANCE—This insurance is to indemnify the insured for their legal liability, if any, to the amount they are obliged to pay on such merchandise in their care by reason of loss or damage by fire.

COMMON HAZARD means carelessness, unsafe chimneys, ashes in wood receptacles and the hazards of light, heat and power, as found in all risks. See Hazard.

COMMON RAFTERS—See Jack Rafters.

COMMUNICATION—An opening from one building to another, directly or indirectly by an enclosed passageway. A standard communication requires an automatic "labelled" fire door on each side of the wall. See Cut-off.

COMPOSITION FLOORINGS are composed of different mixtures containing such materials as asbestos, magnesite, sawdust, sand, magnesium chloride, etc., and are sold under such names as Alignum, Asbestolith, Asbestos Granite, Rex, Sanita, Monolith, etc. See Flooring (composition).

COMPO-BOARD FACTORIES.—The lumber is dried and reduced to slats about a quarter inch thick. These slats are then laid flat and indiscriminately as to grain, after which straw-board is glued on either side so as to form a large flat board. Sometimes the straw-board is treated with a cement or composition of resin, whiting and wax to harden it and render it water-proof. The hazards are those of wood-working risks. See Fireboard.

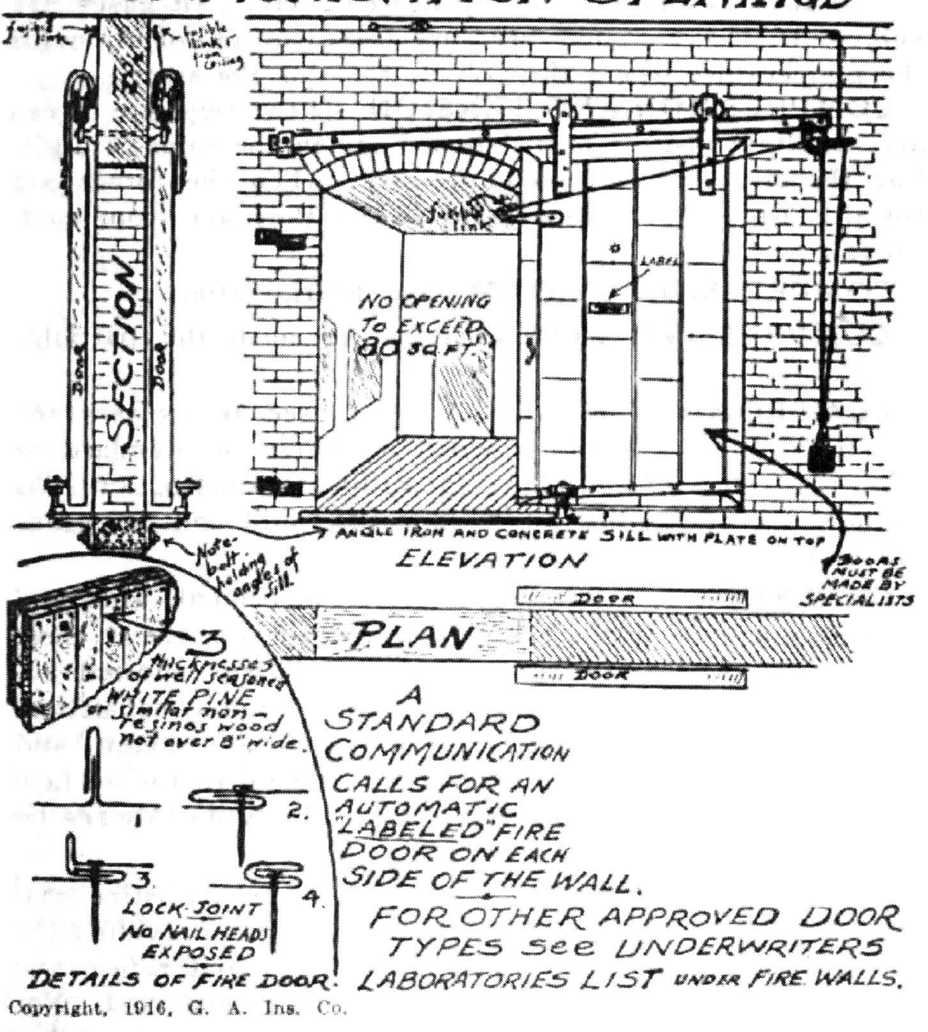

COMPOUND (chemically) refers to a substance containing two or more elements chemically united in such a way that the properties of the compound substance bear no resemblance to those of any of its constituents.

COMPOUND—An expression used by underwriters to indicate a risk having many manufacturing hazards under one roof; usually a loft building.

COMPOUNDING—See Liquors.

COMPRESSED GAS CYLINDERS must not be exposed to the rays of the sun or any heated body. All gases are subject to the law that pressure increases uniformly with the temperature where the volume remains the same.

COMPRESSION AND TENSION—If two opposite forces are simultaneously imparted to a body in the same straight line the stress is either compressive (when the forces act towards each other) or tensile (when they act from each other).

COMPRESSION SYSTEM—See Refrigerating.

COMPRESSIVE STRESS tends to push the particles closer together.

COMPROMISE "MILL"—A term used to express the construction of a building which is below the standard of "mill construction" and above the ordinary construction. The timbers are of smaller dimensions than mill and the spans are of less distance apart.

CONCRETE is a mixture of Portland cement, sand and stone or cinders. In the Edison Phonograph Co. fire at West Orange, N. J., in 1916, the concrete buildings showed superiority over all other forms of fireproof construction. Concrete partially injured by fire may set again and become hard, if there is a gradual cooling off of the surface and if no water is applied; but this result cannot always be relied upon.

CONCRETE, CINDER—An excellent fire resistive material for floor arches in fireproof construction, providing the cinders are of uniform size, free from dirt and refuse and contain not more than 15 per cent. of unburned coal. For good work the cinders should be ground before the other ingredients (sand and cement) are added.

CONCRETE-COVERED FLOORS—Numerous fires have

occurred under dry kilns and hotel or restaurant ranges which have been built on concrete-covered wood floors laid without air space, even though the concrete was three to twelve inches thick. The continuous heat slowly reduces the wood to charcoal and produces spontaneous combustion at a low temperature. The same principle applies to the flooring around anvils and forges due to the continuous dropping of hot iron on wood. Metal-covered floors are necessary at anvils and forges.

CONCRETE FOR CELLAR FLOORS—One part of good domestic cement, one part clean, sharp, gritty sand and five parts of best clean, coarse gravel, thoroughly washed, or clean, broken stone (small enough to pass through a 2-inch ring), the latter preferably. All to be by measure, thoroughly mixed and water then added.

CONCRETE, REINFORCED—Reinforcement consists of plain bars, bars with lugs, twisted bars, those having fins or protrusions, woven wire fabric, expanded metal, perforated sheet metal. Aggregates used are rock, stone, gravel, cinders, broken bricks or tile, slag. Buildings are erected in various types of construction, columns of concrete, walls or floor arches of concrete, or combinations of terra-cotta arches, curtain walls, etc., with concrete supporting members, or all concrete. Buildings of this latter character are rigid, sanitary, durable, fireproof. They have disadvantages, such as faulty design resulting in collapse or cannot be used for intended purposes, careless workmanship resulting in inferior construction; dishonesty on part of contractor resulting in small percentage of cement and therefore weakening of structure; expensive to alter, owing to solidity of material when once hardened; floors and walls apt to become "dusty" due to drying of concrete which has too small a percentage of cement as binder and too much sand, or materials of poor quality or not thoroughly mixed. Building collapse or failure due to removal of forms too quickly before the concrete has set properly; frozen concrete; overloading new structures; electrolysis.

CONDENSER—An apparatus for changing vapor into

liquid, usually a series of iron coils, cooled by running cold water.

CONDENSER, STEAM—A part of a steam plant in which the steam, after doing its work by expansion in the cylinders, is condensed by coming in contact with a jet of cold water or with the outer surface of tubes in which cold water circulates.

CONDUIT, RIGID—Sometimes known as galvanic duct and loricated. A rigid steel pipe chemically treated for the express purpose of providing a concealed method of running electric wires from place to place and so confining these wires as to prevent any fire resulting from short circuits.

CONDUIT SYSTEMS of electric wiring are far superior to open work, for the reason that the wires are better protected against mechanical injury and also because novices cannot very easily tamper with the installation.

CONES AND WAFERS—Made of flour, lard and sugar, mixed and baked. Machinery consists of gas-heated moulds, revolving automatic bakers and lard heaters. See Wafers and Cones.

CONFECTIONERS—Have motor or gas engine or boiler for power for ice-cream machine and ice cracker. Gas stoves and gas candy warmers used in candy manufacturing should be properly protected.

CONFECTIONERS' STOVE—A round iron or sheet metal stove with open or removable top to accommodate large kettles. Gas, coal or charcoal fuel.

CONFETTI is made of paper. The sheet paper is run through a perforator. The process is not hazardous, but the premises are usually filled with loose waste paper, presenting a very untidy appearance.

CONFLAGRATION BLAST—If you light a match the flame will mount so high. Light a second and a third match, hold them beside the first and the flame will mount successively higher. Blow gently upon the flame and it will have a steady striking range of an inch or more. Now, if you have a quarter mile of buildings all afire at once, the uniting flame from them will reach to a height corresponding to the area of the fire, and correspondingly great must be its

This sketch represents a fire caused by invisible heat, as shown in the candle sketch above, and also by flying brands lighting on the shingle roof in the distance.

striking range. In San Francisco in the language of one of the official reports: "Until the wind arose the heated column reached almost half a mile in height." (Arthur E. McFarlane.) See Flames.

CONFLAGRATION BREEDERS (remedy for) — First, that owners of existing buildings (defectively constructed), which are so located as to form conflagration areas, be required to suitably protect roof, floors, party walls, and exposed openings. Second, that automatic sprinkler equipment with outside siamese hose connections and controlling valve near the main in the street be required in all buildings which by reason of their size, construction or occupancy, singly or combined, might act as conflagration breeders. (National Board of Fire Underwriters.)

CONFLAGRATION PROBLEM—Extracts from address by Franklin H. Wentworth, Secretary, National Fire Protection Association, before the Newark Association of Credit Men:

There is a way to solve this conflagration problem—not absolutely, but at least relatively. You cannot be expected to tear down your city and rebuild it of fire-resisting material; or even to tear down enough buildings to allow broad streets or parkways—by which open spaces, conflagrations might be arrested. The cities must be protected as they stand. What then can be done by you beside furnishing water supplies and fire departments; keeping your city free from rubbish, and prohibiting forever and always the shingle roof as if it were a public crime? I would suggest this plan: In the heart of nearly every city there are streets crossing at right angles, along which for a very considerable distance are buildings of brick, stone or concrete. Looked at upon the map this shows a more or less complete Maltese cross of buildings which are not wooden, and which operate to divide the wooden-built district into quarter sections, and which might hold a fire in any one of these sections if they were equipped to do so. These brick and stone buildings are ordinarily valueless as firestops, because their windows are of thin glass and their window-frames of wood. At Chelsea the conflagration attacked such buildings easily, breaking out the panes, consuming the frames and converting every story of these brick structures into horizontal flues full of combustible contents. Brick and stone buildings are logical and capable firestops if the fire can be kept out of them. If you will trace out your Maltese cross of such buildings and equip them with hollow metal window-frames and wired glass, you will immediately possess the equivalent of substantial fire walls crossing at right angles in the centre of your city, dividing it into four sections. By such a simple, inexpensive, but yet strategic procedure you may be able to save your city from destruction which now awaits—only the right kind of a fire on the right kind of a night.—Franklin H. Wentworth.

The prohibition of the shingle roof, which is now generally recognized as a conflagration breeder, is today almost universal within city fire limits, and from the more enlightened communities it is excluded altogether. Burning shingles can be carried great distances by the wind or draught of a conflagration, and when they may alight in their turn upon other dry shingles they make fearful havoc.

CONFLAGRATIONS—Double fire engine companies are valuable in congested sections, the second company being available for second alarms or as a reserve to answer calls to simultaneous fires in the same district, thus rendering unnecessary the calling of apparatus from other districts.

CONGOLEUM is a form of linoleum in which a composition is used in place of cork.

CONNECTING ROD—A piece which connects a crank with something which moves or to which it gives motion.

CONSEQUENTIAL LOSS IN COLD STORAGE RISKS—According to some underwriters' bureau, if a cold storage building contains a source of refrigeration, no clause is necessary on the policies assuming consequential loss and no additional charge is made in the rating. If the source of refrigeration is derived from the outside, the policies must either include or exclude the consequential loss by the use of the following clauses:

Clause No. 1 excludes the consequential loss.

Clause No. 2 includes the consequential loss with an additional permit charge.

The insurance companies in order to avoid payment for a consequential loss occasioned through partial or total disablement of a refrigerating plant (except when same is located in the insured building) demand clause No. 1 on the policy. If it is desired to cover against consequential loss, clause No. 2 is attached and the premium advanced.

Up-to-date refrigeration plants should have "duplicate" refrigeration systems. Not long ago a fire broke out in the cold storage stores, 2286-2298 Twelfth avenue, New York City, which are equipped with a duplicate refrigeration system. Only a very slight consequential loss was sustained owing to the temperatures rising from 33 deg. F. to 51 deg. F. The damage was greatest in the basement refrigerators, due to the presence of the water on the floor, which quickly absorbed the cold air in the rooms, while on the upper floors very little damage resulted, owing to the frost on the piping and the insulation of the refrigerator walls, floors and ceilings maintaining a sufficiently low temperature to prevent serious damage until the auxiliary plant was put in operation. See Cold Storage.

CONSTANTINOPLE, a city characterized by uncleanliness, the apotheosis of filth, the most fire-stricken city of the world, has burned down ten times since 1792. It seems unnecessary to state that over 50 per cent. of all fires are caused by untidiness coupled with carelessness.

CONTINGENT LIABILITY—In New York City if a frame building is damaged more than one-half of the value, exclusive of foundations, the building cannot be repaired or rebuilt but must be torn down. To offset this, policies can be written to include liability for loss occasioned by the operation of ordinances or laws requiring the replacement of entire buildings in case of fire damage exceeding a given percentage of value, the rate on such buildings being double the regular fire rate. The endorsement should read: "It is understood and agreed that the fire limit laws is one of the hazards insured against loss." See Tax Lien Insurance.

CONSTRUCTION—The difference between a frame building and one of ordinary brick is the walls. The difference between a brick building and one of fireproof construction is the floors.

CONTOUR, to follow closely, as for example, covering the beams of a floor so completely as to cover all accessible parts of the beam. Metal or asbestos generally used.

CONTRACTORS—Subway, tunnel or other underground work. Usually occupy light temporary frame structures. The heating and lighting arrangements are make-shifts. Workmen have rooms where they smoke and have wooden lockers for their clothing. These risks sometimes have power plants with air compressors, large motors, switchboards, transformers, machine shops, oil and gasoline storage sheds. Fire on January 28th, 1917, of the Degnon Contracting Company was probably caused by spontaneous combustion of oily overalls in wooden lockers. Fire swept through entire plant, putting entire electrical apparatus out of commission.

CONTRACTORS' STABLES are not considered as good as ordinary stables, as they have a considerable amount of shoring material, tackle, hoisting engines and paraphernalia.

CONVECTION—Property of matter controlling the rate of transmission of heat, i.e., if a bar of iron is heated at one end, the heat will be conducted rapidly to the other end, whereas a rod of glass can be heated to melting point without the opposite end becoming heated.

CONVENTS are classed same as boarding-schools. See Schools.

CONVERTER OF COTTON GOODS—One who buys goods in the "gray" or unfinished state and dyes or otherwise conditions them into finished goods.

COOKING AND HEATING APPARATUS (oil burning) usually have an auxiliary supply tank of about five gallons capacity. They should be ten feet from burners and have overflow pipe draining back to main supply; also a vent pipe. These equipments introduce an additional hazard, and care must be exercised in their maintenance. Only approved apparatus should be installed. Burners must have an overflow pipe arranged to draw off any excess oil by gravity to a reservoir. No dampers to be used in smoke pipe between burner and chimney. All parts must be kept clean and the apparatus not used when not in proper order. Unless installed rigidly in a fixed place the handling is apt to loosen joints and fittings.

COOPERAGES are shops for assembling staves, hoops, heads and bottoms, producing barrels and pails. Regular wood-working hazard; also use direct fire heat, or in some cases steam for bending, shaping and setting the parts. This class should be written cautiously. Second-hand (recoopering) considered very undesirable by most underwriters. See Barrel Storage.

COP—The top or head of a thing. The conical roll of thread formed on the spindle of a spinning machine.

COP YARN (used for weaving cloth)—A loose-twisted thread of cotton, silk, wool or mixture.

COPING—The flat stones, iron or terra-cotta tile placed on top of a wall to protect it from the weather.

COPPER—A metal of red color which does not tarnish or oxidize easily.

COPRA—The dried, broken kernel of the cocoanut after it is split and ready for shipment.

CORBEL—A bracket usually of brick, consisting of several courses built out from the face of a wall usually for a chimney support.

CORDAGE—See Fibre.

CORDEAU DETONANT is a fuse consisting of a thin-walled lead tube filled with trinitoluol.

CORDITE—A form of gun cotton. Very explosive.

CORDUROY is not easily damaged by clean water providing the material is a good grade. The cheaper grades are coated with a gummy substance and do not allow much salvage if thoroughly wet.

CORE—Anything serving as a mould around which something else is to be formed.

CORE OVENS are usually constructed of brick with perforated metal floors and are either heated by hard coal fires, fuel oil or gas. Flasks should never be placed (if of wood), on top of the ovens. The fire record shows 15.3 per cent of foundry fires are traceable to core ovens. The heating of the ovens in drying the cores, which are sometimes mixed with a molasses compound, drives off a heavy smoke which causes a black, sticky deposit to form on the vent pipe or stack. See Foundries.

CORK—The bark of a tree. Pieces are soaked in water, pressed flat, dried and baled. It burns with dense smoke. Cork is bleached with oxalic acid or chloride of lime.

CORK (Agglomerated Cork), known as Silax, used for cork discs. Ground cork is placed in ordinary bread-mixer and mixed with boiled solution of albumen and glycerine.

CORK BOARDS COMPOSITION—Cork received in bales, ground in high-speed knife grinders, the dust removed in separators and then mixed in steam-heated mixers with pitch (mixers resemble dough-mixers), then cooked in steam cookers and cooled in iron air-cooled moulds. The edges are trimmed with saws and sometimes planed smooth.

Ordinary cork board is made from ground cork with no other ingredients. The natural resin in the cork is sufficient as binder when drawn out by heat (about 500 deg. F.). The cork is fed from a steam box through blower system to hydraulic presses of iron construction and passed on endless conveyor to a bake oven, a long affair of brick walls heated by coal, producer gas or coke, similar in appearance to a lehr in a glass works. Cork grinding is the greatest hazard in cork works. The cork should be screened and have magnets attached to screens or hoppers to attract foreign substances as the high-speed machines cause sparks and ignite the dust. After grinding, it is bagged and sold. Grinding should always be done in fire-proof cut-off sections or in detached buildings properly vented. The mills produce heat through friction and are preferably water-cooled. They should be of iron construction and have banking devices under the rollers similar to a malt mill in a brewery. A dusty process; requires vapor-proof electric light globes and good ventilation. See Bottle Stoppers.

CORK CEMENT—Chiefly crude shellac and wood alcohol and cork.

CORK DRYERS or ovens are of high temperature, and fire heat may ignite edges of cork blocks being dried.

CORK DUST is said to be subject to spontaneous combustion if moist. Cork dust is of explosive character when in suspension mixed with proper amount of air.

CORK LEATHER is powdered cork and india-rubber.

CORK PUTTY—Asphalt, cork and heavy oil.

CORK VARNISH, used extensively to protect the interior of ships from undue humidity due to sudden changes, is made of a mixture of ground cork mixed with litharge and copal and other similar substances.

CORK WORKS—See Cork Boards.

CORN CURE, made by some druggists by dissolving scrap celluloid with acetone.

CORNER BUILDINGS, from an underwriting standpoint, are more desirable than buildings in rows, as a fire can always be fought from at least two sides.

CORNICE—The ornamental projection at the eaves of a building or at the top of a pier.

CORNICES and cornice bulkheads should not be continuous. At least a six-inch open space must be obtained between properties adjoining. Fires have been known to travel across fronts of rows in this manner and not be discovered until it has broken out in some remote place.

CORNSTALKS are now being used in paper-making.

CORRODED PIPES—See Gas Explosion.

CORRUGATED IRON on wood stud is considered practically the same as frame construction.

CORRUGATING PAPER MACHINE—A machine with two sets of steam-heated corrugated iron rollers through which the paper is run after being glued at a glue tank.

CORSETS, especially of cheap grade, will not give much salvage if wet on account of the steel frames, which rust very quickly. Better grades of corsets offer good salvage, providing they are dried immediately. Foreign-made corsets are generally embroidered and specially designed, hence a greater water damage is looked for in this class. Where bone stays are used instead of steel stays, the salvage is greater.

CORSET STAY (Description of)—Steel ribbon (corset steel) is coated by a squeeze process (similar to rubber coating of electric wires) with a composition similar to pyroxylin (celluloid). This is applied in two coats. The pyroxylin is evidently of a different composition from that usually manufactured, as some composition other than camphor is mixed with the nitro-cellulose. This composition on being tested shows that same will disintegrate without flame upon moderate heating, showing a strong similarity to pyroxylin in this particular. This composition is highly inflammable, and the ignition point is apparently very low.

COSMOS—A fibre from flax and hemp.

COST PRICE—See Sound Value.

COTTON, once ignited, is capable of maintaining smoldering combustion for a number of days. Baled cotton often ignites from friction in center of bale and will not flame at surface for several weeks after so igniting. Not believed to be subject to spontaneous combustion See Boll Weevil.

COTTON BATTING MILLS—Raw stock is mill waste and sweepings from cotton mills. Pickers, cards, lappers, garnetts, constitute the machinery used. A poor fire-record class.

COTTON—DIPPING COTTON—A secret, non-inflammable process is now on the market which, it is claimed, will eliminate the hazard of fires in this class. One of the railroads has decided to have all cotton dipped which travels over their roads, so that the same can be placed on open flat cars. A recent experiment; a flat car loaded with cotton, traveled nearly 100 miles without a fire resulting, although the car containing the cotton was next to the engine. Shipping cotton on flat cars will release many freight cars for other commodities, and by fireproofing it, a large sum of money will be saved annually.

COTTON GINS—The processes usually divided into three sections, the warehousing of the cotton containing the seeds (seed cotton), the gin-room proper, where the separation is made, and the lint pressed into bales, and the warehousing of the seed after the lint has been removed. Most gin fires are caused by hot bearings, cotton wrapped around the rapidly revolving brush shafts and cotton clogged at the end of brush drums. Underwriters write this class warily.

COTTON MILLS—The cotton is taken from the storehouse to the opening room, where the ties are removed and the bales pulled apart, sometimes by hand, at other times by machinery. The cotton is then blown in the picker room, usually by an approved system similar to the blowers in a wood-working plant. The machines in the picker room are known as breakers, intermediate and finisher lappers. They consist of a cylindrical metal box, inside of which is a steel shaft, to which are attached arms which beat the cotton to a loose, fluffy state, all foreign material going to the bottom of the enclosure. The cotton is delivered through a slit in one side of the box in the form of a sheet, and is then rolled around a steel rod in a roll known as a lap. After leaving the picker room, the cotton goes to the cards. This process consists of passing the cotton between rapidly revolving cylinders covered with wire teeth to straighten out the cotton fibres and lay them parallel to one another. The remaining process of drawing, slubbing, speeding, spinning and weaving are merely preparatory processes and present little, if any, fire hazard. The main hazard in a cotton mill is the picking.

COTTON-PICKER FIRES are commonly attributed to "foreign" substances in the stock. This foreign substance is supposed to be stones, pieces of metal and matches. Statistics show that there are more picker fires in the winter time than in summer, and more in "dog days" than in May, June or October. Some believe the humidity of the picker room itself has something to do with it. When the relative humidity of the picker room is below 25 degrees the cotton may become so dry that it is readily ignited by a small spark, and when it is above 80 degrees, cotton becomes so limp that it winds up and packs on moving parts of pickers, thereby causing fires. It is claimed that a part of these fires could be prevented by avoiding both extremes of humidity in the picker room. See Humidity a Factor in Cotton Picker Fires, Vol. 9, N. F. P. A., April, 1916.)

COTTON PIERS—Sprinklers are absolutely necessary to prevent "flash fires" spreading over the surfaces of baled cotton. In May, 1916, a fire started in about 1,200 bales of cotton stored on one of the Bush Terminal piers, Brooklyn. Sixty-five heads operated and held the fire in check until the arrival of the fire department. A few hours later fire was discovered in a cotton warehouse about half a mile away. The fire department would have been severely taxed with two cotton fires at one time had the pier and warehouse not been sprinklered.

A great many fires are caused by matches being dropped on piers and docks by careless workmen, and fires are started by the friction of moving the bales. Such a fire is liable to smoulder for several days before it is discovered, by which time it has had the opportunity to spread, so that its extinguishment is a difficult task. There is never any surety that a cotton fire is out until every piece of each bale has been hand-picked and thoroughly water-soaked. A great many cotton fires have been traced to compress and gin owners who entered a low-grade cotton on their books, then burned it to collect the insurance. See Piers.

COTTONSEED OIL MILLS—Fires are sometimes caused by spontaneous combustion in old filter cloths. The special hazards of this class are spent or used fuller's earth, filter-press cloths, storage of oleo-stearine and refrigeration.

COUNTERFORT—Vertical projections of masonry or brickwork built at intervals along the back of a wall to strengthen it.

COUNTERMAN—The person who attends the counter of an insurance office and passes on the merits of the business which is offered to the company, by the "placers" from the various brokerage offices, binding and committing his company to liability on the risks offered. It is necessary that he be a good underwriter, as he must perform that duty with snap judgment, basing his calculations of line on his knowledge of conditions in his particular field, and the known hazards and construction of the risk to be covered. This position requires not only one possessing expert insurance knowledge, but a pleasing personality, so that placers and others offering business may be attracted to the office. See Examiners; see Underwriting.

COUNTER-SHAFTING—The shafting operating or actually driving the machinery, and itself being driven by the main or jack shaft.

COUNTERWEIGHT or counter balance. Any weight used to balance another.

COUNTRY STORES—Usually contain a miscellaneous stock, chiefly general merchandise. The heating apparatus is usually defective. Risks often isolated in frame rows with poor protection. See Business Blocks.

COUPLINGS—A term used to express the arrangement for connecting two shafts so that they will revolve together.

COURSE OF CONSTRUCTION risks are usually good fire risks, especially if of brick or fireproof construction. Theatres, churches and halls in course of construction are not considered as good as ordinary buildings, owing to the great amount of lumber scaffolding necessary to complete the high interior of building. Many fires have been caused in buildings in course of construction by the use of salamanders, stoves and careless mechanics using gasoline torches. See Builders' Risks; see Platforms.

COUTCHINE—See Caoutchoucine.

CRADLE—Applied to various kinds of timber supports which partly enclose the mass sustained.

CRANE—A hoisting machine consisting of a revolving vertical post or stalk.

CREAM OF TARTAR—Made from argols, the scrapings from the wine casks. Process is as follows: Ground in mill, cooked with hydrochloric acid and hydrated lime in wooden, steam-heated tanks, precipitated, screened to remove liquor, mixed with bone black to bleach, filtered, dissolved, granulated, crystalized, dried, washed in hydrochloric acid to remove lead and lime, crushed, ground, sifted, barrelled. Hazard of dryers, storage of bone black and lime, grinding in stone and iron mills. Tartaric acid, in the juice of the grape, is combined with potash forming a salt called cream of tartar.

CREAMERIES AND DAIRIES—Although the up-to-date

risks of this class are all steam process, the fire record is poor. See Dairy Farms.

CREMONITES—Detonating preparations, partly composed of picrates.

CREOSOTE—Produced by the distillation of wood tar. Used to impregnate wood. Nearly as inflammable as kerosene.

CREOSOTE OIL—See Heavy Oil.

CREOSOTING RAILROAD TIES—The Reuping process, with blow-back system. Under this system, the railroad ties are placed in impregnating cylinders and subjected for about an hour to an air pressure of 75 lbs. filling the cells of wood with compressed air. Without reducing the pressure in impregnating cylinders, creosote at a temperature of 180 deg. F. is forced into impregnating cylinders. When cylinders are full of creosote, the air pressure is raised to 200 lbs. Under this pressure the creosote penetrates into the cells of the wood, soaking the cell-walls and compressing still more the air formerly put in at 75 lbs. The pressure of 200 lbs. is maintained from 2½ hours to 4 hours, depending upon the nature of the wood. When wood is sufficiently impregnated, the air pressure is released and the expansive energy of the air in the wood forces as much of the creosote out of the wood as does not adhere to the cells of the wood. The surplus creosote is then blown back to supply tanks with a pressure of 8 to 10 lbs. The creosote is manufactured from bituminous coal, having a specific gravity of 1.178, and a flash point of about 500 deg. F.

CREOSOTING WORKS—The finished lumber should be piled a considerable distance from the plant as it burns very rapidly. Storage tanks containing the creosote fluid, ought not be nearer than 50 feet to the plant, with underground piping and gravity return. No open lights or fires allowed in treating room, which should be a detached structure. The boiler should also be detached.

CRIB CONSTRUCTION—Made of superimposed planks laid with broken joints and spiked together. See Piers.

CROCKERY (porcelain)—Kiln burning hazard, grinding, moulding, cutting, dry rooms, hand decorating. Use turpentine and varnish from individual bottles for decorating. Machine shop repairs, carpenter shop, storage of packing material. Large area risks predominate. See China Decorating.

CRONSTADES—The pasty shells made of flour, water and sometimes eggs, fried in grease. Used in hotels and restaurants in serving cut-up meats, fruits or sauces. Where these are made, the floors are apt to be grease soaked.

CROSS-BRIDGING—Each pair of floor beams should be cross-bridged at intervals of seven feet in their length.

CROSS SECTION in an elevation drawing is an imaginary line cut through the center.

CROWN—A term applied to the uppermost or highest part of an arch, that in which a keystone is fixed.

CRUCIBLE WORKS—Crucibles are used for refining metals. The metal is placed inside of crucible and then same is placed in furnace. Crucibles are made of French clay and plumbago (which is black lead or graphite). It is moulded and then baked in brick (wood fuel) retorts.

CRUDE OIL—See Petroleum. As it comes from the well is a heavy, oily liquid, very inflammable, coming from Eastern wells. From Western wells, flash point is above 100 deg. F. to as high as 210 deg. F.

CRUDE PETROLEUM is crude oil.

CRYSTALLIZATION—When crystals are formed from solutions, we term it the process of crystallization. When the substance used dissolves as freely in cold as in hot water, as is the case with common salt, crystalization is produced only by evaporation; as the water goes off into the air, the crystals form.

CRYSTALLIZING is really evaporating. When chemicals are in a state of solution in water or other liquid they can be crystallized by evaporating the liquid. This work is done in low pans, steam heated. Hazard is considered very light.

CUPOLA—As used in foundries. The upright cylindrical stack of iron, lined with fire brick into which is dumped the scrap iron and fuel for melting. The molten mass flows through a trough to buckets, which are carried to the foundry.

CUPOLAS and towers on public buildings are frequently the depository for old records, furniture and fixtures. The City Hall (New York City) tower has been destroyed three times. The last fire in May, 1917, causing $20,000 loss, was caused by a careless workman leaving a charcoal furnace unattended while he absented himself.

CURB—The term "Curb" when used in connection with defining the height of a building is the established mean curb level at the front of the building. If the building fronts on more than one street, the datum for measurement shall be taken at the established mean curb level on the street of greatest width. When this width is common to more than one street, the datum for measurement shall be taken at that having the highest curb. The term "Curb" when used in fixing the depth of an excavation is the established curb level nearest to the point of the excavation in question. Where no curb elevation has been established, or the building line does not adjoin the street, the average finished ground level adjoining the building shall be considered the curb level.—(N. F. P. A.)

CURTAIN BOARDS—Metal or other non-combustible shields placed around openings in the floor so as to bank the heat and allow the sprinkler heads to operate. The heat waves travel similar to water waves, rebounding when striking an obstruction.

CURTAIN WALL is the wall placed on the outside of steel skeleton frames merely to keep out the elements. No structural parts depend upon these walls.

CUSTOM OR MERCHANT TAILORS—Make clothing to order for individuals from measure. Tailor shop hazard.

CUT GLASS is first blown into the general shape intended from the brilliant crystal and then ground into a cluster of glistening facets. Grindstones, continually moistened by streams of wet sand, cut the rough pattern, and emery wheels and putty powder finish the brilliant angles. After the glass is cut it is given an acid bath after the inner surface has been coated with paraffine and beeswax. The wax prevents the acid from eating into or staining the glass. Alundum (a composition of carborundum) and craigleth (natural hard stones) are used for cutting. They crack under action of fire and water.

CUTLERY STOCKS—Apt to rust from moisture or dampness. Should be salvaged immediately after a fire. See Tools and Instruments.

CUT-OFF—A term used by insurance men to signify that buildings are separated by brick division walls with standard or non-standard doors at openings. See Communications.

CUTTING AND WORK TABLES should have galvanized fire stops or partitions firmly set and fastened under the same. These are to prevent flash fires from sweeping swiftly under the entire length of the table in the cuttings.

CUTTING BOARDS—See Shoe Factories.

CYANATES are cyanic acid compounds.

CYANIDE OF POTASSIUM—Deadly poisonous. Used by electroplaters in forming solutions of gold, silver, etc., and by photographers for "fixing." Liable to cause spontaneous combustion.

CYANIDES—Compounds of cyanogen with elements or metals.

CYANOGEN is one of the most volatile of the distillates from crude petroleum. Flash point zero F. Classed as very inflammable. Cyanogen compounds (carbon and nitrogen combine to form cyanogen), a combustible gas which forms with chlorine. Sometimes used for fumigating purposes.

CYCLONE is a centrifugal collector made of iron, shaped like the inverted frustrum of a cone depending upon gravity and centrifugal force to separate the dust from the air containing it. Cyclones are usually on the roof of the shavings vault of a woodworker. See Shaving Vault. See Blower.

CYLINDER PRINTING PRESSES have a large flat bed for the form containing the type, which passes back and forth under a revolving cylinder; the latter receives the paper from the feeding board and brings it into contact with the form beneath. See Printers.

D

DAILY REPORT—The copy of the policy, together with all other necessary information concerning a risk, sent by an agent to the Home office of a company for the guidance of the examiner.

DAIRY FARMS—Bad fire record. Health board restrictions are said to have taken considerable of the profits of the business. In some states, if an epidemic occurs, the entire herd is confiscated. The State reimburses the owner to only fifty per cent. of the value of the animals destroyed. Hazards of large area barns, large quantity of hay and straw on storage and boiler. See Creameries and Dairies; also Milk Depots.

DAMAR—A resin similar in appearance to gum arabic.

DAMMARA—A gum or resin similar to copal.

DANCE HALLS—See Halls.

DANGEROUS GOODS—See Storage Lines.

DANGEROUS PROCESSES—Most manufacturing risks would be desirable insurance if the dangerous processes in them were isolated or cut off from the balance of the plant by heavy brick walls and "labelled" automatic fire doors at communicating openings. Automatic sprinklers in these rooms would also greatly aid in the protection of the plant.

DAVY SAFETY LANTERN merely has a wire mesh above the light, which prevents fumes from coming in contact with flame.

DEAD ENDS—Any pipe scheme containing a dead end should be corrected where possible by completing the parallelogram. See Water Mains.

DEAD OIL—A heavy oil distilled from coal tar after the distillation of the light oils. Not very inflammable.

DEAD RISER—In sprinkler equipments. Is the riser which drops down from the tank supply to the basement without any openings and connects in the basement to the live riser which supplies the heads. See Sprinkler Equipment.

DEAD STORAGE—Automobiles are said to be on dead storage when they are not in use, and laid up for the season. Gasoline should be drained from the tanks, but this is seldom done.

DEAFENED FLOORS prevent sound from traveling from floor to floor. One of the best methods to deafen floors is to have a layer of cinders and concrete underneath the top flooring carried by thin deafening-boards resting on cleats fastened to the side of beams or joists as shoulders.

DECALCOMANIE crockery decorating.—Impression transferred from copper plate to paper by passing it through a roller, then transferred to crockery by hand. Mineral oils and turpentine are used in transferring work. Firing kilns and packing material constitute the hazards in this class. See China Decorating.

DECARBONIZE—See Tempering.

DECLINE—A notice, verbal or written, from the company to the insured or his agent, stating the company's refusal to assume liability.

DECK-FLOOR—The main floor of a pier. A narrow mezzanine floor or gallery between floors.

DECK-NOZZLE—The main nozzle for fire hose on a boat.

DECORATORS AND PAINTERS—Busiest season April to October. Oily waste and oily overalls left by workmen when decorating the interior of buildings have caused many fires. See Painters.

DEGREE OF INFLAMMABILITY is determined by the attraction of the substance for oxygen.

DELIQUESCE—A salt which gathers moisture from the air is said to be deliquescent.

DEMOLITION OF FIREPROOF BUILDING—Gillender building, 20 Wall Street, New York City, part sixteen and part nineteen stories high, skeleton steel construction, terra-cotta floor arches, all ironwork protected by 1½-inch terra cotta. It was observed that the steel work during removal was practically in as good a condition as at the time the building was originally built in 1896. The conclusions obtained from this rather unusual case were: 1st—The presence of corrosion in several small places where the steel work was exposed to the weather (this emphasizes the importance of proper protection against moisture). 2nd—A covering of cement mortar protects steel from corrosive influences better than any form of paint at present in use. 3rd—It is important to paint the steel both at the mill and after being erected at the building before the cement coating is applied.

DENATURED ALCOHOL consists of grain alcohol to which some substance is added, rendering it unfit as a beverage, usually contains wood alcohol, pyridin or benzine. Flash 40 deg. F. Classed as inflammable.

DENATURED OLIVE OIL—Olive oil with about 3 per cent. rosin oil, mineral oil, distilled wood turpentine, pyridin, creosote, aniline oil or oleic acid.

DENITRATION—Removal of the NO_2 radicle from nitrocellulose, rendering it non-explosive.

DENSE TILE—Hard terra-cotta tile of little porosity.

DENSITY—See Specific Gravity.

DENTAL GAS—Nitrous oxide gas, colorless, incombustible, not hazardous.

DEPARTMENT STORES—Much of the stock displayed is of a highly inflammable nature, and as different in character as celluloid combs, ammunition or calcium carbide are from crockery, china and glassware. The stock is very susceptible to water damage and breakage, and may be ruined by smoke. The large well-holes, open stair and elevator shafts have been responsible for the spread of fire in most of these risks. If building is fireproof and sprinklered, with curtain boards on ceilings at openings, this danger is somewhat reduced.

DEPRECIATION OF BUILDINGS—There is really no set rule, in some cases a sliding scale may be applied, whereas sometimes an average figure is the better way. If the structure is badly worn, the depreciation would be correspondingly greater than a building kept in good repair. See Values of Buildings.

DEPRECIATION OF MACHINERY—For a great many

kinds of machines, experts have arranged a percentage table whereby a regular deduction each year is applied. In some machines there is practically no important depreciation for several years while others must be entirely rebuilt after very little wear.

DETACHED—A structure which does not adjoin another structure. Not necessarily isolated. Number of feet detached should always be mentioned on inspection report.

DETERGENE—A benzine substitute, classed as non-volatile.

DETONATING FUSES usually contain several ounces of a high explosive such as picric acid or nitrocellulose.

DETONATORS—See Fuses.

DEVILING—The picking apart of fibres or similar materials by machinery.

DEXTRINE—Made from starches. The best is made from potato starch from Japan, tapioca and sago from Java and Sumatra, and cornstarch or similar starches. Received at mills in bags, mixed in agitator where a one per cent. solution of various acids such as muriatic, acetic, nitric; salts, hypochloride of soda, magnesium chloride and similar materials are added by a sprayer as the machine revolves, then roasted in brick-enclosed coal fuel roasters, ground in centrifugal crusher or grinder and bolted. Roasters are similar to brick-enclosed coffee roasters, with a revolving drum enclosed in brick. Hazards of roasters, grinders and dust. The dextrine in roasters will take fire if the drum ceases to revolve. The dust will settle on bearings and shaftings of machinery. Used as a stiffening substance and as food. Sometimes called British gum.

DIAMOND METAL POLISH—Flash point 204 deg. F. Classed non-volatile.

DIAMYL, obtained during the distillation of coal, very inflammable.

DIAPHRAGM—A single or double-movable plate or partition placed across or inside of a tube, pipe or other hollow body to record fluctuations in pressure or heat, to hold back liquids and gases or to allow variations in pressure without impairing the efficiency of the device.

DIE—A hard block of metal or that part of a stamping machine which cuts out or makes an impression on an object, such as a coin. Those with a fine cutting edge are classed as "edged tools," owing to their susceptibility to fire damage.

DINITRO-CHLOR-BENZOL in crystal state will feed fire, not very inflammable and only slightly explosive.

DI-NITRATES are classed as explosives.

DI-NITRATING is a hazardous process.

DIP BLACK—See Shoe Factories.

DIP TANKS with automatic covers. (Inspection Dept., Factory Fire Ins. Co.)—Should be in a 1-story high building. Floor to be incombustible and should pitch to one side and have drain pipe leading to underground well (drain pipe 6 inches and have coarse strainer ¼-inch mesh at first floor). Dip tank should be steel or iron plate riveted together. Should have wrought-iron overflow pipe leading outside of building to a well, these pipes to be at least 3 inches where tanks hold less than 100 gals., and 4 to 6 inches for large tanks, overflow to have coarse strainer at tank; the well, to which overflow pipe leads, should be ventilated, and should be at least four times the capacity of tank. Well should be at least 15 feet from building, located down-hill and be so arranged that any overflow therefrom cannot endanger buildings. Tanks should have automatic covers; a folding hinge cover is generally most convenient. Cover to be metal or wood covered with lock-jointed tin, and overlap the sides of tank, and be secured with strong metal hinges, the hinges being offset and projected against gumming. A fusible link and chain and counter-balanced weight makes a satisfactory arrangement. In addition to above, it is often advisable to locate a metal hood directly over tank, hood to have a metal flue pipe, which discharges into a properly constructed brick chimney. The hood should extend well over sides of tank and should be as low down as feasible, the hood answering the double purpose of preventing, at least to some extent, water being thrown into the tank by sprinklers or hose, and, also, taking off flames from the burning liquid in case the automatic cover should fail. (H. A. Fiske.) See Lacquer.

DIPPING ARTICLES in tanks containing inflammable liquids, such as japan, enamel, varnish, etc., no matter how well guarded, constitutes a severe hazard. No open lights are permitted in same room.

DIPPING COTTON—See Cotton.

DIRECT CURRENT—See Alternating Current.

DIRECT FEED TO BOILERS from blower systems for fuel shavings. The feed pipe connects directly with the blower system; the feed end placed at the boiler feed door and the shavings blown in. Automatic dampers in the feed duct prevent back-fires from racing up the duct in case of clogging of the shavings or shutting down of the blower. See Shavings Vaults.

DIRECT LOSS—The loss of capital due to damage or destruction of the buildings, machinery, stock or other real or personal property; and this loss to the owners is usually minimized by means of fire insurance.

DISINFECTANTS—Ingredients used are creosote, glycerine, sugar, camphor oil, resin, charcoal, Texaco spirits, sulphur, euchrelytum, Russian turpentine, caustic soda, bicarbonate soda, chloral, mineral oils, nucoline (cocoanut oil), carbolic acid, coal tar, acetic acid, kerosene and essential oils.

DISPLAY FIGURES AND FIXTURES, as used to display clothing, dry goods, furs, etc. A complete figure consists of a wax head, false hair, glass or celluloid eyes, bust of papier-mache (enamelled), body of papier-mache (cloth covered), arms of wood, wax hands with celluloid finger nails, wooden or papier-mache legs, iron feet and a wire frame for skirt. Hazards are metal working with foundry, painting and japanning, wax heating by direct fire, making depressions in wax, such as dimples with heated tools, woodworking, painting complexions with air or hand brush, inserting hair by first warming the scalp near a stove. Papier-mache form making, drying, enamelling, painting and lacquering. Class of help is inferior. Early fall and early spring are the busiest seasons. This class is, as a rule, a poor one.

DISTILLATION—See Distilleries.

DISTILLERIES—Distilling is separating the lighter parts from the heavier parts of a substance by vaporizing in a still and recondensing same into liquid form by sudden cooling. High proof liquors, such as whiskey or brandy, are made in distilleries. Alcohol, cologne spirits, fusel-oil and other alcohol by-products, are produced in the process. Except brandy, most are made from grain. Distilleries embrace many of the brewery hazards. The grain is reduced to a meal, mixed with water, cooked in steam kettles at high temperature, run to fermenting vats where yeast is added. The liquid drawn off and mashed, is then pumped to a so-called beer-still (usually copper), at the top of which is an opening to which is attached a long copper tube, one end of which is inserted into a vat and connected to a worm (a spiral copper condensing coil), immersed in water. The mash is boiled until the liquid is vaporized and recondensed in the worm. The product of this distillation is known as high wines. Direct heat, sometimes used for stills, is more hazardous than steam. Coal, coke, oil or gas are used. Setting of furnaces is important hazard. The liquid produced by the first distillation is redistilled and the vapor therefrom passes to a column, which is a cylindrical separator containing several cells which are designed to condense certain of the spirit vapors. Some of the cells are connected to "leaches" or rectifiers, which are receptacles containing powdered charcoal through which the liquid is forced for cleaning or filtering. There are various methods of distilling, some being a continuous operation. Hazards are open lights in the presence of alcohol vapors, charcoal storage, putting stoves inside of charring vats for drying, painting, branding and coopering barrels or kegs; the method of still heating and alcohol handling. See Liquors.

DISTRIBUTION CLAUSE—"It is understood and agreed that the amount insured by this policy shall attach in each of the above named premises in that proportion of the amount hereby insured that the value of the property covered by this policy contained in each of the said premises shall bear to the value of such property contained in all of the above named premises." When this clause is attached to the policy it distributes the insurance over the property (at the time of the fire) in the same proportions as the values are distributed and the policy immediately becomes specific insurance for the amounts so ascertained. Example: Insurance carried, $10,000. Merchandise in building, "A," $5,000; in building "B," $5,000; in building "C," $10,000. Total value, $20,000. Building "A" gets 5,000/20,000 of $10,000, or $2,500; building "B," 5,000/20,000, or $2,500; building "C," 10,000/20,000, or $5,000.

DISULPHIDE OF CARBON (carbon bisulphide) is a very inflammable liquid. When its vapors mix with the air, hydrogen or carbonic acid, highly explosive gases are produced. A mixture of air and the vapors from bisulphide of carbon will explode at about 300 deg. F. The flash point is very low and under certain conditions the liquid may be exploded by shock. It is made by passing sulphur vapor over red-hot charcoal and when burned it produces quantities of suffocating gases. It is a colorless, heavy liquid, with an odor resembling rotten eggs. It is a serious fire hazard and should never be allowed inside of main buildings. It is sometimes used to fumigate stocks of tobacco. It is also used as a solvent for gums and resins, extracting grease from wool; also oil from various seeds. It may also be used as a disinfectant and germicide insect killer. (F. J. McFarlane.)

DIVI-DIVI—A vegetable product from Venezuela used in tanning and dyeing.

DOCKS—See Piers.

DOLLS—Indestructible dolls. Any or all of the following materials may be used to make the "dough"—ceresin wax, paraffine, glue, whiting, wheat-paste, linseed oil and rosin, colored with oil colors. Moulded in forms under die presses, dried, sandpapered to remove roughness, enamelled in dip tank (enamel thinned with turpentine or benzine), painting complexions with air sprayers or hand brush, and lacquering. Heating of wax mixture by direct heat, use of benzine, enamel, lacquer are main hazards.

DONKEY ENGINE—A small steam engine attached to a larger one and fed from the same boiler.

DOOR FRAME—The case in which a door opens and shuts, consisting of two uprights and one horizontal piece connected together by mortices and tenons.

DOORS—See Collapsible, Revolving and Fire Doors.

DOORS—Safety releasing latch for exit door. The latch combines in a unit the usual locking devices, the door lock and top and bottom latches. The usual hardware trim is applied on the outside of the door. On the inside, about waist high, a solid bar stretches across the door. This bar stands away from the wood and connects directly with the mechanism of the latch. Pressure applied to any part of the bar instantly releases the lock and latches simultaneously and permits the doors to open. The operation of these latches under conditions of a panic is evident. The occupants of the building rush toward the exit doors and the leaders are forced against the bar across the doors, thus operating the latches automatically and opening the doors to safety.

DORMER WINDOW—A window which projects out of the wall just under the roof.

DOUBLE BACKING MACHINE—Used in paper box making. A long iron table heated by steam coils; on one end a large glue pot which glues one side of each of two sheets of paper which runs between wood or iron rollers, is dried while passing over the steam-heated table and reeled at opposite end. Glue pots should be steam heated.

DOVE-TAILING MACHINE—Used by woodworkers for cutting the fan or wedge-shaped grooves or projections used in making joints. The term dove-tail being given to the joint in question because of the resemblance of the interlocking projections to a dove tail spread out. The cutting tool, also shaped like a dove tail, is fixed in the end of spindle projecting up through a table mounted upon an iron frame and rotating very rapidly. Danger of overheating bearings.

DOWEL—A straight pin of wood or metal inserted part way into each of two faces, which it unites.

DRAGON'S BLOOD—A resinous substance obtained from tropical trees.

DRAWING—See Sketching.

DRAWN STEEL—(Drawing steel from a flat piece into cup-shaped pieces and tubes.) The machines used are similar to huge stamping presses. The thick plate of steel is placed on the bed of the press and a plunger, by repeated thrusts, makes an indentation which enlarges as the process proceeds and eventually presses out a cup-shape piece. These machines are called "reducing" or "drawing presses." Each press has a different sized plunger, the largest plunger being used first. After each reducing process, the steel is heated in a rotary annealing furnace before it is placed in the next press. When the tube is finally drawn out, it is washed in a rust-proof solution, and threaded to receive the nut. Heavy machine-shop hazard.

DRESSMAKING—Usually locate in dwellings without salesrooms or show rooms and the owner lives on the premises. Called "parlor shops." Sewing and pressing on small scale. If under five hands working, without show room, and if owner lives on premises no extra rate is charged for this occupancy by some rating boards.

DRESS PATTERNS (paper)—If kept in cardboard boxes in the open may be counted on to suffer a bad loss from smoke and water. They are usually made of the cheapest grade of tissue paper, and should always be kept in metal cabinets. In dry goods and notion stores they form considerable of the value. A full set of dress patterns as sold by most large dress pattern firms is worth $250-$300, and are kept in pigeon-holed cabinets with open fronts. See Patterns.

DRIP CUPS should be placed on all shafting, gearing and sewing machines to catch oily drips. They are usually made cup-shape of cast-iron. Drip pans are necessary under spigots of oil and paint barrels in paint stores.

DRIP VALVES on sprinkler equipments must be sealed shut. They are used for draining the pipes.

DROP FORGINGS—Forgings whose shape is impressed upon them by dies on which a heavy weight is allowed to fall.

DRUGS AND CHEMICALS—The present European war has caused a scarcity of certain chemicals and drugs hitherto imported. As a result, local concerns have hurriedly erected small plants for the manufacture of such goods. These equipments are for the most part built for temporary use and their crudity and lack of stability makes them unsafe. See Chemistry; also Chemicals.

DRUG STORES (retail)—Usual drugs and chemicals in small quantities. May bottle benzine, gasoline or alcohol, or make ointments and salves by direct fire heat (grease hazard). Basements should be inspected on account of packing material, empty boxes, surplus stock and untidiness.

DRUGS (wholesale)—Risks of this class not only carry large quantities of dangerous drugs and chemicals, but they may also do the following work: Drug grinding in stone or steel mills, cutting, compounding, separating, bolting, sifting, mixing, drying and packing. All combustibles should be kept in an underground vault, cut off from the main building by standard fire doors. Drugs and chemicals such as ether, nitric acid, chlorate of potash, etc., should not be packed in the same box or in close proximity to each other, as a sudden jar, sufficient to break the bottles, may cause an explosion. Some of the causes of fires, according to fire reports, are spontaneous combustion in barrel of powdered charcoal, explosion in chlorate of potash storage closet, explosions of carboys containing nitric acid and barium dioxide, explosion in barrel of tar, fires in or near grinding and pulverizing machines probably due to friction of foreign substances or grinding, substances containing phosphorus, ignition of inflammable vapors in compounding room. Fires in this class are extremely dangerous because the action of radiated heat or the application of water in contact with certain chemicals, will cause fires or explosions of chemicals which of themselves would not be dangerous otherwise. Phosphorus should be stored under water outside of main building. (J. Younes.) See Chemicals.

DRUID ROOF is cotton duck soaked in paraffine, borax and sulphate of magnesia, then painted with a composition of liquid asphaltum, soapstone and graphite. Said to be both water and fireproof.

DRUMMOND LIGHT, made by causing the burning gases, hydrogen and oxygen, to strike against a piece of lime. The lime becomes intensely heated and shines with a dazzling brilliancy.

DRY CLEANING AND DRY DYEING (benzine or naphtha process). Always a dangerous exposure. Buildings should be detached from surrounding properties, the greater the distance the better. Entire construction should be fireproof; no basements; and areas as small as possible. Dry rooms should be cut off from main buildings and cleaning rooms, and only steam heat used. Steam pipes should have screens of wire mesh to prevent goods coming in contact with them. Racks for clothing should be iron. Entrance to washing room should be from outside only. Perforated pipes or steam jets are recommended for extinguishing fires in these rooms; the control valve located outside of building and easily accessible. Ventilators should be near floor as the vapor falls, being heavier than air; vents to be about 10 inches by six inches with wire mesh screens. Distilling apparatus for reclaiming dirty liquids is usually located in cleaning room. Centrifugal extractors for drying washed goods generate electricity through rapid motion, and a spark is liable to explode the vapor in the machine. Naphtha and benzine to be stored underground as per requirements. See Dyeing and Cleaning.

DRY COLORS—See Aniline Dyes; also Color Works.

DRY DISTILLATION—Heating without access to air, in closed receptacle.

DRY DOCKS—Fires have been caused by shavings and portable furnaces, soldering devices, oakum storage, painting and spontaneous combustion of oakum and oily waste.

DRY KILNS—The most common causes of fires are overheating, faulty construction and uncleanliness. The intense heat fosters the fire when started. An efficient steam jet is the best fire extinguisher. Modern kilns are made of concrete with tile roofs. See Kilning.

DRY PIPE SPRINKLER EQUIPMENT—In unheated buildings where the water is liable to freeze sprinklers are installed "dry pipe," i. e., instead of water the piping contains air under pressure which holds shut an automatic water-control valve. This valve opens and admits water into the pipes when the pressure is weakened by the escape of air through sprinklers opened by fire. **Test of, in Fireproof Cold Storage.** Test number one was made with the circulating refrigeration system in full operation and started with an initial temperature on the floor of approximately 30 deg. F. The first sprinkler head operated 17½ minutes after the lighting of the first pan of alcohol. Alcohol pans were lighted in succession every 30 seconds. Test number two was made with the circulating system completely cut off by starting with initial temperature of 30 deg. F. The first sprinkler head operated 15 minutes after lighting of the first pan. Extracted from detail report made by E. S. Clayton, March 19, 1913. See Sprinklers (Dry Pipes). See Dry Valves.

DRY POWDER EXTINGUISHERS—Their use is not encouraged. They are inferior to water or chemicals. Composed of about 85 per cent. bicarbonate soda and 15 per cent. iron oxide, silica, starch, fuller's earth, venetian red; yellow ochre is added to prevent caking. Will cake in damp places and powder may lose its strength. They are, however, better than frozen water pails in unheated buildings. See Chemical Extinguishers.

DRY ROOMS should be of all-metal design and steam-heated. Wood dry rooms, even if lined with lock-jointed metal, are not approved. See illustration on page 134.

DRY ROT—Decay in such portions of the timber of houses as are exposed to dampness. The best preventive is creosote.

DRY VALVES—Attached to sprinkler systems in buildings without heat. Ten pounds of air is sufficient to hold back sixty pounds of water, but most engineers have the air-gauge show 25 pounds of air to be positively safe.

DRYERS—Usually made of soaps composed of lead and manganese in some form or other, usually as the linoleate or the resinate. They are needed in all paints. It is assumed that they exert no chemical action, but attract oxygen from the air by virtue of their presence. May contain volatile oils. (See Japan Dryers.)

DRYING OILS—The chief one is linseed oil, derived from flaxseed. Subject to spontaneous combustion, especially if mixed with organic matter.

DUALIN—A foreign make of nitroglycerine. Explosive.

DUMBWAITER DOORS in the basement of apartment houses are usually blocked open or tied open so as not to inconvenience the errand boy delivering orders. Boys stand at these shafts and smoke. The bottoms of shafts are sometimes filled with waste paper and rubbish even in the "high-class" apartment houses. Sometimes large wooden packing

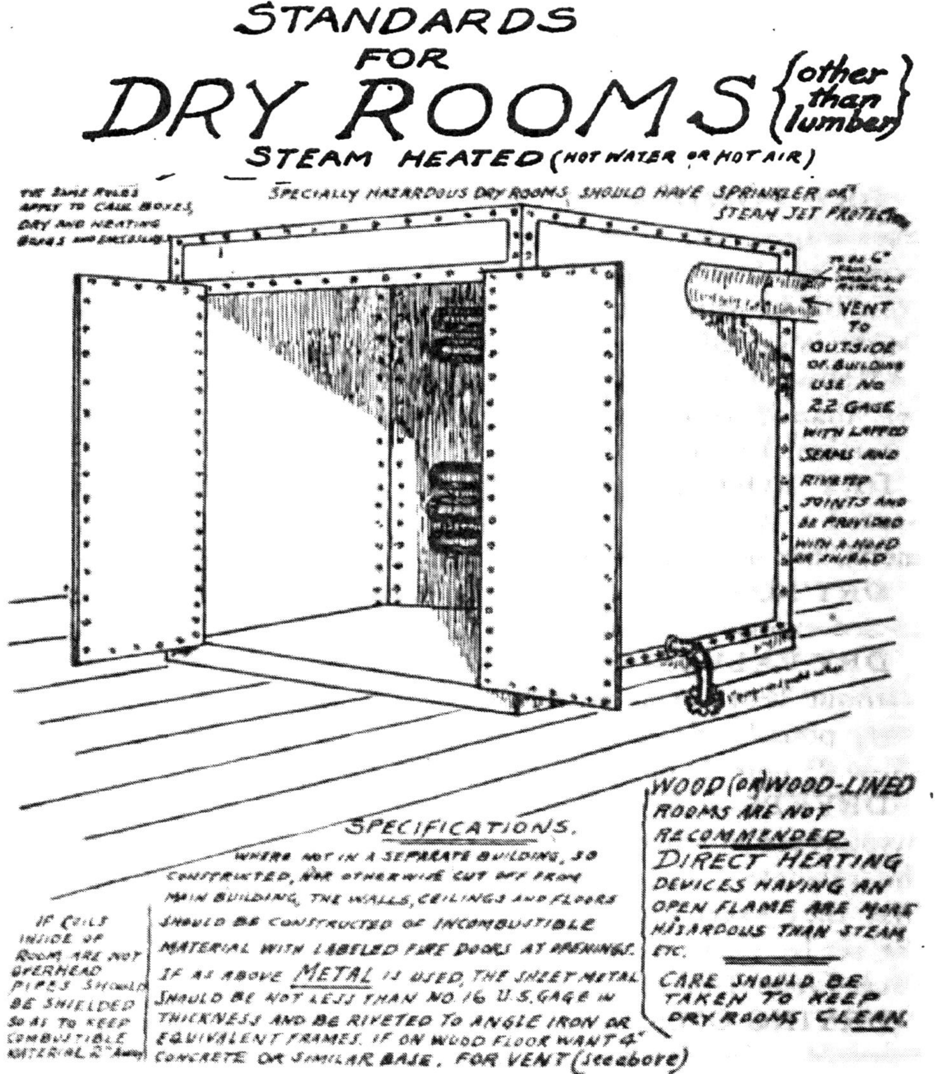

boxes filled with paper adjoin these shafts. "Fire patrol" reports show numerous fires from these causes. Dumbwaiter shafts should be of terra-cotta, concrete, common brick or plaster block with labeled self-closing fire doors at all openings. See Shafts.

DUMPS FOR STREET CLEANING DEPARTMENTS, especially on water fronts, are littered with debris and rubbish scattered all around, and underneath piers and docks in the vicinity. All such piers should be enclosed from low-water line to pier floor, so as to prevent waste floating underneath. Many fires at these places.

DUPLICATING CARVER—The work is clamped to frames in a similar position to pattern or model, and by a parallel motion a blank tool and small cutters are made to pass simultaneously over the outline and surface of the pattern. Machine parts rotate 5,000 to 15,000 a minute and heat up. See Spindle Carver.

DURABOLD, a waterproofing compound. Flash 110 deg. F. Classed as non-volatile.

DUST—Accumulations of dust on bearings of machinery cause undue friction and numerous fires. Fires flash along dust-covered shelves or woodwork. The presence of much dust denotes poor housekeeping. Ordinary dust, such as found in offices, office buildings and schools, consists of human hair or hair from soft hats, wool and cotton from clothing, sand and dirt tracked into building, wings from dead flies, paper, iron from nails in shoes, carbon from coal smoke, salt from perspiration. The presence of bacteria in dust, aside from the fire hazard, is the reason boards of health and labor departments demand proper ventilation.

The most hazardous, the most easily ignited and the most explosive dusts are sugar, dextrine, starch and cocoa. Almost any finely divided material will explode if mixed with air in the proper proportion and ignited—dust of coal, soot, grain, bronze powder, celluloid, lycopodium, dust from buff wheels. Where dust is produced in any process, proper ventilation with blowers to conduct the dust from the machines to a safe place should be provided, and if the dust is of an explosive character, explosion vents (small boxes or openings provided with covers kept in place with spring hinges) should be provided on the conveying pipes. As with sugar dust, there is often sufficient violence in explosions to wreck buildings where the quantity of suspended dust is sufficient to explode. See Fly.

DUSTLESS DUSTERS—Principally flannel saturated with linseed oil and paraffine. Subject to spontaneous combustion.

DWELLINGS—There are more fires in dwellings than in any other class of risk. Were it not for the millions of them insured they would not be written at current rates. Although many lives are at stake, building and fire departments and insurance companies give less supervision to them either

In case of fire, close every door you pass through on your way out of a burning building. In this manner the oxygen necessary for combustion is reduced to a minimum.

before or after completion or occupancy than to other classes of buildings. There are more defects of common hazards in the ordinary dwelling than in the owner's factory. The tenants are, through familiarity, blind or indifferent to the need of fire prevention. As winter approaches fires are started in stoves or furnaces with no thought of the need of cleaning chimneys of birds' nests or soot, replacing rusted smoke pipes, protection under stoves or the general condition. Unsafe gas jets, which are penalized ten cents in nearly all rate schedules of factories, are numerous in dwellings and cause many fires. See Apartment Houses.

Palatial Country Houses (Journal of Commerce, Nov. 27, 1916), owing to the lack of fire protection, open country and the high values contained therein, are now looked upon by underwriters as business to be avoided if possible.

DWELLINGS (fireproof)—Rating Bureau Requirements. All floor openings leading from the basement to the upper floors must be cut off in the basement by brick, terra cotta or concrete shafts at least four inches thick with solid kalamein or kalamein and wired glass doors; also kalamein trim. If there is a continuous shaft from basement to upper floors, the former must be cut off in similar manner. Large air ducts used in indirect heating systems need no cut off, unless they have openings in the basement, in which case automatic dampers must be installed. Elevator drum and motor room must be cut off in a standard manner.

DYE can be made from the roots, leaves and stalks of nettles. Used in woolen stuffs.

DYE WOOD—Extracted from logwood and fustic. Fires are sometimes caused from the union of chemicals used. Where stock is kept, especially in ground or powdered form, even small fires usually results in severe losses owing to water making the colors run. An unprofitable class.

DYE WOODS, such as logwood, are prepared for extracting by first cutting the logs in small pieces the size of kindling wood. These are put in an all-iron knife grinder, revolving at about 950 r.p.m., then ground finer in corrugated iron roller machine, revolving at about 1,100 r.p.m., which reduces the wood to finely divided particles ready for the steam vats. Hazards of high-speed grinders, high-tension electric currents, transformer. See Logwood.

DYE WORKS—See Bleach, Dye and Print Works.

DYEING AND CLEANING WORKS—Equipment consists of revolving washing drums using soap and water, centrifugal extractors, dye tubs and kettles, drying rooms, gas or electric pressing irons, gas-heated crimpers (or steam), mangles and finishing. Materials used are chloroform (for removing spots) alcohol, benzine, acetic acid, sulphuric acid, ammonia, oxalic acid, sal-soda, glycerine, neatsfoot oil, peroxide of hydrogen and blue stone. See Dry Cleaning.

DYERS, as a mordaunt, use thin solution of nitrate of iron and water for loading green cotton goods. See Dry Cleaning and Dyeing.

DYNAMITE—A high explosive formed by mixing nitroglycerine with an absorbent material to form a plastic solid. **Frozen Dynamite** should never be used. Most high explosives freeze at temperatures between 45 and 50 deg. F., and when frozen will explode only imperfectly or not at all. When frozen it is thawed out before being used. See Explosives.

DYNAMITING BUILDINGS to check the path of a large or sweeping fire is seldom employed in the city, although more or less explosives have been used for this purpose in all conflagrations.

DYNAMO CLAUSE—See Electrically-driven Machinery.

DYNAMOS—See Electrically-driven Machinery.

E

EAGLE SOLVENT—A benzine substitute, classed as non-volatile.

EARNED PREMIUM—That portion of the premium representing the length of time the company has assumed liability; the premium for the length of time the policy has been in force, and retained by the company in case of cancellation. See Premium.

EARTH OIL is petroleum.

EAVES—The edge of a roof which overhangs a wall. It is designed to carry off the water without flowing down the side of the wall.

ECCENTRIC—A circular plate or pulley surrounded by a loose ring and attached to a revolving shaft and moving around with it but not having the same center, for producing an alternate motion.

EDGED TOOLS—See Instruments.

EDGE-RUNNERS—See Chasers.

EFFECTIVE LOAD—The effective span in feet multiplied by the weight of the distributed load per foot run.

EGG DEALERS—Hazards of candling eggs and packing material. See Candling.

EGGS—If eggs are thoroughly wet while in storage they are liable to become spoiled in a short time. Water removes from the shell of the egg a gelatinous covering which helps to keep air and germs out of the inside of the egg. See Candling; see Consequential Loss.

EJOO—Called Indian hemp, a black fibre.

ELECTRICITY, properly installed, is the safest kind of light. Repairs or extensions should be made only by experts. Regular examination is necessary to detect defects. Amateurs are responsible for many of the electric wire fires. Electric power is safer than other forms because all the power is transmitted through stationary wires and not rapidly moving belts or shafting which have friction gearing, overheated bearings and which necessitate floor openings.

When repairing or altering, all old wires or "dead ends" should be removed as they are apt to become charged and cause fire.

A large percentage of the so-called "unknown cause" fires are directly traceable to poor insulation, poor wiring, overloading wires without proper fuses, or poor installation of motors. Overfusing is a common happening. Direct current (brush motors) should be carefully protected from dust. Induction motors, while not subject to this dust hazard, should be very carefully wired because the hazards from currents are greater than at brush motors.

Among the **conductors** are metals, charcoal, animal fluids, water, vegetable and animal bodies, flame, smoke and vapor. Among the **non-conductors** (called insulators) are rust, oils, phosphorus, lime, chalk, rubber, camphor, marble, porcelain, dry gases and air, wool, silk, glass, transparent stones, wax and amber. Some of these become conductors when wet.

Defective insulation, such as wires hung on nails, is apt to cause short circuits through abrasion or the wearing off of insulation, the arc setting fire to surroundings. Conduits are the best form of wiring. Wires strung loosely are dangerous and apt to become damaged. Water in leaky conduits and wires in contact with dampness, such as underground wires, causes blowouts.

ELECTRIC ARC—The intensely bright arc produced between two carbon points in air, when a current of electricity passes from one to the other across a gap.

ELECTRIC CABLE DUCTS—See Pipe Shafts.

ELECTRIC DEVICES—The National Board states that 30,000 fires a year are caused by carelessness in using electric devices. A new form of peril is coming into prominence as a cause of much destruction, and its fires are so directly associated with carelessness that it has been deemed necessary to issue a special warning. Because of their convenience small electric devices, such as pressing irons, curling irons, toasters, electric pads or blankets, electric plate warmers and electric sterilizers or heaters, are now to be found in nearly every community. If these were used with proper care the danger would be negligible; but, unfortunately, a proportion of their users do not realize the peril of leaving them in circuit when not in use. In such cases these devices tend to become overheated, whereupon they are liable to set fire to anything combustible with which they come in contact. Most of these fires are small, but the aggregate loss is large, and occasional instances show extensive damage, as in the case of the $350,000 fire in a Boston residence. This was traced to an electric plate-warmer in the butler's pantry. Fires of this class furnish a special peril to life, being most frequent in dwellings, and often breaking out in the night. A characteristic example is that in which an electric pressing iron is left upon the ironing board with the current turned on and then forgotten. In such a case the fire may not occur until some hours later. It is safe to say that most of these fires are entirely preventible and can be charged to nothing but carelessness on the part of the user. Various safety devices have been added by certain of the manufacturers of these articles, and among them are some that are fairly effective, but there is one absolute precaution which should be borne in mind at all times by every user, namely, that of shutting off the current when not personally and continuously supervising its use. See Electric Iron.

ELECTRIC HAZARD—In the eyes of the underwriter it is a question of heat and not light. Heat is caused by wires carrying too great a current; therefore it is necessary to find out if wires are overloaded or provided with proper fuses.

ELECTRIC IRON—An electric iron in use in Dayton, Ohio, was left on a table and burned its way through the table, through the flooring, then through a joist that supported the flooring and was found dangling by its wire in the room below without firing the building. They should have a thermostat switch placed in the iron to automatically cut off the current whenever the temperature exceeds a predetermined point, usually 400 to 600 deg. F. See Electric Devices.

ELECTRIC LAMP SHADES—These shades are made of colored fabric, and have shaped corrugated sides designed to stretch to snugly fit naked incandescent electric light globes with which they come in contact. The use of these shades is fraught with danger as electric light bulbs readily heat sufficiently to ignite material with which they may come in contact. Unsuspecting customers are apt to purchase these shades and install them in their homes for decorative purposes near curtained windows, drapery or other inflammable material where the light might be left burning indefinitely and thereby cause a fire.

ELECTRIC MOTOR—A machine by which electrical energy is transformed into mechanical energy to rotate a shaft.

ELECTRICAL SUPPLY STOCK—Work is repairing and assembling fixtures, repairing motors, winding armatures, buffing, soldering, relacquering. Use considerable packing material. Numerous portable electric light wires for displaying domes and globes is a poor feature. The insulation wears off by continuous use and careless handling, and short circuits are frequent.

ELECTRICAL TERMS — Broadly speaking, ampere means volume; volt, pressure; and watts, the resulting quantity. A volt is the measure of pressure. Amperes multiplied by volts equals watts. The quantity (watts) of electricity delivered over a single circuit is the direct product of the volume (amperes), multiplied by the pressure (volts). A thousand (kilo) watts are the mechanical equivalent of one and one-third horse power. Lighting circuits usually carry 105 to 120 volts, although some towns have 220 volt systems.

ELECTRICALLY-DRIVEN MACHINERY—If fire takes place within the machine itself, the fire policy is not liable for damage to the machinery. If, however, the fire extends to other property, the company is liable for the property so destroyed. If fire starts elsewhere than in the machinery, the company is liable for the damage to the machinery.

ELECTROLYSIS—The destructive effect upon metals of an electric current. The most common form is the effect upon underground pipes, lead-covered cables, and metal work of building foundations. The effect is the pitting or erosion where the electrical current leaves it. Stray currents from power houses seeking return to the power house utilize pipes, metal structures and cables in their path (usually because the return feeders are of insufficient capacity). The damage occurs where the current leaves these structures.

Electrolysis (electrolytic corrosion) is disintegration caused by stray electric currents attacking underground steel work. Where the electrolysis is severe or continuous, it may cause the collapse of steel skeleton buildings.

ELECTROPLATES—Inspection should be made to see if wood backed, also whether kept in fireproof vault, in stacks or in boxes.

ELECTROTYPING—Wood cuts, half-tones, and zinc etchings are so much in use at the present time that it is necessary to describe briefly their manufacture, and also to mention some of the hazards found in their production. These cuts are sometimes placed in the press with other type, as in ordinary printing, but quite frequently electrotypes are made from them; this is especially true of wood cuts. The electrotype is then placed in the press while the original is preserved for future use. In wood engravings, Turkish boxwood is cut into pieces of the desired size and the surface to receive the design is finished so as to be perfectly flat and smooth. The next step is to have the design or picture traced or drawn on the block to enable the engraver to begin his work. Sometimes this is done by hand, but now-a-days most of this work is accomplished by the use of photographic negatives. The object to be reproduced is photographed by means of the negative, the design or picture is printed on the face of the block which has previously been covered with a sensitized solution. Arc lights are generally used to do this printing; this makes it unnecessary to depend upon the proper weather condition. The engraver then takes the design, and with hand tools cuts away those portions of the face of the block which must be removed to produce the design in relief. Nothing but hand tools are used in this work. A "lining" machine is used to produce the fine parallel lines appearing on these cuts. No hazard of much importance presents itself in this business, except that of arc lights, which should be, and generally are, protected by glass globes.

ELEMI—A composition of resin used in lacquer making.

ELEMINE—Rosin boiled in water containing carbonate of soda.

ELEVATION—In reviewing plans it is the drawing which shows the height of the building with all the stories combined.

ELEVATOR BOOT—The lowest part of a "lofter" or elevator (also termed elevator leg), enclosing the pulley under which passes the carrying belt.

ELEVATOR BUILDINGS—All buildings such as grain elevators, used in the handling of any combustible substance, especially where finely divided dust is liable to be produced, should be built of fireproof materials. Non-fireproof construction type have a bad loss record.

ELEVATOR HEAD—The opposite end to the "boot" enclosing the driving pulley. See Strut Board.

ELEVATOR LEG—The narrow, continuous boxing, enclosing a belt-and-bucket or chain-and-bucket elevator, through one or more floors.

ELEVATORS are used in grain warehouses or breweries to convey grain from one floor to another, and also from boats to cars. In the latter case, it is called a "marine leg."

EMBOSSERS—Used by woodworkers for pressing patterns on wood in imitation of carving. The machine consists of a plate or roller bearing a design in relief with a device to hold the work to be embossed and another device for heating the plate or roller. Gas heat is generally used, although live steam and sometimes gasoline have been used.

EMBOSSING PRESS—Similar to a cylinder press. One type is the revolving press, the revolving portion of which is covered with fine needles which make impressions on the paper. Others are similar to a screw press, in which case a die is used for making the impression. Both are usually gas heated, and flexible connections are sometimes necessary unless the "bed" or stationary part of the press is heated, in which case a rigid iron pipe connection can be made. See Printers.

EMBROIDERIES—Dress goods, lace, netting with braids, cords, spangles or beaded cord are embroidered on a "Bonnaz embroider," a type of machine similar to the ordinary sewing machine. The best of machines are imported. Hemstitchers, scalloping and imitation hand embroidery machines are similar to the ordinary sewing machine. A "braider" is a circular all-iron machine similar to a knitting machine for making bodies of sweaters. On it round, flat, elastic or soutache braids are woven. The rough edges of braids are singed over a gas flame, alcohol, gasoline or kerosene torch or lamp. "Chenille" machine: a machine designed to make cords, tassels, etc., as used on portieres or draperies, dress goods or millinery trimmings. Usually of wood, a small affair, the yarn being drawn through the machine to a large wheel on opposite side of room, the reverse action of the wheel and the chenille machine making the twist. The machine is usually very oily and covered with lint. Swiss embroidery: Swiss machines are large, 5 to 15 yards long, weighing 2 to 18 tons. Should always be set on substantial bases, preferably in the basement or first floors of buildings, the foundation resting on terra firma. The pattern is placed on a board at one end of the machine, an operator tracing the design with an arm (called pantograph), which also regulates the action of needles and punches which embroiders the goods. The goods are stretched along the entire length of the machine, which is motor-driven. An "automat" attached to a Swiss machine takes the place of the operator. It works on the same principle as a player-piano, having a perforated pattern instead of a music roll, which makes the design, and is also motor-driven. Oily, lint covered motor, oily floor and swinging gas brackets are the hazards of these Swiss machines.

Passementerie is the edging, bead work, or lace trimmings for dress goods. All hand work; no material hazard.

Stamping is transferring a pattern to piece of goods to be embroidered. The transferring is done by rubbing a piece of colored chalk, wax or lamp-black thinned with benzine over the perforations of the patterns similar to a "pounce."

Carbonizing—Braids are frequently sewn on buckram which has been treated with sizing of diluted sulphuric acid. Heat tends to disintegrate the buckram. The goods are placed on a wire mesh over a gas flame in an oven. The heat carbonizes the buckram and leaves the braid intact. A source of danger, unless the oven is properly constructed. Carbonizing is also done by passing a hot iron over the buckram.

Plaiting, Ruching, Fluting and **Crimpers** are gas-heated. Unless the rollers become overheated, thereby burning the goods, there is little hazard if the gas connection is of iron.

Bleaching is done with benzoin or hydrogen peroxide; cleaned with alcohol, turpentine, benzine or chloroform; dyed in aniline colors. Important hazards are heating of sizing kettles, rubber tubes at gas-heated machines, swinging gas lights at Swiss machines, stamping with benzine and lamp-black, and the carbonizing ovens. Very susceptible stocks. Water will streak the goods, mildew, or make the colors run. After a fire they should be immediately sorted and dried. Wash embroideries generally yield a good salvage. Imported machinery with necessary loss of time in replacing parts must be considered in "use and occupancy" lines. (W. O. Lincoln, "Live Articles on Special Hazards," The Weekly Underwriter.)

EMERY AND SANDPAPER MFG.—Hazards of crushers for raw materials, dry rooms, pulverizing. Paper is coated with glue and by continuous process passes through a steam heated machine where the dust is deposited on the paper.

EMPTY BOXES—All kinds of fire wood, boxes, etc., in yards and alleys should be stacked neatly and kept free from rubbish.

ENAMELS are mixtures of pigments, varnish, oils and japan.

ENCLOSED—Surrounded by partitions to prevent draughts and fires from spreading from floor to floor. See Shafts.

END CONSTRUCTION—As applied to laying terra cotta, is the same as side construction, except the blocks are laid on ends instead of sides. See Side Construction.

ENDORSEMENT—A term expressing a change in the original contract of insurance, thus: change of location, name, increasing or reducing amount, etc., are noted on policy and signed by agent or officer of the company.

ENEMY ALIEN CLAUSE—The Executive Committee recommend and urge all members of the N. Y. F. I. Exchange to employ **on all policies hereafter issued in this area** the following clause in order to make reasonably sure of avoiding violation of the so-called Trading with the Enemy Act of the United States Congress, approved October 6, 1917:

"This entire policy shall be void if the insurance hereunder, directly or indirectly, is for, or on account of, or on behalf of or for the benefit of an 'enemy' or 'ally of enemy' (as defined in the Act of Congress, approved October 6, 1917, known as the 'Trading with the Enemy Act,' or amendments thereto, or in any proclamation of the President pursuant thereto), or is for any person who is acting for, on account of, or on behalf of, or for the benefit of any 'enemy' or 'ally of enemy' unless the interest of the 'enemy' or 'ally of enemy' has been conveyed, transferred, assigned and delivered to the Alien Property Custodian, or unless with a license from the President of the United States permission is granted to insure the 'enemy' or 'ally of enemy.'"

The foregoing has been agreed upon in conference with the representatives of the National Board of Fire Underwriters and other company organizations and interests for adoption in all cases where policies appear to protect an unnamed beneficiary such as would be covered by the trust and commission clause, the expression "heirs of" or "estate of" or "as now or may hereafter be constituted" or "on storage or for repairs," etc., etc. (Author's Note—The situation regarding the trust and commission clause has not been definitely settled.)

ENGINE OILS—Hydrocarbon oils of gravity 32 to 33 degrees. Flash point 300 to 400 deg. F. Animal or vegetable oils are only used in mineral oil compounds.

ENGRAVERS use plate printing presses somewhat similar to transfer presses in printing risks (only much larger). To keep the ink warm a gas jet is usually used, but kerosene oil lamps may be found. Use of kerosene oil lamps should be discontinued. Benzine is used for cleaning. Metal should be placed under the presses. Oily waste to be kept in safety can.

EPSOM SALTS—See Sulphate of Magnesia.

EQUAL TO—An insurance term meaning the adjoining building is higher, therefore being equal to a parapetted wall. A very high ceiling building or story of a building, such as a church, may be described as being one equal to two (or more) stories in height.

ERADELINE—Flash point, 100 deg. F. Classed non-volatile.

ERADICATOR PAINT OR GREASE may contain ether, gasoline, alcohol, acetone, etc.

ERWIN AUTOMATIC EXTINGUISHING OUTFIT—For extinguishing oil or naphtha fires in tanks. Briefly—a white foam is ejected on the surface of the burning material from standpipes containing a chemical solution. A lead-lined thimble containing acid is closed with a fusible link which in burning allows the thimble to fall in the chemical solution in the standpipe and the chemical mixture is forced out under pressure.

ESSENTIAL OILS—Liquids which give the odors peculiar to plants from which they are derived, or are produced by the combination of substances in the plant which react when brought into the presence of water. They have strong odors, and are generally volatile.

ETCHING—A process of engraving by means of hydrofluoric, nitric or hydrochloric acid. If glass, hydrofluoric acid only can be used.

ETHER—Prepared by distilling alcohol and sulphuric acid in retorts. Volatile, highly inflammable. When mixed with oxygen it explodes. Flashes at 29 deg. F.

Petroleum Ether—Very light and volatile petroleum distillate. Used as a solvent. More inflammable than gasoline.

Sulphuric Ether—Highly inflammable and volatile. Flashes at zero F. Made by treatment of alcohol with sulphuric acid.

Spirits of Nitrous Ether—More inflammable than alcohol.

ETHILENE—A colorless gas which burns with a luminous smoky flame.

ETHYL ACETATE—See Acetate of Ethyl.

ETHYL ALCOHOL—See Grain Alcohol.

ETHYL CHLORIDE—A gas at ordinary temperature. Stored under pressure in small tubes and used by dentists for freezing purposes. Not as hazardous as ether. Volatile and inflammable. Boils at 55 deg. F.

ETHYL-METHYL KETONE—A colorless inflammable liquid. Flash point 30 deg. F.

ETHYL NITRATE—A thin yellow liquid. Boils at 61 deg. F. Volatile and inflammable. May ignite spontaneously at 194 deg. F.

ETHYL OXIDE is ether.

EXAMINER—One who examines and passes on the risks submitted by special agents, or agents through a daily report system. He is an underwriter and should have a good knowledge of building construction and hazards. See Counterman.

EXCELSIOR, if damp, is subject to spontaneous combustion if the natural sap still remains.

EXCLUSION—The standard policy does not permit of excluding any portion of an insured building (insured as a whole), except the cost of foundations and excavations below the level of the ground.

EXOLIUM—A benzine substitute. Flash point above 100 deg. F.

EXPANDED METAL—A steel plate slit in one operation and pulled and enlarged into diamond or other shape meshes. Also slotted or punched steel plates.

EXPERIMENTS or experimental works or manufacturing risks should be declined unless their objects are clearly understood. In case of failure, the insurance collected is often all that is back of the enterprise.

EXPLOSION—When gas or vapor is released so suddenly

as to cause a loud noise, an explosion is said to occur, as for instance, the explosion of a steam boiler or a cylinder of compressed gas. Great and increasing use is made of explosive processes in gas, petrol and oil engines for driving machinery of all kinds. In these engines, the material that explodes is a mixture of air with combustible gas, vapor or finely comminuted liquid and, in the explosion, these are suddenly converted into water vapor and the oxides of carbon, which latter are gases. Although all these things are liable to explode, none of them are called explosives; this term is confined to liquids and solid substances which produce much more violent effects than exploding gaseous mixtures, because they occupy much smaller volumes originally. (A. Marshall.) See Velocity of Explosions.

EXPLOSION (Black Tom)—New York Harbor, July 30th, 1916. Two explosions resulted from a fire that was started maliciously or accidentally among freight cars that had been placed on the terminal tracks of the Lehigh Valley Railroad at Black Tom preparatory to a transfer of their contents to barges for export movement. The more severe of the two explosions occurred on the land and involved about 400,000 pounds of dry trinitrotoluol packed in wooden cases, while the second explosion on the water involved 100,000 pounds of dry picric acid. Black Tom was occupied by the warehouses of the National Storage Co., and the Lehigh Valley Railroad had therein its office, float bridges and tracks. Practically all of the brick warehouses were demolished by the explosion. As explosives are essential in peace as well as in war, and must be transported, all restrictions that promote safety and are practicable must be enforced, in other words, uniform regulation by the Federal government of the water as well as the land carriers of dangerous articles. Ocean going ships must sacrifice more of their conveniences to the cause of safety in tidewater terminals. (Extract from Bureau of Explosives report.)

EXPLOSION INSURANCE—Policies cover property damage due to explosions of every name and nature, except from boilers and flywheels, originating within such apparatus, which insurance is covered by casualty companies only.

Form reads as follows: On all buildings of their manufacturing plant, including chimney, also sprinkler tank and fixtures, and yard hose houses, all situate.............., and on contents thereof (except accounts, bills, currency, deeds, evidences of debt, money, notes or securities) therein or on premises above described, through explosion (excluding boiler and flywheel explosions originating within said apparatus), occurring on said premises. Note.—When boiler or flywheel explosion is included the rate is 25 per cent. higher.

The policy also covers machinery or stock belonging to others which the assured are under obligations to keep insured; also machinery or stock consigned to them, or held in trust, or on commission, or sold but not delivered by being removed; but this policy does not cover machinery or stock on which there is specific insurance.

This company shall not be liable for any loss caused by explosion originating from any of the materials and/or processes incidental to the business of the assured. Note.—If this clause is eliminated, the rate is increased according to occupancy.

It is warranted by the assured and made a condition of this contract that constant nightwatchman service shall be maintained; furthermore, that at times when plant is not in operation, constant day watchman service shall be maintained during the life of this policy. Note.—Not required on dwellings and mercantile.

Other insurance permitted without notice until requested.

The policy does not cover any automobile which may be within the premises of assured.

50 per cent. co-insurance mandatory. Allowance made for 80 per cent. co-insurance.

EXPLOSIONS from static electricity. See Static or Frictional Electricity.

EXPLOSIVE—An explosive is a solid or liquid substance, or mixture of substances, which is liable, on the application of heat or a blow to a small portion of the mass, to be converted in a very short interval of time into other more stable substances, largely or entirely gaseous. A considerable amount of heat is also invariably evolved and consequently there is a flame. (A. Marshall.)

EXPLOSIVE GELATINE is about 90 per cent. nitroglycerine and 10 per cent. gun cotton.

EXPLOSIVES should be stored in a dry, well-ventilated place, not warmer than 80 or 90 deg. F. They should be kept under lock and key, so that children or irresponsible persons cannot have access to them, and should not be stored in locality where hunting or other shooting may be done, unless they are kept bullet proof. Most high explosives freeze at a temperature between 45 and 50 deg. F., and when frozen will either explode imperfectly or not at all. Low explosives are exploded by a spark; but a spark will not explode high explosives, although it may ignite them, and the heat and pressure caused by burning in a confined space may result in an explosion after a time. High explosives can only be properly exploded by a powerful shock. This shock is brought about in their use by exploding a detonator inserted in the charge of explosives. This detonator is either a blasting cap, which is exploded by a spark from a fuse, or an electric fuse (pronounced fu-zee) which is exploded by a fine wire superheated by an electric current. See Dynamite.

EXPOSURE (EXTERNAL)—A condition, structure or material which increases the hazard of a risk through burning or exploding. It defines the likelihood of a building becoming ignited without its walls. The exposure depends upon the width of streets or alleys, the space between buildings and the nature of the construction and occupancy of such buildings. The hazard may be reduced by the use of standard wire glass windows, shutters, doors and skylights and outside sprinklers. About one-sixth of the losses are caused by exposure fires.

Inspectors should carefully note all exposures, the distance away and whether outside openings of risk are protected by labelled wire glass windows or standard shutters. The following is the fire record of exposure fires in Greater New York as taken from the New York Board of Fire Underwriters' report:

BUILDING—

Year	Insurance	Loss	%
1910	$ 6,362,822	$169,468	.026
1911	10,811,063	148,507	.014
1912	14,742,149	171,442	.011
1913	6,862,499	98,781	.014
1914	11,422,651	82,344	.008
1915	8,181,076	52,782	.006
CONTENTS—			
1910	4,684,224	263,327	.056
1911	8,567,924	350,289	.04
1912	5,729,133	738,799	.13
1913	3,624,729	234,220	.064
1914	2,422,303	150,697	.062
1915	1,601,119	45,823	.020

EXPOSURE (INTERNAL)—The hazard due to exposing the property of one or more tenants of a building to the danger of fire spreading from the premises of another tenant in the same building. In rating, the internal exposure is the most hazardous occupancy; as paper box making, painters or carpenters, which increase the rate of building and of other less hazardous tenants.

EXPRESS OFFICES AND DEPOTS—Frequently old or dilapidated buildings of various construction. Hazards of unsafe heating and lighting appliances, miscellaneous storage, including chemicals and explosives, smoking by employees, and used as a "hang-out." See Legal Liability.

EXTRACTION PLANTS, NAPHTHA PROCESS—(Oil-seed works, and Refuse Disposal plants). Walls should be heavy common brick with light corrugated iron roof. Screened openings should be provided at floor levels to carry off vapor. Lighting by incandescent lamps, marine type vapor-proof globes, all wiring in conduit with screw joint junction boxes and marine type fittings; no switches should be permitted in the building.

The naphtha tank should be buried outside the building.

The Process—The meats from the oil works are brought into the extracting building and dropped into bins having spouts feeding into the extractors. These are cylindrical steel drums having stirring arms rotated by shaft and gearing. The bottom of each contains a perforated metal false bottom under which is located a copper pipe, steam heating coil and a perforated steam jet coil. Charging doors are located in the top through which the meats are fed, and discharge outlets provided in the sides near the bottom. There are also pipe connections for the naphtha at both top and bottom connecting with vaporizers and discharge tanks, all of which are inclosed vessels. The extractors are partly filled with the meats and then hot naphtha vapor passed through same, passing through the extractors in series, the naphtha vapors forming a solution with the oil. The mixture is pumped from the extractors into a receiving tank and steam is turned into the heating coils in extractors; the vapor from same being condensed in suitable condensers. Live steam is then blown into extractors to remove as much of the remaining vapor as possible. This is also condensed in the condensers. The discharge doors of the extractors are then opened, and the extracted meats dropped into a screw conveyor from whence they drop into another conveyor and are returned to the oil mill plant. The balance of the operation of obtaining the oil from the naphtha and entrained water is one of settlement where the water separates through difference in specific gravity and is then drawn off and distilled, the mixed vapor and oil being introduced into a still heated by steam, the naphtha vapor distilling off and being condensed, the oil remains. The process is hazardous. See Garbage Reduction Plants.

EVAPORATING—See Crystalizing.

EVAPORATION—The conversion of a liquid into a gaseous state by action of heat.

EVERITE PRESSOLINE—A benzine substitute, classed as non-volatile.

EXTRACTS—See Flavoring Extracts.

F

FACING in building construction; a wall or surface covering of stone or similar substance on the outer wall.

FACTORS—A firm or individual who acts as a banker for, or a backer of, another firm or person, advancing money to buy goods or carry on a business. Usually in wholesale woolen, piece goods or dry goods businesses.

FACTORY—According to the Bureau of Fire Prevention, a factory is in substance any mill, workshop, or other manufacturing or business establishment, and all buildings, sheds or other places used in connection therewith where one or more persons are employed at labor. No smoking is permitted in factories in New York City.

FAIR GROUNDS—A group of hastily and flimsily constructed frame buildings of varied occupancy, such as shooting galleries, stables, live stock pens, lunch rooms, display rooms, demonstrating machinery, race tracks. Not considered desirable. Temporary occupancy and on leased land.

FALLING WALL HAZARD—Most rating organizations add a certain charge for this feature; sometimes a percentage of the rate of the exposing risk is taken. Experience shows that in case of a severe fire in a high exposing building with a separated distance, the lower building so exposed is liable to be destroyed by falling bricks and debris. See Wind.

FARM—At piers, is the open space in front of the pier used for open storage of merchandise.

FARMS have been considered as unprofitable insurance by many large companies. Hazards include the use of gasoline stoves or engines, incubators and brooders, feed grinding, lighting by acetylene gas systems, wood burning furnaces, evaporating fruit in a room with red-hot pot stove, garage, threshing machines, unsafe heating apparatus. Stove pipes through floors to heat upper rooms are quite frequently found. In place of scalding hogs with steam, farmers have been known to sprinkle gasoline on the carcass and set it on fire. The quick flash burns off the hair without damaging the hide.

FARRIERS—See Blacksmiths.

FAT RENDERING—Plants buy fat from butchers and deposit same into steam jacketed (covered top) rendering kettles with agitators. The liquid (tallow) derived therefrom is run to a covered sump pit from which it is pumped to a tank on the floor above. The residue or waste material is removed and placed in hydraulic presses and pressed into cakes. The cakes are then placed in a power grinder and made into chicken feed or used as fertilizer. Hazardous. Entire premises usually oil soaked.

FATIGUE OF MATERIALS—The increased weakness produced by frequent bending or by sustaining heavy loads for a long time.

FEATHERS AND FEATHER PILLOWS—Feathers are sorted in a sorting machine, cut up in a high speed knife cutter equipped with a blower system which draws the feathers through a suction pipe to a duster, thence to the storage bins. Bins are usually of wire mesh on wooden frames. The lighter feathers are deposited on the upper portion of the bins and the heavier feathers fall to the floor. The pillow cases are then filled and sewed up. Cotton is sometimes added; in which case a cotton picker may be used. Considerable dust about premises. Knife cutter should have magnets to catch metal particles.

FELT—A rather coarse fabric or cloth, made of fibres of hair, wool, coarse paper, etc., by pressure and not by weaving, treated with resin.

Felt (roofing) is sometimes made from the refuse of flax treated with resin.

Felt (cotton) in bales is considered subject to spontaneous combustion.

FELT PACKING—As used for automobiles and electrical machinery is about 80 per cent. wool and 20 per cent. cotton. The hazard of making the packing is cutting, stitching and gluing. These are usually good risks, unless the felt is manufactured on the premises.

FENCES—If of slatted wood, especially along the line of steam railroads, are considered poor risks. Fires have been known to start at one end and burn for miles.

FERMENT—To allow moistened organic matter to undergo a process of decay.

FERMENTATION—A chemical action brought about by the action of micro-organisms or "ferments."

FERRO-MANGANESE is imported from England. Without it some kinds of steel cannot be made. Produced from ores of iron and manganese in high temperature smelting furnace.

FERRO-SILICON—Compounded of iron and silicon. Non-hazardous.

FERRY BOATS—Should be inspected. Lines are usually offered on the old wooden hulls rather than on the modern type of steel hull.

FERRY HOUSES of frame construction are apt to be a total loss. If barnlike construction, they burn rapidly. Hazard of oil rooms and lamp filling, repair shops, baggage rooms, lunch rooms and heating apparatus.

FERTILIZER—The commercial mixed varieties have very little fire hazard when packed and ready for use.

Fertilizer from fish scrap and crabs. Process—boiling in digesters where all unused agents are removed, drying residue and reducing same to carbon in high temperature dryer, ground, bagged. Subject to spontaneous combustion by absorbing oxygen very rapidly.

FIBRES are divided into two classes, **hard and soft.** Hard fibres, by virtue of their construction, do not absorb water rapidly when immersed and do not heat or decompose as rapidly as soft fibres which, when damaged, must be picked apart and dried at once if any salvage is to be expected. The largest losses are caused by the collapse of the building due to the swelling or expansion of the soft fibre from the excessive absorption of water. Spontaneous combustion is not attributed as the cause of these fires. See N. F. P. A. Quarterly (T. E. Sears), October, 1913. See Bagging Factories.

Hard Fibres—Manilla, Sisal, Henequen, Maguey, Mescal, Istle, Zapupe, New Zealand, Mauritius, Cabinja.

Soft Fibres—Hemp, American, Italian, Russian jute, Sunn, Flax.

Hemp Fibres of all kinds are destroyed if exposed to a heat of 300 deg. F. Hemp is an annual plant of the mulberry family, a native of Asia. Classed as a soft fibre.

Flax is a native of western Asia. Used chiefly in the manufacture of linen sewing thread, fishing lines, etc. Classed as soft fibre.

Sunn Hemp is a base fibre from an annual plant and also known as Conkanee, Indian, Brown and Madras hemp. Used in manufacturing cordage. Classed as soft.

Jute is a base fibre, growing principally in India. Used chiefly in rugs, grain sacks and binding twine. Classed as soft.

Caburya—A fibre produced in Costa Rica and sometimes called Central American sisal, used for binder twine. Classed as hard.

Maguey is a comparatively new fibre on the market, and is produced from the leaves of the Maguey plant, which very closely resembles the henequen of Yucatan. Classed as hard.

Sisal—The true sisal is taken from the leaves of the sisal plant, a native of Central America. Classed as hard.

Henequen is a native plant of Mexico, known in the trade as sisal. It belongs to the same botanical family as the true sisal. Classed as hard.

Manilla Hemp—Known as Manilla or Abaca, is grown principally in the Philippines. Classed as hard.

Mauritius—A hard fibre obtained in the island of Mauritius. It is white in color and more flexible than henequen. Classed as hard.

New Zealand Flax—Sometimes called hemp, is not at all like wither hemp or flax, but is obtained from the leaves of a native plant of New Zealand. Classed as hard.

Zapupe—A fibre which grows in loamy soils and with more moisture and less lime than seems necessary for good results with henequen or sisal. Classed as hard.

Istle—A fibre grown on the high, arid tablelands of northern Mexico. The fibre is shorter than the henequen plant. Classed as hard.

Mescal Maguey—Similar to henequen, finer and softer, produced in Mexico. Used chiefly in cordage and twine mills on the Pacific coast. Classed as hard.

FIBRE WAREHOUSES for the storage of cotton, hemp, sisal, etc., are especially designed. For charges made in rating, see New York Exchange schedule. Buildings should be low, one-story brick buildings, with walls parapetted and coped and areas restricted, limited window openings, walls blank wherever possible. The height to which cotton bales may be piled is restricted, and clear aisle spaces are demanded. See Warehouses.

FIBREBOARD—Made from leather chips, flux, old rope, paper, wood pulp and similar stuff. Ground, cooked by steam in solution of alkalis, mixed with binder of such material as glue or rosin, colored, pressed into sheets, dried, varnished or stained. See Chemical Fibre; see Compo-Board.

FILBERTS—See Nuts.

FILLERINE—A fertilizer ingredient made from iron oxide. Liable to ignite spontaneously.

FILLERS—Used by woodworkers, are made of various combinations of silax, silver white, cornstarch, whiting, plaster paris, raw and boiled linseed oil, turpentine, japan and benzine.

FILM VAULT (Test for Ventilation)—By F. J. T. Stewart, of N. F. P. A., 4-22-'15, Leonia, N. J.

A structure of 12-inch terra cotta blocks having 133 cubic feet was vented with a side opening 285 square inches and filled with films on shelves in and out of cans and space between racks filled with loose films and ignited with electric spark, 1800 pounds of film in all. The tongue of flame which shot out from the vault almost immediately after the ignition of the film projected itself 75 feet, continuing for several minutes, or until all the gases generated within the vault were consumed. The vault was undamaged, proving that the area of ventilation provided was undoubtedly sufficient to prevent explosion from the rapid decomposition of film under similar conditions. See Motion Picture Films.

FILTER CLOTHS should be washed directly after being used.

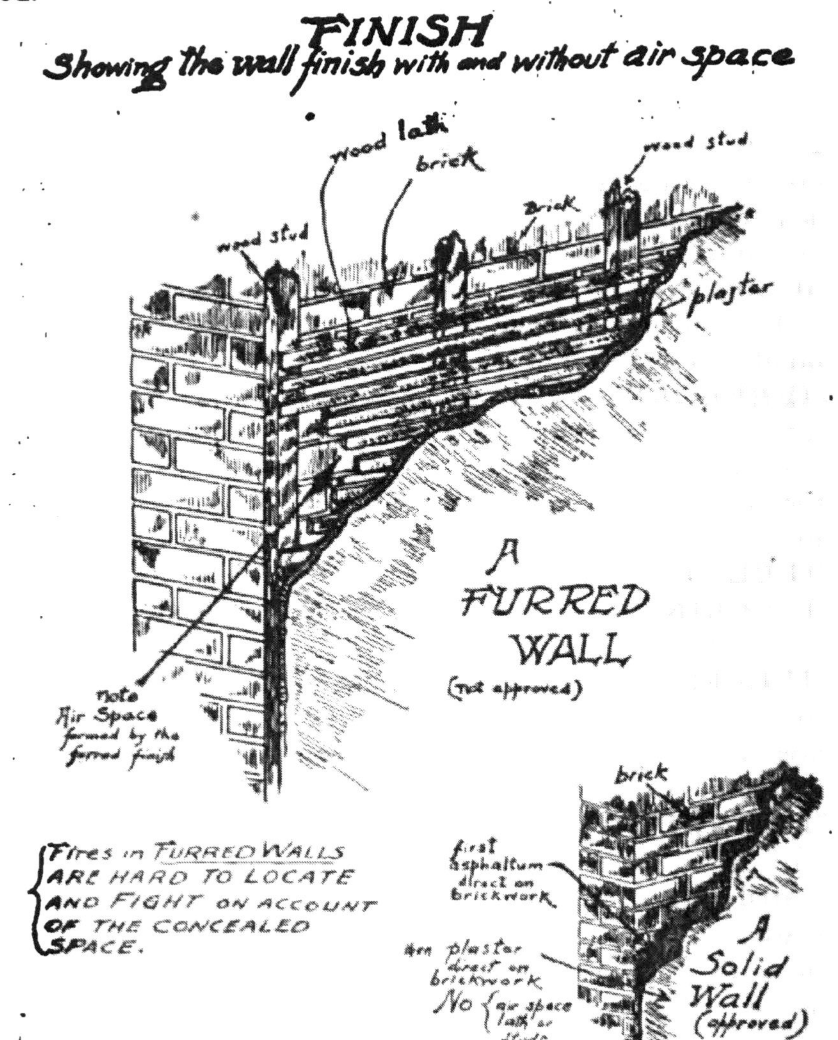

FILTERING—See Liquors.

FILTRATION—This is done to get rid of foreign material of all kinds, or to extract solid matter. The old-fashioned way is by filtering or straining through filter cloths, but the up-to-date method is by means of bone black filters in a large steel tank, partly filled with ground bone black (charcoal), the liquid being fed at the top and strained through the charcoal.

FINISH (plain or hard)—A wall plastered direct without furring or no finish at all. See Furring.

FINISHING—As the name implies, is the last process in manufacturing an article.

FIRE—According to the Standard dictionary, is heat and light emanating from a body.

Fire is rapid oxidation formed by heating carbon substances to a point where they combine rapidly with oxygen. All ignitable substances, such as wood or paper, are carbon substances. Consider the amount of such material entering into the construction of a frame building and realize that a heat force of a few hundred degrees of heat will overbalance the fire equilibrium, and the wonder is that we have not more fires.

FIRE—Buildings do not burn because of the material entering into their construction, but from carelessness, inflammable contents or faulty design.

When certain chemical substances unite rapidly a large quantity of heat is generated and we have the phenomenon which we call fire. See Chemical Substances; see Water Puts Out Fire.

FIRE ALARM SYTEMS are various in character. In crude form, consist of bell ringing, whistle blowing, hammering on locomotive tires severed in the center, or other metallic substances. The modern method is, open the door of street fire alarm box and pull down once only the hook that is in view, letting it slide back to its original position by its own momentum. This act causes a disc in central fire station bearing number of box pulled to drop, and a man on duty telegraphs said number to fire companies who are supposed to respond. Automatic and pneumatic alarms are installed by placing series of thermostats on ceilings which operate by having the fuse within them melted by excessive heat contact, by which action alarm is given at central fire station. See Combination Red Fire Alarm Box; also Alarm.

FIRE APPLIANCES (freezing of, precaution against)—Unless extreme vigilance is exercised the very best installation of fire appliances may suffer temporary disablement from frost. Automatic sprinkler systems, hydrants and all appliances using water for fire extinguishment naturally require special care and attention in winter. The following precautions should be taken; inspections being thorough, with nothing taken for granted.

1. Ascertain if all portions of buildings are properly heated at all times to prevent freezing in any of the sprinkler pipes, particular attention being given to exposed places, such as hallways, entries, stair towers, under sidewalks, show windows, shipping rooms, attics, roof monitors and skylights.

2. Examine tanks and all pipes, fittings and valves, whether for steam heating, general water service, or fire protection. **See that none is frozen** or has been frozen, and that they are **all in operative condition,** and where there is any liability of freezing, provide the necessary protection. All metal work supporting tanks should be thoroughly cleaned from rust and painted, also tank hoops.

3. Examine carefully and provide suitable boxing around any pipe lines which may be in an exposed location (either between ground and first floor, between buildings, or near windows, doors, etc.). Make frequent tests during the winter of such sprinkler systems in order to make sure the piping is not frozen.

4. Ascertain if sprinkler dry valves are in working order, not leaking, and piping thoroughly drained; if alarm connection and gong are in order; if air pumps can be depended on for the winter.

Note.—Do not overlook low points on dry system not controlled by main drain. Blow low points out occasionally to free from condensation.

5. See that **all valves are open that should be open,** and try water outlets to ascertain if all pipes are free and ready for service.

6. See that **extra sprinklers** are on hand in case of need to replace frozen or melted heads.

7. Be sure that engineer or supervising employee is fully posted as to the purpose and intention of every valve and pipe.

8. Try pumps and see that they are in proper working order.

9. Test all of the **hydrants** and **indicator posts**, and see that they drain properly.

10. Examine inside standpipes and connections.

11. **Instruct the night watchman** thoroughly in the use of all fire apparatus and the operation of all valves.

12. Examine the end of suction pipe to see that leaves or other refuse matter have not clogged up the holes in the strainer. The capacity of the pump may be greatly reduced by this defect.

13. Take measures to prevent freezing of water in casks and pails in cold buildings.

14. Empty and recharge chemical extinguisher to insure their being in perfect working order.

A thorough examination should be made of the entire heating system before putting it into service. All heating pipes should be carefully brushed down, and, where the piping is located along walls, any rubbish or litter which may have accumulated should be removed and pipes kept free from dangerous contact with walls, partitions, etc.

When it becomes necessary to close a sprinkler valve during working hours, a competent man should be stationed at the valves, so that the water can be turned on immediately in case a fire occurs.

When necessary to make changes in sprinkler system, extra care should be taken to have the least possible portion of the equipment out of commission at one time.

Whenever it is necessary to shut water off sprinklers, or in any way modify the fire protection, the inspection department having jurisdiction should be first notified. (N. F. P. A.)

FIRE BOATS (New York City).

Name	Horsepower	Capacity, gals. per min.
Zophar Mills	550	6,000
New Yorker	750	12,000
Seth Low	240	3,500
A. S. Hewitt	450	7,000
G. B. McClellan	500	7,000
James Duane	900	9,000
Thomas Willett	900	9,000
C. W. Lawrence	500	7,000
Wm. J. Gaynor	950	7,000
D. A. Boody	240	5,000
Launch, Velox	250	5,000

FIRE CLAUSES—Those attached to leases usually read as follows:

Form No. 1.—It is understood and agreed that should the premises be damaged so as to be totally destroyed, lease is to be cancelled. Note.—This form is acceptable to most companies.

Form No. 2.—It is understood and agreed if the building be so damaged that the lessee or owner elects not to rebuild, then this lease shall come to an end. Note.—This form is not acceptable to most companies, as the lessee or owner can rebuild or cancel the lease as they may choose. See Leasehold Insurance.

FIRECRACKERS made by the Chinese consist of potassium nitrate or saltpetre, sulphur and charcoal. American made firecrackers contain potassium chlorate, sulphur and carbonaceous materials.

FIRE DAMP (Marsh Gas) occurs in nature during the decay of organic matter. Usually in coal mines. Inflammable, but will not support combustion. When mixed with oxygen it is very explosive.

FIRE DEPARTMENT CONNECTIONS—See Siamese.

FIRE DOOR—A door built under specifications of the Underwriters Laboratories, with approved sill, frame, hangers and attachments, as per tests made at the laboratories, showing such a door will resist fire for at least one hour. approved installations, to protect an opening in a fire wa one automatic and one non-automatic door is required, b two automatic doors are preferred. An automatic door is o designed to close automatically through the release weights due to the melting of fusible link as the result fire heat. A self-closing door has a fusible link attachme but is generally kept closed when not in use, or, if open, automatically closes when released; counterweights bei used.

The melting point of fusible link is usually 165 deg. The fire-resisting value of a wood door encased in tin d pends upon the exclusion of oxygen from the wood, ther fore retarding or preventing combustion, and also upon t degree to which bulging in the covering can be prevent while the door is exposed to fire. To obtain these resul the covering must be so applied that the joints between t plates will remain intact and provision made for the esca of the gases generated from the wood core. See Alignu Fire Door.

FIRE DOOR MANUFACTURING, whether lock-joint or kalamein, are no better than other wood and metal wor ing shops. Frequent fires. See Kalamein Door Manufactu ing.

FIRE DRILLS in factories. In New York State t law requires fire drills at least once every three months u der the supervision of the local fire department, in every fa tory employing 25 or more persons. The Fire Preventi Bureau of New York City offers the following suggestion

Definition of Fire Drills—The orderly vacating of a buil ing by its occupants in the least possible time in case emergency, panic or fire. This to be by nearest safe mea of exit, and the use of such auxiliary fire appliances as m be provided for the extinguishment or retarding of fire.

Suggestions for Drills:

1. All employees shall be formed into squads or comp nies. A monitor or captain shall be designated to ta charge of each squad for the purpose of conducting the from the premises; also a monitor or captain to take char

of each squad designated to operate auxiliary fire appliances for the purpose of retarding or extinguishing the fire.

2. On receipt of alarm of fire all employees shall assemble on their respective floors at such point and in such manner as shall be designated by the monitor or captain in charge of that floor; remove all work and portable articles from aisles; form in double files with arms linked, and when ordered, shall march from the floor in a rapid but orderly manner to such exit as may be designated by said monitor or captain.

3. There shall be a sufficient number of employees designated by the owner, lessee or tenant of the premises to take charge of the drill and to operate auxiliary appliances.

4. Guards shall be stationed at the head and foot of each flight of stairs to preserve order and keep the line in motion, or retarding same as may be necessary.

5. Squads shall be designated to search for those who have fainted or fallen.

6. All drills shall be conducted in silence, save for the orders issued by those in authority.

7. An employee shall be designated to transmit the alarm for fire to the city department from the nearest fire alarm box.

FIRE ENGINE—An engine, pumping one full stream from a six-inch service main, will often reduce the pressure on the line below a serviceable point for another effective fire stream.

FIRE ESCAPE—See Fire Tower.

FIRE EXIT PARTITION—A partition subdividing a story to restrict the spread of fire, and sufficiently stable to provide an area of refuge for the exit of the occupants thereof. See Horizontal Exit.

FIRE EXTINGUISHERS—A siphon of soda in the home can be used as a fire extinguisher. The carbonic acid gas in the water helps to extinguish the flames. See Extinguishers; also Fire Appliances.

FIRE HEAT from wood is estimated to be from 800 to 1,400 deg. F.; from coal, 2,200 deg. F.; charcoal, 2,400 deg. F.

FIRE HOSE (care of)—Aside from the general care necessary to observe when the hose is not in actual use, it must be thoroughly overhauled after a fire to detect such defects as scorching, cracking, cuts due to dragging hose over cornices or rough edges, and then neatly placed on racks. See Friction Loss.

FIRE INSURANCE will only cover a small part of your loss if you have a fire. Insurance is a partial repayment, not a guarantee against fire occurring. It is indemnity against loss or damage by fire.

FIRE INSURANCE AS COLLATERAL (Fireman's Fund Record)—The importance of fire insurance as collateral security can be understood when we are told that 97 per cent. of the commerce of the world is carried on by paper exchange, and 3 per cent. of it for cash.

Fire insurance is the support of commerce, the endorser, the collateral security for the protection of credit.

A cargo of Pacific Coast salmon, wheat, fruit, wine or other products, shipped to Europe, is balanced by a cargo of manufactured articles shipped from Europe to China or Japan, and the latter shipment is balanced by tea and silk shipped from China or Japan to San Francisco, Los Angeles, Portland or Seattle, the coast products being thus paid for by the tea and silk. This is credit, no cash being used, but the credit being guaranteed by fire and marine insurance policies, makes the transaction cash, as a loss of either cargo would be made good by the insurance.

Fire insurance as a collateral is the basis for credit. It enables the wholesale merchant to extend credit to the reliable trader, to the extent of five times the trader's capital, at the same prices as for cash in sixty days; for if the trader sells the goods, he will pay his bills, and if his goods are destroyed or lost, his insurance collateral will pay his debts. In either case he is practically a cash man, gets his goods at cash price, and can sell to the consumer at less than if he bought at credit prices without collateral. The reduced prices at which the trader gets his goods (the sellers taking no risk) also pays for his insurance over and over again. Furthermore, as the fire insurance policy covers all stock that goes into the store during the term of the policy, $5,000 insurance on a $7,000 stock may in the course of a year have under its protection $30,000 or $40,000 worth of merchandise, thus reducing the cost of his insurance by distributing its protection over large values.

Fire insurance as collateral security also reduces interest rates and increases the purchasing power of capital.

The owner of a lot who wants to build a house can hire a greater sum of money from the bank on the property and at a lower rate of interest, when his mortgage debt is secured by insurance on the building, than he could without insurance. A warehouse receipt for wheat, fruit, wine or other produce, backed by an insurance policy, will, as collateral, command money at a much less rate, including the premium paid, than a mortgage on real estate will in the same locality.

A buyer with a capital of $20,000 invested in wheat or other produce in a warehouse can insure that produce for 95 per cent. of its value; then, with the warehouse receipt, and the insurance policy as collateral, he can get $19,000 from the bank, and with this $19,000 go into the market, invest that sum in more produce, and, repeating the operation, compete in the market for $150,000 or $200,000 worth of produce on an original capital of $20,000.

The exporter who places a cargo of wheat, fruit, wine or salmon on a ship insures it under a marine policy, with which and the bill of lading he commands money immediately, at the European rate of interest, to buy another cargo; and by repeating the operation not only increases the purchasing power of his capital, but he has the advantage of cheap money to operate on. This enables the producer to get a better price than if he had to depend on the competition of local capital, and emphasizes the benefit of insurance as collateral.

Fire insurance as collateral also protects invested capital from unnecessary disturbance.

Millionaire capitalists who manage large mining, manufacturing or other enterprises in which stockholders are interested, seek the protection of fire insurance for collateral security, as it enables them to obtain cash for immediate repair of any fire damage to the property, without using funds that can be applied to better advantage by continuing uninterrupted dividends to interested people, many of whom need the money.

This idea of protecting investments by the man of millions should be applied by the man of hundreds.

The rebuilding of San Francisco following the earthquake and fire is the best evidence of the value of fire insurance as collateral security for investments and loans that the business world ever experienced. Without the $180,000,000 paid by the fire insurance companies as indorsers (under their policies) and the credit obtained for as many more millions based upon the collateral security of their policies, San Francisco, instead of now being a city of skyscrapers, would be a city of shanties and ash-heaps.

It is asserted by economists who have studied the value of insurance as collateral security that the saving in interest rates to the borrower, and on the cost of goods to the consumer, amounts to a much greater sum than the total premiums paid by the insured, and that the loss collected is all clear profit.—(The Weekly Underwriter.)

FIRE INSURANCE TECHNOLOGY is the art of knowing the special features of a risk and how to inspect the premises.

FIRE LOSS (Extract from Lecture by W. N. Bament)—The fire insurance contract is based on a contingency, and rates are made to cover the contingency, and any omission of that which good faith demands in connection with it is sufficient to warrant a court in declaring the contract void. In these days, however, no underwriter thinks of contesting a claim that is due even to pure negligence. The irresponsible act of an insane person is no bar to recovery under a fire insurance policy, neither is the intentional destruction of the wife's property by the husband, or the opposite. Claims for loss due to property falling in a stove are not recoverable, although loss due to curtains blowing into a gas jet flame must be paid for. Both are friendly fires, the difference being that in the case of the curtain a new and hostile fire begins at the time of contact. Spontaneous combustion, until it becomes so rapid as to produce a flame or glow, cannot be classed as fire, otherwise many kinds of decomposition, which is in fact combustion, would have to be paid for. Damage due to smoking lamps is likewise not recoverable, else thousands of homes would have to be redecorated at the expense of the companies.

Damage to steam boilers, due to lack of water in the boiler, is not covered, although in the case of a fire being kindled under a dry boiler by a stranger a judgment was rendered in favor of the insured. A Wisconsin case furnishes the only departure from the harmony of opinion, and it declared that violent and unusual heat in a furnace loses its friendly nature and judgment was awarded against the insurer.

Proximate cause is sufficient. A flywheel explosion due to a short circuit caused in a remote part of the building by fire attacking a cable of insulated wires was held a loss by fire under the Massachusetts standard policy. Damage done by firemen under the mistaken impression that a fire exists is not covered. The preponderance of court opinion is that explosions occurring during a fire are incidents of the fire and their damage is covered.

The concussion of air which destroys adjacent property upon an explosion is held to be an intervening cause such as will defeat recovery. Damage from explosion due to lightning striking a powder magazine has been held to be not covered, while payment of damage to adjoining property done by the falling wall of a ruin blown over by a high wind seven days after the fire was enforced upon the company. Where a city ordinance prevents the repair of a building damaged more than a certain percentage the insurer is liable for the value of the property less any salvage. The insurer is also liable for extra expense required by city ordinance in the making of repairs to a partially burned building.

FIRE LOSSES IN UNITED STATES, 1875-1916 (from The Insurance Year Book)—

Year	Aggregate Fire Loss	Aggregate Insurance Loss
1875.............	$78,102,285	$39,327,400

1876.............	64,630,600	34,374,500
1877.............	68,265,800	37,398,900
1878.............	64,315,900	36,575,900
1879.............	77,703,700	44,464,700
1880.............	74,643,400	42,525,000
1881.............	81,280,900	44,641,900
1882.............	84,505,024	48,875,131
1883.............	100,149,228	54,808,664
1884.............	110,008,611	60,679,818
1885.............	102,818,796	57,430,709
1886.............	104,924,750	60,506,564
1887.............	120,283,055	69,659,508
1888.............	110,885,665	63,965,724
1889.............	123,046,833	73,679,465
1890.............	108,993,792	65,015,465
1891.............	143,764,967	90,576,918
1892.............	151,516,098	93,511,936
1893.............	167,544,370	105,994,577
1894.............	140,006,484	89,574,699
1895.............	142,110,233	84,688,030
1896.............	118,737,420	73,903,800
1897.............	116,354,575	66,722,145
1898.............	130,593,905	73,796,080
1899.............	153,597,830	92,683,715
1900.............	160,929,805	95,403,650
1901.............	165,817,810	100,798,645
1902.............	161,488,355	94,775,045
		(Estimated by publishers of The Insurance Year Book)
1903.............	145,302,155	104,000,000
(From Nat'l. Board Tables)		
1904.............	229,198,050	144,000,000
1905.............	165,221,650	116,000,000
1906.............	518,611,800	292,000,000
1907.............	215,084,709	127,000,000
1908.............	217,885,850	157,000,000
1909.............	188,705,150	143,000,000
1910.............	214,003,300	175,000,000

(Continued on page 174)

Per Capita Fire Loss Figures Analyzed. Strictly Preventable (Black), Partly Preventable (Shaded), and Unknown (White).

States	Per Capita Fire Loss
Rhode Island	$3.71
New Hampshire	2.54
California	2.57
Massachusetts	2.60
Nevada	2.62
Connecticut	2.63
Florida	2.72
Delaware	2.76
New Jersey	3.52
Montana	3.37
Georgia	3.18
Maine	2.97
Texas	2.95
Washington	2.42
New York	2.41
Illinois	2.30
Iowa	2.28
Minnesota	2.26
Oregon	2.24
North Dakota	2.23
Nebraska	2.23
Michigan	2.15
Tennessee	2.06
Maryland	2.02
Wisconsin	1.83
Arizona	1.79
Idaho	1.75
Kansas	1.70
Missouri	1.65
Louisiana	1.62
Pennsylvania	1.58
Indiana	1.55
South Dakota	1.54
Virginia	1.52
Ohio	1.48
Oklahoma	1.48
Arkansas	1.42
Alabama	1.39
Vermont	1.37
Kentucky	1.35
South Carolina	1.34
Mississippi	1.32
West Virginia	1.22
North Carolina	1.13
Dist. of Columbia	1.05
Wyoming	1.04
Colorado	1.03
Utah	.95
New Mexico	.84

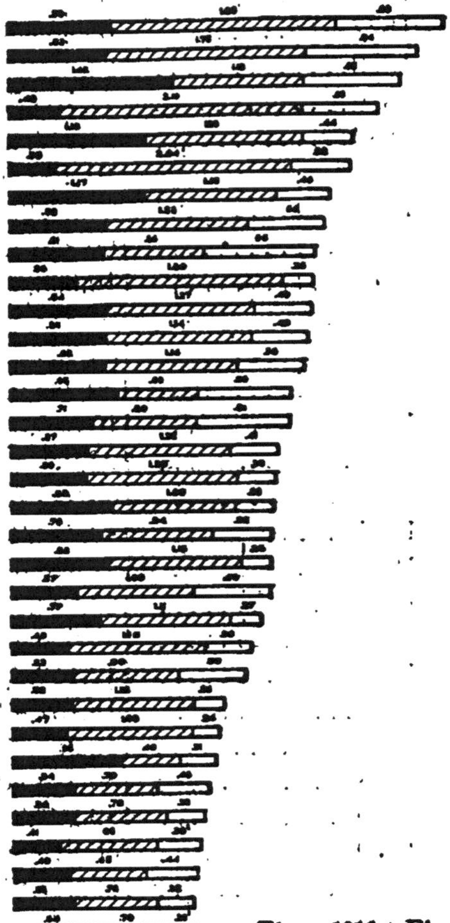

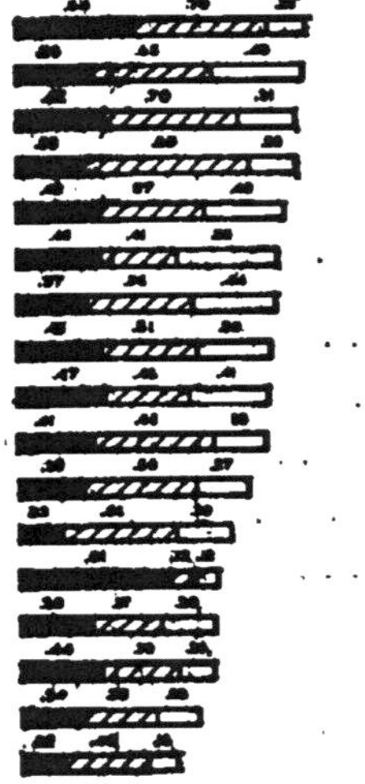

The 1916 Fire Loss figures here shown are in dollars and cents. They represent more than [illegible]% of the total fires in the United States. The figures for several states would be somewhat increased if full statistics were available. — From "Safeguarding America Against Fire," Nat. Board of Fire Underwriters.

United States $2.10

France $0.49

England $0.35

Germany $0.28

Italy & Austria $0.25

Switzerland $0.15

Holland $0.11

How the Fire Losses Compare

(Year of 1916)

1911	217,004,575	190,000,000
1912	206,438,900	194,000,000
1913	203,763,550	196,000,000
1914	221,439,350	210,000,000
1915	172,063,200	167,500,000
1916	214,530,995	195,000,000
1917	250,753,640	230,000,000

Fire Loss Per Capita in United States

1915	$1.71
1916	2.10

FIRE LOSSES IN VARIOUS COUNTRIES

Fire Losses Per Capita Year 1911

United States	$2.62
England	.53
France	.81
Germany	.21
Ireland	.58
Italy	.31
Russia	1.17

FIRE LOSSES (per capita) 1916—Boston seems to enjoy the unfortunate distinction of topping nearly all the cities of the world in annual fire losses. For 1916 its loss was $3.30 for every man, woman and child in the city. Taking all cities of the country of about 400,000 population and upward, the per capita losses figure as follows: New York City, $1.56; Bronx and Richmond, $1.59; Brooklyn and Queens, $1.52; Washington, $1.06; Chicago, $2.05; Los Angeles, $1.11; New Orleans, $1.13; Baltimore, $1.05; Detroit, $2.24; Minneapolis, $3.84; Kansas City, $2.76; St. Louis, $2.03; Newark, $2.70; Buffalo, $2.27; Cincinnati, $1.51; Cleveland, $1.13; Philadelphia, $1.63; Seattle, $1.96; Milwaukee, $2.41, and Pittsburgh, $2.98.

Of these municipalities, it will be noted, Minneapolis is the only one that exceeds Boston's startling record. Moreover, the average per capita fire loss of 329 cities in the United States is but $2.20, which is $1.10 below that of the Hub.

United States Geological Survey statistics state that:

1. During year 1907 fire caused the death of 1,449 persons and the injury of 5,654.

2. Each year $250,000,000 of tangible values are wasted by fire.

3. Each minute of each day of the year sees $500 in value rising in flame and smoke, leaving an ash-pile as its pyre.

4. Each year the fire loss equals $2.65 per capita of our 95,000,000 population.

5. Each year this needless loss equals a tax of $13.00 per each family of five of our population.

6. Each year shows a record of forty fires to each 10,000 of our population.

FIRES, LARGE, IN UNITED STATES SINCE 1897—From The Insurance Year Book.

Newport News, Va.	$2,000,000	1897
Pittsburgh, Pa.	2,000,000	1897
Pittsburgh, Pa.	2,000,000	1898
San Francisco, Cal.	2,000,000	1898
Victor, Col.	2,000,000	1899
Philadelphia, Pa.	3,000,000	1899
Hoboken, N. J.	5,500,000	1900
Bayonne, N. J.	4,500,000	1900
Jacksonville, Fla.	11,000,000	1901
Waterbury, Conn.	3,000,000	1902
Paterson, N. J.	7,000,000	1902
Cincinnati, Ohio	2,000,000	1903
Baltimore, Md.	50,000,000	1904
Rochester, N. Y.	3,000,000	1904
New Orleans, La.	3,200,000	1905
San Francisco, Cal.	350,000,000	1906
New York, N. Y.	2,500,000	1908
Chelsea, Mass.	12,000,000	1908
Chisholm, Minn., Etc.	5,000,000	1908
Wallace, Idaho, Etc.	4,500,000	1910
Cedar Spur, Mont., Etc.	6,000,000	1910
Minnesota	3,500,000	1910

Albany, N. Y.	5,500,000	1911
Bangor, Me.	3,500,000	1911
Coney Island (Dreamland)	2,500,000	1911
New York	3,000,000	1912
Houston, Texas	4,500,000	1912
Hamilton, Ohio	2,000,000	1913
Hot Springs, Ark.	2,250,000	1913
Salem, Mass.	14,000,000	1914
Newport, Va.	2,000,000	1915
Chicago, Ill.	2,000,000	1915
Brooklyn, N. Y.	2,000,000	1916
Fall River, Mass	2,000,000	1916
Paris, Texas	5,000,000	1916
Augusta, Ga.	5,000,000	1916
Canton, Md.	2,000,000	1916
Marshfield, Ore.	2,100,000	1916
Black Tom Is., Jersey City	11,000,000	1916
Swissvale, Pa.	4,000,000	1917
Pittsburgh, Pa.	2,000,000	1917
Kingsland, N. J.	12,000,000	1917
Atlanta, Ga.	5,000,000	1917
Drumwright, Okla.	2,000,000	1917
Brooklyn, N. Y.	2,000,000	1917
Baltimore, Md.	3,500,000	1917
Pittsburgh, Pa.	2,000,000	1917
Jersey City, N. J.	2,000,000	1918
Kansas City, Mo.	3,000,000	1918
North St. Louis, Mo.	2,500,000	1918
Noxen, Pa.	2,250,000	1918

FIRES IN FRANCE—See Responsibility for Fires.

FIRE IN PERSON'S CLOTHING—Throw the person down and, commencing at the head, wrap a rug, mat or any woolen cover around him and roll him on floor. A woman attempting to extinguish such a fire should be careful that her own clothing does not become ignited, and should hold the covering in front of her, and beginning at the person's head, throw the covering toward his feet. If alone, lie on floor and roll to nearest rug and wrap yourself in. Do not run to an open window, door or to the street, as this will fan the flames.

FIRES AT SEA—One of the most promising of the new methods of fighting fire on shipboard at sea is to fight the fire with fire. By this system the hot gases that come from the boiler flues and ordinarily go up the smokestack are used to smother a fire.

A vessel is equipped with great pipes running from the boiler room to all parts of the ship, and at any time the flue gases can be switched from the smokestack to these pipes. The pipes would pour these flue gases into the hold or the sections of the ship where the fire was raging and smother it.

Flue Gas contains only 9 per cent. of oxygen, and 15 per cent. of oxygen is required to support fire. Consequently if great quantities of flue gas are poured into the burning hold the oxygen there will soon be reduced to a point where combustion cannot continue and the fire must die out. Automatic sprinkler protection is the best known method of extinguishing fires and is particularly applicable to ships. There are numerous small compartments on all ships where a fire can smoulder a long time before discovery. A sprinkler in one of these rooms would insure rapid extinguishment.

FIRE PAILS are the simplest, handiest and best extinguisher for incipient fires. One standard fire pail is required for each 500 square feet of floor area. Pails to be galvanized, painted red with word "Fire," of 10 or 12 quarts' capacity. So that they may be easily accessible, pails are to be placed not less than two feet from the floor to the bottom of pail; nor more than five feet from floor to top of pail. In fire insurance ratings, one fire extinguisher is considered equal to six pails; but one-half of the equipment must be pails. Fire bucket tanks holding six pails are approved. One-half the required number of pails in grease or oil risks to be filled with sand. On piers, or roofs of sheds or buildings, oak casks or tanks of 50 gallons capacity, each having three fire pails, casks staggered 50 feet apart, are accepted. Hasty filling of fire pails while the inspector is waiting in the office for the manager may be detected by finding spilled water on floor under them, swinging pails, or water in agitation. This trick is often resorted to. See Pails and Casks; also see Staggered.

FIREPLACES—Open fireplaces should be provided with screens to keep sparks in and to prevent children's clothing coming in contact with the fire, and to keep sparks from flying into the rooms. Most fires are caused by radiating heat to combustible floors or mantels. A safe fireplace will have a fireproof hearth of an area and thickness to prevent radiated heat igniting the floor, and the mantel should be of incombustible material. Ornamental hearths have been responsible for many fires. They are mostly made of flat tiling or cement laid on the floor boards in a thin layer. Tenants, unaware of the danger, frequently build fires on them with disastrous results.

FIRE PREVENTION OBSERVATIONS of Fire Chief Kenlon of New York on the needs of fire prevention. A few of the great needs are:

"1. **Fire Walls in Factories.** I would have every loft and factory building with more than 5,000 square feet of floor capacity to a floor divided by fire walls. If light is needed, and a wall would shut it out, let the wall in part—say 40 per cent of it—be built of polished wired glass. This material would withstand an intense heat for thirty minutes or more. Doors through the fire wall, built of thoroughly fireproof material, would allow the persons on one side to flee for safety past the fire wall if fire should break out in their portion of the room.

"2. **Fire Escapes in Enclosed Towers.** There is absolutely no doubt that the present form of fire escape is doomed to go as inadequate. The inclosed staircase in a fireproof tower, built outside the building, is the one sensible solution of the problem. Entrance is had in this type of fire escape only through doors reached by balconies and not directly from the building where a fire may be raging. Thus the fire tower is not only fireproof, but is smoke-proof as well.

"3. **Automatic Sprinklers in All Department Stores, Storage Warehouses and Manufacturing Lofts.** The sprinkler has already proved its efficiency, and its installation should be made compulsory.

"4. **A Sane Alteration of the Law Regarding Exits.** At present staircases are required to be the same width whether the building be four or forty stories high. Owners should be compelled to widen the staircase in large buildings toward the bottom, following a carefully graduated scale, so that the people rushing down from above would not jam into people from below above the maximum capacity of the staircase. With the adjustment of staircases to the fire needs should come the 'certificate of occupancy,' under which an owner would be prevented from changing the character of his building after having been inspected and approved—so that an inspection for mere storage purposes should not cover the putting of hundreds of girls to work in factories on upper floors.

"5. **A Rigid Enforcement of the Regulations Requiring the Removal of Rubbish.** A good janitor and an efficient engineer in a factory building are the firemen's best friends. I would like to see an incinerator in the basement of every large building, in which rubbish could be thrown as soon as it reaches the cellar. This would insure its destruction. In the absence of the incinerator, the next best substitute is a receptacle for rubbish of fireproof material which would prevent its accumulation in a condition to serve as fire food.

"6. **The Abolition of Heavy Fireproof Roofs.** The fireproof roof of slate and metal is itself a menace, as it is especially liable to crash through the building, carrying floor after floor with it to the ground. The heavy roof of the Equitable Building is what did the damage and smashed in the floors that killed Fire Chief Walsh. Before that fire I would not have thought to include the making of lighter roofs as a great necessity."

FIREPROOF—The term used to express a building built of fire-resisting material, such as steel or concrete, which of themselves are not combustible and will withstand the ravages of an ordinary fire without rupture or impairment for at least four hours. The term "fireproof" is a popular expression used to denote "fire-resistive." See Unprotected Iron.

FIREPROOF APARTMENT HOUSE (Alwyn Court

Building)—Fire, March 4, 1910. Ordinary glass windows allowed the fire to leap from floor to floor on the outside of building. Wired glass windows in standard sash and frame would have prevented this.

FIREPROOF BUILDINGS (Weekly Underwriter)—"A so-called fireproof building bears about the same relation to its contents that a furnace or stove does to the material put into it to burn. As a rule the fireproof building will prevent the spread of fire to other buildings just as a fire will not spread from one stove to another placed near it; but the contents of a fireproof building will be consumed once the fire is well under way just as thoroughly as the coal and wood in the stove. Further, the heat will be retained in the fireproof building and human beings, if they fail to get out quickly, will be killed. This is particularly true of a building filled with merchandise, and to a very much less extent to an office building. If there is only the ordinary office furniture in an office building, the danger to life is not great; but if there is a large amount of inflammable material, such as partitions, office records, etc., stored in some dark floor, you would not want to be in the upper part of some tall structure where the stairs and elevators are in open shafts and carry the heat chimney-like to the upper floors."

A building constructed entirely of fire and heat-resistive material is fireproof as long as it contains no inflammables. The contents of such a building are more liable to destruction than the same material in a frame building. Underwriters frequently overestimate the amount of salvage to be derived from a stock on the floor of a fireproof building and frequently have an "over-line" when fire comes. See Demolition of Fireproof Building.

FIREPROOF CONSTRUCTION, according to insurance requirements. A building shall be deemed fireproof construction if it conforms to the following requirements: All the walls constructed of brick, stone, concrete or terra cotta; all floors and roofs of brick, terra cotta or reinforced concrete placed between steel or reinforced concrete beams and girders; all the steel entering into the structural parts encased in at least two inches of fireproof material; excepting the wall columns, which must be incased in at least eight inches of masonry on the outside and four inches on the inside; all stairs, elevators, public hallways, corridors or other shafts inclosed in fireproof partitions or enclosures; all doors of fireproof design and labelled; all stairways, landings, hallways and other surfaces of incombustible material; no woodwork or other combustible material used in any partition, furring, ceiling or floor (the latter may be wood if laid on sleepers without air space) and all doors and sash trim and other interior finish of incombustible material; all windows (side walls and in courts), shall be wired glass in labelled sash and frame. Note.—In factories the floors should be inclined and cement covered with scuppers to carry off water. See Wood Finish and Trim.

FIREPROOF ROOFS—See Fire Prevention.

FIREPROOFING CHILDREN'S CLOTHING—Dissolve 25 cents worth of ammonium phosphate in one gallon of cold water for five minutes. If an ounce or two of alum is added to the last water in which the clothing is washed, they will be less inflammable. See Fire in Person's Clothing.

FIREPROOFING COTTON GOODS—Use sodium stannate and ammonia sulphate.

FIREPROOFING OR STAINING WOOD—Lumber is piled on iron cars and run into large steam cylinders, and by means of a vacuum the air is drawn out of the lumber. It is then put into a solution of ammonia and salts for fireproofing except for cheap work when alum is used. For staining, salts and bark extracts are used. After lumber is entirely saturated, it is taken out and placed again on trucks and run into brick and frame hot air kilns at 125 deg. F. See Burnettizing.

FIRE PUMPS—National standard sizes:

Steam Pumps

Diameter of Steam Cylinder.	Diameter of Water Plungers.	Length of Stroke.	Gals. per Minute.	No. of 1⅛" Fire Streams.	Suction.	Discharge.
14 in.	7½	12	500	2	8	6
16 in.	9	12	750	3	10	8
18 in.	10	12	1000	4	12	8
20 in.	12	16	1500	6	14	10

Centrifugal Pumps

Capacity and speed. The four standard sizes for centrifugal pumps will be as follows:

Size of Pump

Gals. per Min.	No. 1⅛" Streams.
500	2
750	3
1000	4
1500	6

	Size of Pump (gals. per minute)			
	500	750	1000	1500
Suction Inlet..........	6 in.	8 in.	8 in.	10 in.
Discharge Outlet	6 in.	8 in.	8 in.	10 in.

A centrifugal pump is usually named 4-inch, 5-in, 6-inch or 7-inch, according to the size of its discharge outlet. This outlet, also the inlet, should be enlarged to the Standard Underwriter outlet, either in the casing pattern or by reducing casting bolted to the pump casing, so as to bring the openings up to the sizes given in the table above.

Rotary Pumps—Standard Sizes for Rotary Fire Pumps.

Nominal Gals. per Min.	Approximate Width of Buckets.	Approximate Distance Between Centers.	Approximate Speed Rev. per Min.	No. of 1⅛" Streams.	Approx. H.P. Required for 100 lbs. Pressure.
500	8 in.	7 in. or 8 in.	275	2	60
750	9 in. or 10 in.	8 in. or 9 in.	275	3	90
1000	10 in.	9 in. or 10 in.	250	4	120
1500	12 in.	10 in. or 12 in.	250	6	180

Suction and Discharge Openings.

The openings in pump casing for suction and discharge must not be less than as given below:

Size of Pump.	500 gal.	750 gal.	1000 gal.	1500 gal.
Suction Inlet	6 in	8 in.	8 in.	10 in.
Discharge Outlet	6 in.	8 in.	8 in.	10 in.

FIRE PUMPS should be in separate fireproof buildings or a section so isolated that a serious fire will not put the pump or source of power out of commission. Fire pumps for standpipes using electric power, should have their source of current supply so protected that fire in building they are designed to protect, will not put them out of commission. Likewise, discharge pipes should be buried underground with post indicator valves to control the risers in the various sections. Lessons learned at Brooklyn Eastern District Terminal fire, November 25, 1912. See City Mains and Reservoirs.

FIRE RECORD—A careful underwriter will not only look up the financial standing of the applicant, but will refer to the fire record book which contains the names of people who have had one or more fires of sufficient importance, which might indicate that they should be under scrutiny. The records are furnished by bureaus which collect this data and furnish it to company subscribers.

FIRE-RESISTIVE—See Fireproof.

FIRE-RESISTIVE CONSTRUCTION is a better name than fireproof construction. It means that buildings and all of the parts of buildings are designed and arranged to retard the action of fire. There is really no such thing as a fireproof building.

FIRE-RESISTIVE SOLUTIONS—Asbestos paint possesses the valuable property of retarding the action of fire. Coating of sodium tungstate also retards the action of fire.

FIRE RISK of a substance depends upon two properties: 1st, upon the amount of inflammable vapor that it will liberate or furnish in a given time; 2nd, upon the temperature at which this vapor will ignite. Dangerous substances possess both these properties; the absence of one vastly increases the safety.

FIRE RISKS—See Bad Fire Risks.

FIRE RUINS—It is not considered good judgment to write lines on a risk which has suffered a fire and the damage not repaired or in process of repair.

FIRE SHUTTERS are built in the same manner as fire doors if metal clad. Iron shutters have "flat bar" or "angle iron" frames.

FIRE-STOPS—Furred walls or partitions may be fire-stopped while the building is being constructed, if the workmen place all the broken brick, loose mortar and other incombustible material (which is usually carted away) at the floor levels of all stories where the furred walls communicate to other floors. An incombustible partition of fire-resistive property between sections, cornices, frame walls, etc. (Not a complete cut-off nor a fire wall), or may describe intermediate walls or buildings between risk and exposing risks. See Furring.

FIRE STREAM—Standard fire stream; by this is meant the delivery of not less than 250 gallons of water per minute through a 1⅛-inch, smooth-bore nozzle, and to secure this volume it requires a pressure of not less than 45 pounds to the square inch at the base of the nozzle, which will give approximately a reach of 63 feet horizontally and about 70 feet vertically. (John R. Freeman.)

FIRE STREAMS—The quality of fire streams depends directly upon the pressure at the nozzle and the form of nozzle used.

By good fire streams are meant streams which carry the calculated distance retaining to a reasonable extent their solidity and without excessive spray. Costly experience has shown that in serious fires a small stream is evaporated as it falls in spray through the flames while if a large stream is thrown, enough may escape the evaporation to pass through the heated gases and reach the burning coals themselves. John R. Freeman, C. E., after exhaustive tests on streams from nozzles set forth the following specifications for a good fire stream, which up to the present have been considered as outlining fairly the requisites of such a stream:

(a) A stream, which at limit named, has not lost continuity of stream by breaking into showers of spray.

(b) A stream, which up to the limit named, appears to shoot nine-tenths of whole volume of water inside of a circle 15 inches in diameter, and three-fourths of it inside of a ten-inch circle.

(c) Which is stiff enough to attain in fair condition the height or distance named, even though a fresh breeze were blowing.

(d) Which a limit named will, with no wind, enter a room through a window opening and barely strike ceiling with force enough to spatter well.

From the above, it may be assumed that with a certain named limit the stream would be good, while at another it may be poor. This is just the case. For instance, a stream which holds its shape for a distance of fifty feet may be completely broken up at seventy-five feet. (Fred. Sheppard, in Fire and Water Engineering.)

FIRE TOWER—A brick or other masonry tower or shaft enclosing a stairway of fireproof material. The walls must extend from ground to at least three feet above the roof. No openings are permitted except fireproof windows over a court or street. The entrance is indirect, i. e., a "lead" such as a balcony outside of main building connects to an open air vestibule entering the stairway enclosure. Stairs must open on a street or a passage to street. Affords a sure exit from building and a vantage point for firemen, as no flame or smoke can enter the tower directly.

FIRE WALL—In strict sense should be a masonry wall of sufficient thickness, height and width to withstand the element of fires confining them to a prescribed (theoretical) area. Not less than 12 inches thick, without openings, extending above roof at least three feet and projecting from side walls of protected buildings. A wall subdividing a building to restrict the spread of fire. It shall have such thickness as to prevent the communication of fire by heat conduction. It shall have such stability as to remain intact after the complete combustion of the contents of the building on one side of the wall; and its structural integrity shall be unaffected by any wreckage of the building resulting from such fire, or its extinguishment. In fire-resistive buildings with full protection floors and roof, a fire wall need not be continuous through all stories, nor need it extend through the roof. In all other buildings it shall start at the foundation, be continuous through all stories, and extend three feet above the roof. (N. F. P. A.) See Fire Prevention Observations.

Fire Wall, An Outside—A solid, blank, masonry wall at least 12 inches thick. It is either part of a building or a separate wall built to protect a building against an exposure. In case of frame buildings, the wall should extend five feet beyond building walls. The fire record shows that many serious losses have been averted by the use of specially built fire walls.

FIRE POINT—Temperature at which oils become permanently ignited. Usually several degrees above the flash point.

FIRE WINDOW—A window (wired glass) installed as per Underwriters' requirements, and constructed of materials which have been tested and approved by the Underwriters' Laboratories. The sash, frame, glazing, automatic closing device are included in test.

FIREWORKS depend upon nitrates to support combustion and not upon chlorates.

FIREWORKS (special) contain red phosphorus, a fulminate, and are explosive.

FIRE ZONES—Localized fire zones are found in nearly every large city. They are localities which seem to attract a certain class of tenants bent on incendiarism. There is a set of people who move from one city or section of a city to another with the avowed purpose of incendiarism. They change their names but not their habits. The class is not confined to any one race or nationality. Too much care cannot be exercised in scrutinizing the records of antecedents of applicants whose term of residence in any particular section or city is very short.

FIRELESS COOKERS—Report of a fire—Fire was probably caused by spontaneous combustion. This was very likely due to the sides of the receptacle sweating and dampening the sawdust, or to the disc in being dropped into the bottom, broke the solder and allowed grease or water to get through into the sawdust. Only vacuum cookers should be used or the manufacturer should do away with all solder joints in the tin and otherwise safeguard the device against fire. (N. F. P. A., Vol. 4, 1911.) Mineral wool is a good packing.

FIREMEN'S SEARCH-LIGHT (acetylene torch)—A

portable acetylene torch consisting of a generator (water to carbide type), using calcium phosphate as an ignition agent, and a burner. Designed for use when a strong, not easily extinguished, portable flame is desired; such as, around fires and in smoky rooms. Its hazards are in a class with those of commoner forms of open flame kerosene torches.

FISH PLATES—Splices of inch-board, three feet in length, nailed like splints for a broken limb, on both sides of a splice.

FISH STORES—In frying fish lots of grease is used. Ranges become very greasy. The entire top should be enclosed in metal hood, ventilated to proper flue.

FISHING TACKLE—Manufacturing hazards are metal and woodworking. Use celluloid cement and amyl acetate when binding rods.

FIVE AND TEN CENT STORES—Stock consists of almost anything from a pin to a white elephant. Very susceptible, hard to adjust losses, seldom insured by knowing underwriters. See Variety Stores.

FLAMES (Candle Structure)—The flame of a candle is a curious thing as it teaches one of the best lessons possible to the student of fire protection. Every lighted candle is a gas factory. If you will look carefully at the flame when the air is still, you will see that it is hollow, like a shell, and the space inside of this shell is filled with dark gas not yet afire. There are three principal regions to a candle flame, the interior region is dark and consists of coal gas, the next region is where oxygen is being united with the gas (the luminous part), while the last is the oxydizing region, the hottest part of the flames. The flames seen in burning buildings have the same structure. See How Water Puts Out Fire. See Conflagration Blast.

FLANNELETTE is generally used for nightgowns on account of its long loose nap. If it becomes ignited, it is almost certain the wearer's life is doomed as it flashes up immediately. It should be treated with a lasting chemical fireproofing process. See Fireproofing Children's Clothing.

FLANGE—A projecting ledge or rim.

FLAP-CHECK VALVE—A valve with a flap hinged at

upper side, allowing the passage of liquids in one direction only. See Ball-check Valve.

FLASH POINT of a substance is the temperature at which it gives off inflammable vapor. The lower the flash point, the more dangerous. See Burning Point.

FLASHER—A device for throwing circuits in and out to the lights for intermittent electric signs.

FLASHING—Broad sheet of metal with one edge inserted into the joints of brickwork and projecting out several inches and fastened down close to the roof to prevent leaks.

FLASH-LIGHT POWDERS—Aluminum and magnesium powders mixed with chlorate of potash and other carriers of oxygen for intensification ignite readily and are highly explosive; should be kept in cool, dry places.

FLASKS—Boxes which contain the mould into which melted iron is poured for casting. Used in foundries.

FLAT ARCH—In floor construction, an arch with flat upper and lower surfaces. Generally not as strong as segmental arches. See Floor Arches.

FLAT ROOF—A roof which has a pitch not exceeding 20 degrees.

FLAVORING EXTRACT MANUFACTURING—Use steam and gas percolators, mills, mixers, alcohol, fruit juices, essential oils. Care of packing material, method of heating kettles and grinding are main hazards. Not considered a desirable class.

FLAX—A fibre yielded by a certain plant. See Fibres.

FLAX STRAW—Formerly a waste by-product of the flax industry of the Southwest, is now utilized in paper making.

FLESHING—Consists of removing, by machinery or hand, the fatty tissues clinging to the flesh side of skins or hides.

FLOATERS—A policy that covers goods wherever located without specifying any designated locations, except that it excludes goods in the main plant or factory. Not all companies care for floating insurance.

FLOATING FOUNDATION—Is an entire flat bed of concrete and steel reinforced. Used only when a solid foundation cannot be reached.

FLOCK—The refuse fibre from rag-grinding machines.

The Flock which is used for covering wall paper is ground felt. The dust made in grinding flock is heavier than air and said to be non-explosive. Flock dust thrown into the air spreads rapidly, but quickly falls to the floor.

FLOOR ARCHES—Columbian System consists of a combination of rolled steel bars and concrete. The bars are of cross-shaped section and are hung to the floor beams by steel stirrups cut to the exact shape of the bar used. The bars and stirrups are then surrounded by cement concrete. Two forms of this system are in use, the "panelled," in which there is only one plate (the floor), and the "flat ceiling," in which plates are employed for floor and ceiling. Beams are protected by a concrete slab, made at the building and held on the beam flange by malleable iron clips moulded in the blocks and held in place by longitudinal wires. These blocks are placed on the beams first and concrete filled in to make the plate and haunches at the same time. The concrete used is generally 1 part cement, 2½ parts sand, and 5 parts broken stone.

Columbian Beam Plate is made of concrete moulded generally at the building. There are two ties running through the block lengthwise and two malleable iron clips set right in the block. Then, when block is laid, the concrete is run right in on the top. It is a straight concrete arch. Columbian Iron Bars are made either single, cross or double-cross in section and about 5 inches deep. These run from beam to beam, hung in stirrups. The malleable iron clips are protected by the concrete. There is a ¾-inch air space below the beam between the concrete protection. The ceiling consists of a concrete floor plate as in the previous form with the addition of lighter bars, resting on the lower flanges of the beams on which bars the concrete ceiling slab is cast. An air space is left between the two plates (floor and ceiling), but the exposed webs are either left exposed or are encased in concrete.

Expanded Metal Company's System Flange Type, when used for wide spans (from 8 feet to 15 feet), has arched channels about 4 feet apart, sprung from girder to girder to reinforce and stiffen the floor plate. Concrete ribs are then built up on these channels to the level of the tops of the girders, and sheets of expanded metal are laid flat on the tops of the beams and the concrete ribs to receive the concrete floor plate.

Another form designed to give a level ceiling for plastering is constructed by laying sheets of expanded metal on the lower flanges of the I-beams. A 3-inch concrete plate is then placed and tamped and a lighter cinder concrete is filled up to the tops of the beams.

The concrete used is generally made of 1 part cement, 2 parts sand and 5 to 6 parts furnace cinders, the mixture varying somewhat with the character of the sand and cinders.

Fawcett System consists of hard-burned terra-cotta lintels running from beam to beam and filled on top with a cinder concrete. For convenience in setting, the ends of these lintels are cut diagonally and they are laid at such an angle to the beams that the shorter diagonal is at right angles to them. These lintels bear on and fit around the lower flanges of the beams so as to leave an air space of about ¾-inch under their entire length. This space connects with the interior of each lintel, and theoretically there is a connected air space under all beams and through all lintels. Air flues or thimbles may be built into the exterior walls, thus connecting these spaces with the outside air.

In erection, the lintels are set without mortar. No reliance is placed on them for ultimate strength as they are employed only as centers to receive the load-bearing concrete. For the supporting metal work, small I-beams are used, usually 4 inches to 7 inches, spaced from 2 feet to 2 feet 6 inches on centers.

Guastavino System consists of arches of hard-burned tiles laid in three courses and is used more generally in public or semi-public buildings. These tiles are 1 inch by 6 inches by 12 inches, and are laid in neat Portland cement, breaking joints.

The arches are designed especially for each building and may be either dome or barrel-shaped. The dome arches have been used for rooms as large as 70 feet square and may be laid with a decorative tile requiring no finish. The essential point of this system is, that the best cement must be used. The concrete is simply a filling. There are no steel supporting members in the arch.

Hennebique System—The armature of the beams is formed by steel bars placed at the lower flanges, and by vertically placed stirrups which embrace the bent steel tension bars. The columns have the steel rods near the corners and tied together at close intervals with hoop steel ties or collars.

Herculean System reinforced floor arch is composed of terra-cotta blocks held in place between each row of tile with "T" irons.

Kahn System—Made by Trussed Concrete Steel Co. Use a truss bar. The cross-section shows two horizontal flanges or wings, projecting at opposite sides. These flanges are sheared up at intervals to form rigidly connected diagonals, making a unit of main bar and shear members. Resembles a straight bar with iron bars sticking upward at about 45 degrees.

Lee Hollow-Tile and Cable-Rod Floor System—Combines terra-cotta blocks with suspension cables for use in long spans in place of other reinforcement.

Mackolite Floor System consists of moulded blocks made of plaster of paris, mixed with water and chemicals. The mixture is moulded in forms, left a short time to set, and kiln-dried for about four days. These blocks are made up to a maximum length of 5 ft. Flange protection tiles are held under the beam flanges by dove-tailed projections from the main blocks. Cinder concrete with nailing strips and finished floor is employed as usual and the ceiling may be plaster directly on the blocks. The floor differs materially from most of the construction in general use in that the material is designed to act as a beam or lintel instead of an arch. No centering is required for erection, and as there is no end thrust, no tie-rods are needed.

Melan Arch System depends mainly for its strength on the use of steel ribs (usually T's or light I-beams), or by latticed iron rods bent to the shape of the arch, and sprung from the lower flanges of the I-beams. A curved "center" is applied close to the underside of the ribs and then, starting at one beam, coarse concrete is filled in and rammed toward the haunches for a depth equal to about two-thirds of the depth of the curved beam. The remaining one-third is filled with a finer mixture of cement and sand. Each side is built and rammed separately, and the key is then filled in and rammed vertically. This system has been used on spans of from 12 to 16 feet with the curved rib spaced 3 to 5 feet, according to strength required. The rise of the arch is from one-tenth to one-twelfth of a span. Tie-rods are used to take up the thrust. The use of this system may be criticised as the concrete is used as a beam and an arch at the same time. The closer the ribs are spaced, the less objectionable does this feature become.

Metropolitan System consists of a composition plate with wire suspension cables instead of metal bars for the metal members. These cables are anchored to the walls and laid across the tops of the beams and spaced from seven-eighths to one and one-half inches on centers according to the spans and loads, and are laid parallel. Lengths of seven-eighth round iron rods are laid on the cables below the top of the beam, so as to deflect the cables uniformly three inches below the tops of the beams in a six-foot span. Centers are then placed between the beams and one inch below the iron rods. A composition formed of about one part plaster of paris by bulk to two parts of spruce or hemlock planer shavings, with sufficient water to mix thoroughly, is then poured into place and tamped, and brought to a level one-half inch above the tops of the beams. This forms a floor plate four inches thick ready for filling, screeds and wooden floor. The portions of the beams below the ceiling line are protected by a two-inch thickness of a composition poured at the same time the plate is made, into forms left in the centers. The flanges of the beams are wrapped with wire netting before the composition is poured.

Sawdust is used in the composition of the Metropolitan floor. They use plaster of paris and one or two-inch long planer shavings. This construction is used somewhat in apartment houses. They put heavy plank floors on top and anything of weight is screwed through the plaster to the floor. In the Metropolitan floor the under side of beams or girders is protected by making a mould between the "center" and pouring right around the beam. The stuff is mixed up in such a liquid form that it can be poured right on. This type has been tested and accepted by some city building departments.

Ransome System—Use square steel rods, twisted cold, for reinforced concrete construction.

Rapp System uses rolled sheet iron T's laid on the bottom flanges of the beams spaced 8½ inches on centers, held in position by spacing-ties. Bricks are then laid between the T's and grouted, and the space up to the beam top filled with cinder concrete made about one to eight. The lower flanges are wrapped with wire lath and plastered when the ceiling is finished.

Roebling System uses a steel-ribbed wire cloth centering and a cinder concrete arch or plate. This centering is permanent and is sprung into place between the lower flanges of the beams, and the adjoining sheets are lapped or laced. Cinder concrete is then filled in up to the top of the beam giving a thickness of not less than three inches at the crown. A wire lath ceiling may be suspended under the arch of the beam flanges, or the beam flanges may be protected by wire lath filled with concrete. The latter is much better. If no suspended ceiling is used, the lower flanges of the beams are protected by only the plaster on wire mesh about one inch thick.

"Trussit" System—For light concrete roofs, curtain walls and solid partitions. Trussit is corrugated, expanded steel, reinforcing sheets, made in form of continuous "V's," erected without forms or centering. Made by General Fireproofing Co.

FLOOR AREA—See Area.

FLOOR LIGHTS—Heavy glass in wood or iron frames inserted into the flooring to give light below. In non-fireproof buildings if the glass is at least ¾-inch thick in iron frames, no charge is made in some of the local rating schedules.

FLOOR OILS—See Mops.

FLOOR OPENINGS should be protected in a standard manner. See Illustration.

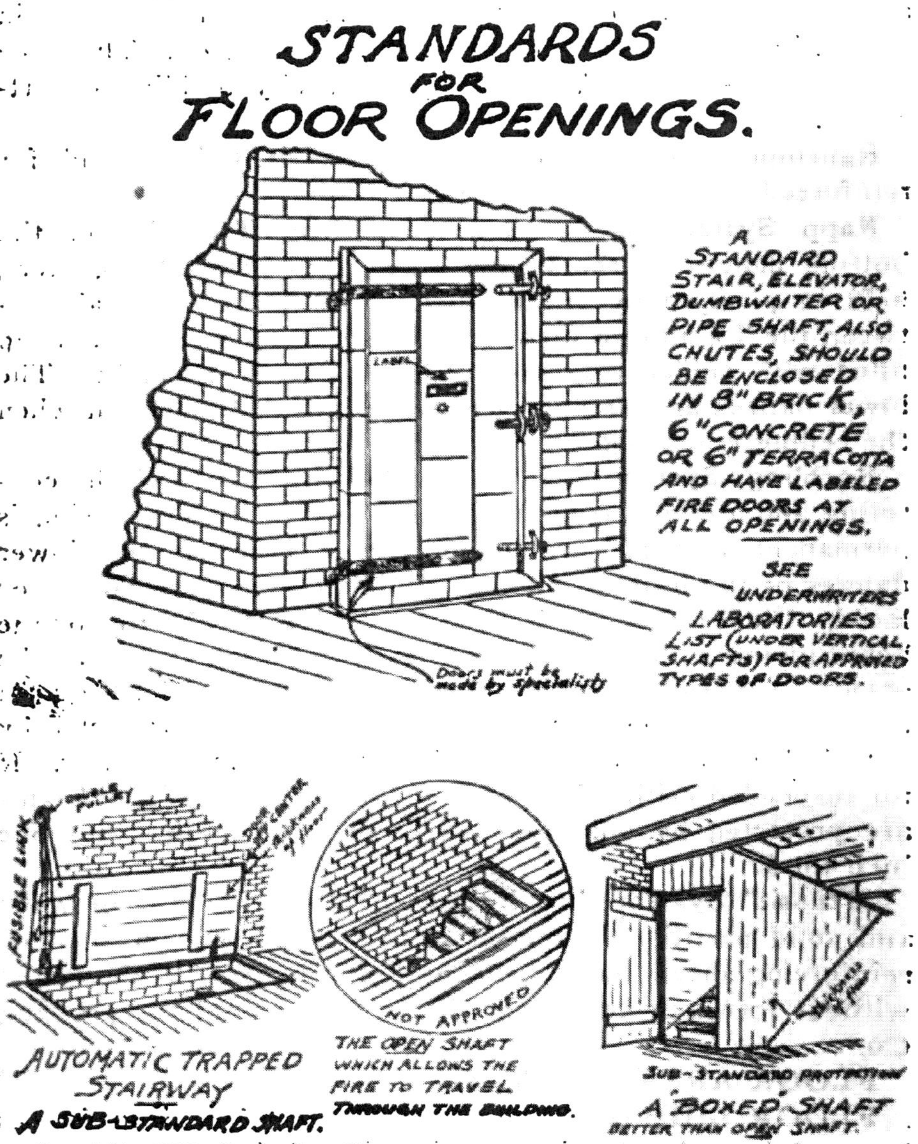

FLOORING, COMPOSITION—Used in place of linoleum or cement-finished floors in office buildings. The compositions vary, but the ingredients are asbestos pulp, wood flour (pulverized poplar), paraffine oil, cement, silax, manganese, chloride of magnesium, graphite, talcum, marble dust, iron oxide, chrome and earth colors, aniline colors, magnesite, lamp-black. The majority of the compositions contain 25 to 40 per cent. asbestos. The hazards are mixing, blending and cooking the various ingredients. Steam kettles usually employed. Some (burr stone) grinders for powders, pressing in hydraulic presses. Usually air dried. The dressing, applied after the flooring is laid, consists of linseed oil, oxide and aniline colors and turpentine. To clean the surface of coloring matter foreign to the composition and also for a dressing or polish a mixture of linseed oil, resin, acetone, alcohol, nitric acid is used, then waxed with paraffine. Asphaltum is or may be added for waterproofing. Direct heat for wax is objectionable.

FLOORS—See Waterproof Floors.

FLORISTS—The fire record of this class is good. Few companies write stock of live plants as a very little heat will ruin the entire stock. Owners, therefore, cannot afford to have a fire. Storage of large quantities of moss and painting of frames are principal hazards.

Florists occupying small buildings, at times decorate the entire interior and front of building with white birch bark or similar fast burning material, adding to the hazard of spreading fire. See Hot Houses.

FLOUR is one of the best extinguishers for a fire caused by the spilling of and ignition of kerosene. Flour in bags, if wet, will cake, spoil and constitute a heavy loss. In barrels, considered good insurance.

FLOUR MILLS—After the grain has been thoroughly cleaned it goes to the roller mills to be ground, the stock being separated by sifting machines. After each grinding, the coarse stock goes back to the "breaks," and the fine passes to the purifiers and between smooth rollers, and then to the flour bins. In short, flour making is a process of separation, the desirable parts being slowly subtracted until only the waste or by-product is left. The hazard consists of dusty bearings and dust-laden atmosphere. This class is not very attractive as a fire risk.

FLOWERS AND FEATHERS—Artificial flowers and

feathers. Busiest season, September and October, January and February. **Leaves:** Mainly of muslin, sized with gum arabic, glycerine and paraffine, varnished and shellaced. Cut out of large sheets of cloth previously painted and dried. **Veins** are made in die presses either cold or gas heated. Painted with air brush, coated with paraffine (waxing), sprinkled with tinsel (ground glass and mica), for frosting and dew. **Tubing:** Hollow muslin for stems. The muslin is treated in a bath of warmed linseed oil, cut into strips and drawn through a "tubing machine." This resembles a metal box on an iron table, two rows of holes in the sides through which the strips are drawn, and heated by gas. Gas connection should be iron piping.

"**Flock**" tubing is ordinary tubing covered with hair or wool flock. "**Ciroleum**" tubing is made of a mixture of glycerine and gelatine to which is added small seeds. When made up, resembles rubber. Steel wires are covered with the mixture, allowed to cool and wires withdrawn, leaving a hollow tube.

Flowers are made of silk, brocaded cloth, velvet, etc., cut by hand or power die presses, colored with anilines by hand or air brush. "**Goffering**": Goffer irons are small gas-heated tools, with ball-end and wooden handle. Used to round out petals. "**Gripping**," or pinching and crimping, are very similar, all gas-heated. Some flowers are of paper, worked cold, dipped in wax. The heating of the wax kettle important. **Metal flowers**, stamped out of sheet tin, painted and soldered to wire frames. Painted in dip tank.

"**Peps**" are small berries, pollen stems or flower centers. Made in automatic machine of a heavy thread, stiffened with sizing of gum arabic and starch, dipped in paste paint and dried in gas-heated machine. Cherries and fruits made of cotton, moulded in treadle machines, dried, painted and varnished.

Preserving and Fireproofing of Natural and Artificial Foliage—Mixture contains sulphate of ammonia, silicate of soda, rock salt, sugar, glucose, and chlorine. Mixed in wooden tanks in which the foliage is immersed. Delicate plants first dipped in gelatine and paraffine bath. This process does not fireproof, but renders the foliage slow burning at ordinary temperature. Plants are bleached with diluted sulphuric, hydrofluoric and acetic acids.

Feathers used in millinery are mainly ostrich, chicken feathers being used for quills and wings. **Raw ostrich feathers** are kept in bins according to quality. They are sorted, washed, whipped by hand to open up the flues, dyed and dried. "**Branching**" is the term applied in making up feathers in bunches or branches. Rubber cement is used from open cups. Tips are colored by hand or air brush with aniline colors, and dried in gas-heated ovens.

Ramie—Used in making artificial plumes. It is sewed on knitting frame, steamed, curled, tinted with aniline colors by air brush. **All flower stocks are very susceptible to fire, smoke or water.** In making leaves the handling of acetone, amyl acetate, turpentine, alcohol, benzine, liquid bronze, dry boxes, celluloid for leaves, gas-heated machines, waxing, and dyeing are the main hazards.—(Live Articles on Special Hazards. (W. O. Lincoln, "Live Articles on Special Hazards"—The Weekly Underwriter)

FLOWING PRESSURE—See Static Pressure.

FLUE—The enclosure by means of which heated air or gases are conducted to the outer air, as a smoke flue from a smoke pipe.

FLUE DUST may be very inflammable if metallic zinc dust is present.

FLUE FIRES—Four or five pounds of common salt poured down the chimney will probably put out the blaze. The carbonic acid gas so generated is a fire extinguishing agent.

FLUORIC ACID—A corrosive acid used by glass etchers.

FLUORIDES—Compounds of fluorine with metals (calcium fluoride).

FLUXES—Various substances used to prevent the instantaneous formation of rust when welding two pieces of hot metal together.

"**FLY**"—The linty dust produced at textile (woolen, cotton, etc.) working machines. It is one of the main features to be watched by the inspector when inspecting a knitting mill. It is always present in the card room, more especially where all cotton or cotton waste is used. See Knitting Mills. See Dust.

FLY WHEEL—A heavy revolving wheel used for equalizing the motion of machinery.

FLY WHEEL PITS are the cause of many fires. In one instance a steam syphon was located in the pit and the engineer entered the pit with an open torch and an explosion and fire resulted. The real cause of the fire was the oil and grease which had been allowed to accumulate in the wheel pit. The oil and grease had become volatilized by the heat from the steam syphon so that when an open flame was introduced, a fire immediately occurred. These wheel pits should be kept clean of oil and litter.

FOAMING—An undue amount of boiling, caused by grease or dust in the boiler.

FOLDING BOX MANUFACTURING RISKS are better than solid box makers because less gluing is done, fewer machines used and goods are packed flat instead of in solid form. Flat packed stock offers more salvage and presents a less crowded condition. See Paper Box Factories.

FOOT-POUND—This term can be easily understood as follows: If you lift a weight of one pound to a height of one foot you have done a foot-pound of work. If you lift it two feet you have done two foot-pounds, and if you lift three pounds six feet you have done eighteen foot-pounds of work. In other words, the product of the weight and the height give the foot-pounds. Or force times distance will also give the foot-pound measurement. If you exert a pressure of 10 pounds through a distance of ten feet you will have exerted 100 foot-pounds. Watt discovered that a dray horse when not tired could do 33,000 foot-pounds in one minute and this unit is called a horse-power. Thus if an engine hoists a weight of 330 pounds through a distance of 100 feet in one minute, it is exerting one horse-power. See Horse-Power.

FOOT-VALVE—The check in the lower end of a pump section pipe preventing the backward flow of water once raised in the suction. See Strainer.

FOREIGNERS, who are natives of countries where long

names predominate, frequently abbreviate or entirely change their name to one of American pronunciation, usually for no ulterior purpose, but proper name should be ascertained, if possible. See Names.

FOREST FIRES—In New York state, the Bureau of Foresty has inaugurated a system of telephone communication from about fifty stations on high peaks from whence the fire rangers can call for help if fires are discovered, supplanting the old method of having the ranger ride to the nearest settlement for help, thereby giving the fire a chance to spread. The Bureau reports state, that causes of fire in order of their importance are: Railroad locomotives, lightning, careless campers, fishermen and hunters, settlers clearing land. There are three kinds of forest fires—the "surface fire," which merely runs in the leaves and ground litter; the "ground fire," that covers the underbrush of dense forests, and the "crown fire," the most dangerous and terrifying of all. A "crown fire" is usually caused when the ground or surface fire reaches the top of a ridge or knoll and the increased draft carries the blaze up the trunks of the trees to the tops of the "crowns." It is the crown fires which have made the great forest fires of history. Surrounding the burning area by a trench from which everything down to the mineral soil has been removed, is the only kind of a fire line which will stop a ground fire, and it will often stop a surface fire. For surface fire "whipping" or using brush branches or water soaked sacking to whip the burning leaves at the edge of the fire back into the burning area is most effective. Sand as well as water is valuable in fighting this kind of fire, too. There is only one way to fight a crown fire. That is by back firing—fighting fire with fire. This method is extremely dangerous, consisting of setting a counter fire far enough from the main body of the original fire so that all inflammable material will be burned by the time the fire reaches that point and the fire will die from lack of material to feed on. The backfire is set far enough from the main fire to escape the draft which is fanning the blaze.

FORGE HAMMER—A heavy hammer for forging large pieces, and worked by machinery. See Anvil Manufacturing.

FORMALDEHYDE—Used by embalmers and also as a preservator and fumigator.

FORMATES—Formic acid compounds.

FORMIC ACID—A colorless liquid of pungent odor.

FORMS—From the brokers' or companies' standpoint, see "Live Articles on Special Hazards."

FORSITE—An explosive material. A foreign make of nitroglycerine. Considered more dangerous than dynamite.

FOURDRINIER MACHINE—A paper-making machine in which the pulp is screened and made into sheets.

FOUNDATIONS—The bases of walls, piers, columns, etc., directly supported or kept in equilibrium by the earth.

FOUNDATIONS FOR SKYSCRAPERS are sometimes laid as follows: Heavy, hollow steel piles are driven through quicksand and to rock. They are then cleaned out with compressed air and then two-inch steel rods inserted to act as reinforcement for the concrete which will eventually be poured in. This system of foundation work is used because it is much quicker than the former method of sinking an open pit to rock.

FOUNDATION WORK—(Robert H. Pearson.) Foundation work calls for the best engineering skill, and the design and construction involved requires much study, as each problem demands a special solution. The best condition from an economical point of view is to have the level rock just below the cellar floor of a building; if the rock is higher the expense of excavating is large and if lower the footings must be carried to bed rock. Ordinary ground will maintain safely a load of 2 to 4 tons per square foot, dry clay from 4 to 6 tons per square foot, and gravel from 6 to 10 tons per square foot. Having these figures in mind, the necessity for footing buildings on good bed rock will readily be seen, if we consider the fact that one of the N. Y. skyscrapers weighs approximately 120,000 tons, with a wind pressure on building surface computed at 40,000,000 pounds. The cellar flooring of high buildings usually runs from 30 to 45 feet below the street, and if rock is not encountered at that depth, it becomes necessary to foot the foundations on concrete piers sunk to meet the bed rock, and if the rock is below the water level, or at a considerable depth below cellar excavation, the only known way to reach it is by means of the **pneumatic caissons.** These caissons are simply air-tight bottomless boxes, rectangular or cylindrical in cross section, and equipped with a steel reinforcement on bottom which is known as the cutting edge, the interior being large enough to accommodate a gang of men whose duties are to excavate the space within the area which it covers.

Prior to putting the caisson in place, a pit sufficiently large to allow for its entry is dug in the ground on the site which the finished pier or monolith will occupy, a derrick is installed and the caisson seated accurately in place to a depth usually 6 feet below the main excavation. When in place the caisson is provided with a strong decking which allows a height of about 6 feet for workmen within the chamber. On top of the caisson decking vertical sections of air shafts are set up, these sections being usually circular in form, three feet in diameter, made of steel plate, each section measuring about 10 feet in length, and forming a means of passage to the working chamber for men and material.

The air lock is placed at top of shaft and usually consists of a steel cylinder about 5 feet in diameter, 7 feet high and bolted in position.

There are two doors in this chamber, one at the top and one near the bottom; an attendant is stationed on a platform near the upper door, whose duty it is to regulate the air pressure, attend to signals from working chamber and open and shut the air-lock doors as required.

When the outer door is opened, the inner door is closed and vice-versa, thus retaining the pressure in the caisson. Signal is made by whistle operated by compressed air within the chamber, a valve and the necessary piping being provided for this purpose.

A ladder is installed within the shaft and workmen travel to and from the working chamber by this means.

Excavated matter from working chamber is loaded in small canvas bags and carried by workmen to air lock, or it is blown out by the compressed air through special pipe, but these methods have been improved on recently and it is now possible to use half a cubic yard bucket without interfering with the caisson efficiency.

When the caisson and its appurtenances are put in place, concrete is poured around the air shaft so as to form slabs about 12 inches thick, this having sufficient strength to support a mass of wet concrete on caisson walls; sections of airshaft are added and concrete is filled within the forms in 5 foot courses until the pier is built up to about one-half its full height. As the top of the piers are to be sunk below the temporary surface of excavation they are enclosed within coffer-dams placed 3 or 4 feet beyond, these coffer-dams serving to exclude the earth from the column piers until such time as the open excavation is completed.

Forms are set up within the working chamber and concrete is built up to the desired height, after which it is sunk through the water-bearing ground, compressed air being used as the sinking progresses below water level, when another section of concrete is added, and so on until the anchorage point has been reached.

Owing to frictional resistance it is necessary to use cast iron blocks to weight the caisson for the purpose of sinking and this, in addition to the weight of the caisson, forces the work downward until the footing is reached, when the surface of the rock is cleaned and leveled, after which the whole interior of the caisson and shaft connecting the working chamber with the atmosphere is filled with concrete well rammed into place, thus forming a monolith upon which to support the superstructure.

FOUNDRIES—Usually large area frame buildings. Hazards of pattern and flask making; preparation of the mould, including core making, melting and reduction of the metal to a proper fluidity, pouring the molten metal into the mould, and cleaning and finishing the casting, also core ovens and painting iron or wood patterns. When casting, a man should be stationed on the roof to detect flying sparks alighting on the roof or on nearby structures. Casks of water with fire pails should be placed every fifty feet on the roof. There should be 12 inches clearance around floors or roof where stack from melting furnaces passes through. See Core Ovens and Cupolas.

FOUNDRY FIRES—Carbon dioxide is a very good extinguisher, providing the seat of the fire can be enclosed. Water thrown on the glowing metal will form oxy-hydrogen gas and should therefore not be used.

FOUNDRY FLASKS—Frames of wood or iron, four sided, no top or bottom. Used to hold the sand moulds in position. Wooden ones frequently become charred from molten metal. Fires arise from storing flasks inside of buildings or against wood partitions where hidden sparks break out into fire.

FOUNDRY SAND—"Water-proof" sand used by founders when casting in sand moulds is composed of ground resin, flour and secret white powder. Prevents the molten lead from adhering to mould. Process is grinding, mixing, heating resin by direct heat. Non-hazardous.

FRAME—A term used when pieces of timber are put together so as to form a truss or other structure.

FRAME CONSTRUCTION—See Balloon and Braced Frame.

FRAME ROWS—Many of these rows have open spaces called cock-lofts, roof spaces or small attics, which are open from one building to another. This space is between the top floor ceiling and the roof. It may be from 6 inches to 5 or 6 feet in height. Besides containing considerable dust, shavings left at the time the building was built, they are sometimes used for storing old mattresses and junk of all kinds. Fires once started, entering these concealed spaces, are hard to locate and put out. The tendency of a fire to go through spaces is greatly increased by the pressure of the air and hot gases produced by combustion. Hot gases always rise, therefore the danger is greater directly under the roof. Partitions of incombustible material to under part of roofboards should be placed on each side of the studs between buildings at roof spaces. See Attics; also Roof Spaces, Cock-Loft, and Brick-filling.

FRAMING AND TIMBER WORK—See Braced Frame and Balloon Frame.

FREEZING WEATHER—See Fire Appliances; also Fuel.

FRENCH POLISH is a polish formed by dissolving shellac in spirits of wine.

FRETWORK MANUFACTURING—See Cabinet Makers.

FRICTION (revolving) is the friction of journals and bearings of every description. **Roller friction** is the resistance offered by the circumference of the wheel of a vehicle to the propelling power. **Sliding friction** is the friction of two flat surfaces as in a planing machine. Friction is worse in suction pipes than in discharge.

Friction Wheels—Wheels so placed that the journals of the shaft may rest upon their rims and thus be enabled to revolve with diminished friction.

FRICTION LOSS in fire hose. From experiments of J. R. Freeman. In pounds per hundred feet, with various amounts flowing. Nominal diameter 2½ inches; actual approaches 2⅝ inches.

	Gallons Flowing					
	100	150	200	250	300	350
Unlined linen	5	12	21	33	46	62
Rubber-lined, fair	4	10	18	29	40	54
Rubber-lined, good ..	2	5	9	14	20	27

3-inch hose about 40 per cent. of the above.

FRICTION LOSS in water pipes is determined by loss in pounds pressure per square inch for each 100 feet of length on different size clean iron pipe discharging given quantities of water per minute.

FRICTIONAL ELECTRICITY—See Static Electricity.

FRIENDLY FIRE—One that does not leave its seat of origin, as, for instance, a smoking oil stove or oil lamp, charring from radiated heat (unless fire ensues), like charred beams under a furnace. The damage caused by soot is not covered by the fire policy.

FRIEZING MACHINES—Sometimes called a shaper, used by woodworkers. These machines consist of two vertical spindles projecting up through a table and rotating rapidly in opposite directions. Each spindle carries cutters of various designs as desired. They are used for beveling, making edge mouldings. Considerable dust and refuse made.

FROZEN WATER—No receptacle has been made with sufficient strength to resist the bursting power of frozen water.

A Friendly Fire.

FRUIT EVAPORATORS—Fruit is pared, cored, trimmed, bleached with sulphur fumes, sliced and dried, packed. Evaporators resemble a brick kiln; steam or furnace heat, with furnace set in kiln, fruit on slatted floor above.

Bleaching with sulphur fumes, in separate building, or by putting same on belt-conveyor passing through a bleaching box. Both use a pot of burning sulphur. Fruit-preparing usually by machinery. Busy season, September to January.

FRUIT JUICE MANUFACTURING—See Flavoring Extracts.

FRUIT PRESERVING AND CLEANING—Raw materials consist of tapioca, currants, dates, raisins, citron, etc. Machinery consists of raisin-seeding machines, currant-washing machines, steam kettles, dry-rooms, tubs of syrup. Not a desirable class.

FRUIT STORES—Owing to health board regulations, requiring certain fruits, shelled nuts, etc., to be covered, dealers are using sheets of celluloid for a covering. In large stores, considerable quantity is kept on hand. If well established, considered a desirable class. Salvage in case of fire is very small.

FUEL is a substance whose combustion in atmospheric oxygen can be utilized as a source of heat energy for commercial or domestic purposes.

In zero weather, the supply of coal should be carefully noted by inspectors as experience has shown that a lack of supply may lead to the crippling of the automatic sprinkler equipment due to lack of heat. See Fire Appliances.

FUEL OIL—Crude oil with some of the lighter hydrocarbons (gasoline, benzine, etc.), removed, leaving the heavy tar oil. Flashes usually at about 150 deg. F. Classed as non-volatile. In large units, tanks preferably buried under ground rather than above ground. Should have a steampipe or other device such as a blanketing gas or foam for extinguishing fires. Conveyor pipes to be run underground with accessible gate valves to shut off supply. See Petroleum, also Oil-burning Equipments.

FULCRUM—The point about which a lever turns.

FULL RISK—A risk on which a company is committed to the full limit of its acceptances. In other words, the company has written all the insurance it cares to accept on the particular risk. See Lines; also Risk.

FULL WAR COVER—See War Risk Insurance.

FULLER'S EARTH RECOVERY—Earth saturated with oil is removed from filter presses and placed in steam stills where oil is driven off and recovered as refined oil. The earth thus freed is calcined to remove all volatile and organic matter, and, after cooling, is ready for use again.

FULMINATES—These metallic salts are explosive with heat or friction. Should be kept from mineral acids, carriers of oxygen, liquefied oxygen, organic substances and sulphur. If water or other liquid with which a fulminate has been mixed is sprinkled about and the drops left to dry, the slightest residual traces of the fulminate will explode of themselves, the greatest violence being exhibited when they are exposed to the rays of the sun. Even the dust swept up in fulminate works has a tendency to explode spontaneously.—(W. D. Grier.)

FULMINATE OF MERCURY is made by dissolving mercury in strong nitric acid. It is extremely sensitive to the heat of friction and is handled immersed in water or alcohol to prevent explosion. Used in ammunition works.

FULMINATE OF SILVER is a grayish white crystalline material used in torpedoes. More sensitive than mercury fulminate. Liable to spontaneous combustion.

FULMINOSE—Cellulose changed by heat.

FUMEXER—Trade name for an apparatus for venting vapors from inflammable liquids. It is a curved metal hood with wire glass side and back, equipped with suction fan for drawing off vapor from air brushes, and a drip pan for catching excess liquid.

FUMIGATION—Carbon bisulphide is sometimes used in tobacco factories to exterminate insects.

FUMING SULPHURIC ACID—Used in fortifying the mixed acids used for nitrating. See Oleum.

FUMOTH—Used in fumigating as a protection against the Mediterranean or flour moth. The process is: Slow-burning paper is saturated with a secret material (claim non-hazardous). This paper is slowly burned in a coal stove or other receptacle which has ducts leading to the machinery or elevator legs, etc. The fumes are forced through the machinery parts by means of a slowly-revolving fan. The outlet from these burning fumigators is protected by a double wire gauze, and the intake air is also protected with wire gauze.

FUR INDUSTRY (**Charles E. Jahne**)—The fur industry is very extensive. The class of employees is largely of foreign type. The larger and more important shops are well cared for, and attention is given to the matter of cleanliness; but the middle or smaller classes are generally crowded and untidy, and the employees are addicted very much to cigarettes. It is a common occurrence to open the shop door unexpectedly and see an employee smoking while standing with a "SMOKING PROHIBITED" sign directly in line of his vision, then ask the shop foreman if he allows smoking and receive his innocent reply, "Never." Then the inspector leads the foreman to the offending employee, who, of course, claims he was never told not to smoke in the shop, and then the matter closes with a promise from both foreman and employee that it will never happen again, and the inspector knows as well as they do that neither one expects to make good his promise.

There are many failures and fires in the fur trade. The manufacturers of small means are severely handicapped. There are, practically speaking, three grades of furriers. The first grade usually has first selection of importations; the second-raters, the second choice, and the third-rater takes what is left and usually pays as much as others for an inferior article. It is in the last class that most failures occur. The better the skins, the more easily they are manufactured at less expense, and the third-rater therefore has an added expense to cover up defects.

The fur industry is divided into many parts, namely, the sale of raw skins, the dressing of skins, the manufacturing of hatter's furs, of dressed skins into garments, of muffs and boas, of robes, of caps, of fur tails and heads; also, the trade of the taxidermist, who by his art of dressing and stuffing, produces the animal hide in a form representing its natural outline.

We will endeavor to consider these departments and point out the hazards connected with each, so as to give at least a faint idea of them.

In the capturing of the animals, it is most desired that they shall be trapped rather than shot because in trapping only the feet or neck of the animal is punctured, while in shooting, the body skin is usually damaged, and thereby reducing the value.

Skins are known as the **seasoned** and the **unseasoned.** The better of the two are the seasoned, because they are captured during the coldest weather, that being the time when the hair is the strongest and most oily and the skin the toughest. In skinning the animal, the punching process is the best, because there is less liability of cutting the skin or having the flesh cling to it. After removing the skins, they are dried by natural air, and if the pelt is soft, it is sprayed with water to harden it. They are then baled for shipment, except the finest grade of seals, which are often salted down and packed in casks. When they are received by the dealers in raw skins, they are examined to determine whether they are **firsts** or **seconds** (those without knife cuts from the skinning process being the first).

Dealers in Raw Skins usually have drying and fleshing rooms. Herein lie the hazards in their class. The drying of the skins is usually done by gas heat and in frame enclosures with the skins hung on wooden racks. The room should be made of some fireproof material, the hangers of metal and the skins so arranged that if one or more should fall from their supports, they would not come in contact with the heating apparatus. Steam heat for the drying room is the most preferable from a safety point. All scrapings from the fleshing work should be placed in metal receptacles. Sawdust is often used for the grease absorption on the floor of the fleshing room. Sand is preferable; but no matter which is used, the sweepings should be removed at least daily.

The next to consider is the fur-dressing trade. The skins are received here in bales generally, but very often in loose form, and stored in piles awaiting the process. In case of fire in the storage rooms, and the skins should not be burned but thoroughly water soaked, they should not be allowed to remain in piles over seven or eight days (the time being governed by the temperature), as they are liable to become heated and then fermentation would be rapid, and this would render the skin practically useless. The skins are in turn examined, and fleshed if particles adhere to them; then, if dirty or sandy, they are washed in plain water and dried by artificial heat, preferably gas. They are then **tramped.** This means placed in a barrel (one skin at a time) containing sawdust, and tramped upon by a man with light slippers on his feet. This makes the skin soft and pliable and also works out the grease which is absorbed by the sawdust. The skins are then **rolled**, e. g., drawn back and forth over round sticks by means of which they are stretched and flattened; and if any humps or ridges still exist they are skived, or trimmed down with a sharp knife. They are then cleaned in **drums**, which are large cylindrical-shaped casks practically resembling squirrel cages, which contain quantities of sawdust, preferably cedar wood dust. The drums are rotated by power, and the forced contact with each other, and the mingling with the dust, all serve to clean the skins and remove all remaining greases (at times charcoal stoves are placed under the drums in cold weather), and lastly, comes the hand beating with rattans, which serves to fluff up the fur.

There are times when the skins must be bleached or dyed. To dye them, aniline or logwood dyes, sumac, ammonia, sulphuric and nitric acids are used, and this is not a hazardous process. In the bleaching process, an air-tight room is needed; sulphur cakes are put in a crucible or pot which is set on some fireproof base, and the sulphur which is set on fire with a match, burns very slowly without a flame, practically smoldering, and gives escape to dense fumes which penetrate the hair and hide. Many firms have fireproof vaults in which the more expensive furs are stored. See Hides.

Manufacturing of Hatters' Furs is a very much more hazardous process than fur dressing, on account of the high-speed machinery used. Hatters' furs are usually shipped in burlap-covered bales. Water, if clean, will not damage the stock very heavily if immediately salvaged, and providing the stock is not scattered about. Smoke has a bad effect on the stock because it is very hard to remove the odor. The stock on the pelts is a different proposition, and offers only small salvage. Felt hats are made of hatters' fur.

This specific work is the producing of the animal hair in a proper condition for use by the manufacturers of felt hats and felted fabrics. The preferable skins to be used are the beaver, coney, rabbit and hare; because they are the most susceptible to the carroting process, which is intended to stiffen the hair for the cutting machines. **Carroting** means a spraying, usually with a hand brush, of a weak solution of nitric acid, carrot oil and water on the hair, and the skin then passes to the dryer, which is heated to about 150 deg. F. At one time it was thought that only coal fires were proper for this drying, but that severe hazard is now eliminated by the use of steam. Previous to the carroting, the skins are examined and fleshed, if necessary, and after the carroting they are trimmed; that is, the irregular edges are straightened; then they go to the **combers** and then to the **shearing** and **blowing** machines. These machines remove the hair from the pelt and blow all foreign particles free from it. The blowers have separators attached and the hair and foreign particles are carried to different receptacles. The possibility of overheated journals covered with dust and hair and resultant combustion causing rapid flash fires is a serious feature. The finished product is packed in paper bags and burlap bales. The pelts are sold to tanners.

Fur Garment Manufacturing contains practically a tailoring hazard, with the additional feature of stretching and drying skins by nailing them on boards and standing them around coal stoves, or in small gas-heated drying rooms. After the drying, they pass in turn to the cutters, sewers, liners and finishers.

Muffs, Boas and Caps are made largely by pieced skins for the cheap grade stock, and of whole skins for the high-grade stock. You find the hazards of the fur garment shop here with the additional and serious hazard of the use of cotton bats and shoddy, which are used for stuffing or filling purposes. The latter very naturally increases the possibility of an untidy shop.

Fur Tails are made from the clippings and waste. This class includes the poorest type of fur manufacturing, both from the standpoint of tidiness and rank of employees. Cutting and sewing are the only operations.

The Taxidermist is in a sense a part of the fur trade, in that he receives the skins from the fur dresser for mounting. The serious feature in his shop are the storage and handling of materials for stuffing; use of waxes and paints for tinting and finishing, and the woodworking in the making of moulds, frames and bases. Materials used for stuffing are cotton, shoddy, excelsior and sawdust.

In conclusion, let us sum up the brief hazards of the fur trade:

Dealers in Skins—Fleshing and drying.

Fur-Dressers—Fleshing skiving, tramping, cleaning in drums, dyeing and bleaching, benzine for removing grease from heads.

Hatters' Furs—Carroting, cutting, blowing, drying.

Garment Manufacturing—Drying, cutting, sewing.

Muffs, Boas and Caps—Cutting, sewing and filling and drying.

Taxidermist—Drying, stuffing, decorating and woodworking.

The above all have a grease hazard to some degree.

Fur Tails—Cutting and sewing.

Fur Pointers—Use fish glue for setting seams.

FUR COLD STORAGE VAULTS—Rooms should be of small area and each equipped with ice house door entering vestibule and the inner door of two thicknesses of sheet iron interlined with 4-inch cork block. Direct pumping brine system with coils on walls. No blower or suction fans.

Regular watchman and clock service, sprinklers on dry pipe line with control valve outside of vault. Automatic alarm, expansion thermostatic operating at about 130 deg. F. and connected with central station. Trouble alarm, consisting of electric thermometers. Approved electric wiring, outside switch with pilot light to indicate when lights are on or off. Masonry walls 12 inches thick, insulated with 4-inch cork block and cemented. Floors insulated and water-proof with two layers of felt (tarred), 1-inch corkboard alternating and finished off with 2-inch concrete. See Consequential Damage.

FUR HAT FACTORY—Fire, caused by watchman opening door of alcohol recovery oven, the vapors therein being exploded by the watchman's lantern. An approved watchman's lantern should always be used.

FURS IN COLD STORAGE—Underwriters should be careful not to authorize "too high" a line, as considerable value may be concentrated in very small space. See Consequential Damage.

FURNACES—For installation of temporary kerosene oil burners. See Kerosene Burners.

FURNACES (portable hot air type) should be placed at least four feet from any combustible partition or ceiling. If protected by metal shield, not less than two feet. Wood floors under furnaces should have sheet metal or one-eighth inch asbestos covered with two courses of 4-inch hollow tile or equivalent, this in turn with at least three-sixteenth inch boiler iron plates. Three courses of brick, top course laid on edge, producing a ventilating air space, may be used in lieu of the terra-cotta. See Cold Air Boxes.

FURNISHED-ROOM HOUSES—Contents are usually undesirable, owing to the great inroads made by apartment hotels taking the better class of roomers, and the rapid deterioration of furniture from wear and tear. The furnishings in the cheaper grade houses are bought from second-hand dealers. Many fires are caused by smoking, carelessness with matches, swinging gas jets, cooking on gas, alcohol or kerosene oil stoves. See Actors; also Boarding Houses and Lodging Houses.

FURNITURE POLISH is usually made of clay, petroleum, varnish, linseed oil, benzine, acetic acid, glacial acetic acid, nitro-benzol, lemon oil, oil of citronella, turpentine.

FURNITURE STOCK—If stock is all new and only occasional "touching up" is done, packing material in standard bin, safety waste can for polishing rags provided, this class appears to be acceptable. Cabinet making or re-upholstering may be done.

FURRING is the finish applied to a wall to prevent dampness. The usual method is to lay furring strips on wall about 16 inches O. C., then place the wood lath over the stud and then finish with plaster. This leaves a concealed space of about 3 inches. Fires getting into this space are hard to locate and put out. The up-to-date method is to place asphaltum directly on the naked brick walls and then coat with plaster, leaving no concealed space. See Finish; see Fire Stops.

FUSE—Device for breaking an electrical circuit which may become overloaded.

FUSE (ammunition) forms the point or nose of the projectile. It is made of machined brass and aluminum parts enclosing a powder train and detonators. Platinum fuses cause ignition when exposed to coal gas or alcohol vapors.

FUSE (powder) is a train of powder or a fuse which leads to a charge of powder.

FUSEL OIL (amyl alcohol)—Colorless to yellow liquid, produced in the fermentation of starch and sugar, and is separated from grain alcohol. Commercial flashes at over 80 deg. F.

Fusel Oil—The refuse from the distillation of spirits.

FUSIBLE LINK, as used on fire doors, etc., made of bismuth, tin and lead and antimony. The ordinary link fuses at 165 deg. F. Even though a cord is used in place of wire to hold open a door or packing bin, a fusible link is needed, as it melts when temperature rises sufficiently, whereas direct heat is required to burn a cord.

FUSION POINT OF METALS—

Blast furnace slag	2500	deg. F.
Bessemer retort slag	3100	"
Brass	1600	"
Bronze	1450	"
Cast iron (pig)	2000-2400	"
Copper	3000	"
Ferro-nickel steel	2250	"
Gold	1950	"
Iron (pure)	3275	"
Iron (wrought)	3300-4000	"
Lead	630	"
Manganese steel	2300	"
Nickel	2700	"
Silver	1750	"
Solt, Solder	340	"
Steel	2400-3300	"

Tin .... 450 deg. F.
Zinc .... 750 "
Glass ....2000-2300 "

N. F. P. A. (May 7, 1914). Reprinted from Western Actuarial Hazards report.

FUSTIC—A dyestuff from wood or venetian sumac. See Dye Woods.

G

GABLE ROOF—A sloping roof forming a vertical triangle.

GALENA—An ore, compound of lead and sulphur.

GALIPOT—A white resin obtained from turpentine.

GALITH—A substitute for bone, horn, ivory or celluloid; produced from milk; nearly pure casein.

GALVANIZED IRON is iron which has been coated with zinc to prevent it from rusting. The iron is simply dipped in zinc and is not coated by any galvanic process. Zinc, after a short exposure to air, becomes coated with a fine film of oxide which does not increase, and this preserves the zinc itself, as well as the iron beneath it. The setting of ovens should be on non-combustible bases. The acids used are hydrochloric, sulphuric and muriatic.—(The Weekly Underwriter.)

GALVANIZING KETTLES are brick set kettles, usually 5 feet wide 12 feet long and 4½ feet high. The walls are about 20 inches thick, the inner 6 inches being enclosed on the four sides by a boiler iron compartment containing the coke fire, while the top is covered with metal plates. The fires are kept going continuously as long as six years, for it would take a long time to get the zinc in proper form if it once became chilled. No woodwork should be near kettles.—(Live Articles on "Special Hazards," The Weekly Underwriter.)

GALVANIZING DRY—Metal is packed in zinc dust in sealed iron drums, placed in gas heated kilns and subjected to high temperature for about six hours, which deposits a coat of zinc on the metal.

Drying Ovens (for galvanizing) are usually enclosed in brick walls with a steel beam and boiler iron top, while the base is half-inch iron plates, underneath which are the various flues, with a coke fire at each end of the oven.

GAMBIER—A vegetable tannin, extracted from the leaves of an Indian tree. Used in tanning.

GAMBRELL ROOF—A roof with four sloping sides.

GARAGE—A housing place for automobiles. Gasoline feature important. Hazards of repairing batteries and sealing same with pitch, which is generally heated by gas; brazing, cleaning parts with gasoline, burning out carbon cylinders of cars, storage of oils, smoking. Oily waste should be placed in proper cans. It has been found that by placing fire pails two to five feet above the floor as per Underwriters' requirements, they are often broken by automobiles backing into them as they hang on the wall. Some rule should be adopted by rating bureaus to allow full allowance for fire extinguishers without pails, or to have a barrel of sand with fire pails nearby instead of hanging pails where they can be easily broken. A "bumper rail" along the wall is recommended. See Sewers.

GARBAGE REDUCTION PLANT—The garbage arrives in scows. Grab buckets deposit it in hoppers; it drops to traveling conveyors on which it is carried to digesters and receiving tanks, and to the presses, which expel the water and grease. The water and grease run off to catch basins and the solid matter (vegetable garbage) is taken from the presses and shoveled to a traveling conveyor, which deposits it in dryers. From the dryers, the material is sent to the degreasing plant (naphtha extracting process), which extracts nearly all of the remaining grease by means of percolators, which are horizontal tanks, steam heated, with strainers. From the percolators it is run to the evaporating tanks (steam 280 deg. F.), where the vapor (naphtha) is taken off by means of piping to the condensers. After condensing, the naphtha is again returned to the storage tanks. At this stage the mass (garbage tankage) is again conveyed to the dryers, where it is redried and put through the percolating process, after which time the mass (tankage) is practically free from grease and deposited into storage house in dust form to be used for fertilizer. See Extraction Plants.

GARBAGE TANKAGE—A product from digesters and extractors of garbage reducing plants. Subject to spontaneous combustion.

GARMENT WORKERS—Many fires have been caused by smoking, untidiness, gas or electric pressing irons, individual motors. Considered an unprofitable class. See Cutting and Work Tables; also Pressing Tables.

GARNET—A machine which winds cotton bats on cylinders in sheets. A type of wool card.

GAS BLACK—The soot produced from the combustion of hydro-carbon fuel or illuminating gas. Also made from natural gas burned under revolving cylinders, the deposited soot being removed by scraping. It is nearly pure carbon.

GAS BRACKETS should be 3 feet below any combustible or open ceiling. If shielded with suspended metal shield, they may be 18 inches distant. No gas bracket shall be nearer than 5 inches measured from the burner to the woodwork or other combustible material. No swinging or folding gas brackets allowed against any combustible partitions; same must be protected by wire cages and metal placed on walls where brackets swing. If gas brackets over sewing machines are nearer than 2 feet they must have wire globes. No rubber hose is permitted to be attached to any gas jet.

GAS CYLINDERS—See Compressed Gas Cylinders.

GAS DISTRIBUTING PLANTS—The gas is made elsewhere and comes through pipe lines to gas holders and is then distributed to various sections of the city under pressure. Many buildings comprise one of these plants. Power house with boilers, dynamos, generators, exhauster house with pumps, water cooling tower, condensers, carpenter shop, oil storage house, lamp storage shed, battery recharging and repairing, machine shop, meter repair shop, linemen's storage and supplies, including lubricating oil, conduits, cables, paint, ladders, tackle; blacksmith shop, arc lamp repairing, paint shop. See Gas Works.

GAS ENGINES—The hazards. Rubber gas bags are dangerous because escaping gas, due to accident or leak, may cause an explosion or fire. When used they should be 3 feet in a lateral direction from ignition chamber. Exhaust chambers or pots become very hot. Frequently they set on wood to reduce vibration incident to the operation of the engine, and for support. No wood should be allowed. The chamber or pot should be raised at least four inches above the floor or set on incombustible base. The exhaust pipe should be two inches from all woodwork and enter a proper flue, extending at least six inches above the flue or chimney. Floors under and 24 inches outside of engine should be metal clad with flanged edges. Woodwork back of engine should be sheathed with metal as the wheel throws considerable oil.

GAS EQUALIZERS—Galvanized iron gas equalizers are now being used in connection with gas engines in place of the old rubber bags. They insure a steady and uniform gas pressure to the engine and are practically indestructible. The old style rubber gas bag was the cause of many fires.

GAS AND VAPOR FIRES can best be fought by closing all doors or other means of ventilation, thereby excluding the air, and then turning on steam.

GAS FIXTURES AND GLOBES—Stocks usually kept in basements. Stock is crated or in barrels packed with straw or salt hay. Hazards are overcrowded stock, unsafe gas brackets without wire cages, untidy premises due to packing material. See Chandelier Manufacturing.

GAS HOLDERS—Large steel tanks, usually near gas works. Used for storing the gas after it is manufactured. These holders are really reservoirs from which gas is constantly being taken and constantly replenished, as a gas plant never ceases manufacturing its product.

Gas Holders (gasometers), holding millions of cubic feet of gas are a menace to surrounding buildings in case of destruction by wind storms or other agencies.

GAS LIGHTS—Inverted gas light mantles have caused many fires by reason of red hot carbon dropping on combustible material. A wire mesh should be placed under the burners or an enclosed globe used. **Gas Lights** which are two feet or less above sewing tables should be caged. See Cluster Gas Lamps.

GAS METERS—Fires have melted off the connecting pipe

and caused a jet of burning gas to be projected into the room, setting fire to surrounding woodwork. An outside shut-off valve is recommended for business buildings. Leaky meters are responsible for numerous fires. Meters should not be placed near gas jets. Looking for leaks in meters with a candle has caused many explosions. See Gas Safety Valves.

GAS OIL—A residue from the process of making gas. Flash point over 100 deg. F. Not volatile.

GAS PIPES—Fires have been caused by leaky service pipes which have become so corroded that scales could be picked off with the fingers. Holes appear in the pipe and quantities of gas fill the premises. If an open light is near, an explosion is apt to follow.

GAS PRESSING IRONS left with gas burning cause fires by burning through tables, unless on iron stands three inches high. See Pressing Tables.

GAS PURIFYING WASTE—A fertilizer ingredient. See Iron Mass.

GAS RANGES—Vents from gas ranges should be of three or four-inch tile, extending through roof to the outer air. Usually they are of galvanized iron and set in between studs of frame walls and terminate in attics. It takes but a short time for this flue or vent to become heavily coated on the inside with grease. Should a pan of fat boil over, fire would ensue and pour out into the attic. See Ranges.

GAS STOVES should be placed on iron stands and be connected with rigid iron piping. Rubber tubing should never to be used. Stoves must be six inches from combustible partitions and shielded to 12 inches above the stove. See Baffle Plate.

GAS SAFETY VALVE—A safety device to prevent the escape of gas from meters during fires. The danger of escaping gas from meters supplying fuel to a fire and endangering lives of firemen is too apparent to need comment. The gas-valve safety device for preventing the escape of gas consists of a valve plug of any size desired with a hard steel ball soldered into hollow of plug with solder that will melt

STANDARDS FOR LOW GAS STOVES

NO. 1
AN UNSAFE ARRANGEMENT
NOTE— THE RUBBER TUBE and the wood bench.

iron pipe connection

want 4 inches from burners to shield

need 6" from burners to base of table

metal shield to catch hot carbon—

metal covered wood table

NO. 2
AN Acceptable Arrangement
approved by the N.Y. Board and the Exchange

iron

solid iron top

pipe legs

angles

No. 3
An Ideal Arrangement (all iron Construction)

at 120 deg. F. No special fittings are required, ordinary gas tee being used in place of elbow over the meter.

The valve will automatically shut off the gas in case fire burns off the lead meter connections or melts the soldered joints on the meter itself. When the solder melts, the ball drops into the mouth of the pipe and the gas pressure is on top of the ball and not against it. The nipple or pipe in the bottom of tee should be reamed just a little to make it perfectly round as seat for the ball. This device was invented by John P. Doyle, a fireman.

GAS TUBING MANUFACTURING—Raw stock is wire, cotton and silk yarn, glycerine, glue, litharge, venetian red, metal parts, rubber tips. Hazards are steam heated kettles for glycerine, glue dipping mixture, wire drawing and spinning.

GAS WELL—How Mr. Guerin, of the New York Fire Department, extinguished a fire in a burning gas well. Put men behind shields, push the shields to within ten or fifteen feet of the well, raise the pressure in the two seven-eighths of an inch nozzle to forty or fifty pounds and have the streams played on the base of the well casing so that they converged from an angle of 90 degrees.

"This was done. Then I had the streams slowly raised up to and through the column of gas until they reached the base of the glare. At this juncture the men who were handling the hose were ordered to squeeze their thumbs against the stream at the nozzles so that the water spread like a fan. They followed instructions.

"Striking the flame where it merged with the column of gas, the water became steam, the roar of which exceeded that of the gas itself. The fire went out like a snuffed candle. The steam had simply cut off the flame from the gas."

GAS WORKS—Pentone used for standardizing light instead of candles is a hydro-carbon, very volatile and inflammable. In the reviving room, chips, sawdust and iron filings that are being revived should be not spread more than 12 inches deep, because the mixture may spontane and set fire to woodwork. See Gas Distributing Plants.

GASKET—Rope, yarn or hemp used for stuffing the joints

of water pipes, or rubber bands for making connections water tight.

GASOLINE—Flash point 84 to 88 deg. F. Ordinary gasoline boils at 113 deg. F. Its vapor is power producing; when pure will not explode, but when mixed with from 2 to 6 parts of air becomes explosive in the presence of an open light or flame. When stored above ground it is constantly vaporizing due to the changing temperatures of the atmosphere. Should be stored underground in approved tanks where the temperature remains nearly stationary. When stored in this manner, it will not explode. It is often used for cleaning automobile parts by means of a brush. When used in this manner around the engine, a spark from the motor is apt to explode the accumulated vapors, enveloping the car in flames. Cleaning chamois skin gloves with gasoline by rubbing them, or cleaning silk in the same way, or filtering gasoline through a chamois cloth when filling an automobile tank, generates static electricity which will ignite the vapor. See Benzine. See Petroleum.

Gasoline vapor is about three times as heavy as air, and therefore the greater portion will be found near the floor, and travel to an open flame, flash back to the container, and cause an explosion. One pint of gasoline will make 200 cubic feet of air explosive.

Gasoline, benzine, naphtha or other fluids which emit an inflammable vapor below the temperature of 100 deg. F. should be stored outside all buildings in steel tanks buried at least two feet underground.

Storage tank shall be constructed of steel at least one-quarter of an inch thick; shall have a capacity of not more than two hundred and seventy-five gallons, and shall, under test, stand a hydrostatic pressure of at least one hundred pounds to the square inch.

Tank shall be coated on the outside with tar or other rust-resisting material, shall rest upon a solid foundation, and shall be embedded in and surrounded by at least twelve inches of Portland cement concrete, composed of two parts of cement, three parts of sand and five parts of stone.

No storage tank shall be placed under the sidewalk nor in front of the building line.

Storage tank shall be equipped with a filling pipe, a drawing-off pipe and a vent pipe; provided, however, that no storage tank installed as part of an hydraulic or pressure storage system shall be required to have a vent pipe. All pipes shall be of galvanized wrought iron and shall have malleable iron fittings. All screw joints shall be made with litharge and glycerine.

The filling pipe shall be at least two inches in diameter, and shall be laid at a descending grade from the sidewalk in front of the garage to the tank.

The intake of the filling pipe shall be located in a heavy metal box, which shall be sunk flush with the sidewalk at the curb level and fitted with a heavy metal cover, which shall be kept locked when not in use.

The filling pipe shall be closed at the intake by a cock or valve fitted with a coupling for attaching to the hose of a barrel wagon, and with a screw cap to close the opening when not in use.

Each filling pipe shall be provided with a screen made of two thicknesses of 20-mesh brass wire gauze, placed immediately below the filling cock or valve.

The vent pipe shall be at least one inch in diameter, and shall run from the tank to the outer air at least ten feet above the roof of the garage and at least ten feet from the nearest wall of any other building, and shall be well braced in position.

The vent pipe shall be capped with a double goose-neck, hood or cowl, and provided with a screen made of two thicknesses of 20-mesh brass wire gauze, placed just below the gooseneck or cowl.

Regulations of the Municipal Explosives Commission of the City of New York. See Petroleum; also Liquid Tank.

GASOLINE ENGINE fires occur largely from exhaust pipes and from "back-fires." The small engine generally has its gasoline supply in the base, and very often the unions of the pump connections become leaky, and gasoline drips from them. If possible, when inspecting a risk having a gasoline engine, the machine should be seen in operation. The main cause of trouble is the exhaust. Carbon very quickly collects in the muffler and exhaust pipe, and is likely to give trouble if the exhaust pot is confined or near inflammable material. The engines burning fuel oil or distillate should be treated same as gasoline engines. In practice, the exhaust pipe from big engines is run to a concrete muffler, usually built underground outside of building with wooden tops. Sometimes these concrete pits burst open or the tops burn off. This is a severe hazard to buildings of frame construction or where any combustible material is adjacent to the muffler.

GASOLINE SPRAY FOR CLEANING AUTOS—A process employed for cleaning oily automobile machinery without dismantling. To meet this demand a gasoline spraying machine has been placed on the market. This machine is made of galvanized iron and resembles a 2½-gallon chemical extinguisher in appearance. It is provided with about 5 feet of ¼-inch rubber hose, a ⅛-inch nozzle, a pressure gauge and an air pump fastened to the tank. For cleaning purposes about 2 gallons of gasoline is placed in the tank and then an air pressure of from 50 to 150 pounds is pumped up. To clean the automobile parts, from one to two gallons of gasoline under pressure is sprayed on the machine parts. It is understood that, after the car has been sprayed, the gasoline is allowed to vaporize and the vapor to blow away before the machine is started. Notwithstanding this supposed method of procedure several fires have occurred due to premature starting of the automobile. At some garages this is done inside of the buildings, and at others it is done in the street. An extremely hazardous process.

GASOLINE STORAGE TANKS—One type to prevent the accumulation of vapors. Water is poured in tank forcing the gasoline to the top. The water is drained off to admit of more gasoline. Tanks are also equipped with froth or foam extinguishing apparatus, consisting of a glass bottle containing acid which is broken by a hammer when the fusible links melt, letting the acid mix with chemicals such as bicarbonate of soda and soap bark, which, under pressure, forces the resulting foam or froth on the surface of the burning liquid. Gasoline is also stored under gas, such as nitrogen or carbon dioxide under pressure.

GASOLINE STOVES—Considered more dangerous than kerosene stoves. The storage and handling of supply is important. Leaky stoves are dangerous.

GASSING—Passing material through a gas flame or over rows of Bunsen burners in order to remove the down or fuzz.

GATE VALVE—The valve used on sprinkler equipments to control the water supply. They should always be sealed open. The latest type, O. S. & Y. (outside screw and yoke), enables the inspector to see at a glance if valve is open. The old style "target" valve depending on a plate marked "open" or "shut" is not looked upon with favor by inspection departments. Emergency gate valve at base of tank should not be sealed. This valve is used to drain the tank in case of accident. See Valves; see Sprinkler Equipments.

GEARING—A train of cog-wheels.

GELATINE—A substance obtained from one of the boilings in the manufacture of glue.

GELATINE CAPSULES FOR MEDICINE—Gelatine is boiled in kettles, usually Mott kettles (by direct heat), to a thick mass and moulded into capsule form by hydraulic presses, dried in dry rooms. Oily floors frequently found.

GENTS' FURNISHING stocks, if damaged by water, have a fair salvage as they can, in most cases, be relaundered and pressed and sold at auction sales.

GEORGIA PINE TURPENTINE—See Turpentine Spirits.

GERMAN SILVER—An alloy of copper, zinc and nickel. It does not contain sterling silver.

GILSONITE—A high-grade asphaltum, mined in the western states. Melts at 300 to 350 deg. F. Used in making cable insulation. Is useless if water comes in contact with it before being compounded.

GIN—A machine for separating cotton from its seeds. See Cotton Gins.

GINSENG ROOT—A yellowish root, imported mainly

from China. Used extensively by the Chinese for medicinal purposes. Susceptible to water and smoke damage.

GIRDER—A timber larger than a common beam and on which the floor beams rest.

GLASS OR CHINA is usually packed in barrels or boxes with plenty of straw or salt hay. In case of fire, the place might resemble the after effect of a "bull in a china shop."

GLASS DEALERS—Have stock of ordinary sheet glass, art glass, wired glass, and plate glass. Turpentine is used for cleaning off old glass brought in from jobs. There is little salvage in large sheets of glass, as heat and cold water applied will crack them.

GLASS WORKS—Glass is composed of silica and alkalis. The principal ingredients are sand, lime, soda ash, potash, cullett, charcoal, oxide of lead, kelp, saltpetre, and cobalt. The process is as follows: Materials are mixed together to form a "batch," which is placed in a fire clay pot, inserted in a brick-enclosed furnace and heated by soft coal. When the batch has cooled to a temperature of about 1,900 degrees it is ready to be "gathered." This is accomplished by means of an iron blow pipe which is inserted into the fire clay pot, the molten glass clinging to the end of the pipe resembling a ball. The glass blower then blows through the pipe which inflates the glass ball, soap bubble fashion. The glass design is then placed in a water jacketed mold, after which it goes to a brick set tempering oven or "lehr" in order to give the glass the proper temper. See Annealing Furnaces.

GLASS (Colored)

Amber is produced by the addition of carbonaceous matter, i.e., grain, coke, coal, or other organic matter. It is also produced by sulphur and certain sulphites.

Black is produced by an excess of coloring matter such as manganese, cobalt, or iron.

Blue can be produced by cobalt or copper.

Canary is produced by uranium.

Green, chromium or iron alone will produce green, though it is usually made by combining several oxides.

Purple is produced by manganese dioxide.

Red or ruby is produced by gold, selenium or copper,

(C. C. Dominge, "Live Articles on Special Hazards," The Weekly Underwriter.)

GLASS, FROSTED—Made by treating the glass in a solution of hydrofluoric acid with ammonium carbonate or with a sand blast.

GLASS, LEADED—The shop hazards are crimping, cutting and soldering. Gas mufflers are used for soldering irons. Glazing and painting in small way.

GLASS AND MIRROR WORKS—Fire which causes much smoke ruins the glass by cracking and smoking. Smoked glass, especially plate, is useless unless ground down. This process exceeds the cost of the glass. The white glass, resembling marble, is very expensive. Such glass is ruined if smoked up. The grinding stones are made of a composition, very hard, varying in thickness from one to two inches. They crack under the action of heat. Cutting stones are carborundum, which also crack under heat.

GLAUBER SALT—See Sulphate of Soda.

GLORY HOLES (in glass factories) are small brick-enclosed circular furnaces using fuel-oil heat. These small furnaces heat the glassware so as to trim the edges. Setting and clearance should be carefully inspected. See Glass Works.

GLOVES—Cotton Gloves. Cut by hand or machine or die presses; stitched on sewing machines; pressed and formed into shape by steam-heated glove forms. Light hazard.

Men's gloves, being heavier than women's, are not so susceptible as the latter and, if slightly damaged, can still be used as work gloves, whereas women are very loath to wear any glove which is spotted or defective. Kid Glove stock very susceptible.

GLUCOSE occurs naturally in most fruits, honey and corn. Sometimes made from potato starch.

GLUE—Gelatine produced by boiling the parings of hoofs, and also from fish. Factory hazards of boiling and evaporating. The arrangement of drying ovens and sulphur burners is important. Usually a nuisance to neighborhood. A class avoided by most companies.

GLYCERINE is formed when natural fats decompose by treatment with alkalis or superheated steam.

GLYCOL (or ethylene alcohol) is a liquid between glycerine and alcohol, the vapor being inflammable.

GLYOXILINE contains gun cotton, very inflammable.

GOLD BEATERS—The first process is to beat the gold in a "shodder," which consists of pieces of specially prepared skin, with which the metal is interleaved. Though the hammer used is 14 pounds in weight, the elasticity of the skin causes a rebound, which considerably reduces the exertion of lifting.

The "shodder" during the beating process looks rather like a pack of cards, only a little larger, and the "cutch" into which the pieces of gold, already thinned out to several times their original size, has much the same appearance. At this stage, however, much finer skins are used—so fine that the 700 or so of which the "cutch" is composed make a thickness of less than one inch. After some hours more of beating, the gold leaf is again cut and put between yet another book, or pack of skins, known as a "mold."

The "mold" is beaten on for about four hours with hammers of varying weights and sizes, according to the stage of the beatings. The transferring of the incredibly thin leaves of rich, yellow metal from the "mold" to the books bought by the gilders is done with a very fine pair of clips, or pincers, made of the lightest wood.

The leaf is laid on a cushion of soft leather, and then delicately cut to the size of the book with a simple-looking instrument of wood with sharpened sides, known as a "waggon."

GOLD PAINT—See Bronzing Liquid.

GOLDSMITHS—Hazards of melting pots, metal working, gas blow pipes, polishing.

GOLF BALLS—The core is gelatine or soap and water or an acid resembling sulphuric in a rubber bag around which is wrapped a tight rubber strip, then follows a layer of rubber strips and an outer shell of gutta-percha and composition.

GOODS IN HANDS OF—A term signifying that goods

belonging to one party are in the hands of another party, presumably to be made up, as for instance, cloth in the hands of a contract tailor to be made up into garments. Considered desirable insurance at current rates, even in sweatshops, as quite often it is found that prior to the fire most of the goods have been returned to the owner. See Sweatshops.

GOOSENECK—The inverted end of a cast iron or other pipe used at the end of vent pipes above the roof of garages, etc., to prevent rain from getting into the pipe.

GOVERNOR—The part of a machine which regulates the speed; usually by two balls attached to springs on a revolving axis. Increase in speed causes the balls to fly outward, which action regulates a valve, which in turn reduces the amount of power consumed by the machine.

GRAHAMITE—An asphalt used in making cable insulation compound. Contains carbon and has caused mine fires in West Virginia and Utah.

GRAIN ELEVATORS or Warehouses. Grain is usually received from barges or trains, elevated to top of building and dropped into receiving bins, called "garners." Thence it is cleaned, mixed, bleached and perhaps cooked. From the steam cooker the grain is conveyed in worm conveyor to a hopper, through rollers to squeeze out water, then to grain dryer, and through an exhauster, where dust is conveyed by blower to a cyclone.

The **bins are usually "cribs"** made of planking, and extending from first to top floor. When the warehouses are built in rows they are usually connected by endless belt conveyors on which the grain travels from one building to another. Standard automatic drop doors should be at each side of openings at fire walls. Cleaners and other machinery are usually located on first floor. The "scourers" (smut removers) and mills should have magnets, as they revolve at high speed, as do the "clippers," which clip the ends of the grain. Sulphur fumes are used for bleaching.

Dryers are invariably steam-heated. Cleanliness about the plant and machinery is essential. Dust in machinery and elevating machinery is more hazardous than that found under ordinary atmospheric conditions from handling of the grain. The use of open lights or of unguarded electric lights lowered into bins to ascertain the quantity of grain therein, has often caused an explosion of the dust in suspension in the bin from the open light or the breaking of the electric light bulb. All lights should have guards. Grain dust explodes from sparks in grinding or milling machines, electric sparks from motors or from static electricity generated by rapidly-moving belts and pulleys. Fires are caused by clogged elevators (sometimes called lofters) or grain accumulating around "strut-boards," also by friction gearing at machinery, journals resting on wood, cyclones, wood pulleys, sparks from motors or railroads. Dust spouts from cleaners should not exhaust on railroad side of building as sparks from locomotives may enter the spouts.

Fireproof grain storage tanks can be built of terra-cotta tile, circular in shape, furred on the outside with tile 2 inches in thickness and 12 inches in height (the furring tile overlap the inner tile), the whole being reinforced by pairs of steel tension bands running through the walls at frequent intervals. The steel tension bands are imbedded in a cement grouting and the outside furring is applied with a cement mortar. The foundation walls and base are built of concrete.

GRAIN FIRES—A great many of the disastrous field grain fires originate when threshing begins. Fires in threshers are mainly caused by static electricity in the machines.

Suggestion of Insurance Department of Washington

This hazard can be guarded against to some extent by keeping the top of the machine open, allowing the smut and dust to blow away. Have shovels and some spaded-up earth handy to the feed, as shoveling dirt into the separator will frequently extinguish the fire. Chemical extinguishers, of 2 and 3 gallon capacity are most efficient.

Threshing-machine engines should be equipped with spark arresters and precautions should be taken to keep the same clean and clear from soot. When the engine is moving from one setting to another a man with a wet sack should follow fifty to one hundred yards behind the machine in order to extinguish any fire which may be started by sparks. A barrel of water with tub and wet sacks should accompany all threshing outfits.

The ash dump should be thoroughly covered with dirt and wet down before leaving the setting. The engineer should not be depended upon to extinguish dump fires, but the grain growers should be on the ground and see that all fires are carefully extinguished.

Sparks from trains—If a field is exposed to railroad, hay strip should be cut about fifty feet wide, and fire guards of at least ten feet of furrows plowed between railroad track and the field. If field is exposed to country road where there is considerable dry grass or the road is strawed, it is well to plow a fire guard between the field and the road.

Old straw stacks which have been burned at the time of plowing frequently cause fires. Precaution should be taken not to set the machine or allow the new straw pile to be near the burned butt of the old straw pile.

Back fire from gas engines—A number of fires are caused by back firing of gas engines. The exhaust should be screened and kept free from dust and precaution should be taken to have a guard follow the gas engine when moving. Exhaust should be at least five feet above separator where used on combines. A chemical fire extinguisher should always accompany the engine.

Smoking—Under no circumstances allow smoking in any field at any time after grain begins to ripen.

Oily rags which are used for cleaning up around machinery should never be thrown aside or dropped in a field, as is sometimes done. Spontaneous combustion may result. All threshing machines should be equipped with metal receptables for oily rags.

Fires in the field are very difficult of control, especially where the straw is heavy. Every precaution should be taken to eliminate the cause. A very large proportion of the fire loss can be prevented if farmers will plow at least ten feet of furrows around stacks as soon as the grain is cut, making a circle large enough to take in both the setting and separator and leaving the engine outside the furrow. By use of a harrow or other means, the stubble should be removed from the ground. It is not sufficient to plow two or three furrows that do not fully cover the stubble. It is little less than criminal to allow a fire to spread in this manner when it can be largely controlled by following these suggestions.

Fighting field fires—The most effective way is with wet sacks. Men should go out on all sides with wet sacks and beat it toward the centre. A barrel or tub of water should be put in a machine or wagon and immediately driven to the fire fighters so that they can keep their sacks wet at all times.

Fires in setting—Grain sacks burn very slowly, especially when in large piles. If work be started immediately most of the damage can be prevented. Straw should never be piled on sacks until after the engine has been moved and it is made absolutely certain that no fire can spring up.

Combined harvesters—When grain is harvested by a combine, the sack grain should be taken care of promptly. There is a large and useless risk in leaving sacked grain scattered about the field. Remember, it is your duty under the policy conditions to prevent and put out all fires and save grain after the fire. Do not be misled by the impression that you should not touch the grain until the adjuster arrives. You violate the policy conditions if you do not use due diligence to take care of it.

GRAIN STORAGE WAREHOUSES—Old type brick construction are lined with continuous planking of crib construction forming bins. This peculiar construction, together with the enormous height and almost total lack of windows or fire escapes, makes this class a hard one to fight in case of fire. Fires in this class usually are of a "flash" nature and sprinklers may not prove effective. Even though heavy blank fire walls separate the various buildings, if much water is thrown on the grain the walls are apt to bulge and come down when the wet grain expands. (Lessons learned from Dows Store Fire, Oct. 14, 1917.) See Cleaning Machinery.

GRANITE—Under fire will explode and fly off in fragments or it will disintegrate into a fine sand.

GRANULATING—Forming into grains or small masses; separating molten substances by dropping or pouring into moving water.

GRAPHITE, or **Black Lead,** as it is called, is a form of carbon. It is used in lead pencils. The name "black lead" is misleading, for there is no lead in this substance, which is purely carbon with a very small amount of iron.

GRAPHITE (artificial)—Made from anthracite coal, can be used as a lubricant in graphite grease form.

GRAVITY AND PRESSURE SYSTEMS for Fuel Oil—Inspectors should ascertain if gasoline or fuel oil system is supplied by gravity or pressure. The former is not approved, because the supply is above the point of use and the supply pipes continually contain oil whether system is in operation or not. In the latter case, the system depends on a pump to bring the oil to the outlet, the supply pipe pitched to drain back to supply tank.

GRAVITY SUPPLY of water is the best thing for fire purposes. A reservoir of good capacity or a large standpipe gives a reserve supply already stored at the higher elevation and available to meet any sudden large demand. Water thus stored is, we may say, capital on hand, giving strength to meet any emergency, whereas, the best pumping equipment must depend on the right action promptly taken when special demands arise, and there must be very large reserve capacity to meet possible heavy calls which would come but rarely. (French.)

GRAVITY TANKS—The usual requirement for sprinkler tanks is an elevation of 20 feet above roof to give about 15 lbs. pressure on top lines. Ordinary sized tanks are made of 2½-inch first grade dressed lumber, or steel. Round hoops are used, as flat hoops burst from rust. Water is kept from freezing by steam coil; but at times steam jets are used. Exposed piping must be packed frost-proof. "Tell-tales" are used to indicate height of water, although mercury gauges may be used. These latter are connected to tank riser on tank side of check valve and installed inside of building.

GREASE FIRES in hotels and restaurants are caused by the ignition of grease which has collected in the ventilator pipe connected with large ranges. The grease slowly condenses on the inside of the pipe until it is thickly coated, when it may ignite, and because the pipe has not ample clearance from combustible material, start a fire. Some authorities recommend **steam jets**. Water thrown on grease when afire will scatter the fire. Sand or even sawdust is preferable. See Oil Fires.

GREASE ERADICATOR—See Eradicator.

GREEK FIRE—A colored fire mixture, classed as fireworks.

GREEN HIDES—See Hides.

GREER OIL—Made from sediment of gas oil, volatile.

GRILLAGE—A sort of net work of timbers laid crossing each other.

GRILLAGE FOUNDATIONS—See Floating Foundations.

GRISSETTES—Plain triangular pieces of plate iron riveted by their vertical and horizontal legs to the sides, top and bottom of box girders for strengthening their angles.

GROCERS—See Canned Goods.

GROIN—An arch formed by two segmental arches or vaults intersecting each other at right angles.

GROOVED-AND-SPLINED—Planks grooved at both edges instead of tongue and grooved. When laid, a strip is driven in between the planks, which takes the place of tongue.

GROUND (Made Ground)—Cinders from smelting furnaces or others which contain a large percentage of unconsumed coal should not be used for filling under buildings. Plant of the Tottenville Copper Co., Staten Island, April 14, 1910, suffered a loss of approximately $20,000. Fire discovered near the melting furnaces and was probably started by hot coals finding their way through a crack in the bottom of pot melting furnaces or flue and thereby coming in contact with the unconsumed coal in the cinders of which the filling under the floor of the building was composed. N. Y. Board of Underwriters.

GROUT—The mortar poured into the interstices between stones or bricks.

GUANO (manure)—If wet is liable to cause spontaneous combustion. Although the hazard is very mild, inspectors should always suggest that pigeons and chickens be removed from the attics or cupolas of buildings.

GUARDS—During war times when incendiaries are active, the question of sufficient armed guards plays even a more important part than the construction of the building and the hazards contained therein. The year 1917, with its heavy loss record, shows that many plants were not properly guarded. See War Conditions.

GUAYULE—A form of rubber.

GUNCOTTON—Cotton soaked in nitric and sulphuric acid mixture. The stronger the nitric, the more powerful the guncotton. A weak solution produces collodion or celluloid. See Nitro-cellulose.

GUN METAL (or Bronze)—A compound of copper and tin.

GUN POWDER—A mixture of potassium nitrate or saltpetre, powdered charcoal and sulphur. The explosive quality of gunpowder is due to the fact that it will burn with great rapidity without contact with air and that in burning it liberates large volumes of gas.

GUTTA-PERCHA—Making in sheets, steam-heated mixers and calenders are used. When mixed, beeswax is added to keep the gutta-percha from sticking to the rollers, and oxide of iron and oxide of zinc is also added. The sheets are sprinkled with talcum powder to prevent adhering when rolled up. Hazard is mild. Gutta-percha is rubber.

GYPSUM is **sulphate of lime.** Found in rock formation. It is a slow conductor of heat, as it contains in its mass a multitude of infinitely fine air cells. Gypsum manufacturers claim that three inches of gypsum properly applied to steel or ironwork will hold the temperature of the metal to about 300 deg. F. when exposed to 2,200 deg. F. for a period of four hours.

GYPSUM ARCH (Fire Test)—A 4-inch panel flat arch of gypsum and shavings reinforced with Clinton Wire Cloth, two inches cinder concrete fill on top and soffit of arch covered with 1½ inches of plaster, 1 part cement and 3 parts composition plaster. Span of arch 5 feet 3 inches center of I beams. Furnace of 12-inch concrete, interior about 9 feet above grating on which the fire was placed. Heat averaged 1,700 degrees for 4 hours. The gypsum arch surprised those in charge with its unexpected strength. The arch had been in place about two weeks. The arch was intact—the wire mesh reinforcement exposed where water from hose stream washed the plaster off, about 3 inches remaining show result of calcination; the lower flanges of I beams were exposed. The sawdust showing in arch is natural in color showing heat did not penetrate through arch further than one-half inch. No load test applied.

Water Application—At intervals of 5 minutes the following was applied: $2\frac{1}{2}$-inch hose with $1\frac{1}{8}$-inch nozzle, 100 pounds pressure at hydrant. First, stream of one minute duration at each of two doors to quench fires, one minute streams on arch, outside flushed for one minute, hose applied three times to interior of furnace to cool and wash down.

GYPSUM PLASTER MILLS—Reduce gypsum to the finest possible powder or flour before passing it to the cookers or calcining kettles and then to apply only such degree of heat as will serve to carry off such proportion of its contained moisture as will prevent the voluntary setting or hardening of the finished material when exposed to the atmosphere. Inspect carefully before binding lines.

H

HAIR—Human hair stocks are not considered desirable, owing to susceptibity of stock.

HAIR CURLERS are made of piece or scrap leather, cut and sewed with a cotton filling through which runs a wire. Hazards are storage and sorting of scrap leather into which considerable quantities of rubbish find their way; sewing machines, storage and use of cotton batting or tow. Usually untidy appearance.

HAIR-DRESSERS—Use alcohol for massage purposes, and in lamps for curling irons, electric curling irons and hair dryers, gas-heated hair dryers. Some use benzine for cleaning hair goods and also make cosmetics on the premises.

HAIR FABRIC as used for nets or braid. The hair is reduced to a paste by a solvent, run through an artificial silk spinner and drawn out in threads. Can be braided or woven like horse hair.

HAIR GOODS—Manufacturing—The hair is, washed in hot water with or without disinfectant, bleached (usually with peroxide or hydrogen), dried in dry room, curled on irons, hand combed, or dyed. Use aniline dyes, muriatic and sulphuric acids. See Dry Rooms, also Bleaching.

HAIR NETS are made by hand from Chinamen's queues or from combings of women's hair.

HAIR ORNAMENTS are usually made of celluloid, ivory, imitation ivory, vegetable ivory or bone. Involves hazards of celluloid working on power machinery. See Celluloid.

HALLS—Buildings used for halls and lodge rooms are usually of large, open area; either frame or ordinary brick construction with unprotected floor openings. May have miscellaneous stores on ground floor. The hall proper usually has a complete stage equipment; the stage constructed of wood or other light material; makeshift dressing rooms and an abundance of old properties and scenery which accumulate and are rarely ever removed. The dance floor is highly polished, and care should be exercised in storing of oil and floor mops. Gangsters frequent the poorer class halls. Many fires are caused by smoking. Fires once started in this class are hard to extinguish. Poor fire record.

HALVING—To notch together two timbers which cross each other so deeply that the joint thickness shall only equal that of one whole timber.

HANGERS—Fixtures projecting below a ceiling to support the journals of long lines of shafting, or piping.

HANDKERCHIEFS—Fancy handkerchiefs are mounted on colored pasteboard which, when wet, may stain and thereby reduce the value of the goods. The manufacturing consists of cutting, sewing, hemstitching and ironing. Classed as white goods manufacturing. The nature of the business requires cleanliness.

HARD COAL is almost wholly composed of carbon.

HARDWARE—Heavy hardware stocks are mostly unpolished wares and are preferable to light hardware, which is polished and therefore more susceptible to rust from moisture.

HARD WOODS—Generally classed as those cut from broad-leaved trees. Underwriters prefer hardwood and write larger lines than on soft woods. See Soft Woods.

HARDENING AND TEMPERING—Known as **Heat Treatment Process** in machine shops; consists of hardening and tempering tool steel. The steel is first placed in gas-heated hardening ovens until a certain temperature is reached and then plunged into an oil trough with agitator. The oil used is principally fish oil, flashing at about 550 deg. F. Care should be taken to see that the furnace is properly set.

HARNESS-MAKERS—Work consists of stuffing collars, sewing and oiling harness. Tow, straw, hair, or hay may be used as stuffing material.

HARNESS OIL is mainly neatsfoot oil.

HARTIN—A resin obtained from lignite.

HARTITE—A fossil resin found in coal beds.

HARTSHORN—See Ammonia.

HATCHWAY—A horizontal opening in a floor. Should be automatically trapped in order to prevent fire from gaining access to other floors. See Shafts.

HATS (FELT)—Busiest season is summer. Made of wool or fur felt. The hats are shaped from the felt in gas or steam-heated presses over plaster moulds, then laured (putting on the nap) by brushing the felt so that the hair lays in one direction and greasing with a cloth pad which is applied until a gloss is obtained. The lining is then put in. Heating of lauring stoves important, gas being principally used but sometimes kerosene oil.

Buckram frames for hats are sized with shellac, varnished and glued. See Buckram.

HAT STOCKS are very susceptible. **Derby and other** stiff hats are practically ruined as far as sale is concerned if damaged by water or smoke. **Soft hats** are not so easily damaged. **Straw hats** are usually a total loss.

HATS (STRAW)—Straw braiding is usually a separate business. In making hats, the braided straw is sewn by machinery and blocked, i. e., moistened, formed over plaster or spelter moulds and pressed in gas or steam-heated presses, then bleached or dyed, varnished or shellaced and dried. Bleaching is done by peroxide of sodium or sulphur fumes. Glue or shellac is used for sizing. Blocking presses require several rubber tube gas connections. There may also be a foundry for making spelter moulds. Paper boxes may also be made on the premises. The arrangement of glue kettles and construction of dry rooms and bleaching rooms are most important hazards. See Bleaching, Dry Rooms, Sulphur.

HATTERS' FURS—See Furs.

HATTERS' SUPPLIES—Stock consists of embossed or plain lining or those stamped with maker's name, sweat bands and trimmings. Use rubber cement for cementing leather, gas crimpers for linings, embossing presses and stenciling presses.

HAUNCHES—The parts of an arch from the skewback to the keystone.

HAY—Spontaneous combustion in sweating hay is one of the chief causes of the large barn loss. According to the Ohio bulletin, spontaneous combustion in hay originates in the following manner:

"The cells in hay continue to live and breathe for some time after it is cut, and they alone in a close mow, heat the hay to a temperature of 132 deg. F. Added to this is the heat from the microscopic spores of fungi which continue to grow in the blades of hay during its fermentation, the heat created by the development of the hay seeds and the heat of the sun upon the roof. These three causes, acting together, may heat closely packed hay stored where there is no ventilation to a temperature of 212 deg. F. The hay then begins to char; the charcoal formed absorbs oxygen and the mass grows still hotter. The hay reaches 265 deg. F., and then the mass blazes. Bran, grain and silo material may ignite spontaneously if placed under similar conditions."

HAY AND FEED STORES—Generally crowded to the doors with baled hay with more or less of it loosely scattered about. Smoking prohibited. Method of heating and lighting important. Dust hazard is mild.

HAZARD—The word "hazard," as applied to fire insurance, carries the same meaning as in ordinary usage, and means the point of danger, or to be in jeopardy or danger. The fire hazard is the inherent quality or surrounding of a risk or piece of property which makes it more or less liable to contagion or destruction by fire. Powder or gasoline is hazardous. Frame dwellings are more hazardous than steel structures. The risk is the thing insured, the hazard is the danger which surrounds the risk. (Fire Facts, issued by Washington Surveying and Rating Bureau.) See Risk.

HAZARD, PHYSICAL—Any feature of a risk which affects the risk, either structurally or from conditions therein.

H. C. TYPE AND PLATE CLEANING FLUID—A benzine substitute acceptable to underwriters as not dangerous.

HEADER BEAM—(Also see Chimney Construction). The beam on which is fastened the stirrups for beam supports or into which is framed the joist It is also used in floor opening construction.

HEADER COURSE—A course of brick laid with end outward in wall to form a bond. At least every sixth course in brick wall should be a header course.

HEAT is a physical property obtained by mechanical energy; by passing an electrical current through a substance; from the sun, or by chemical means.

HEATERS (Water Heaters)—The gas flame flaring out, caused by wind blowing down vent pipe, has caused fires. Vents should be carried above roof and be equipped with wind deflector. Vents should never terminate in an attic or concealed space—the heat is apt to bank up and cause fire. If in contact with wood, the continued heat, while even at low temperatures, carbonizes the wood which is apt to burst into flame.

HEATING APPARATUS—If in doubt as to whether it is unsafe or not, place the hand on the combustible material nearest the heater. If the hand cannot remain because of the heat, be on the safe side and consider it unsafe.

HEATING, COMBINATION SPRINKLER HEATING SYSTEMS—See Sprinkler and Heating Systems.

HEAVY OIL—The fractional distillate obtained from coal tar between 225 to 270 deg. C. Inflammable.

HEELBALL—Composition of lamp-black and wax. Used by shoemakers. Manufacturing process is hazardous.

HEMSTITCHING (manufacturing), employ ordinary sewing machines and gas-heated crimpers, which usually have rubber tube connections.

HEIGHT OF A BUILDING is the distance from the curb or street level to the highest point of the roof in case of flat roofs, or the average height of the gables in case of roofs having a pitch of more than 20 degrees. The height of a building seriously affects its insurance. It is very difficult to fight fires "up in the air" as the ordinary fire steamer or tower is not designed for excessive height. In very high buildings inside standpipes are relied on for furnishing water for extinguishing purposes. (N. F. P. A.)

HEIGHTS AND AREAS IN FACTORY BUILDINGS—Factory buildings of excessive height and area have long been recognized by underwriting organizations as a grave danger to life and property, owing to the difficulty of controlling fires in them. It is logical to assume that the men best fitted to determine safe limits of heights and areas are the men who have made a life work of combating fires under all conditions of weather and hazard. The following is the average of the replies of 50 fire chiefs throughout the country.

Type of building	Stories	Area between fire walls in sq. ft.
Brick or joisted construction, not sprinklered	3.2	5,200
F. P. construction, not sprinklered	5.3	9,300
Brick or joisted construction, sprinklered	4.8	10,500
F. P. Sprinklered	7.5	21,600

(From booklet, Ira H. Woolson.)

HEMP—Hemp without a prefix such as manila hemp, sisal hemp, etc., is generally understood to mean the fibres from the true hemp plant. The basis of all vegetable fibres is to be found in cellulose; a compound belonging to a class of naturally occurring substances known as carbohydrates. Ordinary hemp is classed as a soft fibre which must be handled at once, if damaged, if any salvage is to be expected. From the underwriting standpoint, fibres may be divided into two principal classes, i. e., hard and soft fibres. Hard fibres, by virtue of their construction, do not absorb water rapidly when immersed and do not heat or decompose as rapidly as do the soft fibres. Hemp requires about 110 days for its growth, and is cut either by hand or special machinery. The hemp stalks are dried, set in shooks and sometimes bundled and stacked. Later the shooks or stacks are opened and the hemp again spread out for exposure to action of the dew, frost, and sun, which dissolves the gums holding the filaments together and makes the inner woody stem dry and causes it to fall away readily when passed through the breaker. Hemp exposed to a heat of 300 degrees practically destroys the fibre. Fibres in storage warehouses, if thoroughly wet down after a fire, have been known to cause the collapse of the building walls due to the swelling and expansion of the fibre from the excessive absorption of water. Large masses of this fibre, when wet, heat rapidly and soon decay, and unless steps are taken at once, very little or no salvage can be effected. Authorities seem to be divided as to whether fibres are subject to spontaneous combustion, although the following authorities are quoted as follows:

Hemp, especially if gathered in wet seasons, is very liable to get heated. Experience at Maysville, Kentucky, indicated that wet hemp is a very dangerous neighbor. Many of the fires that occurred there in hemp could not be satisfactorily traced to any other cause than spontaneous burning. (Harris' Ins. Chemistry.)

Hemp in a pure and thoroughly dry condition may attain such a degree of desiccation, under the influence of moderate warmth, the radiant heat from a stove or piping, and in summer from the rays of the sun, that pyrophoric carbon is formed, and the mass takes fire. (Von Schwartz in "Fire and Explosion Risks."—(D. Van Nostrand Co.)

T. E. Sears, an authority on fibres, states that as far as he could learn, no positive proof has ever been given that fibres are subject to spontaneous combustion. Hemp mills as a class, are not very desirable insurance. Hemp in the field is a rather new feature for underwriters and very little information is available, owing to the lack of experience with this class. Owing to the nature of the soil in California, perhaps only the tall-growing single-stalk variety can be grown. The tariff rate of 6 per cent. in some locations is charged and this would indicate somewhat the hazard involved. Aside from the spontaneous combustion (probable) hazard, inspectors should see that the fields are cleared of all stubble or foul stuff which would permit a fire to communicate from stack to stack; find out whether the insurance also covers in the factory or shredding building; carefully note all exposing buildings and distance from the railroad tracks on account of sparks from locomotive; gasoline tractors used in the fields; lightning, and smoking by the employes. See Fibres.

HEMP HURDS—Formerly a waste product, is now being used in paper making.

HENEQUEN—See Fibres.

HERAKLIN—Used for blasting purposes; explosive.

HERROLIN—A liquid used in the gasoline motor industry. It is diluted with gasoline to make the gasoline vapor more explosive. It is really nothing more than highly purified and distilled gasoline which seems to regenerate other gasoline when mixed.

HELICAL STAIRWAY—A spiral stairway.

HIDES AND SKINS (T. O. Gildersleeve)—The name "hides" is commonly given to the undressed skins of the large domestic animals, such as oxen, horses, etc., while those of the smaller animals are called skins. See Tear-offs.

Green Hides are salted and dried. The salt acts as a preservative, keeping the albumen inactive. The dried hides are dried in open air and the albumen becomes inactive and in both cases they can be kept for a long time. They are receiving today in New York City hides from Japan and China. (Considered good insurance.)

If **Salt Hides** become wet, the water washes out the preserving quality or salt and the albumen becomes active and they decompose very soon if not resalted, especially in hot weather. (Considered good insurance.)

Dry Hides wet with water become soft and the albumen becomes active and will decompose very soon if not dried almost immediately. The actual loss in both cases, salt and dry, should be small. (Considered good insurance.)

Dressed Hides such as harness and sole leather undergo various processes in tanning and are more susceptible to fire damage on account of the oils used in finishing. Water is apt to cause stains, but if immediately refinished the salvage should be large. (Not as good as undressed hides.)

Pickled Hides (brine solution) are skivers and thin hides. If dried will crack and break. These are shipped in brine in barrels. (Good insurance.)

Undressed Hides are not as susceptible to fire as dressed hides, but if exposed to excessive heat they become so hard that they will crack and break. (Not so good as pickled hides.)

Water would not have any bad effect on hides in barrels unless the barrels are open, then it would weaken the brine and possibly discolor the top hides. Fire possibly would not effect stock in closed barrels, and if open would only damage the top hides if salvaged at once. Should fire burst the barrels a large loss may result. Water has a damaging effect on skins, especially if not dried at once.

HIGH PRESSURE STEAM—Most rating bureaus consider 15 lbs. to the square inch as high pressure. Below this pressure they are classed as low. Sometimes the safety valve can be adjusted so that when 15 lbs. is exceeded the steam will blow off.

HIGH PRESSURE SYSTEM (New York City)—This system is supplied by pumps. Six of 5,000 gallons capacity each, in each Oliver and Gansevoort street pumping station. As soon as the alarm of fire is sounded the pumps are started and 125 lbs. pressure is immediately ready. By 'phoning the pumping station, this pressure is increased according to the nature of the alarm, in 25-lb. installments until a maximum of 500 lbs. is reached. See Water Mains.

HIGH WINES—See Distilleries.

HIP ROOF—One that slopes four ways, thus forming angles called hips.

HIPS—Pieces of timber placed in an inclined position at the corners or angles of a roof.

HOARDING—A temporary closed fence of boards placed around a building in course of construction.

HOG-CHAIN BEAM—A beam strengthened by tie-rods under same sprung from end to end of beam, with straining posts below, under which passes the tie-rods. Used to prevent bending or buckling.

HOLD DUST (a substitute for sawdust)—Composed of sawdust and wood fibre treated with a solution of ammonium phosphate in dilute triatonic alcohol, certain salts, a disinfectant, traces of iron and aniline coloring matter. Will not burn at ordinary temperatures.

HOLLOW FINISH—Sheathing, lath and plaster, etc., for walls, ceilings or partitions, which allow a hollow space back of same.

HOLLOW METAL DOORS AND TRIM—These are considered next in merit to standard fire doors, which are too ungainly to be used in office buildings. Some time ago a fire on the 26th floor of the Singer Building, New York City, completely burned out the entire contents of a room used for the storage of old records; but was confined to the room by the hollow metal door.

HOLLOW SQUARE—A group of adjoining or adjacent buildings arranged in the form of a square with a yard or court in center. Fires communicate through the windows or other openings (unless protected) at the angles formed by the buildings.

HOOD—A metal canopy placed over a gas range, coal range, retort or other stove to catch vapors, smoke or gasses and pass them out of the buildings through a vent pipe. Hoods, if covered with two inches of asbestos, may be placed not less than nine inches below a combustible ceiling. If without asbestos covering, the distance should be eighteen inches. See Ranges.

HOOPS FOR SPRINKLER TANKS should be round. The flat hoops rust, and their condition cannot be ascertained until they rust through.

HOPPER—A container such as a bin with spout, used for feeding grain, etc., to mills or machinery. A temporary storage bin.

HOPS are hand picked and dried in kilns on screen floor over furnace having a pan of sulphur on top. When baled, and in warehouses, are difficult to burn. When wet, will expand sufficiently to burst the walls of buildings. Susceptible to smoke or water damage.

HORIZONTAL EXITS—Openings or means of egress from a floor to the corresponding floor of an adjoining building by means of a doorway cut through a fire wall and protected by standard fire doors. See Fire Exit Partition.

HORN BLACK or animal black is almost identical with bone black, but is generally in a more finely divided form. Animal refuse, albumen, gelatine, horn hoof shavings, etc., are subjected to dry distillation in a still or retort; the black carbonaceous mass which is left is washed with water and powdered in a mill. Used for printers' ink, blackening, and the cheaper grade of varnishes and paint.

HORN AND FERTILIZER FACTORY—Concerns sometimes use celluloid scrap. This is mixed indiscriminately with the horn, etc., and ground by the "pressed horn and meal worker," then placed in dryers. While the temperature will not ignite the horn dust it readily fires celluloid dust and frequent fires are likely to occur.

HORSE OIL—Obtained by boiling down flesh and fat; used in making palm or rosin soap.

HORSE-POWER—This term is intended to express the amount of work that a power plant will do. The word was coined by James Watt, the father of the steam engine. He finally decided that a dray horse was capable of doing 33,000 foot-pounds of work in one minute, and so this amount of work he called a horse-power. Example—Horse pulling 3,300 pounds vertically upward 10 feet in one minute exerts one horse-power. See Foot-Pound.

HORSES—The sloping timbers which carry the steps in a staircase.

HORSES AND OTHER LIVE STOCK—The policy form usually limits the amount payable in case of loss for each animal; thus, $2,000 on horses, in case of loss, no one horse to be valued at over $200. Numerous losses have been paid where unscrupulous dealers have substituted old "skates" for good stock and then set fire to the stable. After a serious fire it is hard to determine the true value of stock. The bodies of horses which have been killed in a fire become bloated. This, and the fact that all the hair and skin have been burned off, make it almost impossible to judge the value of the animal. See Stables.

HORSES STABLED ABOVE GRADE—See Stables.

HOSE—In the manufacture of fabric-covered rubber hose, the hazards are those of rubber working with vulcanizing, weaving and covering. If covered with flexible metal, there is a machine shop hazard, with metal spinning. This hose is vulcanized in a very long vulcanizer sometimes 30 feet long. See Rubber Works.

HOSE STREAMS (Effective height of), according to E. V. French.

1⅛-inch smooth nozzle Length of hose	Limit of height, with moderate wind With 100 lbs. at hydrant	With 80 lbs. at hydrant	With 60 lbs. at hydrant
ft.	ft.	ft.	ft.
100	88	82	67
200	82	72	59
300	74	65	52
400	67	58	44
500	62	52	40
700	53	43	33
1,000	42	34	25

HOSIERY AND UNDERWEAR STOCKS—Usually in pasteboard boxes. Woolens are subject to shrinkage or stain if wet. Cotton goods can be washed and salvaged.

HOSPITALS—Usually consist of a group of ordinary constructed brick buildings with frame roof structures or cupolas, and freely communicating, and with unprotected floor openings, especially stair wells. Fire hazards are laundries, kitchens, paint and carpenter shops, medicines or oils boiling over on stoves, storage of drugs and chemicals, including ether, Columbian spirits and alcohol, and other common hazards. In cities, hospitals have fire drills of all employees, including nurses and staff, with fire alarm systems and standpipes with hose.

HOSTILE FIRE is one that leaves its seat of origin. See Friendly Fire.

HOT BLAST—Is a term used in conflagrations. In the Chicago fire, the fire started outside the congested district, developed into hot-blast form, then swept through and beyond the congested district, and finally burned out for lack of fuel. These fires cannot be stopped by firemen while the wind holds out, but they have been checked and deflected upwards by barriers consisting of two or more fire walls, or their equivalent, with a free air space between as in the case of fires out of control, which have been stopped by a mere alley, with buildings fully shuttered on each side. (From paper by Albert Blauvelt, Before American Society of Mechanical Engineers.) See Flames; see Conflagration Blast.

HOTELS, especially of the better class, are considered

good risks. This is due mainly to the superior management and careful scrutiny given by all in charge, day and night. As a general rule the construction of the non-fireproof hotel is not so good on account of the large well-holes, furred walls, and poorly protected floor openings. They are inspected regularly by city departments on account of the lives at stake, and the fire fighting equipment is usually in good order. Fires have been caused by chefs pouring grease on top of ranges for the purpose of hastening cooking by getting top of range red hot. See Apartment Hotel; also Seashore Hotels.

HOT HOUSES connected to florist shops, fair risks if heating apparatus is safe.

HOUSEHOLD INVENTIONS—Consist of kitchen utensils of tin, aluminum, enamelled, plated and japanned ware. Hazards include wood and metal working with japanning by spraying or dipping. Fire record of class is poor.

HOUSEKEEPING—This expression is used to denote the care and cleanliness about a plant. See Dust.

HOUSE WRECKERS OR MOVERS—Equipment consists of ropes, rigging, tackle, lubricating oils, second-hand lumber, shoring timbers, building materials.

HOUSINGS—In roller mills, the vertical supports for the boxes in which the journals revolve.

HUMIDOR—A box or room (usually of wood), in which cigars are kept moist by using wet sawdust on the floor or by sprinkling water on the floor.

HYDRANT PRESSURES according to E. V. French.

The following table shows the hydrant pressures needed with various lengths of hose to discharge 250 gallons per minute through a 1⅛-inch nozzle:

Length of Hose	Pressure at Hydrant
100 feet	63 lbs.
200 "	77 "
300 "	92 "
400 "	106 "
500 "	120 "
700 "	149 "
1000 "	192 "

HYDRANTS—The approved fire hydrant or fire plug is so constructed that when the valve is closed by raising a flange on the rod all the water remaining in the hydrant is allowed to escape through an opening at the bottom where it runs to waste into the ground, through the open lower end of the frost jacket. This jacket is a hollow cast-iron cylinder surrounding the working parts of the hydrant. Without this arrangement, water remaining in the hydrant would freeze and burst the hydrant. Upon the approach of winter all hydrants should be tested for proper draining to prevent freezing.

HYDRATE composed of salt, oxide or acid with water.

HYDRAULICS is the science of the flow of water through pipes and the raising of water to various heights.

HYDROCARBON is a liquid composed of carbon and hydrogen. Flashes at zero F. Classed as inflammable. Hydrocarbons: all compounds of carbon and hydrogen.

HYDRO-CARBON OIL is obtained from crude petroleum and from the tar obtained from bituminous coal. Flash 200-500 deg. F.

HYDROCHLORIC ACID (muriatic)—A corrosive liquid formed by combining hydrogen with chlorine. Not inflammable. See Acids. Usually kept in carboys.

HYDROCYANIC ACID—A colorless, volatile, very inflammable liquid, used for fumigating to destroy the flour moth in flour mills.

HYDRODYNAMICS—There are four important but simple considerations which must be kept in mind for understanding the dynamics of water pressure. **First**, water, like other liquids, exerts equal pressure in all directions owing to the fact that its molecules move freely over and upon each other. Pressure exerted upon water in a hollow ball with numerous perforations would expel the water from all the perforations with equal force. This, it need not be explained, is the principal of the hydraulic press, where the pressure of a small pipe of water exerted over a wide surface shows the same pressure for every square inch of such wider surface. It is the principle upon which an inch pipe inserted tightly in a barrel full of water will burst the barrel when the water reaches a certain height in the pipe, although the weight of water in the pipe may be trifling. **Secondly, water** like any solid, has a known weight for a given quantity. **Third,** water will flow with less or greater velocity through pipes according to the pressure exerted upon it, which pressure may be simply that of its own weight, due to its elevation above the point of escape from the stored body or the pressure exerted by a force pump. **Fourth,** water, like a solid in motion, is subject to the retardant effect of friction of its surface against the surfaces rubbed against. Consequently water flowing through a pipe is retarded in its flow by the friction of its particles on the sides of the pipes what is known as "skin friction," naturally greater in rough interiors of pipes than in new, smooth ones. (From lecture F. C. Moore.)

HYDROFLUORIC ACID—A fuming corrosive liquid made by treating a mineral, known as flourspar, flourite or calcium flouride with sulphuric acid. (See Etching Acid.)

HYDROGEN, the lighest of all gases, burns with a pale, blue flame, giving out much heat. Hydrogen gas is inflammable.

HYDROSTATICS is the science which treats of quiet water or water at rest in a reservoir.

I

I BEAM—An iron or steel beam, the cross section or end view of which is the shape of the letter "I".

ICE CREAM CONES—See Wafers and Cones.

ICE FORMATION—(In sprinkler piping in risks involving mechanical refrigeration). As a preventive measure, up-to-date plants have an apparatus for reducing the amount of moisture in the air used in charging the dry pipe system. This apparatus consists of an air pump taking air from a small refrigerator room constructed especially for the purpose. It is called the air chiller, and discharges back through coils and a settling drum located in the same room. A valve is placed at the bottom of the settling drum for drawing off the accumulation of water removed from the air. See Ring Ice Formation.

ICE HOUSES—Usually large, light frame construction and filled with salt hay, sawdust or hay between each cake of ice. Inspectors should note if located near water that is pure and not contaminated. Sweating hay is subject to spontaneous combustion. Instances have been known where the owner has kept the ice so long that it froze into one mass and could not be removed except by blasting, in which case the ice has no market value. The moral hazard should always be investigated.

ICE-MAKING—There are two distinct methods of freezing the water by the same evaporating agents. One is the **Can System,** whereby the filled cans are almost entirely immersed in brine which is kept cool by ammonia expansion coils. An agitation of the brine is secured by means of propeller wheels in the brine, usually operated by a motor.

The other is known as the **Plate System,** where cells are filled with water. The walls of the cells are iron plates forming a chamber, inside of which coils are placed through which brine is circulated or in which ammonia is expanded. With this system, the freezing progresses from each side and toward the center, but so as to form two plates of ice, the freezing process being arrested before the center is frozen. Iron bars are frozen in these cakes, with which they are raised out of the cells by cranes and pulleys. The cakes of ice are loosened from the plates by turning warm water into the coils. It is claimed for the plate system of ice-making that the product more nearly approximates natural frozen water, and that artificial cooling of the ice storerooms is not necessary whereas with the can system a temperature of about 28 degrees must be artificially maintained to prevent the ice from melting.

IFE—A white fibre from which cordage is made.

IMITATION LEATHER—Paper, cloth, wood pulp, celluloid, fibre and cloth sheets are the main bases. These are sized, impregnated with nitrated cotton in paste form in a calender (set of steam rolls), dried, varnished, painted or embossed or enameled. This is a hazardous process, including picking cotton and drying nitrated cotton (the same process as in making cellulose). The mixture is inflammable, and the vapors are explosive. The cellulose is mixed with substances like clay, with oils to add to the spreading qualities and then colored. As in making oil-cloth, the coating process is repeated for desired thickness. This latter feature should be in fireproof cut-off section. Embossing press and corrugating machines are mainly gas-heated. The nitrating building, picker house, boiler room and storage buildings should be detached. See Leather.

IMITATION MARBLE AND ONYX are usually made at slate quarries. The slab of slate is cut, ground and polished smoothly, and gradually submerged in a vat or tub of water. The water is streaked with paint which adheres to the slate as it submerges. When removed, the slate is baked in a kiln, polished, varnished, dried and rubbed with oils to obtain a high finish. Benzine or turpentine paint are sometimes used.

IMPOST—The upper part of a pier from which an arch springs.

IMPROVEMENTS—This class of insurance should be written with extreme care, and should, wherever possible, be included in the building or contents items. Where the improvements to buildings are written separately from the insurance on the building, they usually take the building rate with an additional charge added thereto when written separate from building insurance. Insurance complications are likely to ensue after a loss unless the same insurance company insures both the improvements and buildings. Inspection should always be made to determine the nature of the improvements. It may develop as very good insurance such as a new brick front, or on the other hand, it may be very poor insurance such as highly ornamental plaster ceilings, mirrored side walls, fresco work, wall paintings. Tenants who install permanent improvements such as mentioned above have an insurable interest in same although they properly belong to the owner of building, who (by virtue of ownership) may claim damages in case of fire. In this instance it is possible that the same loss might be paid twice, both to tenant and owner. Only competent underwriters should accept "Improvements" insurance.

INCANDESCENT ELECTRIC LAMPS called in the trade "carbon lamps." They are being rapidly replaced by Mazda and Tungsten lamps. An extensive detail process but briefly described is as follows: Glass bulbs received with collars attached, two copper wires tipped with platinum are inserted and the filament put on. The filaments are of ordinary absorbent cotton in solution of zinc chloride, injected into wood alcohol under air pressure in a bulb which solidifies the filament; placed in carbonizing furnace where it remains until carbonized. The temperature is about 4000 deg. F. Flashing follows, which process is, passing an electric current through the filament in the presence of gasoline vapor. The flashing apparatus consists of a glass container of gasoline from which is passed a rubber tube to a vacuum vessel containing the filament which is held by clamps connected with electric current. The current passing through the filament brings it to incandescence, and the gasoline vapor passed into the vacuum, the vapor being broken down and a black metallic appearing covering of hydrocarbon deposited on the filament. It is then cemented to the platinum (or substitute) wires. The bulb and the mount are fused together and the air exhausted from the bulb. A more perfect vacuum is created by the use of amorphorous phosphorus and alcohol. (Numerous spark fires due to friction are caused at this point more than at any other in the process.) The lamps are tested with electric current, to determine the candlepower and defects, packed and shipped. Electric hazard severe. Glass blowing, blow pipe work, use of alcohol, zinc chlorides and amosphous phosphorus, carbonizing ovens, flashing with gasoline vapors, buffing and packing are the usual hazards.

INCENDIARISM—The act or practice of maliciously setting fire to buildings. See Pyromaniac.

INCENSE—The material is a mixture of powdered charcoal, starch and perfumes, molded into small cakes and dried. The only severe hazard is the grinding of charcoal.

INCOMBUSTIBLE—Materials which not readily ignite when subjected to ordinary fire.

INCOMBUSTIBLE BUT NOT FIREPROOF—The term refers to steel skeleton construction built with unprotected iron work.

INCREASE OF HAZARD—The policy states that if there be any increase of hazard, the assured shall notify the insurance company. The courts have liberally interpreted this clause, giving the insured the benefit of the doubt in most cases. An increase of rate does not necessarily signify an increase of hazard.

INCUBATORS AND BROODERS—The most popular is the type heated by kerosene oil lamps. The end of the incubator should be protected with non-combustible material plus an air space of at least 1 inch between the metal shield and the incombustible material. The heater should be all metal with riveted joints. The heated air pipe entering the incubator ought not to be in contact with the woodwork. All woodwork should be protected with metal or asbestos. The lamp should be of metal bowl type, rigidly set, and arranged so that it cannot be filled while lighted or while it is in the incubator.

Brooders should be of non-combustible material. In place of kerosene oil type, some employ hot water, gas or electricity, and the rules governing the installations of these are those of approved general practice. Kerosene oil-heated types of brooders or incubators have a poor fire record.

INDEPENDENT WALL—An outside wall carrying loads of but one building.

INDIA RUBBER is the solidified sap of the rubber tree. See Caoutchouc.

INDIA RUBBER CEMENT is India rubber solution of coal tar naphtha.

INDIAN COTTON, called **Lintus** or **Linters,** is similar to shoddy.

INDIAN SPIRITS—A benzine substitute; acceptable to underwriters; has a flash point of about 105 deg. F.

INDIGO—A blue coloring substance originally obtained from the indigo plant; now artificially prepared as a coal tar product. In underwriting, care should be taken to see that this stock is kept away from other stocks. A hose stream played on this material will cause colors to run through the building and damage other stocks.

INDIGOTINE—A dyestuff used in the color blue.

INFANTS' AND CHILDRENS' WEAR—Usually white goods. Susceptible, but if attended to at once after a fire, considerable salvage can be derived. Subject to mildew and the colors running from ribbons. Usually kept in glass show cases.

INFLAMMABLE LIQUIDS should be stored in rooms constructed of 8-inch brick or 6-inch tile walls with similar roofs and doors with sills raised 4 to 6 inches to prevent the liquid from running into other rooms. All doors should be standard automatic, and windows wired glass (double glazed preferred) in hollow metal sash and frame. Good ventilation is a primary requirement. All liquids flashing under 100 deg. F. are classed inflammable.

INFLAMMABLE VAPORS—Those heavier than air settle close to the lowest level and are present in an invisible stream leading to an opening of any kind such as a door or stairway. An open light 100 feet away may be sufficient to ignite this vapor. Precautions as to ventilation, electrical devices, vent fans, etc., are the necessary requirements.

INGOT—A lump of cast metal, as for instance: a pig of cast iron.

INHERENT HAZARDS—The hazards found in the ordinary risk of a given occupation aside from the common hazards of light, heat and power or of special processes. See Hazard.

INITIALS—It is well not to pass a line of insurance without ascertaining the first name of the assured. Many women use the initial of the first name without prefixing Miss or Mrs. This is often resorted to as a subterfuge to mislead the insurance company into believing that the insured is a man. See Woman's Names.

INK (Printing Ink)—Ordinarily made of linseed oil, lampblack, soap and nut oils, dry colors, Japan, varnish and rosin oil. Manufacturing requires the use of grinding mills, mixers, calenders, kettles and furnaces. Ink mills usually consist of three calender rolls, steam-heated, one revolving in the direction opposite to those above and below. The paste is ground between the rolls for mixing and smoothing.

INSECT AND VERMIN EXTERMINATORS—May contain carbon bisulphide, gasoline, or other similar substances. Rat exterminator can be made of ground sponge saturated with flour, sugar, grease, barium carbonate.

INSPECTOR—One who inspects the risk on which a company assumes liability. He should have a good knowledge of building construction and hazards and also know something about machinery, electricity and chemistry.

INSPECTORS should "train their noses" as well as their minds and eyes. In these days of new processes, the olfactory sense will often indicate and detect the use or presence of substances which may not be visible but which can be detected by smell if the inspector is familiar with odors.

The best inspector is not always the one who boasts loudly of his education and finishes his day's work in spotless clothing, immaculate linen and with lily-white hands. There are many inspectors arrayed thusly who can only be dubbed, "The Sign Readers." The ambitious, conscientious and successful inspector will always endeavor to obtain all the information due him, in probing for causes, conditions and results, with the manner of a gentleman, the speech of a diplomat and the common sense of a man. He will always attempt to investigate "concealed spaces," whether he begrims his skin or his clothing. And last but not least, he will never allow himself to think, or act as though he believed, that he owns any person's property, because he bears the title, Inspector. The assured invariably judges the company from the speech or actions of its representative. In conclusion, let the Inspector who thinketh he knoweth it all, take heed, lest he be made ashamed; because that type of an Inspector is usually a pronounced failure. Inspectors should always point out the defects of a risk to the tenant and offer suggestions toward their correction. All processes, special machinery, common hazards and exposures, should be set forth in the report. There is a wide difference between inspection work by rating bureaus and the work done by individual companies. In the former, construction and the physical hazards as relating to rate-making are noted while in the latter the "human element" enters, i. e., the moral hazard, general appearance, prosperity, class of help and other features which a company requires for underwriting purposes and which are not brought out in the rating schedule.—(Chas. E. Jahne.)

INSTRUMENTS (SURGICAL)—The hazards are those of machine shops with forging, annealing, emery wheels, blow pipes, engraving. The parts are usually cleaned with benzine to remove grease or oil and treated in a bath of nitric and sulphuric acids.

Instruments and razors are subject to rust from dampness and do not necessarily have to become wet.

INSULATE—To cover with a non-conducting substance.

INSULATED—A body is insulated when it is separated from other bodies by a non-conducting substance.

INSULATING COMPOUND—For electric wires and cables, the composition is principally rosin, pitch, parafin, gilsonite, montan wax, grahamite and prepared asphalt. These are heated in steam kettles or Mott kettles with direct fire heat. Such a composition has a very high flash point.

INSULATION, on electric wires, in burning give off fumes which are injurious to or will suffocate firemen when fighting fire.

INSULATORS—Substances which do not conduct electricity such as glass, gutta-percha or porcelain. See Air Space; also Asbestos Insulators.

INSURANCE—A system of collecting sums of money (called premiums) from a number of people to pay the losses of a few. The rate therefore should be graded according to classes of trade to effect an equal distribution of the cost (premium) among those businesses which have shown a larger percentage of fires than some others.

INTERIOR DECORATORS—Those occupying small shops or grade floor stores are in some cases considered desirable insurance risks when they have only a few pieces of furniture or draperies on display while other shops may be crowded with furniture to be remade, antiques, odds and ends, draperies, stocks of wall-paper and present an untidy condition. The higher class concerns usually occupy several floors of a building in a good section with offices, showrooms and workrooms. Here we may find upholstering, drapery-making, sewing, furniture repairing, also retail stocks of fancy goods or notions. See Painters.

INTERTIE—Small pieces of timber placed horizontally between, and framed into vertical pieces to tie them together.

INVERTED ARCHES are frequently built under openings in order to distribute the pressure more evenly over the foundation.

INVERTED GAS-LIGHT mantles have caused many fires owing to the red-hot carbon dropping on combustible material.

INVISIBLE HEAT—See Flames.

IODIDES—As chlorine forms chlorides with many of the metals, so iodine forms iodides with them.

IODIDE OF NITROGEN—A highly explosive black powder, used in combination with drugs.

IODINE is produced to some extent from the ashes of deep seaweed, but mainly from crude Chile saltpeter or Caliche. It is bluish-black, lustrous crystalline solid, slightly volatile and sparingly soluble in cold water. Melts at about 114 deg. C. (238 deg. F.) and boils at about 184 deg. C. It is usually imported from South America in small hardwood kegs bound with iron hoops, covered with dried skins which are said to be intended to keep the kegs from falling apart should the destructive action of the contents on the wood and metal weaken the keg to the point of collapse before the iodine is ready for use.

Owing to its great tendency to stain everything with which it or its vapor comes in contact it should not be stored in buildings containing other merchandise, unless it is on a floor lower than those on which the other stocks are kept.

Iodine Extract presents a better insurance proposition, as it is kept in bottles packed in wooden boxes.—(W. J. Tallamy.)

IRON—**Cast Iron** has considerable carbon, **Wrought Iron** no carbon, **Steel** about one per cent. carbon. When an iron band or hoop is first heated and then at once placed upon the body which it is intended to surround, it shrinks or contracts as it cools and thereby fits very tightly.

IRON BED AND SPRING MANUFACTURING—Mainly a machine shop hazard with drills, presses, rolls, stretching and special machines. Parts are sometimes dipped in black asphaltum or coated with aluminum or bronze paint. Excelsior pads used for wrapping. The class has a poor fire record.

IRON BORINGS, TURNINGS AND FILINGS, are more or less subject to spontaneous combustion when moist. Should be kept in metal receptacles. Sometimes called "swarf."

IRON CLAD—A frame wall sheathed with corrugated iron, replacing the clapboards.

IRON FRONT BUILDINGS—If in rows are apt to have a hollow space back of the iron fronts. Fire is likely to travel from one building to another unless this concealed space is backed up with brick or other fire-resisting material.

IRON MASS—A mixture of wood shavings with hydrated ferric oxide. Used to remove sulphur from coal gas.

IRON MASS (SPENT)—Called spent-iron sponge. Is iron mass after saturation in gas purification. Subject to spontaneous combustion on exposure to air.

IRON RUST—Oxide of iron.

IRON-ON-STUD WALL—Corrugated iron or sheet iron fastened directly on studding.

ISINGLASS—Bladder of fishes. The better grade is made from the giant sturgeon of Russia. See Mica.

ISOLATED—A building is isolated when it stands alone with no other building in vicinity.

ISOMETRIC DRAWINGS—All vertical lines are 90 deg., while all other lines are 30 deg.

ISOPRENE—The raw product from which artificial rubber is produced.

ISTLE—A fibre of a tropical American plant, grown abundantly in Mexico. Used in brush making. See Fibres.

IXTLE—Same as Istle.

IVORY BLACK—Made by burning or charring chips of elephant tusks and other hard bones free from fat.

J

JACKETED—A means to prevent "direct" heating by placing a steam or water jacket around the kettle or other receptacle containing the substance to be melted, thereby preventing such substances as glue, pitch or wax from overflowing onto the fire. Also an insulating covering on steam pipes.

JACK-RAFTERS—Small rafters laid on the purlins of a roof for supporting the shingle laths.

JACK SHAFT—Intermediate driving shafting. Usually driven by main shafting and drives the countershafting.

JAMBS—The sides of an opening through a wall, as door, window and fireplace jambs.

JAPAN BLACK—A varnish made with tar and alcohol, or lamp-black and resins.

JAPAN DRYERS—Made of linseed oil and gum shellac cooked in a varnish kettle. Litharge, burnt umber, sugar of lead and turpentine may be added. Naphtha and benzine may be used, especially as a thinner. When cooked to a thick substance called a "pill" it is cooled and thinned. Baked Black Japans, made of linseed oil and asphalt, copal resins, kauri gums and turpentine.

JAPAN WAX—A solid wax extracted from the berries of the Japanese lacquer tree. Melting point 120-125 deg. F.

JAPAN, ENAMEL AND LACQUER OVENS—To be of all metal, double wall, with air space filled with insulating material; vented to the outer air and heated by steam or electricity. Direct fire heat is a serious hazard. If gas is used, the heat should be radiated through an all-sheet metal flooring between burners and lacquered goods to prevent the vapors in oven being ignited by exposed flames. Vent pipe and oven not to be near woodwork. See Dip Tanks.

JEWELRY—Novelty jewelry is mostly imitation ware,

such as imitation pearl (glass), pins and trinkets. Shops use gas blow-pipes, small metal working machines, gas or electric-heated dry-boxes, lacquer and celluloid-enamel.

JEWELERS use benzine for watch and clock cleaning, by dipping the mechanism in an open dish of the liquid.

JEWELERS' PUTTY—An oxide of tin.

JIG SAW—A very narrow thin saw worked vertically by machinery and used for sawing curved ornaments in boards. It jigs up and down.

JOBBERS—Their method of conducting business differs in various lines. They can be classified as speculative wholesalers and are the middlemen betwen the mill or mill agent and the retailer or small manufacturer. For instance, a jobber in piece goods, silks, woolens or cotton, buys direct from the "mill agent" or commission merchant, on say a 30-day basis, or buys up small lots or "jobs" for cash. In turn he sells to the small manufacturer or retailer whose business is too small to be recognized by the "mill agent," on a longer term basis and in smaller lots as desired. For this accommodation, the buyer is willing to pay an advanced price for the goods, of say 5 to 10 per cent. which represents the jobber's profit. Also some jobbers take advantage of a manufacturer's temporary financial embarrassment and offer him a low figure on a cash basis for his product. For instance, in the cloak and suit line, a manufacturer may need some ready money to meet a note before his garments can be marketed in the regular way. A jobber may buy the garments for cash at a figure which would permit him to resell to a retailer or wholesaler at less than they could ordinarily buy direct from the manufacturer, and still make a profit for himself.

JOINTERS—Woodworking machines used to make a true surface or edge for gluing, also for trueing up smoothly, chamfering, beveling. Similar to planers except without feed rolls, the work being held against cutters by hand, producing a great deal of refuse. Cylinder head rotates rapidly and is liable to overheat bearings unless clean and properly aligned.

JOIST—A beam set on edge to which the flooring is fastened.

JOURNAL—The end or other part of shaft which rests on or against a bearing and supporting the ends of a horizontal revolving shaft.

JUNK SHOPS—While of one general class, may be subdivided into classes such as those who carry all metal, metal and rubber, or those who include paper and rags. Sometimes used as a "fence" for stolen goods, and frequently as "hangouts." Very poor fire risks.

JUTE—See Fibres.

JUTE RISKS—Raw stock consists of hemp, istle, jute, sisal, old burlap, tar, mineral oil, starch, borax, soda, tampica, talc and ammonia. Process consists of opening, picking, lapping, carding, roving, drawing, twisting, spinning, rope preparing by laying, coloring, tarring, polishing, weaving, calendering and honking. This class has a very poor fire record and should be written with extreme care. Jute is bleached by exposing the fibre to the action of permanganates and then sulphuric acid.

JUTE SHODDY is made by macerating burlap bags, sacks, etc. See Hemp; see Cordage.

K

KAKODYL—A heavy fuming liquid which takes fire when coming in contact with air.

KALAMEIN DOOR—A metal-clad door, the metal being in large sheets pressed over the wood door. Unless labeled, not considered very good in case of fire.

KALAMEIN DOOR MANUFACTURING—Metal and woodworking hazards. The metal is placed over the wood and power saws then cut through metal and wood, sometimes causing sparks to drop into the oil-soaked sawdust under the saw table. Poor fire risks.

KALAMEIN IRON is a trade name for open hearth sheet steel covered with a thin alloy of tin and lead.

KALSOMINE—A sort of lime or whiting used to coat walls.

KAPOK OR COPAC—A cotton or silky fibre covering the seeds of a tropical tree found in East and West Indies. It is a substitute for hair and cotton and used for pillows, mattresses, life preservers and linings for aviators' coats. It is non-absorbent. Heat expands it. It costs more than cotton but can be renovated simply by steaming. When loose burns very rapidly. Not subject to spontaneous combustion. Classed as a fibre. Sometimes called "Silk Floss."

KEROSENE BURNERS—Specifications for the Temporary Installation of Small Kerosene Burners for Emergency Use in Fire Boxes of Cooking Stoves, Heating Stoves, Furnaces and Boilers—Permission may be granted for the temporary use only as an emergency measure of special burners in stoves and furnaces as a substitute for coal or other fuel.

The capacity of gravity tanks containing kerosene shall not exceed 2 gallons for stoves and 5 gallons for boilers or furnaces. The tanks should preferably be located outside of building; if inside, they shall not be within 5 feet measured horizontally from any fire or flame. Pressure tanks shall not exceed 10 gallons total capacity (air and kerosene), and if inside shall not be within 10 feet measured horizontally of any fire or flame.

Tanks for kerosene shall be constructed of galvanized sheet iron or steel; all joints to be riveted and soldered or made tight by some equally satisfactory process. The shell of tank shall be properly reinforced where connections are made. The tanks shall be sufficiently strong to bear without injury the most severe strain to which they are likely to be subjected in practice. Tanks for systems under pressure shall be designed for six times the maximum working pressure and tested for twice the maximum working pressure.

Gravity tanks shall be readily accessible for filling, and be set in a drip pan constructed of galvanized sheet iron or steel, with joints riveted and soldered or made tight by some equally satisfactory process. The tank and pan shall be supported on a shelf rigidly secured to wall or partition. The drip pan shall be at least two inches deep and extend four inches beyond tank at sides and front. The wall or partition back of tank shall be covered with sheet metal, which shall extend four inches beyond the sides and twelve inches above tanks; the sheet metal shall also overlap the side of and extend to bottom of pan.

Each pressure tank shall be set in a drip pan on the floor at a safe location and protected from injury. The tanks shall be placed in a pan two inches deep and extend at least four inches beyond the tank on all sides.

A drip pan capable of holding the full capacity of supply tank shall be placed below oil burner.

Piping—Standard, full-weight wrought-iron or steel or brass pipe with substantial iron or brass fittings shall be used and connections made tight with well-fitted joints. Piping to be run as directly as possible and be protected against injury. Systems under pressure to be designed for six times the maximum working pressure, and installation, when complete, to be tested to twice the working pressure.

Any storage of oil outside of a buried tank shall be limited to 60 gallons in an oil barrel or its equivalent.

A shut-off valve should be placed in the pipe line as near as possible to oil receptacle and one near burner. (Recommendations of New York Board of Fire Underwriters.)

KEROSENE OIL—A petroleum distillate; flash point about 115-125 deg. F. See Mineral Burning Oil.

KEROSENE OIL STOVES or lamps should not be filled while lighted, or even when hot.

KETONE—Chemical group, sometimes called acetones.

KEYSTONE—The center stone in an arch.

KID GLOVES—Not considered attractive stocks because only a slight moisture will class the stock as seconds.

KILLED ACID is made by dissolving zinc in hydrochloric or muriatic acid.

KILNING is merely drying on a large scale. Inspectors should note construction of side walls, roofs and floors, and whether cut off in separate building or communicating. The heat used is preferably steam or hot air; if the latter, fan and motor should be carefully inspected. Pipes should be preferably above or at the sides of the material to be dried, not below, on account of the light material falling on the pipes and being ignited. Steam jets can be used to advantage to extinguish fires in kilns. **China kilns**, used for decorating, are mainly of brick construction; coal or coke fuel. Numerous small gas-heated kilns of special design are found in art decorating establishments. See Dry Kilns.

KILOWATT—A thousand watts. A watt is the electrical unit of power, being the product of one volt by one ampere; 746 watts equal one horse-power. See Electrical Terms.

KINDLING WOOD FACTORIES use heavy wood-working machinery, chiefly cross-cut saws. Generally crowded, and untidy with loose bark. Usually occupy old buildings and employ cheap labor. Not considered as good as ordinary woodworkers.

KING POST—The center post, or rod, extending vertically from the collar beam to the ridge board. All those on each side of it are queen posts or rods.

KIPS are the hides of young animals. See Hides.

KIRKER-BENDER SPIRAL FIRE ESCAPE consists of a spiral slide incased in a cylinder six feet in diameter. Entrance is by a passage from each floor to the tower. Persons slide to the foot of the tower on the spiral incline.

KITCHEN RANGES—When the kitchen range is placed eighteen inches from a wood lath-and-plaster or stud partition, partition must be shielded with metal extending from the floor to three feet above the range. See Stoves; also Ranges.

KNEE—A piece of timber bent to receive some weight, or to relieve a strain.

KNIT GOODS are very likely to be stained by smoke; will shrink if wet; if colored, the colors are apt to run.

KNITTING MILLS are mills making sweaters or knit goods. Process consists of washing, dyeing, picking, cutting, finishing, carding, spinning, knitting and drying. The hazards of the picker room consist of the light, inflammable stock, sometimes containing foreign matter, passing through high-speed machines. A full-fledged picker room contains a burr picker, mixing picker and duster, and lappers which discharge the stock after it passes through them into the gauze or blow room. The card room: After the raw stock is cleaned and mixed in the picker room it is transferred to the cards, which lay the fibre straight and form it into a loose roving, preparatory to spinning process. The main hazard in card rooms is the presence of foreign matter in stock, which emit sparks when coming in contact with the rolls of cards. The other processes present only mild hazards. Always remember the higher the grade of the output the better the risk. Avoid the mill with a low-grade cotton and cotton waste, especially if the picker room is not properly cut off and the card room is over the finishing room. The fire record (unsprinklered) is not very good.—R. G. Potter.

KNOCK-DOWN—Parts of an object before assembling, as chairs in knock-down condition.

K. O.—A term used by insurance men to denote a poor risk. Means "Keep off."—Gene Eagles.

KOHOLIA—A form of alcohol used as a fuel for heating in place of small portable gas or oil stoves.

L

LABELLED GOODS—See Canned Goods.

LACE CURTAINS—Cleaners and dyers use nitrate of iron, permanganate of potash, sulphuric acid and benzine. The dry room is the main hazard.

LACE PAPER WORKS—The lace paper is perforated in revolving machines, then sized or varnished. The perforating dies are mostly hand-made and many are imported. It takes from one to three months to engrave a large die ,some of which are two feet long and cylindrical in shape. Dies should be kept in vaults. All scrap paper should be baled daily. Use and Occupancy insurance should be written with caution.

LACE WORKS—The hazards are weaving, sewing, knitting, twisting, bobbin-winding, sizing, silk-throwing, embroidering, lace-making, dyeing and drying. In dyeing use muriatic, acetic and sulphuric acids. For sizing, use glycerine, gelatine, gum arabic and starch. These are heated in a steam or gas-heated kettle. Goods are bleached with chloride of lime and caustic soda. At times do considerable repair work and use benzine and alcohol for removing stains, and gas or electric irons for pressing. The needle lead pot is gas-heated. Machine repair shop work is extensive in most plants. Expensive silks should be kept in vaults. Imported machinery forms a large proportion of value. White laces are "dry dyed" by refinishers, who place them in wooden tumblers containing a yellow powder called "Dutch white," which turns the laces a creamy white.

LACES in some cases will be almost unimpaired after a serious clean-water damage if they are what is known as wash laces; but fancy laces will not, as a rule, give near as much salvage.

LACQUER FLASHES at about 75 deg. F. The preparation, storage and manufacture is very hazardous. Should not be stored in large quantities. Usually consists of nitro-cellulose dissolved in volatile solvents. Classed as inflammable.

Dry rooms for lacquered goods should have drip pans under or on steam pipes to catch excess liquid, as fires have been caused by steampipes covered with lacquer.

LACQUER FIRES—Sawdust, if spread over the surface in sufficient quantity will readily and successfully extinguish fires of inflammable liquids, especially lacquer, when contained in moderate-sized tanks, such as those ordinarily used in manufacturing plants, or small fires in these liquids on the floor. The efficiency of the sawdust is undoubtedly due to its blanketing action in floating for a time upon the surface of the liquid, thereby excluding the oxygen of the air. The sawdust itself is not very easily ignited, and when it does become ignited it burns without flame. The burning embers are not sufficient to reignite the lacquer. In sixteen fire tests the fire was put out in from 11 seconds to 1 minute 55 seconds. See Dip Tanks.

LACQUERING—See Varnishing.

LACQUER SHELLAC is a mixture of shellac and lacquer. Inflammable.

LACTEIN—See Casein.

LADIES' FURNISHINGS, if not kept in cardboard boxes or in cases, will suffer severe damage from smoke and water. Considered no better than millinery.

LADIES' TAILORS are in the same class as dressmakers. They make suits, coats and skirts for individual customers. Use gas irons for pressing and benzine for cleaning.

LAGGING—A covering of loose plank, as that placed upon centers and supporting arch stones.

LAGGING—A covering of felt or other poor conductor of heat applied to steam boilers, pipes, etc., to prevent radiation.

LALLY COLUMN consists of a steel outer shell filled with concrete under hydraulic pressure. Some rating bureaus require an outside insulation of from two to four inches of concrete or tile.

LAMP-BLACK—A kind of soot made by letting the smoke

of burning substances, such as oil, pitch or rosin, collect in a chamber lined with leather. If moist, is subject to spontaneous combustion. See Carbon Black.

LAMP EXPLOSIONS—Many of these may be prevented by trimming the wick daily. When burned for several evenings without trimming, the wick becomes black, clogged and incapable of supplying the oil clearly and uniformly, and the chimneys are sometimes filled with flame and smoke, to the embarrassment and alarm of those present. Some explosions would be prevented by never extinguishing the lamp by blowing down the chimney; for if the wick happens to be too small, the flame may be driven down into the oil. The best way is to turn it down with the button until it is extinguished.

LAMPS smoke when the wick is too high because of insufficient oxygen. Smoke is made up of little particles of carbon, because oil as well as wood contains carbon. It smokes because more oil rises in the wick than can unite with the oxygen supplied, making an imperfect combustion.

LAMP SHADES of celluloid or paper should not be placed on electric lamps or bulbs. Many bad fires have been caused by these flimsy articles.

LANTERN SKYLIGHT—Similar to monitor. A raised roof with glass sides, usually extending the entire length of a building.

LAPPER—A machine which combs out or cleans the stock, passing it over a wire mesh cylinder, and laying it in the form of a lap.

LATHE—A machine for shaping wood or metal parts by causing them to revolve while acted upon by a cutting tool held in place by a slide rest.

LATTICE GIRDER—A type of girder in which the web is made-up of diagonal iron or steel bars, which form a lattice between the flanges.

LAUGHING GAS—A mixture of one part oxygen and four parts nitrous oxide. Used by dentists.

LAUNDRIES (Chinese)—A class to be avoided. The hazards are swinging gas brackets, coal stoves of laundry type, with clothing hanging over and around them; improvised dry rooms, gas bosom ironers with rubber tube connections, gas irons, gas and coal stoves for heating irons.

LAUNDRIES (Collar, Cuff and Starched Goods)—Washing drums are revolving wood cylinders into which the goods are placed for washing. The goods are dried in centrifugal extractors, then starched and ironed. Starch kettles are either steam or gas-heated. Dry rooms are usually metal-lined and steam-heated, having an iron track on which a rack of wet goods travels which is pulled in and out on the tracks. Some dryers have an overhead traveling track with a rack, to which the goods are hung and dried by the traveller passing slowly through. Dryers should have wire mesh over steam-piping to prevent goods coming in contact. There is less dust and lint in this class of laundry than in those doing general work. **Ironers (called mangles)** are large steel rollers, cloth-covered and gas-heated. Gas mufflers are used for hand-irons. "Tipping" machines are used to finish off the fronts of collars and are gas-heated.

Power Laundries—Process consists of washing, rough-drying by wringing, and drying in centrifugal extractors, starching, ironing, and drying in dry rooms. There are special ironers, such as "art edge" ironers and "moulding ironers" for turn-down collars, both gas-heated. The old style sadiron is only used in the small store laundries. If used they should be set on a solid iron stand at least 18 inches from all woodwork. If the plant machinery is all steam process and the boiler is cut-off in a standard manner and the building is of fair construction it should be a desirable risk. Only write a small line on the stock, which is equivalent to second-hand stock.

LAUNDRY STOVES—The rule for setting is the same as for hotel ranges. When set on legs, two courses of four-inch tile are required.

LAURING—See Hats (felt).

LEAD—Derived principally from an ore called galena and has a bluish gray color. It oxidizes or tarnishes easily and melts at low temperatures.

LEAD DROSS—Material skimmed from the surface of molten lead. When cold it is non-hazardous.

LEAD NITRATE—A white, heavy, translucent salt. Not an oxidizing material.

LEASE is a contract for the use of a building for a year or term of years. If the terms of the lease are complied with, the lessee is virtually the owner during the term mentioned in the contract. A lease is a valuable holding, therefore the lessee should provide for indemnity in case the building is destroyed by fire. See Leases; see Leasehold Insurance.

There are two forms of leases. First, value of a lease, where the building is occupied by the lessee. Second, profits of a lease, where the lessee sublets the building to make a profit.

LEASES with the "self-reducing" clause are commonly written and the premium is obtained in the following manner: Policy written for eleven years for the full amount of $110,000, the tenth year for $100,000, and so on to the first year, $10,000, which added together, equals $660,000, divided by 11 years, equals $60,000, and the premium is figured on the $60,000 amount, but in case of loss the first year, assured could collect $110,000, the second year $100,000, and so on, deducting $10,000 for each year the lease has to run. It is also customary to write this insurance specifying so much reduction per month. In this case the premium may be computed upon an amount representing the average between the policy amount at the beginning of the first month and at the beginning of the last month of its term. See Leasehold Insurance.

LEASEHOLD INSURANCE—This class of insurance should be written cautiously and follow the same adjustment as the building losses. The form should be carefully scrutinized to ascertain what restrictions are included, as for instance, "building is not to be used for a certain class of business or tenants." In this instance the neighborhood may change and property could not be leased for said purpose, making leasehold insurance very undesirable. Leases should not be insured unless the assured has a good bargain. An assured may take a building during prosperous times and later be losing money in consequence of change of trade. The fire clause should always be carefully reviewed. If no fire clause appears in the form it would be acceptable as no fire restrictions would then appear. If total destruction cancels the lease the form is also a good one, but if the form reads "it is optional with the lessee or the owner," the proposition is a poor one and should not be entertained. In this latter case the building may only suffer a very small damage and the lessee or owner decide not to rebuild, in which case the company would be forced to pay a total loss up to the amount of the policy. Only competent underwriters should accept "Leasehold" insurance. See Profits of a Lease.

LEATHER—A skin is cut into three thicknesses. The top is the **"skiver"** or grain, the middle is the **"splits"** and the bottom the **"flesher."**

The wholesale leather dealers term **fancy leather,** any leather used by the bag, case, strap, belt, trunk and novelty trade.

The word fancy is used in quoting trade prices; in such cases it refers to colors.

You cannot strictly determine the limits of fancy leather, as ordinary leather is used by the bag, etc., trade. In such cases it comes in the fancy class. Pigskin used by a harness-maker is only pigskin, but if used in the bag, etc., trade, it is fancy leather.

Insurance underwriters usually put all kinds of leather in the **fancy leather class,** except sole and harness, yet some have put the latter in this class, especially if highly finished and of light weight. They would possibly be correct, from an insurance standpoint, or at least be on the safe side, to class all leather as fancy, except sole and harness. Probably the latter is less subject to damage.—T. O. Gildersleeve.

Leather (Finishing)—Received at tanneries in dry state, soaked in water and in lime pits (called beam house), washed again in water, the water squeezed out by "putting-out" machines, dried, "staked," and "seasoned" by use of ammonia and albumen, tanned, dried, softened by machinery, ironed and dressed. If raw hides are received they are "fleshed" and "unhaired," i. e., the hair and flesh adhering to the hide is removed. Tanning and finishing differ for different kinds and qualities of leather. There may be used gambia, sumac, tanbark, chrome, neat's-foot oil, soap, salt, sulphuric acid, aniline or logwood dyes. See Celluloid (Imitation Leather); also Imitation Leather and Patent Leather.

LEATHER BELTING—Some factories use celluloid cement instead of glue for waterproofing or finishing. Celluloid is apt to be dissolved on the premises with acetone and used from open cans.

LEATHER CEMENT is a solution of rubber in gasoline or carbon bisulphide. Flashes at zero F. Very inflammable.

LEATHER DECORATORS do painting, embossing, staining, sewing, cutting. Use amyl acetate, japan, lacquer, turpentine, benzine. Coloring is usually done by airbrush (spray). Write this class cautiously.

LEATHER DOG-COLLARS—Work consists of cutting, splitting, skiving, creasing (creasers, gas-heated), eyeletting and riveting machines for brass ornaments, cementing with rubber cement, shellacing, varnishing and buffing metal parts.

LEATHER DUST is attributed as the cause of a fire in a shoe factory recently. Rapidly revolving drums covered with emery or sandpaper produce a fine dust; also a good deal of lint was made by the cloth-covered buffing wheels. The fire was possibly caused by sparks from the machines. After the fire the floor was dotted all over with lumps of glowing dust resembling lumps of incandescent charcoal. These balls or lumps could be picked up without falling apart, when handled gently.—Fire Chief Soule, Coatesville, Pa.

LEATHER FINISHERS—Some bag makers use alcohol, acetone, benzine, shellac, linseed oil, glycerine, lampblack and turpentine.

LEATHER LININGS—Bag linings are the inner side of split sheep skins, called "skives"; usually tanned with sumac, dyed with anilines, tacked on boards to stretch, softened either by hand or power machines. Before tacking they are "slicked up" to remove all loose or rough surfaces by laying same on a glass washboard and being scraped with a knife. Graining is done in a machine similar to a mangle, having a copper roller with indentations, heated by steam over which the skin is rolled.

LEATHER (PATENT)—In making the varnish for the patent leather, linseed oil is heated by wood or coke fires to about 580 deg. F. The temperature of the oil is lowered in open air to about 250 deg. F. and then thinned or reduced with naphtha and turpentine, which are slowly added. Fires have occurred in this process, due probably to adding the naphtha and turpentine before the oil is properly cooled. The "daub" consists of linseed oil, lampblack and benzine.—Adamson.

LEATHER SCRAPS and remnants from factories are used for fertilizer by reducing same to a pulp and extracting the animal ammonia. Leather remnants burn very slowly, in fact in bags they have stopped the progress of fire.

LEATHER SOFTENERS may contain inflammables.

LEATHER (SOLE)—Will easily stain from water to such an extent that the spots cannot be removed.

LEATHER—(TRADE NAMES) for leather substitutes, Leathertex, Neolin, Textan, Keratol, Fabrikoid, Texoderm, Pantosote.

LEGAL LIABILITY—Forms are sometimes written for expressmen as follows: $.... on their legal liability in, or for all merchandise and for baggage held in their custody as common carriers, warehousemen, forwarders or freighters. It being mutually understood and agreed that if claim is made against the assured hereinunder for merchandise or baggage held for them, the insurers shall have the option of either admitting such claim for payment, or if resisting it in the court, the legal expenses incurred in such resistance to be borne by the insurance companies interested, in the proportion that the total amount of insurance shall bear to the total amount of such claim or claims. Only competent underwriters should accept "Legal Liability" insurance.

LEHRS OR LEERS (tempering furnace) in glassworks have a solid brick wall at sides and a flat brick-arched top. They are either coke or gas-heated. The hot ware from the glassblowers is placed on iron trays at the receiving end and then slowly propelled through the length of the lehr on a traveling belt.

LEMON OIL—Composed of lemon grass and paraffine; used by piano polishers.

LEPTYNE—A substitute for turpentine in thinning paint or varnish. Classified same as turpentine. Flashes at 99 deg. F. Fire test, 120 deg. F.

LIABILITY—Where a tenant occupies a number of floors in a fireproof building with fair cut-offs between floors, the usual practice is to carry the full line authorized for one floor and a half line on each of the additional floors. This same rule applies to a row of buildings or well-constructed ordinary brick buildings with heavy floors and standard floor openings.

LIABILITY OF A COMPANY is primarily divided into two classes, contingent and actual or accrued. Contingent liabilities are based on the possibility or likelihood of being called upon to meet claims such as losses. When these losses occur, the liability is then actual or accrued. Policies in force are the principal liability. See Assets.

LICORICE (stick manufacturing)—Process is crushing, grinding and pulverizing of licorice root in chasers. It is mixed with sugars in paste form, boiled in tanks, where other ingredients are added, made into various shapes by machinery and dried on trays in dry rooms.

LIGHT SHAFT—A shaft in the interior of a building for the admission of light; usually has thin glass windows. A light well is a large open or enclosed light shaft. See Shafts.

LIGHTNING (scientifically known as static electricity) is caused by the disruption discharge of the positive electricity in the clouds rushing to equalize the negative electricity in the earth, or vice versa. Discharges upward are by no means uncommon, although not often observed.

LIGHTNING RODS, if properly installed, effectually protect buildings. Prof. Dodd says: "Let us see how a flash of lightning is made, for there is always something at work ahead of the lightning flash, getting things ready.

"Before a house is struck with lightning, the house is first charged by induction.

"'Induction' is taken from the word 'induce' and induce means to 'coax or pull your way.'

"Before a house is struck by lightning an electric strain is placed upon it. That is, a condition has been coaxed into it, and it is this condition we have to deal with if we would prevent it from bursting into a lightning explosion.

"Now the air is a poor conductor of electricity, and things that stick up from the earth into the air, like houses and barns, become discharging points for the earth's electricity, and in this way the house gets ready to be struck.

"So the lesson we wish to impress here is this: 'Lightning is due to causes.' Electricity first gets in its work and loads up a cloud. Then this cloud fixes up things on the earth and induces an opposite electric condition, and the two electrified surfaces strain and pull on each other, and when the strain gets great enough so that the air cannot resist any longer, off she goes with an explosion through the house, and the undertaker has a job on his hands."

Cattle or other livestock herded in wire-fence enclosures are apt to be electrocuted if in contact with the charged wire.

LIGNITE—Carbonized fossil wood. Subject to spontaneous combustion.

LIGROIN—A volatile distillate from crude petroleum. Inflammable. Flash zero F. See Petroleum.

LIME—Obtained by calcining marble or by adding a solution of carbonate of ammonia to a solution of chloride of calcium. See Calcium Oxide.

Lime (unslaked) should be kept under a water-tight shed or building on proper skids. Many fires have been caused, especially along the water front, when the rising tide causes the lime to slake, creating enough heat to set fire to the structure. Firemen playing hose on lime will slake it with the same result. Usually found in builders' material yards.

LIMESTONE FRONTS of buildings are damaged by heat more than any other granular building stones. They become calcined under intense heat, or are decomposed into lime.

LINE—The amount of liability which a company carries on a risk. The amount is determined by the loss ratio according to the company's underwriting experience or judgment. See Average Risk, also Block Lines.

LINCRUSTA—A wall covering. See Wall Coverings.

LINENS offer very good salvage if only damaged by clean water and are dried immediately.

LINIMENTS usually contain crude petroleum, ether, alcohol, chloroform, turpentine.

LINOLEUM—The foundation of linoleum is burlap. This is impregnated with ground cork, linseed oil and oxide of lead in a calender roll. A heavy coating is then applied and printed in various designs. The coating mixture is made of scrim (light cotton fabric) which is hung on racks and saturated with linseed oil. The oil which adheres at about 100 deg. F. rapidly hardens. This process is repeated until there is a thick coating (called skin). The roll is then cut down and ground between rollers. A cement is made of oil, resin, kauri gums and ground cork, colored if desired. The mixture is cemented on the burlap foundation. The printing of designs is a continuous process, the sheets passing through a machine under blocks of different colors which, rising and falling, do the printing. Hazards of cork grinding, dry rooms, oil soaked premises, spontaneous combustion in oily materials.

Linoleum (ground) is subject to spontaneous combustion when moist.

LINOTYPE MACHINES resemble huge typewriters and set up one complete line of type at a time. The operator sits at a keyboard, strikes a letter and the matrices (brass slugs on which is an impression of the desired character) fall down through a channel until a line of type is made up. Metal followers push the line across until it is dropped in front of a pot of hot type metal. The lead is forced by air pressure against the matrix. The only hazard is the lead pot, which is usually gas heated. The gas connection should be rigid iron piping. Metal should be placed on the floor under the machine. See Printers.

LINSEED OIL—Is pressed from flaxseed by either cold or hot process. Moderate steam heat is required for kettles and presses where the seeds are cooked and pressed. Floors usually very oily.

LINTEL—A horizontal beam across the opening in a wall over windows, doors, etc. When of wide span and supportting heavy brickwork or masonry it is called a "breast-summer."

LINTERS (unbleached)—The cotton scraped from the cotton seeds after the best or loose cotton has been removed.

LINTUS—See Indian Cotton.

LIONITE (Used for Backs of Brushes)—Made from powdered asbestos with resin, shellac and lampblack in small proportions (not hazardous).

LIQUID AIR is air condensed into a liquid at high pressure and low temperature. A powerful explosive.

LIQUID BRONZE—See Bronzing Liquid.

LIQUID CEMENT—A rubber cement used for roofing.

LIQUID GAS—Obtained by the dry distillation of raw petroleum and by-products of the lignite and oil industries. The vapors and gasses are obtained by the decomposition of the material in retorts, passed through tar separators and cleaned. The gases are liquified by cold and pressure, carbureted and put in cylinders for shipment.

LIQUEFIED PETROLEUM GAS is liquid condensed by compressing the gas from petrol oil wells. Classed as inflammable.

LIQUID TANKS (For Gasolene or Other Inflammables)—**Burning liquids** can best be extinguished by forming a blanket of gas such as generated when carbon tetra-chloride or bi-carbonate of soda, or a solid is formed on the surface. This cuts off the supply of air and dilutes or breaks up the volume of natural air by introducing a non-inflammable agent with it.

Liquid Storage Tanks—The size of tanks, distance from buildings and location are determined by local underwriters and governed by National Board rules. Small sized tanks are usually buried three feet under ground, and below all piping connected thereto, set on a solid foundation and have filling and vent pipes. Tanks should be of all steel or wrought iron, all joints riveted, soldered or caulked, brazed or welded, **(soldering alone is insufficient)**, and coated on the outside with rust-resisting material such as tar or asphaltum. The fill pipe should be screened with fine wire mesh and the vent pipe not less than three feet from a window or other opening. Only an approved pump or device should be used to draw liquid direct to receptacle, and such liquids not to be in open containers. See Gasoline.

Portable tanks of 40 to 60 gallons capacity are built of solid steel 3/16 inch thick, set on rubber-tired wheels with approved pump and vent pipe. These latter are used mainly in garages.

LIQUOR in barrels will yield a greater salvage if the barrels are laid on their sides instead of ends, as this method will prevent water from seeping through and spoiling the contents.

Liquors—There are two kinds, **fermented** and **distilled.** All spiritous liquors are fermented. Distilling, a hot process, embraces the whole process of making of potable spirit from cereals and grains. This process includes the grinding of the grain, mashing and fermentation, and thereafter the separation of the alcohol from the other constituents. See Distilleries; see Rectifying.

Refining—The purification by redistillation for the purpose of eliminating impurities.

Blending—Mixing together, by a cold process, whiskeys, spirits, gins and other such articles.

Clarifying—For the purpose of clearing the color of wines either by allowing sufficient time for the liquor to settle or by hastening the process by adding such substances as whites of eggs, Spanish clay, gelatine or other ingredients.

Filtering—The straining of liquors.

Compounding or Rectifying—A cold mixing process.

Additional hazards in distilleries are extract-making, coopering, barrel painting, bottle washing, storage and handling of alcohol in large quantities.

LIQUORINE—An approved benzine substitute for cleaning printing presses.

LISTED NON-FIBRE STORAGE—Stores used for the storage of general merchandise. In New York city the rates are figured on the Exchange Mercantile Schedule with an allowance of 35 per cent. for base rate, and 17½ for the building. This final rate, called base rate, to be added to the rate for the commodity desired to be stored. For example: Baking powder is 17c + 10c base, makes 27c proper rate to be charged. See Warehouses; see Storage.

LISTED STORAGE STORE—See Warehouses.

LITHARGE—Is yellow oxide of lead. **Sodium Nitrate** is roasted with metallic lead which form nitrite and litharge.

LITHOFRACTEUR is a foreign make of nitro-glycerine. Explosive.

LITHOPONE—A dry powder used in paint. A combination of zinc and lead.

LITMUS—By boiling blue cabbage or certain lichens in water, a blue solution is obtained. A drop of acid added to this liquid turns it a bright red. Used in experimental labratories.

LITHOGRAPH CRAYON DRAWINGS—Artists draw on stones with ordinary crayon, after which the stone is treated with a solution of sour gum (gum arabic with a few drops of nitric acid). A separate stone is used for each color. When a blue color is desired, instead of drawing with crayon they first sensitize the stone with a solution of bichromate of ammonia and white of egg, then photograph on it. The stones are usually cleaned with turpentine.

LITHOGRAPHING—Most stones used in lithographing are imported from Bavaria and come in all sizes from those having an area of about one square foot to those which have an area of about twenty square feet. They are usually four inches in thickness, but can be used until they are not less than one inch thick. This is made possible by backing them with slate which not only provides the required thickness but also strengthens them as well. The principle of lithographing is the printing from a flat stone surface so treated that ink will adhere to the design only. To get this result it is necessary to have two stones called the engrayed stone and transfer stone. The process is as follows; the stone is polished by hand with pumice and water until its surface is perfectly smooth. It is then given a coating with a gum arabic solution which is left on the stone to protect it. The stone is then engraved by hand, and in doing this the engraver cuts thru the hardened gum solution and removes it while the rest of the surface remains protected as before. When the gum solution on the stone is kept wet, no ink will adhere to it, and when the engraved part is inked no water will mix with the ink. The stone is therefore moistened with a sponge and "rolled up" or inked with a leather ink roller. The stone is now complete and is called the engraved stone, but as mentioned before, the printing is done from a stone having a flat surface called a transfer stone. The next step is to transfer the engraving to the flat surface of this stone. After the engraved stone has been inked a piece of specially prepared paper is laid on the engraving and it is subjected to pressure in a hand press. The engraving is now transferred to the paper which is then laid on the second stone with the ink-side down. The ink under pressure eats into the stone which previously has been polished with pumice stone and water, but has not been protected with the gum solution. The transfer paper is now removed and the stone is covered with the gum solution which adheres to those positions only which have not received the ink from the transfer paper. The stone is now moistened with water and again inked. After being proof read it is placed in the cylinder press similar to those described above and is ready for printing. These presses have both ink and water rollers, under which the stone passes back and forth at each revolution.

LITHOGRAPH SHEETS may be subject to spontaneous combustion if placed in large piles before being thoroughly dried. This heating is caused by the linseed or other drying oils in the ink.

LITHOGRAPH STONES AND PLATES—Very susceptible to fire and water damage, and may crumble almost to dust when so damaged. The stones are imported.

LIVE RISER—The pipe leading from the supply tank with mains and laterals to feed the sprinklers. See Sprinklers.

LIVESTOCK—See Stables; see Lightning; also Blooded Livestock.

LOCK CORNER MACHINES—For cutting tooth-like projections on the end of pieces which are to form the concurrent sides of a box or drawer; vertical or horizontal mandrells carry gauges of saw-like cutters which rotate rapidly. Considerable fine refuse is made.

LOCKERS—In the Metropolitan Museum of Art, New York City, a fire started in the locker room where the artists store their canvases, paints, oils, brushes, etc., evidently caused by spontaneous combustion. All lockers should be of metal on raised legs with open screen front to allow ventilation. In this manner, refuse under the lockers can be readily seen, and a fire can be seen through open front. Oily waste in pockets of workmen's overalls is apt to cause fire.

LOCK-JOINTED—See Fire Doors.

LOCOMOTIVES for Mill Yard Use—Steam locomotives without fires are now being used. The steam is pumped into a reservoir under high pressure. The tank is sufficiently large to run the engine for several hours. This eliminates the danger of spark fires from the ordinary locomotives.

LOCOMOTIVE SPARK HAZARD—This hazard is an ever-present one along railroads, especially where bituminous coal is used for fuel. Buildings, especially with shingle roofs, within a radius of one-half mile should be written with this hazard in mind.

LODGING HOUSES—Usually of ordinary construction with joist floors, open or poorly enclosed floor openings. Individual rooms are usually enclosed in frame partitions extending part way to ceiling thereby adding considerable combustible material to the interior. Hazards are pot stoves for heat, furnaces, use of benzine for exterminating insects, swinging gas jets, and smoking. Usually located in the poorer sections. The fire record is poor. See Boarding Houses; also Furnished Rooms.

LOFT—The first loft of a building is the first floor above the grade.

LOFT BUILDING—Usually interpreted to mean one occupied by omnibus manufacturing tenants.

LOGWOOD is wood from which logwood dyes and extracts are made. Received in this country in varying lengths to 6 feet and small in diameters. The surface under the bark is very splintery. When on fire in dry state it burns very rapidly due to the rough surface, smolders a long time and sparks and embers fly a considerable distance in a wind. When on fire, the smoke is thick, pungent, opaque (making nearby objects invisible) and hard to fight. In small piles it is readily extinguished, but in large piles up to 40 feet, the fire will smolder for days.

The dye is extracted from logwood as follows: The logs are chopped into chunks, sawed by power saws, broken into smaller pieces and ground in machines. It is cooked in steam-heated vats where it remains until the dye is cooked out of the wood. The liquor is separated from the mass by centrifugal extractors and barrelled. See Dye Woods.

LONGITUDINAL SECTION in a drawing shows the object lengthwise as distinguished from transverse or cross.

LOSS ADJUSTMENTS—Many of the unsatisfactory loss adjustments are caused by the failure of the assured to make satisfactory proof of the value of the stock at the time of the fire. Misguided people do not try to salvage any goods after a fire by separating the damaged from the undamaged goods for fear of experiencing trouble with the insuring company. Non-current forms are an ever present source of trouble to an adjuster. See Proof of Loss.

LOSS COST—The relation between the amount of property insured in a certain class and the amount paid in losses. Loss cost is the cost of carrying a certain class of risk.

LOSS RATIO—The percentage that the amount paid in losses bears to the premiums received in any class of risk.

LOST POLICY RECEIPT (or voucher) is a release given by the assured to a company when the original policy has been lost, thereby releasing the company from obligation under the contract.

LOUVRE—A slatted ventilator. Used in place of a window. Built of metal or wood slats, slanting to permit foul air to escape from a room but preventing fire from entering from the shaft because the openings between slats slant inwardly. When used in shafts should be of metal with riveted rather than soldered joints. See Diagram on Ventilating Shafts.

LOWER FLANGE—The under part of "I" beams. These should be protected with at least two inches of approved insulation, although if unprotected, this should not be considered a serious defect in construction if the arch springs from the lower flange and protects the webs.

LOW WINES are classed as alcohol, cologne spirits, fusel oil and other alcohol by-products. See distilleries.

LUBRICATING OIL—Manufacturing consist of mixing different grades of heavy mineral oil with some animal or vegetable oil. The lower the flash point, the more likely is the atmosphere surrounding the machinery to be impregnated with inflammable vapors.

LUDLOW TYPOGRAPH MACHINE—A newly-invented machine for setting lengths of lead type in line lengths similar to monotype work, except that this machine is smaller and the type is cast against a brass matrix.

LUMBER—Second-hand lumber is somewhat better than other second-hand stocks as there is always a market for it. As a class, second-hand lumber yards are not attractive risks. They usually occupy leased ground.

LUMBER YARDS—Inspectors should state whether it is hard or soft wood; note the height of piles, and whether piled solid or with open spaces between, and whether piles rest on earth, shavings, sawdust or skids. He should note the aisle space, whether lumber exposes windows of mill or other buildings, prevailing winds, whether yard is fenced in. If near a steam railroad there is danger from sparks of locomotives. Lumber yard fires are hard to fight. Rating bureaus add a charge for exposure to lumber if the mill exposes the lumber yard, unless 100 feet distant.

LYCOPODIUM—Obtained from certain plants. In powdered form it is inflammable.

LYE—Common name for Hydrate of Potash or Soda.

LYDDITE is a form of gun-cotton; an English trinitrophenol.

M

MACARONI MFG.—The farina and flour are received in bags, then dumped in hopper and conveyed to storage bins according to the grade. From the storage bins, it is brought by worm conveyor to the scales to be weighed according to the batch desired. It is then dumped in the mixing machines which are directly under the scale, hoppered to the kneaders, then passed to the rolling machines where the mass is rolled up into ¼-inch-thick cartridge forms and dropped into macaroni cylinder presses. The plungers of the press are forced down by hydraulic pressure, squeezing the paste through a compartment die which is perforated with a number of circular holes with a core held in the centre. It is dried atmospherically or in heated rooms.

MACARONI SHOPS in basements are usually crowded, and have unsafe dry rooms or heating apparatus. Many of these shops employ direct coal heat for drying purposes.

MACHINERY—Heavy machinery on upper floors, even though normally substantially supported has wrecked many buildings in case of fire because the supports weaken or burn away. Drip-pans should be placed under all oily machinery to catch oil drips and so prevent oily floors.

Machinery in Rapid Motion—See Shaftings.

Machinery (Second-hand)—Even old or unused usually has a market value unless obsolete, badly damaged, or worn out, in which case it has only the value of old iron.

MACHINES of a revolving type, gas-heated, are permitted to have flexible rubber connections instead of rigid iron piping.

MACHINE SHOPS—See Metals Workers.

MADE GROUND—See Ground.

MAGIC METAL POLISH—An approved benzine substitute.

MAGNESIUM POWDER—Will burn readily and is not

easily extinguished by water A stream of water will scatter the burning particles.

MAGNET—A magnetic device placed in grinding mills, hoppers, chutes, feed spouts, etc., to arrest any metal particles and prevent them from entering the machine where, in grinding or milling, they may create a spark and explode the dust in the mill.

MAGNETO MAKING—Machine shop hazard, annealing, nickel-plating, buffing, testing, sealing with wax. Benzine for cleaning parts, lacquering.

MAGNOLIUM—An alloy of aluminum and magnesium 90-98 per cent. aluminum). It is imported in pigs or ingots for casting.

MAGUEY—See Fibres.

MAIL ORDER CONCERNS—They carry nearly every variety of goods. Where no manufacturing is done, the premises resemble warehouses with open stocks and on shelves. Included in the general merchandise there may be calcium carbide, automobile tires, rubber cement, small arm ammunition, lubricating and other oils, celluloid articles. Large concerns usually have repair departments for damaged merchandise.

MALT EXTRACTING—After the above process the grain is soaked in tanks of cold water, then steam is turned into the tanks to cook it, then evaporated and packed in kegs.

MALT ROASTING (for Breweries)—Malt received from breweries, roasted usually in an ordinary coffee roaster which consists of a cylindrical revolving drum equipped with agitator and heated by direct coal heat. It is drawn off in metal-cooling pans, where the heat is drawn out by suction, then "lofted" by cup-conveyor to a hopper which feeds a grinding mill. A magnet should be at the hopper or at the rollers of the mill to catch metallic pieces such as nails. See Brewery Malt Mills.

MANGLE—An ironing machine used in laundries for flat work. They are large steel rollers, cloth-covered and either steam or gas-heated.

MANICURISTS—Usually locate in private dwellings or apartments or in barber shops. Usually have or make small

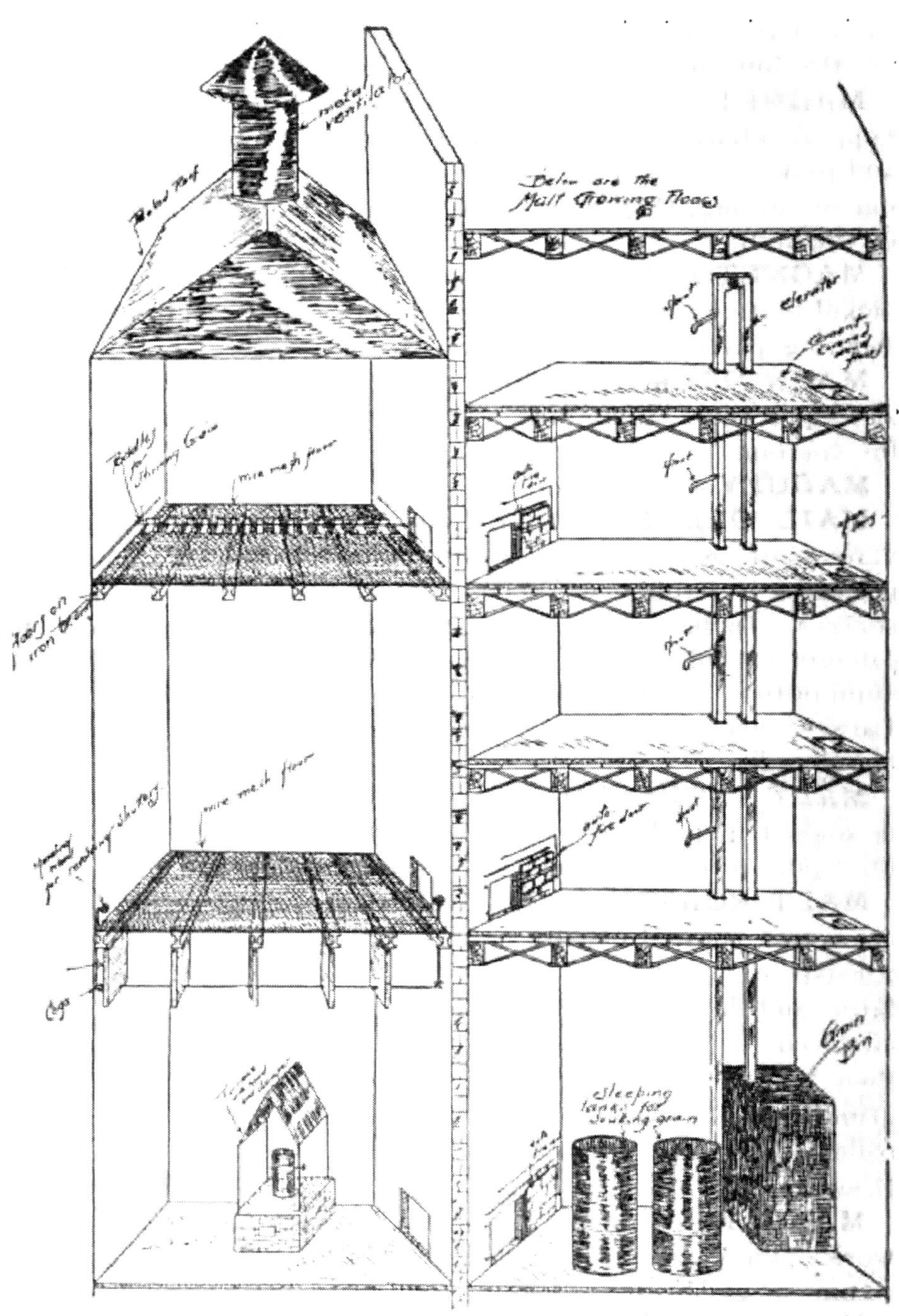

From "Live Articles on Special Hazards," pub. by "Weekly Underwriter."

Malt House.

quantities of cosmetics and pomades. At times use alcohol or gas stoves. If in a dwelling, and not over three hands employed, with the owner living on the premises, there is no extra rate charged for this occupancy in New York City. See Massage Parlors.

MANSARD—The top portion of the outer walls which slope to the roof. The backing is usually of wood or lath and plaster on studding. Termed by fire fighters as " a lumber yard up in the air" because of their inability to locate the seat of the fire once it gains access to the concealed space.

MANUAL ALARM—Usually a small red box with a ring attachment at the bottom, which if pulled down sends in a fire alarm.

MAP CLERK—A junior underwriter whose main duty is to write the "lines" on the map so that the company's liability can be seen at a glance. He must also understand forms and rates and adjust reinsurance. See Underwriter; see Examiner.

MARBLE is easily damaged by fire. Where it forms any considerable part of the building structure such as marble fronts or facings, underwriters usually cut down their "line."

MARBLE WORKERS—Stone and granite such as used in buildings are included. Work is sawing, planing, cutting, drilling, polishing, rubbing. Polishing is done by machinery on flat, soft stones, using a mixture of dry putty and oxalic acid as an abrasive. Glycerine is used for highly polished stones. Broken pieces are cemented with plaster of Paris, beeswax or stick shellac. The latter two are usually heated by gas blow pipes. Gas or gasoline torches are used for heating lead for dowels. Usually occupy large area frame buildings heated by "salamanders." See Imitation Marble.

MARGARIC ACID is obtained from hog fat and potash.

MARINE GLUE—One part India rubber, 20 parts gum lac and 12 parts benzine.

MARINE-LEG—Used in connection with grain elevators located on water fronts. A movable elevator leg, so arranged that grain can be conveyed from the hold of a boat by dipping the elevator boot into the hold.

MARINE INSURANCE—Is a contract whereby one party for a specific sum agrees to indemnify another who has an interest in the property exposed to marine risks, against loss incidental thereto. The policy covers goods from port to port but by endorsement they may be covered from some place in the interior until delivered to the assured's store or warehouse at port of destination. Almost all marine contracts are valued policies.

MARKED OFF—An expression used by insurance men when an application or policy is returned to the company when the insurance is not wanted.

MARKETS (Chicken)—Especially where killing is done are usually untidy with feathers, guano and wooden crates. Stoves are used for heat and for heating water. Not an attractive class.

MARKET VALUE—See Sound Value.

MARSH GAS—See Fire Damp.

MASSAGE PARLORS—Usually in connection with hair dressers and manicurists. Use electric vibrators for massaging, electric baths and various other electric appliances. Some are connected with the lighting system with ordinary sockets. Others are on separate circuits or run by storage batteries. Alcohol and face creams are used extensively. Salves are mainly heated on alcohol stoves. See Manicurist.

MASSICOT—Oxide of lead.

MASTIC—A resinous substance from a shrub. Used in varnish-making.

MATCHES. (Manufacturing)—Many different processes are employed. One of the common being a cylinder of pine or poplar wood, the length of seven matches, which has been soaked in water to make it tough, is placed in a lathe which cuts off a continuous shaving, the thickness of a match. As this shaving comes away from the log, it is cut into seven strips, each as wide as a match is long. As soon as the splints are separated from the block, they are seized in iron clamp plates which form an endless chain. The endless chain carries the splints across a steam-heated drum which warms them nearly to the temperature of paraffine into which they are dipped. From the paraffine bath the splints move on continuously to the rollers that carry the "heading" mixture, phosphorus, chlorate of potash, etc., and as the matches are carried past the rollers each one receives a red or blue head as the case may be. From the rollers they continue on through a room swept by a blast of cold, dry air. The matches move on until just before they reach the starting point, again air automatically thrusts them out and places them side by side in a box.

The composition of match heads varies a great deal in different factories and consists of various combinations of glue, rosin, phosphorus, sulphur, chlorate of potash, saltpetre, red lead, bichromate of potash, nitrate of lead, antimony sulphide and fine sand.

A Prolific Source of Fire Losses.

The **sulphur match tip** is made of a paste consisting of chlorate of potash, sulphur, colophony, vermillion and gum.

The **"strike anywhere"** match tip usually contains phosphorus and potassium chlorate.

The **"strike-on-box"** match head is partly composed of potassium chlorate while the box contains red phosphorus.

Paper match heads are dipped in chlorate of potash, amorphous phosphorus, sulphur and iron oxide.

Incomplete reports of the National Board of Fire Underwriters for the year 1915 show a loss over the country totaling $4,324,596 due to matches.

In New York City alone, the fire department's report of 1915 shows that there were 1,346 fires attributed to matches, causing a loss of $227,886.

The Underwriters' Laboratories of Chicago have made a careful study and test of matches and now issue the label service covering this line of goods. The testing covers the subject of flying heads, ignition temperatures, stability of head and composition, afterglow, strength of splint and method of packing.

The **label service** is divided into two classes. Class "A" is the "strike on the box" type, where the match is struck on a prepared surface and the ignition point is above 340 deg. F. Class "B" is the so-called "strike anywhere" match, and the ignition point is above 300 deg. F. This type of match is double-dipped, the outside bulb being inert and of larger diameter than the tip. It is constructed so that it will not ignite from friction or when it is trod upon. The splints of both types of matches are treated to prevent afterglow, and they are required to be of a reasonable strength.

At this writing there is only one manufacturer who has obtained the label service. This concern manufactures both classes of approved matches.

The hazard from the careless handling of matches cannot be too greatly emphasized and it would be well to advocate stringent laws for those who continue to use them with utter disregard for the loss of life and property that they may cause.—(S. T. Skirrow, "Live Articles on Special Hazards," The Weekly Underwriter.)

MATTRESSES—Materials used are tow, shoddy, sea grass, cotton, hair, moss, excelsior and fibres. Work consists of picking and rolling cotton or other materials in pads, filling and tufting, sewing slip covers. They may also assemble and paint bed springs. Hazards are cotton and fibre picking, storage of upholstering material, dust in the presence of open lights, loose materials about the premises. In small shops, coal stoves are used for heat. Unless the various processes are segregated, the entire floor may become covered with dust. A very poor fire record class.

MATZOTH BAKERY—Matzoths are made of flour and cracker dust. Bakers use sifters, cleaners and occasionally mill flour. The baking oven is brick enclosed with fire box underneath. The dough is placed on a revolving metal drum over the fire and baked in one revolution. When baked, the crackers drop on a woven cloth belt conveyor which takes them to the packing room. Some of the crackers may be burning and if not removed from the conveyor are carried to the packing room where they might set fire to combustible material. Several fires have been attributed to this cause, and also to friction in dust box of flour mill. (Poor fire record.) See Bakeries.

MECHANICS' PRIVILEGE—Allows mechanics to be employed in the building for ordinary alterations and repairs without limit of time. Just when and where a builders risk condition takes place is sometimes rather a difficult question to decide, but most underwriters claim that so long as the building in not weakened or added to but merely altered by means of painting, carpentering and other interior work, the mechanics' privilege is all that is necessary. See Builders' Risk.

MEDICINAL OILS—See Mineral Oil.

MELINITE—A powerful explosive.

MELTING FURNACES—Called "pot" furnaces. Used by glass manufacturers and are generally circular in form with an inside lining bench and crown of fire clay blocks and brick and an outside enclosure tapering above the crown forming a chimney stack. The base is usually brick about 10 feet thick with brick arched cave or tunnel. They use soft coal for heat. There are a number of openings in these furnaces which receive the crucible or pot which contains the "batch" of glass ingredients. Aside from the setting, the only hazard of any importance is the woodwork which should be removed to at least 18 inches.—The Weekly Underwriter.

MELTING POINT of metals. See Fusion Point.

MEMORIAL WINDOWS are part of the building and may form considerable of building loss in case of fire. Few companies will write them as separate insurance.

MEN'S FURNISHINGS—Susceptible stock. When colored goods are water damaged, the colors either run or goods become mildewed and prove total loss. White goods mildew but these can be washed. Cheap jewelry may be included which tarnishes.

MENTHOL—Resembles camphor. Obtained from oil of peppermint by cooling; volatile.

MERCANTILE BUILDING—One occupied by mercantile tenants such as those having stocks, offices and very light manufacturing.

MERCANTILE RATING—When the financial rating of a person or firm does not appear in any of the mercantile rating books it usually indicates lack of capital or credit but may only signify that the bureau has no information on which to base a rating. See Trade Reports; also Blank Rating.

MERCERIZED GOODS—Water will practically ruin stocks of this nature, which are also severely damaged by dampness.

MERCERIZING—A process which imparts a gloss or lustre to cotton fibres by treating the tightly stretched fibres with caustic soda, followed by washing and drying.

MERCHANDISE SPECIFIC FORM—In writing insurance under this form, add to the base rate of warehouse, the amount named in the alphabetical list. Specify the merchandise by name and if the rate is for a particular kind of package, mention the package. See Storage; see Warehouses.

MERCHANT POLICE—In place of the ordinary watchman, are hired by owners of merchandise, usually on docks and piers, to prevent thievery. The merchant police are responsible for all goods lost and therefore are always alert.

MERCHANT TAILOR—Does custom work, and may also have stock. See Custom Tailor.

MERCURIC CHLORIDE—Corrosive sublimate, heavy white salt, no fire hazard.

MERCURY is the only metal which is in liquid form. It is white, having a brilliant metallic lustre. Boils at 660 deg. F. Alcohol is used as a substitute for mercury in thermometer where very low temperatures prevail.

MERCURY FULMINATE—Produced by solution of nitrate of mercury and alcohol. Powerful explosive.

METAL BEDS AND SPRINGS—Busiest season April to July, September to November. Metal working hazards including japanning and enameling. Use considerable excelsior for packing. (Poor fire record class.)

METALIZING—Dipping articles in molten metal.

METALLIC POTASSIUM (and sodium) are kept by nearly all drug houses. Should be kept in oil, because if water comes in contact with them, flames result, as the reaction releases hydrogen.

METALLIC POWDERS such as aluminum and bronze have a great affinity for oxygen and are considered dangerous.

METAL SIGNS (Lithographed)—Sheet metal working and varnishing hazard. Benzine thinned paint used in dip tanks. A roller varnishing machine is sometimes used with celluloid varnish. Dry rooms same as lacquer dry rooms.

METAL TUBING (Manufacturing) embraces the hazards of gas-heated brazers, roller mills, stamping presses, swaging machines and heavy metal working machinery. Floors usually oily and greasy.

METAL WORKERS—Machines used are lathes, shapers, milling machines, drill presses, emery wheels and similar devices. If the floors are of wood, the machines should set on metal with edges curbed to prevent oil soaking into the wood. Waste used around machinery when oily should be kept in self-closing cans with legs so that the bottom of the can is off the floor. Iron filings should be kept in similar receptacles. Some shops do lacquering or japanning. Only a day's supply of such materials should be kept on hand in the building. Dry rooms for lacquered parts should be standard in construction.

METHYL ALCOHOL—See Wood Alcohol.

METHYLOXALIC ACID—Is recovered from the products of dry distillation of wood; inflammable.

MEZZANINE FLOOR—A gallery or half floor, of smaller area than other floors of the building.

MICA—Manufacturing such goods as electrical insulators, lamp chimneys, etc. There are but few plants in the United States. The stock of mica is received in rough state from mines, cut up into small pieces, worked up into several layers using shellac as a cement, pressed into sheets by hydraulic presses, dried in ovens, cut to size, formed in steam moulds. They are gradually cooled in these same moulds by circulating water jackets, then dried in ovens, edges trimmed with jig saws and surface ground down on carborundum wheels and the seams cemented with shellac. When put in ovens to dry, the mica is placed on a sheet of metal previously oiled. Metal parts are riveted on by foot power presses. Hazards embrace light metal working, machine shop for repairs, storage of shellac and alcohol, drying ovens, steam pipes at mould tables in contact with wood.

MICALITE—A substitute for sheet celluloid. Non-inflammable.

MICE—Have long been credited with causing fires and although experiments with mice and matches have been unsuccessful, the following is a true report of a concrete case: A fire was discovered under a floor in a residence. A large quantity of water was poured in. When firemen arrived they took up the floor boards and discovered a large nest between the beams and in it were acorns, chestnuts, pieces of cloth, plumbers' waste, cheese, and—half of a burnt match. See Rats.

MILK DEPOTS—High pressure boiler hazard, which supplies steam for pasteurizers, sterilizers, bottle washers and dry rooms. Crate or box-making for bottles, tinsmith shop for repairing of cans, refrigerating machinery, printing labels and caps are hazards found at some plants. The fire record is not very good. See Dairy Farms; see Creameries.

MILL AGENT—An agent who sells the product of mills

to the trade, receiving a commission for same, although goods are shipped and billed direct to the buyer.

MILL CONSTRUCTION—Briefly, mill construction embraces the following: (1) Consists of making a fire stop of heavy plank between stories so that the spread of fire may be retarded. This necessitates doing away with all openings in floors such as belt holes, stairways, elevator wells, or all such must be in cut-off towers. (2) The timbers and flooring required to give the necessary stability and strength are arranged so as to offer as smooth a surface and as few corners, on which fire may feed, as practical, also doing away with all concealed spaces in walls or floors. This is accomplished by using very heavy floor timbers spaced 8 to 12 feet apart and floors of 3 to 4-inch plank with single or double top flooring. Roof to be 3 inches thick and covered with gravel or tin. In a building of this character fire can be readily reached with water from either hose stream or sprinklers. (3) Floors must be tight as well as heavy so as to prevent fire, smoke or water from working through. This is one of the most important features of a mill building and one to which sufficient attention is not paid. Due to poorly seasoned plank or poor workmanship openings are left around posts, at side walls or elswhere and fire smoke or water spreads through these openings destroying or impairing the efficiency of the floor. See Bay Construction; see Compromise Mill.

MILL WASTE—Odds and ends from fabric mills, macerated and bleached to obtain a resemblance to cotton.

MILLINERY is liable to include almost anything from a delicate chiffon to a stuffed bird, but can be counted on to give practically 100 per cent. loss in nearly every fire starting in this class, because the salvage, once the stock is smoked or wet, is practically nil.

MINE FIRES are caused by ignition of timbers, wooden stoppings and brattic cloths, hay or oil-soaked material by open torches, the ignition of coal by blown-out shots, or explosions of fire damp or coal dust, or the improper use of explosives; surface fires communicating to the mine through the shaft or tunnel, underground furnaces and boiler plants, ignition by friction on oily wooden rollers or rope haulage-ways; fires occasioned by spontaneous combustion of coal, timber or greasy waste. Most effective means of exploring and combating fire is the oxygen helmet. Article, H. M. Wilson, Insurance library.

Mine Fires spread rapidly. Unless extinguished within a few minutes from the start, the closing of the section or mine often becomes necessary. Mines should be patrolled by lookouts and employees, especially English-speaking, and the more intelligent should be organized into a fire brigade for instant service.

MINERAL BURNING OIL—Obtained by the fractional distillation of crude petroleum and shale oil.

MINERAL INDIA-RUBBER NAPHTHA—Produced during the process of refining tar by sulphuric acid.

MINERAL LUBRICATING OILS—See Hydrocarbon.

MINERAL OIL FOR MEDICINAL PURPOSES—Petroleum oil products and Russian white oils are used. Work in compounding risks include mixing the oil with Fullers earth, then refining, distilling, filtering, all by steam heat. Barrelling, bottling, labelling, painting barrel heads and chemical laboratory for testing. Premises usually very oily.

MINERAL OILS are usually products of coal tar and petroleum. They are considered more hazardous than the animal or vegetable oils. The most important thing to know is the flash point. If not mixed with vegetable or animal oils are not subject to spontaneous combustion.

MINERAL WATERS AND BEVERAGES—Work consists of making flavoring extracts, charging or carbonizing water with marble dust, straining, filtering, bottling, labelling, packing. Use steam or gas-heated kettles, steam-heated bottle washers. Bottles are packed in excelsior or straw jackets. See Bottlers.

MINERAL WOOL—The product obtained by forcing a jet of steam or air against a stream of molten slag or molten rock.

MIRROR BACKING—An amalgam of mercury and tin. Tin foil, i. e., tin leaf, is first applied over the glass, then mercury is poured upon this, and it unites with the tin, making an amalgam.

MIRRORS—(Electroplating Mirrors)—A new method of silvering mirrors consists of depositing the metal on the glass by means of a high potential electric current. Electrical hazard.

MITRE SAWS—Used by woodworkers to cut any kind of pieces at an angle.

MIXED ACIDS—Mixture of nitric and sulphuric acids. If in contact with organic matter will cause fire.

MOLASSES DEALERS make rock candy at times using steam vacuum kettles. They may also have benzine for thinning paint for barrel heads.

MOLASSES REFUSE—The ashes of molasses refuse (used for fuel in molasses or sugar factories), contains about 1-3 potash and 5 per cent. phosphotic acid. Is used for fertilizer.

MOLASSES WASTE LIQUID—Used in fertilizer. The waste liquid derived from molasses contains about 60 per cent. water and 40 per cent. substance. The body portion is now reclaimed by the following process: Waste pumped into large wood tanks, then to steam-heated still evaporators with condenser apartments. The heavy liquid is then run into large storage tanks, and then flowed to a hopper, into which ground phosphate is added. It is then mixed and dried. Considered non-hazardous if fuel oil system for dryers is approved and no grinding of phosphate on the premises. Molasses-soaked floors burn fiercely.

MOLLACH—A benzine-thinned stain used by leather goods manufacturers.

MOLYBDENITE—Ore of molybdenum which is used to give hardness to steel.

MONITOR—A raised roof structure of various shapes and sizes, with glass sides. Sometimes called "Texas" or "Lantern Skylights."

MONOLITH—A single piece or block of stone, as a single piece stone column.

MONOLITHIC CONSTRUCTION—An all reinforced concrete building.

MONO-NITRATES are not necessarily dangerous.

MONOTYPE MACHINE—Used by printers for casting and setting up lead type in single letters. First a key board is used, where the different styles of type, spacing and alignment are indicated by perforating a roll of paper. This paper roll is put in the casting machine. Air pressure blowing through the perforations of different sizes and spaces regulates the machine operation so that the lead type is automatically cast and set up. Usually motor driven. The lead pot should have rigid iron connection, and floor under machine should be metal clad. See Printers.

MONTAN WAX—A soft coal distillate from Austria; melts at near 180 deg. F. Not hazardous.

MOPS—Prof. John H. Bryan, principal of the Ward School at Marion, Ohio, on several occasions found mops used by the janitor in oiling the floor burned to ashes, it being evident that the building each time narrowly escaped being burned. To prove the nature of the trouble, he saturated several mops with the floor oil and hung them where there were no inflammable surroundings. A mop saturated with oil at 5 p. m. was found to be very warm at 7 a. m., and in one instance he watched a mop until it burst into flames. It is claimed that the ill-fated Collinwood school fire may have started in this manner.

MORAL HAZARD—The moral hazard of a risk is most pertinently described by Colonel Ducat as "the danger from friction caused by high insurance and low depreciated stocks and property coming together. And just the difference between what would have been the fire loss with no insurance and the fire loss under insurance would be the moral hazard of the risk."

Unoccupied dwellings outside of the police protection of cities or towns, slept in once in a while by caretakers, which, by the way, is not dwelling occupancy unless approved by the agent. They are open to tramps, subject to carelessness of boys and like the family-deserted farm dwelling, are hazardous risks.

Ex-factory buildings that may have cost thousands of dollars, but which, with their machinery removed, have been purchased for a few hundred dollars and converted into barns and warehouses. Such buildings are liable to be overvalued and insured for more than they are worth.

Stocks of merchandise purchased at assignee's sale for 65-cents-on-the-dollar invoice, and insured at 85-cents-on-a-dollar invoice, because the insured got a bargain. Careful consideration of the property as to present cash value from an insurance point of view is necessary.

Long distance over the hills and far away from the agency risks, on which the commission will not pay the agent for surveying them, and the amount of premium will not warrant the expense of the special for inspecting them. When insured "unsight, unseen," as boys swap pocket knives they are often sold (by fire) in a manner that causes the local agent to think the company carrying the business may also have been sold.

Property that has outlived its usefulness, that is unoccupied, that is not adapted for the purpose for which it was intended, that is overvalued, that is offered at forced sale, or that is at a distance from the agency, should be avoided; or, if written after full knowledge of the facts pertaining to it have been obtained, the amount of insurance thereon should be based upon commercial cash values, instead of upon the cost of replacement, and rates should be made to cover the hazard.

In betting $1,000 under a policy of insurance against $7.50 premium or any other amounts, unsatisfactory losses can often be avoided by keeping an eye on the possible amount of loss instead of on the small amount of premium. It is also an excellent plan in such cases to carefully examine the other fellow's stake before accepting the bet.

Losses under the conditions stated are not necessarily criminal; they can arise from legitimate carelessness that would not occur if the insurance was 70 or 75 per cent. of the commercial value instead of the commercial value being less than 75 per cent. of the insurance.

Moral Hazard—(By Samuel R. Weed, in "The Weekly Underwriter.") What is that intangible, but important, part of fire risk which is commonly called the moral hazard?

It exists in other lines of business, and, in fact, it is omnipresent in all vocations where financial responsibility is involved, and is frequently a synonym for a form of dishonesty. If we hear of a bank or a stock broker or a merchant who is dishonest we frequently describe his condition as overburburdened with "too much moral hazard." Consequently we must understand at the outset that moral hazard is a risk which to a greater or less extent permeates all kinds of business. It is the same as short weights in the grocery, or coal yards; it is the same as misrepresentation in merchants' transactions or downwright fraud in manufacturing, or any other dishonest proceeding to deceive the public on the part of the man who has something to sell and finds a market among the innocent purchasers. In the majority of cases there are some ways of discovery and detection, and often of punishment, but in fire insurance the moral hazard risk goes down much deeper because it is a long-drawn-out process of crime which may be conceived months or years before it is actually committed, and it is more generally suspected than proved. It is, however, sometimes confirmed by circumstantial evidence, but even then the victim has no redress. It is intangible because we have to search into the inner motives of man and go below the surface before finding any important proof. Attempts to describe it in general terms have often been made, but the difficulty of a description applicable to each case is increased by the fact that no two instances are precisely alike. . . .

There are certain questions which should be answered by the agent, or which he should answer for himself, which will assist him materially in forming a correct judgment whether the insurance seeker is a safe subject for the company:

1. Has the applicant been long established in business in the place? If not, is he a resident or a newcomer, and if the latter, where was he formerly located, and why did he change?

2. Does his business appear to be prosperous? Has he good local credit? Have any of his notes been protested by the local banks? Has he ever failed, and if so, upon what terms did he settle with his creditors?

3. Was he ever burned out? Where and how did the fire originate? Was he insured, and if so, did he have any trouble in settlement with the insurance companies? Are the same companies willing to insure him again? An inquiry addressed to your head office will often bring out this information, which is inaccessible at your own residence.

4. Is the insured a woman? Or is the active manager doing business as agent for his wife, and if for another, for whom? Has the present owner or manager of the business ever been connected with anyone who has suffered from fire?

5. Is the business of a declining class? Are the premises poorly located in the town for profit? Is the building out of repair? Has there been any difference with the landlord, and is the owner of the building a desirable person to insure?

6. Has the applicant suffered from strikes or differences with labor unions, or been publicly or privately threatened with damage by strikers or discharged workmen? . . .

The companies as a rule dislike to insure property in the name of a woman unless it be one of the small stocks which may properly be managed by her sex, such as a retail haberdashery or a dressmaking stock. But the trouble with a woman in the case lies in the probability that she is being used as a mask for somebody else. It is surprising how many cases turn up where, by the use of a woman's initials only, companies are deceived by the supposition that it is a masculine whom they are insuring. I know an examiner for an important city company who invariably sends out an inquiry when initials only appear for the full name of the person or persons insured. He uses this form of query: "Is the insured male or female? If a female, is she married, and if so, what is the full name of her husband? If a widow, please state the fact." This examiner once told me that in the course of five years he had turned down several daily reports because he learned that the insured was of the feminine gender, and what is still more remarkable, at least one in ten of the risks on which policies had been canceled for this reason had subsequently burned. Probably this should be called a "suspected moral hazard" in which the woman is not directly to blame, and if the whole truth were known it would be found a man profited by the loss of such a risk far more than the woman whose name was used as a cloak for the man's insurance. These instances are easily connected with incendiarism, and I have no doubt that many of them belong to some of the worst classes of moral hazard which have ever come to light.

I presume you will be surprised when I assert that there is a new kind of moral hazard affecting the business of fire underwriting now in vogue quite unknown twenty-five years ago. I mean a sort of reverse action of the moral-hazard principle succeeding a fire quite apart from its origin. I believe the experience of the last twenty years has demonstrated that many an honest loss has been turned into a dishonest loss by the temptation, or whatever else you choose to call it, to indulge in crookedness directly aroused by the fire. Somehow the underwriters are often treated as easy marks who can be plundered by fraudulent claims and robbed of large sums by schemes to cover up the real loss with a layer of fraud which sometimes escapes detection. I believe that the discovery of such schemes is generally possible through patience and perseverance, as well as by skillful handling of the testimony. Some very remarkable evidences of this kind of moral hazard have been gathered by our loss committee, and the former manager, Mr. Robb, could, if he would, tell you of one very extraordinary case in the surrender of policies for a large amount upon a stock of plate glass in this city without any payment at all, after a most elaborate scheme of fraud had been prepared which was exposed by accident. One of the links in the chain was weak, and that broke down all the connecting links. I am obliged to withhold the particulars of this case, but I believe it was one where the rascality really followed the fire.

The temptation to swell loss claims sometimes overtakes men who are esteemed honest and upright in all the walks of life. The peculiar view which some people hold regarding the value of their property after the damage frequently leads to downright perjury, a phase of moral hazard which is generally created, promoted, suggested and carried forward by the new profession known as the public adjusters. I wish it were possible to take up the record of every loss handled by public adjusters in the last ten years. The revelation would, I am sure, astonish you.

MORDANTING—Means fixing the colors of the dyes so as to thoroughly impregnate the material.

MORTGAGEE CLAUSE (full contribution)—This clause is usually placed on policies covering the second and third mortgagee's interest. The object of this clause is to make all policies contribute their proportion of loss in case of fire. If the insurance company controls the insurance for the first mortgagee, the full contribution feature may be omitted.

MORTGAGEE INTEREST—Except in special cases, the interest of the mortgagee is not insured direct or separate, but is covered by the usual mortgage clause.

MORTISE—A hole cut in one piece for receiving the tenon which projects from the other piece. A chisel mortiser, by repeated thrusts, produces the desired hole.

MOTION PICTURE BOOTHS—Usually built of asbestos lumber ¼-inch thick on 1¾ by 1¾ and ¼-inch angle iron frame. Iron booths are now obsolete. Where the equipment is permanent, tile or brick is used. Shutters should close automatically. **Ventilation:** metal pipe should extend to outer air (not to attic). **Hand-operated machines:** the operator is always at the machine and therefore can readily detect any mechanism which might go wrong. If the machine is electrically driven, it may run wild, the film become clogged, and before the operator could shut down the machine many feet of film may be burned. Machines should be fastened to floor to prevent tipping them over. **Automatic shutters** on machines are to shut off rays from the arc lamp when machine stops and thus prevent ignition of the film. The upper magazine in the machine holds the film being shown which is run through a thin slot to a lower magazine where it is wound up. These slot openings are just large enough to accommodate the film. Arc lights at machines should be enclosed in metal box lined with asbestos. **Careless operators** are responsible for most of the fires in picture booths. Extinguishers and sand pails are required in booths.

MOTION PICTURE FILMS are made of nitro-cellulose.

Non-inflammable films are made of cellulose acetate. Those of the pyroxilin type when stored in poorly ventilated vault are apt to decompose and the gas arising, when mixed with air will explode if ignited. The **master film** (**original negative**) is very valuable, especially before copies are made. Sometimes one film will exceed in value the entire contents of the studio. The values run up to half a million dollars for a single film. See Film Vault.

MOTION PICTURE SHOW HOUSES—Note if building is specially designed for this purpose or a converted building, the construction and cleanliness of booth, heating apparatus, lighting system, care of scrap films which are produced when reels are re-joined after breaking, location of re-winding room for films. The ordinary picture show building is a high one-story building and may embrace the theatre hazard by having a wooden stage for vaudeville performances, wooden dressing rooms and a quantity of scenery.

MOTION PICTURE STUDIO—Usually consists of a group of buildings varying in size and construction and communicating with each other. In some, the different departments are in separate buildings or sections; while in others, the dressing rooms, scenery storage and painting, carpenter shop, studio and carpenter shop may be under one roof. The stage and its equipment is usually of a portable or knock-down type. At least one side and the roof of studio is glass. Neither wired glass nor glass with screens can be used for studio lights because the wires would show on the picture if taken by natural light.

Process: Films received in metal cans, washed in benzine, sensitized in glycerine bath. The picture is taken and developed in bath of hyposulphate of soda and hydroquinon, glycerine and water and a thin solution of water and mercury, then air dried. Printing is done in a high speed all metal, electric power printer. An incandescent light is in an enclosed cylinder in center of printing machine with a small aperature to transmit light. The negative and positive films are on open reels and pass through a thin slot about five inches from the light and wound on reels underneath the printer. The film is then perforated, i. e., a row of small holes is made down each side of the film which fit the cogs on a reel on which the film is wound. Perforators are high speed, electric power machines, equipped with a suction pipe to carry off the dust created. The small particles are dropped through bottom of machine to a metal can. The joining of sections of film is done by hand, each worker having a small bottle of cement. The films are then polished on reels on which are fastened flaps of felt saturated with alcohol and operated by hand. They are then projected through a moving-picture machine to detect imperfections. (A moving-picture machine is sometimes called a projecting machine.) Laboratory work consists of making a special cement for joining films composed of carbonate of potassium, collodion, amyl acetate, acetone, iodide potassium, sulphuric acid, ethyl acetone and sulphuret potassium. Joining, printing, developing, perforating, polishing, cleaning, property rooms, carpenter shop, painting, laboratory and projecting should be in separate rooms. Rubber-covered floors are used a great deal to prevent nails in heels of shoes producing sparks and setting fire to film scrap on floor. Care in disposal of film scrap is very important. Film vaults should conform with underwriters' requirements.

National Association of the Motion Picture Industry, Inc., says:

1. Keep plenty of water handy. (a) In an automatic sprinkler system suitable to your conditions; (b) In convenient buckets; (c) In faucets with an inch and a quarter hose and nozzle attached; (d) Have fire extinguishers, which everybody is shown how to use; (e) Keep sand pails handy. Sand will stop a small film fire quickly and will not damage the stock.

2. Keep film in containers when not actually in use. The time lost in replacing it is nothing. Naked film is the one condition that guarantees that a little fire will get beyond control in a few seconds.

3. Throw film scraps into self-closing metal cans, never into open waste baskets.

4. Keep the cutting rooms, etc., well swept. The tiny

pieces of film that fly about make the dust as dangerous as so much gunpowder.

5. Have a professional electrician do all your wiring, in accordance with every city ordinance, no matter how "unreasonable" it seems. Have the light globes caged—a broken globe may make only one spark, but that can ignite $1,000 worth of film. Handle no film by any artificial light but electricity.

6. Box your radiators and steam pipes. The film that touches a hot pipe and crinkles up might just as easily have burst into flame.

7. Enforce the "no smoking" rule. Give the boys a smoking room if they need it, and make the boss and his guests who are looking over the place leave their cigars, cigarettes and pipes outside, as they would if they stepped into a theater for a glimpse of the picture.

8. Banish the "strike anywhere" match. Furnish boxes of safety matches free, if necessary. But don't have anything that will light except when it is intended to.

9. Keep only enough cement, gasoline and collodion on hand for the day's work. They are all highly inflammable, and should be stored where they can do no harm.

10. Appoint one man or woman as fire monitor, and let him know it is all his job is worth to fail to call down the boss, the cutter, or the office boy for any carelessness.

Bad housekeeping and carelessness: Unguarded radiators. Unprotected electric light globe over film. Electric wires wrapped around steam pipe. Film scrap on floor. Lengths of film on floor. Willow waste basket used. Film on fire extinguisher. Too much film on each table. Film not kept in cans. Smoking. Waste paper and newspapers on floor. Posters in same room with film. Lack of order and cleanliness.

Motion picture studio fire, 226-32 West Thirty-fifth Street, New York City, Jan. 3, 1917. The tables on which the films were joined or examined, had an electric light in them, located in a well and covered with a heavy piece of glass. The glass cover in one of the tables was very loose fitting, in fact, it was not the original glass made for the opening.

While an employee was joining a reel on this table, the electric light globe broke. It is thought the heavy glass cover fell on the globe, and as a result the film on the table caught fire. Some of the employees tried to put the fire out by throwing the film on the floor and stamping on it, but were not successful. The flames ignited other films in the vicinity, some of which were not in cases. There were about 59 reels, part in cans, a few of which were in a single wall metal cabinet at the time of the fire. The fire spread over the entire rear mezzanine on the second floor, roof and main part of the studio and filled the premises with an irritating dense smoke. Some of the employees had difficulty in getting to the street, due to the smoke. The importance of segregating motion picture studios and factories and the necessity for automatic sprinklers in connection therewith was illustrated by the fact that the contents of this film department furnished exceptionally inflammable fuel to the fire. This fire would seem to justify the regulations of the fire department requiring a special permit and rigid safeguards for the storage of inflammable films in excess of five reels (5,000 feet) the practice of having electric lights on the film tables, should be discouraged as much as possible. The danger may be somewhat reduced by making the heavy glass over the top of the light well permanent; also the bottom of the well should be removed so no pieces of film can lodge around the electric light globe.—(New York Board Report.)

MOTOR CYCLE AND BICYCLE REPAIR SHOPS— Usually located in basements or on grade floors, with apartments above. Machine shop hazards, with oily floors. Sometimes do painting, enameling, vulcanizing, cleaning with gasoline and have a large stock of acetylene gas cylinders for sale, a stock of automobile accessories, including celluloid articles, and a gasoline supply station. These places are sometimes used as "hang-outs." See Bicycle and Motor Cycle.

MOTOR GENERATOR—A combination of motor and dynamo. The shafts of each are coupled together, so that when the motor shaft rotates it will turn the dynamo shaft.

MOTORS should be enclosed to prevent foreign matter

coming in contact with same. The boxes should be lined with zinc or asbestos and kept clean. Oil pans under same will prevent oil from saturating floor.

MOVING BUILDINGS—Buildings that have been moved should always be inspected to ascertain if the walls have been weakened or if the chimneys have been cracked.

MUFFLER—A type of gas stove with a hooded top to retain the heat. Used to heat soldering or pressing irons.

MULE—A long iron frame spinner used in silk mills.

MULLIONS—Upright bars dividing a window into two or more lights.

MUNGO—Obtained by "devilling" the rags or remnants of fine woolen goods.

MUNITIONS are not necessarily the same as ammunition. Usually denotes war material with the exception of explosives.

MUNITIONS PLANT FIRES—The growth of the munitions business has resulted in greater precautions for safety being taken in many factories that were not operated with success prior to the war. They have since become successful, thus minimizing the moral hazard. Overtime also has a tendency to minimize the risk, inasmuch as when work people are on the premises all the time any incipient fire is more likely to be arrested before actual damage is done. The following are features of the report: prolonged hours of labor, night work, etc., have increased the period of action of the active special or manufacturing hazards. A tendency toward uncleanliness has been created or enhanced by long hours of labor, the difficulty of obtaining satisfactory help, the increased congestion of equipment and material, and, above all, by the failure of superintendents, through pressure of other business, to give attention to matters of housekeeping. The introduction into established risks of new manufacturing or special hazards or processes. In some cases there has been failure to protect these in a satisfactory and permanent manner on the assumption that they were of a temporary character. In other cases there has been failure to realize the true nature of the hazard involved and ignorance of protective measures.—(Weekly Underwriter.)

MUNTINS—See Mullions.

MURIATE OF AMMONIA—See Sal-ammoniac.

MURIATIC ACID—See Hydrochloric Acid.

MURIATIC ACID VAPORS will extinguish fires.

MUSHROOMING—A term used to express the action of fire which travels up a shaft in a building and spreads out on the upper floor. Usually a mushroom fire destroys the roof.

MUSIC STOCKS—Sheet music stock is very susceptible to water damage. Great percentage of the stock is usually obsolete or out-of-date stuff.

MUSICAL INSTRUMENT FACTORIES include wood and metal working and varnishing hazard. (Poor fire record.)

MUSTARD FOR TABLE USE is ground wet in burr mills, mixed with spices and vinegar and bottled. The hazard is mild. (Always inspect this class.)

MUSTARD OIL is pressed from seeds by hydraulic press after crushing and grinding, then filtered. All machinery and woodwork becomes very oily. The grinding of mustard seed is not so hazardous as the grinding of mustard after all oil has been extracted. (Write class with caution.)

MUTUAL INSURANCE—This differs from stock insurance by charging a set premium for each class at the inception of the insurance. At the end of the year, part of the profits of the company are returned to the policy-holders of each class of insurance which has shown a profit.

N

NAILS OR SCREWS packed in kegs suffer severe water damage. In order to get a fair amount of salvage, they must be thoroughly dried at once to prevent rust. Galvanized ware gives greater salvage.

NAKED LIGHTS—See Inflammable Vapors.

NAMES—Business in Woman's Name—A business may be in a woman's name for any of the following reasons: She may be a widow or unmarried, divorced or a "grass widow"; her husband may have broken a lease and to avoid suit transferred the business to her; a judgment may have been entered against her husband and to avoid payment, transferred the business to her; failures of husband; husband may have a bad fire record, or, owing to manner of conducting business, credit is denied him by the trade. Instances are known where the husband has sold a business with the proviso that he would not engage in the same business as a competitor to the new owner, but has started up a business as a competitor in his wife's name. The wife or other female relative may have furnished the capital or owned the business before marriage; it may be a woman's trade, such as corsets or infants' wear, the wife conducting the business and the husband being employed elsewhere. See Moral Hazard; also Foreigners.

NAPKINS—This stock is little affected by water damage.

NAPPERS—Machines designed to brush or pick up the surface of knitted cloth, producing long nap or fleece effect. See Knitting Mills.

NAPHTHA, GASOLINE, BENZINE or other fluids which emit inflammable vapors below 100 deg. F. should be stored outside of buildings in steel tanks, buried at least two feet below ground, or otherwise isolated. In printing establishments permission is given by local boards of underwriters to store these materials above ground outside of building in an approved safety can not exceeding five gallons' capacity if in a box, on a permanent shelf, securely fastened to the wall, but not directly in front of a window; the shelf to be of metal, provided with guard rail, so that the can cannot be readily dislodged by accident. The law prohibits using fire-escapes for storage of such inflammables. Should be used in the building from approved safety can and kept outside on a shelf on nights, holidays and Sundays. A box of sheet iron, under lock and key, or other incombustible material, is recommended as a protection from the weather. The box will fulfill the requirement for a guard rail. See Petroleum; also Inflammable Liquids; see Inflammable Vapors.

NAPHTHA CEMENT—See Rubber Cement.

NAPHTHALENE—Coal tar camphor; white crystalline solid. Usually kept in wooden barrels. Not hazardous.

NAPHTHALIC (or phithalic acid)—A crystalline acid obtained from napthalene. Inflammable.

NAPHTHA SOAP is said to contain a small amount of naphtha.

NAPHTHA WOOD—See Alcohol.

NARROW STREETS—Buildings on narrow streets should be written with caution. The fire department is often handicapped in fighting the fire for lack of room for their apparatus and cannot perform their best work.

NATIONAL FIRE PROTECTION ASSOCIATION—The purpose of the National Fire Protection Association is "to promote the science and improve the methods of fire protection and prevention; to obtain and circulate information on these subjects and to secure the co-operation of its members in establishing proper safeguards against loss of life and property by fire." It is supported by members' subscriptions. There are two classes of members, active and associate.

NATRONA—A form of petroleum.

NAVAL STORES—Turpentine, pitch, rosin and tar. Usually stored in large area frame sheds or in yards along water fronts. Painting barrel heads is sometimes done on premises. Burn fiercely.

NAVE—The main body of a building having connecting wings or aisles on either side of it, as in a church.

NEATSFOOT OIL—Derived from the feet of various animals. Used for leather dressing. Rags saturated with this oil should be kept in self-closing waste cans.

NECKWEAR (especially ladies') is very susceptible to damage from smoke, fire and water. This stock might include the finest grade of chiffon and malines. See Silk Neckwear.

NEEDLES—Made from steel wire, cut into lengths, heated in furnace and rolled. Points are made on grindstone by hand. An automatic machine cuts out the gutters and flattens the heads. Eyes are punched in, and the needles tempered in a furnace. To polish, they are spread on a cloth, sprinkled with emery dust, oil and soft soap, and rolled in the cloth (called "friction" bath) rinsed in water, sorted and packed. Stock subject to severe water damage.

NESTY—A term used by insurance men to describe congested areas of frame buildings.—Gene Eagles.

NET SURPLUS of a company. After all liabilities have been met (including unearned premium reserve and paid up capital) that which remains is net surplus. It is an asset set aside mainly for the purpose of meeting obligations due to large conflagrations.

NETTLES—Fibres grown on plantations are now being used as fabric substitutes for cotton.

NEUTRALIZE—If an acid is deprived of its acid properties by means of an oxide (base) or vice versa it is said to be neutralized.

NEUTRAL SALTS, i. e., Glaubers, Epsoms, etc., are so called because the acid properties of the sulphuric acid are wholly neutralized in them. Neutral Spirits, see Grain Alcohol.

NEWMAN SYSTEM of time recording for watchmen. The Newman System equips the watchman with a portable watch-clock which must be carried in rotation on every hourly inspection round to patrol stations located at the important inspection points, and each having a key, which when inserted and turned in the clock, registers on a paper dial therein the distinctive mark of that station and the exact time at which the station was visited. The keys are fastened and sealed at the various stations. The clock is locked while in possession of the watchman.

NEW VENTURES are usually tabooed by underwriters unless capital is in evidence to promote the business.

NEWSPAPER PLANTS—Printing hazards. Employ day and night shifts and some employees generally about the plant at all times. The last class to want a fire because the success of a newspaper lies in keeping editions going. Considered good moral fire risks.

NICOTYLIA—An oily inflammable liquid.

NIGGERHEAD—A small black box enclosing the alarm mechanism on a water flow alarm attached to a sprinkler system.

NO. 99—Special cleaning fluid, classed as kerosene.

NITRANILINE—Powder used by dyers, cannot be ignited. A subjection to moisture causes it to decompose in which action it throws off heavy fumes and generates heat.

NITRATES—Nitrate of barium. See Barium Nitrate.

Nitrate of Copper Crystals—If bruised or moistened will smoke and may explode.

Nitrate of Lead—See Lead Nitrate.

Nitrate of Strontia—See Strontium.

Nitrate of Potassium—See Potassium Nitrate.

Nitrate of Potash—Formed by the union of nitric acid and potash (commonly called nitre or saltpetre) is one of the ingredients of gunpowder.

Nitrate of Soda—See Soda Nitrate.

Ferric Nitrate is used by dyers.

Silver Nitrate—Used in photo-indelible inks and mirrors.

NITRATING is usually a hazardous process.

NITRATING ACID—See Mixed Acid.

NITRE—See Potassium Nitrate. As soon as emptied nitre bags should be thoroughly washed and dried in the open. Empty bags are very inflammable.

NITRIC ACID—Composed of nitrogen and oxygen, obtained by the action of sulphuric acid upon nitrate of potash. See Acids.

Extracts From a Paper Before the Cincinnati Convention of the International Association of Fire Engineers by Chief Thomas A. Clancy of Milwaukee, First Vice-President of the Association:

If concentrated nitric acid be poured upon powdered charcoal it will take fire under ordinary temperatures.

Paper, cotton, sugar, starch, and certain other organic substances treated with concentrated nitric acid, become thoroughly changed, and though in their outer form they remain the same, they become violently explosive.

Warm nitric acid run into badly annealed carboys will crack them, and set fire to the straw or other packing, or combustible material surrounding them. If this powerful oxidizing acid reaches pine wood, especially pine knots, a fire will result with frightful rapidity.

Nitric acid, while contained in the carboy, is safe enough, but should it leak into organic matter, the mixture becomes spontaneously inflammable.

Like many other chemical substances it is readily affected by light, and many substances formed by its action are decomposed by exposure to sunlight.

Uses of Nitric Acid—Nitric acid is used in a very large number of industrial operations, viz.: in dyeing, in the preparation of lacquers; in the manufacture of picric acid, nitrobenzol, etc.; in the manufacture of many coal-tar colors; in many explosives, as gun-cotton, fulminate of mercury, nitroglycerin, etc.

The nitrates, as the compounds derived from nitric acid by the replacement of its hydrogen by a metal are called, are, like the acid itself, powerful oxidizing agents. They therefore require considerable care in handling, not because they have any tendency to burn in air, but because of their liability, when mixed with oxidizable matter, to produce its oxidation and consequent ignition and inflammation. Slight friction of a nitrate against any dry inflammable matter, such as wood, may be sufficient to start a fire. If the nitrate and inflammable substance be intimately mixed there results a violently explosive combination. Gunpowder is such a mixture.

Nitrates which are specially important on account of their common occurrence are:

Sodium Nitrate—Largely used as a manure and in the preparation of nitric acid, sometimes in the manufacture of mining powder.

Potassium Nitrate, "Saltpetre" or "Nitre"—Used for preserving certain articles of food; in the manufacture of matches and of gunpowder.

Lead Nitrate—Used in the preparation of pigments.

Ammonia Nitrate—Used in the preparation of nitrous oxide, the "gas" of the dentists, and in certain explosives.

The so-called **"Nitrate of Iron"** of the dyer, prepared by oxidizing "copperas" (ferrous sulphate) with nitric acid, consists mainly of ferric sulphate.

"Aqua Fortis" or "strong water" (because of its great solvent power) is the name given nitric acid by Gerber (A. D. 750-800), or one of his immediate predecessors, who made it by heating together saltpetre, copper, vitriol and alum. The first mention of the present process of making it is by Basil Valentine (A. D. 1450-1500) who says, however, that this method has long been used. Nitric acid was, therefore, one of the earliest mineral acids known.

Industrial Importance—Nitric acid occupies a peculiar position, somewhat like that of sulphuric, of great industrial importance as an intermediate step in the production of other products. Its salts are used to some extent in electroplating, since practically every one is soluble; in fireworks and colored lights, because of their high oxidizing power, and it is essential to the manufacture of many organic compounds besides nitrocelluloses, azo and diazo dyes. In tonnage and value, it stands among the leading chemical products. In the form of nitrates or substitution products it is essential in some way to the production of practically every explosive, while its salts (chiefly from natural deposits), are used for fertilizer in this country to a great extent.

Storage—Nitric acid should, if possible, be stored outside of manufacturing buildings or plants. If this cannot be done, then in vaults located in the basements of buildings. Some dealers in this article have separate compartments so that, in case of breakage, the contents may not run over the floor or mix with other acids and form explosive compounds of poisonous gases. Great care should be taken not to have more than what is actually required on any floor of the building and the acid not used should be returned to the carboy and vaults at the end of each working day. Due care should be taken not to jar the necks of the carboys in opening them. A small, cheap saw will readily saw through the plaster of Paris around the stopper, allowing it to come out easily. Heat of any kind will cause the acid in the carboy to expand and, overflowing, will generate heat when it comes in contact with the straw packing of the carboy.

NITRITE—A salt of nitrous acid. See Sodium Nitrite.

NITROBENZINE—Benzine treated with fuming nitric acid, resulting in a heavy, yellow, oily substance. Also known as oil of mirbane.

NITROBENZOL—See Mirbane Oil, also Trinitro Benzol.

NITROCELLULOSE—Formed by the nitration of cotton by treatment with a mixture of nitric and sulphuric acids. Highly inflammable and explosive.

NITROCELLULOSE FILMS—The storage, preparation and manufacture is very hazardous and they should not be stored in large quantities where subject to one fire.

NITROGEN—A gas, which with argon, constitutes four-fifths by volume of the atmosphere, and constitutes the basis of nitric acid.

NITROGLYCERINE—Obtained by nitrating glycerine with a mixture of nitric and sulphuric acids. A heavy oily liquid of yellowish color resembling glycerine in appearance. Highly explosive and dangerous. It freezes at about 40 deg. F. Very insensitive to shock when frozen and for this reason has been shipped packed in ice.

NITROGLYCERINE SPIRITS—A solution of nitroglycerine of not more than 10 per cent. strength in grain alcohol; same inflammability as grain alcohol.

NITRO-HYDROCHLORIC ACID—Mixture of nitric and hydrochloric acids; gives off chlorine gas.

NITROLEUM—Another name for nitroglycerine.

NITROTOLUOL—There are various compounds shipped

as nitrotoluol, for example, dinitrotoluol, mononitrotoluol and trinitrotoluol—some liquid and some solid. None of the liquids are explosive or dangerous. Of the solids, trinitrotoluol is the only one classed as a high explosive.

NITROUS ACID—A compound of four volumes of nitrogen and one of oxygen.

NITROUS ETHER—See Ethyl Nitrite; also Ether.

NON-BEARING WALL—One which supports no other load than its own weight.

NON-CONDUCTORS—Substances that do not conduct or transmit heat or electricity.

NON-DRYING OIL—Chief one is olive oil from olives.

NON-INFLAMMABLE—The term "non-inflammable" applies to materials and substances which will ignite but will not support flame when subjected to ordinary fire.

Alternative Definition—The term "non-inflammable" applies to articles, goods, wares, merchandise or materials of construction which will support combustion, but will not readily burn.

NON-STIPULATED WAREHOUSE—See Warehouses.

NOT WANTED—Policies are frequently written, delivered to the assured, then returned to the company because the insurance is not wanted. Should not be marked off after it has been in force for any length of time because an earned premium is then due.

NOTICE OF LOSS—The first notice sent an insurance company when a loss occurs, stating that a fire has occurred, the date, and approximate amount.

NOTIONS—This stock generally suffers a bad damage from fire. The stock is composed of many different articles, some very susceptible to water and others to smoke or the rusting of the metal parts which are generally on small wares. Celluloid articles may form part of this stock.

NOVELTY JEWELRY MANUFACTURING—See Jewelry.

NUCOLINE—Trade name for cocoanut oil.

NUISANCES—Glue factories, slaughter houses, soap factories, etc., in thickly populated sections are avoided by many underwriters. They may lower the value of surrounding property. May burn from incendiarism.

NUT AND BOLT FACTORIES—Hazards of annealing, tempering, machine shops with heavy and light machines, threaders. Wood floors readily become oil-soaked. Soda-and-water cutting fluid used in place of oil at the threaders reduces the oily floor hazard.

NUT GALLS—An excrescence formed on the leaves of certain trees by female insects. They contain tannic acid.

NUTMEG OIL, if mixed with iodine, detonates and causes fire.

NUTS—Filberts, with solid shell, considered good insurance. Walnuts with parted shells not as good as filberts. Shelled nuts yield very little, if any, salvage, if wet, scorched or even smoked.

O

OAKUM—Fibre tarred with pine tar and mineral oil; should be kept in a standard vault. Process: Fibre is put through an oakum-carding machine and then run between corrugated rolls on which a solution of tar is kept dripping. This saturated fibre is then wound up and pressed into bales ready for shipment. The process is hazardous. The tar pot should preferably be outside of main building and heated by indirect heat or steam. Surrounding woodwork burns quickly when saturated with the drips or scattered tar solution.

OAT CRUSHERS—Used in stables for crushing oats. Should have a magnet attached to keep metallic substances from passing through the rollers and creating sparks which might ignite the dust. If oats are screened before crushing the hazard is lessened.

OATS—Fires have probably been caused by spontaneous combustion due to the fermentation of the grain stored in damp places.

O. C.—The abbreviation for "on centers," meaning the distance from center to center of timbers, as beams "spaced 16 inches O. C."

"OCCUPANCY"—Means the use to which a building is put or the purpose for which it is occupied. The contents of a building determine its "occupancy." The "occupancy" may be a carpenter or paint shop, a garage, school house, theatre or grocery store. One building may have several occupancies, as stores on the first floor, offices on the second, and lodging rooms above. "Occupancy" in fire insurance schedules means the classification of the business of the tenants of any building. (Fire Facts, issued by Washington Surveying and Rating Bureau.) See Loft, also Risk.

OCHRES—Clays tinted with oxide of iron and manganese and small per cent. of water and sulphur. Artificially dried to expel water. Yellow ochre due to oxide of iron; brown, to manganese oxide. They are ground in raw linseed oil.

OFFICE BUILDINGS (fireproof)—The main features are the height, protection of ironwork, and floor openings. Many losses have occurred from old records and files kept in wood cabinets or lockers in rooms where boys go to lounge and smoke. Recommend all-metal construction for lockers.

OIL AND GREASE fires are best fought with ashes, earth, sand or cloths providing they are in well-ventilated places. If in closed places the introduction of steam will be found most desirable.

OIL, BOILING POINTS—Illuminating 212 deg. F. to 450 deg. F. Lubricating, 450 deg. F. to 800 deg. F. Paraffine oil, 600 deg. F. to 800 deg. F. Naphtha, 90 deg. F. to 212 deg. F. Mixture of lubricating and paraffine oils, 450 deg. F. to 800 deg. F. The lower the boiling or flash point the greater the danger of combustion or explosion.

OIL BURNING EQUIPMENTS (except household)—Except in isolated sections, the supply tank should be three feet under ground or three feet below basement floor of building and lower than any of the piping. This allows the oil to return by gravity to the tank. The capacity of tanks is regulated by local underwriters. Tanks (iron) to have a firm foundation, the soil around same well tamped (pounded down), the covering to be dirt with 6-inch concrete topping, tanks coated with rust-resisting paint. Above-ground tanks, oil must be pumped to building and not run by gravity to supply pipes, otherwise, in event of fire, a broken pipe would allow all the oil to drain from the tank and be a source of danger to surroundings. Dikes are built around tanks to prevent the oil running away where gravity feed is used. One-inch vent pipes are required on all tanks to extend 12 inches above any tank car or reservior. Those connected to tanks located inside of buildings should extend outside of building, three feet from any building and one foot above the roof, with screened gooseneck. See Cooking and Heating Apparatus. See Fuel Oil.

OILCLOTH FACTORY FIRE—Chandler Oilcloth Co., Yardville, N. J., May 2, 1916. The cause probably being gasoline vapor in the drying cells and coating room. The recommendations follow: (1) Where drying is accomplished by direct radiation in the drying cells, a system of ventilation by means of air exhaust fan in a separate building, taking suction from the bottom of each cell and discharging to the atmosphere should be employed; (2) Drying cells should be of heavy brick walls (side), but of light fire-resistive roof; fire doors should be at openings; (3) Coating machines should be provided with steam jets and floor should be sprinkled to keep humid condition of air; (4) Coating machine knife rolls, etc., should be grounded together with shafting and machines; (5) Electric light wiring in coating room should be standard in conduit with vapor-proof globes with wire guards; (6) Automatic sprinklers; (7) Quantity of coating mixture and gasoline should be reduced to minimum.—(A. R. Ramsdell, N. F. P. A., Vol. 10, 1916.)

OIL-COOKING AND HEATING—See Cooking and Heating Apparatus.

OILED CLOTHING—Clothing which has been waterproofed with linseed oil. When packed in solid piles is subject to spontaneous combustion. Should be hung on racks so that air will circulate through the stock.

OIL FIELDS—Deep-well drilling particularly is very hazardous because the boiler generally used has an open fire box and is liable to start a grass fire. The forge is usually kept within the derrick, and is safe in small volume wells or when the wind is blowing in the opposite direction. When a large gas pocket is struck, however, and the forge fire is not quickly extinguished, enormous fires usually result.

OIL GAS—Produced from paraffine oil. It is heavier than coal gas and heavier than air, rolls along the ground like a cloud and can be readily observed. It has been known to travel 300 to 400 feet to an open fire, flash back and explode the gasometer. When ignited in this manner, the flame is immense and lasts longer than the same volume of coal gas. See Pintsch Gas.

OIL HOUSES—See Factory Oil Houses.

OIL IN CANS—If cans are soldered, a moderate degree

of heat may melt the solder, allowing the oil to escape, and thus feed the fire.

OIL OF MIRBANE—See Mirbane Oil.

OILPROOF—See Shoe Factories.

OIL REFINERIES—Lightning is the greatest danger to tanks. Direct heat is used, and leaky valves or defective equipment may allow inflammable vapors to escape. After condensing, oil is graded by re-distilling. Gasoline and kerosene are purified with acid in large tanks agitated by steam or air under pressure.

OIL SEPARATORS—Those installed in a garage should be connected to the house drain, and be so arranged as to separate all oils from the drainage of the garage. See Garages.

OIL STORAGE—Risks may include gasoline, and filling of cars. Fires have been caused by back-firing of automobiles in driveways of buildings. Automobiles should be kept outside of buildings and barrels or cans loaded outside. Tanks of small capacity may have a combined fill and vent pipe so arranged that fill pipe cannot be used without opening vent. Oil is conveyed to underground storage tank by means of a fill pipe with inlet on street or yard. The inlet opening should be capped and surrounded by an iron box with cover and kept locked to prevent tampering.

OIL STOVES when on fire should have ashes or wet cloths placed around them, and, if possible, under the same (without moving the stove) and the fire then smothered with wet cloths. It is unwise to move the stove as the oil is likely to spill and spread the fire or explode.

OIL TANK FIRES are mainly caused by being struck by lightning. The tanks should have a permanent electrical "ground" so that in case they are struck this may prevent the ignition of the contents. See Erwin Extinguisher.

OIL TANKS—When on fire, if a sufficient quantity of dry, fine, tough foam (glue and glucose formula) is spread upon the burning oil surface, this foam, being lighter than oil and made of minute bubbles confining carbonic acid gas, will probably extinguish the fire.

OIL TESTING—In testing an oil for its flashing temperature the most rational method would be to heat the oil to a given temperature, aspirate it well with air and apply a flame to the mixture, noticing if an explosion occurs.

OIL OF TURPENTINE—See Turpentine.

OIL OF VITRIOL—See Sulphuric Acid.

OIL WAREHOUSES—Lubricating oil burns with a dense black smoke. Water in tremendous quantities is necessary to extinguish a fire once started in an ordinary-sized building. Barrels burst open, oil and water soak through walls and damage stocks in adjoining buildings.

OILY FLOORS under all kinds of machinery should be cleaned with a solution of ammonia, potash and lye. Under all heavy machinery such as pipe cutters, printing presses, motors, gas engines, a metal base with curbed edges should be placed to catch the oil and prevent it from spreading and soaking the floor. Sand should be used in place of sawdust for catching drips.

OILY WASTE RECLAIMING—Use steam-heated centrifugal machines, similar to laundry extractors, for extracting the oil. Fires have occurred in heaps of oily waste awaiting reclaiming. A class avoided by most companies.

OINTMENTS—Ingredients include lanium, paraffine, petrolatum, cocoa butter and wax. Hazards of heating by direct heat, and oily floors.

OLD METALS—See Refiners.

OLD RECORDS and Files—See Office Buildings.

OLD RUBBER and Metals—See Junk Shops.

OLEOMARGARINE—Made of beef suet and cottonseed oil.

OLEO-STEARINE—A packing-house product derived from beef fats.

OLEUM or N. O. V. (Nordhousen Oil of Vitriol)—The commercial term of fuming sulphuric acid containing anhydride.

OLIBANUM—A fragrant gum resin, readily ignited.

OLIVE OIL—Used in cooking food, soap-making, etc. On the premises of bottlers sawdust is used to catch the drips from barrels. Fires from spontaneous combustion have been thus caused. Sulphured Olive Oil is obtained by the extraction of olive oil by means of bisulphide of carbon.

OLIVOLINE—A non-gumming oil for lubricating.

OMNIBUS RISKS—Those housing a number of tenants with different manufacturing hazards. Companies usually write cautiously.

ONE-FIRE RISK—A risk, either a single building or group of buildings mutually exposing each other and subject to destruction by a single fire. One of the most important features to understand in underwriting.

ONYX (Imitation)—See Imitation Marble.

OPAL OIL—A petroleum distillate treated with sulphuric acid and rape oil.

OPEN FINISH—The absence of any finish so that the studding or ceiling joists are exposed.

OPENINGS TO ROOF SPACE should be boxed to prevent fire entering the same. See Illustration.

OPEN POLICY ACCOUNTS are opened for the convenience of brokers or assureds for the purpose of simplifying the writing of various sums of insurance, covering at various locations for short terms, such as goods in storage. A policy number is assigned to the account and all entries are made in an "open policy book" instead of on a policy. At the end of each month the company renders a bill for the amount of premium due for insurance carried during the month.

OPEN SPRINKLERS (automatic)—There are a number of risks where the successful control of fire is predicated upon an immediate and more general discharge of water, and where the item of water damage is not to be reckoned with. To meet this condition a new idea in sprinkler protection has been installed in the sulphur-grinding room of the National Sulphur Co., at Bayonne, N. J. This room is protected by a system of open sprinklers which are made automatic in action by the introduction of a quick-acting valve which holds back the water, and operated by an approved automatic heat-actuated device. In other words, this new system becomes operative upon the "rate of rise" principle rather than a predetermined temperature as in automatic sprinkler protection. Open sprinklers on outside of buildings are controlled by a valve, operated by hand. The system is dry pipe, and heads are already open, therefore no fusing is necessary. Used also to protect property from exposure fires. Used at the sides of piers for protection against burning vessels. See Sprinklers.

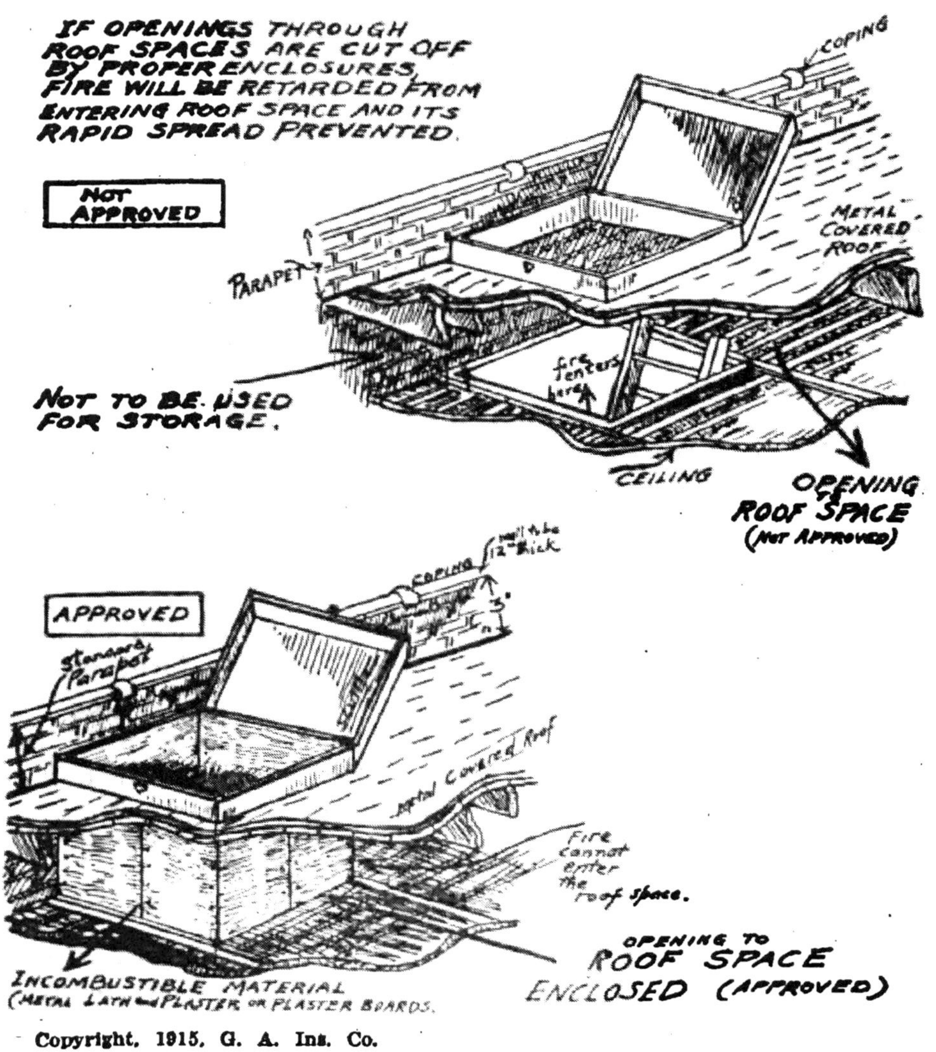

OPIUM—This stock is usually kept in metal-lined cases in the basement on account of the temperature at this point and also to keep away from other commodities. It is very valuable. Fire and heat would be likely to cause serious damage to this stock. Water washes out the morphine alkaloid and renders it valueless. Opium is a milky exudation from the unripe capsules of the poppy plant and this milky substance is rendered concrete by exposure to the air. As found in commerce it is a reddish brown, sticky gum-like body with a bitter taste and a heavy odor. It is used as a medicine and smoked as an intoxicant. Crude opium is usually handled in small lumps (gum-like) about 2 to 3 inches in diameter and are frequently wrapped in tropical leaves and packed in well-constructed metal-lined cases.

OPTICIANS—Principle hazard is lens grinding. A deposit of pitch is put on one side of the lens before grinding. Pitch is usually heated by direct gas heat.

ORDINARY—Designates a brick building constructed in the ordinary manner with joist floors and roofs. Derives the expression from the fact that about ninety-five per cent. of brick buildings are of this type. Briefly speaking, the walls are brick; floors and roof, single one-inch boards on wood beams. Any brick building inferior to semi-mill or mill construction can properly be termed "ordinary."

ORES—Iron is never found in the earth in its metallic state, but always combined with oxygen or some other substance forming ores.

ORGANS—Most companies refuse to write church organs unless receiving a line on the building or other furniture of the church. Very susceptible to fire and water damage.

OSAGE ORANGE—A tree extensively cultivated for hedges. Used by dyers and tanners, the dye therefrom being chiefly used to color khaki uniform cloth.

OSMACO REDUCER—Flash point 110 deg. F. Classed as non-volatile.

OSTEOCOLLA—Glue made from bones.

OSTRICH FEATHERS—If raw, will stand quite some water and smoke, and still give good salvage. Water has very little effect if clean, because the feathers must be washed in water anyway. Finished feathers are very susceptible, owing to dyes used and the prepared quills.

OTHER INSURANCE PERMITTED—The body of the policy states that the company must be notified if other insurance is taken to cover the property insured. The clause is designed to frustrate over-insurance as an inducement to incendiarism. It is now a general practice to include "other insurance permitted" on forms without ascertaining the real value of the property. See Forms.

OUT-BUILDINGS—These innocent-looking structures are liable to contain almost anything from rags to dynamite.

OUTPUT—A business term meaning the product of a factory, irrespective of the sales.

OVERALLS—See Contractors.

OVERLOADING OF FLOORS—Liable to cause sagging and throw shafting out of alignment, resulting in friction and over-heated journals. Buildings with this feature should be avoided.

OVERTIME—Factories which continually work their men overtime have been known to have numerous fires, owing to the sleepy indifference of the tired workmen. According to the terms of the printed policy, it is necessary to have a permit to work later than 10 p. m.

OXALIC ACID—Prepared by heating sawdust with mixture of caustic soda and caustic potash. Used in calico printing, dyeing, bleaching, cleaning brass. Non-hazardous.

OXIDES are so called because they contain oxygen.

OXIDIZING—Combining a compound or an element with oxygen. It may be rapid or very slow, with or without a flame. See Spontaneous Combustion.

OXIDIZING SUBSTANCES should be separated from carbonaceous materials.

OXY-ACETYLENE WELDING—A combination of oxygen and acetylene used for cutting or welding, producing a temperature as high as 6,000 deg. F. Used in most large machine shops and garage repair shops. The acetylene is seldom generated on the premises, but is received in tubes or tanks (cylinders) in the same manner as compressed oxygen. The apparatus is portable. The cylinders are provided with a fusible plug melting at 240 deg. F., to prevent explosions and in case of fire to allow the gas to escape slowly. Special storage places necessary. Cylinders not to be subjected to unnecessary heat, such as near a stove. Exercise care in handling for if break occurs, the acetylene gas under pressure (about 1,800 lbs.), is released and by proper mixture with air is explosive. The oxygen and acetylene cylinders each have a pipe attached, leading to a nozzle where the flame is used, and each cylinder has a pressure-regulating device indicating the working pressure being used and the pressure in the tank. These outfits are dangerous when used by careless workmen. See Autogenous Welding.

OXYGEN—A colorless, odorless, non-inflammable gas. It is needed to support combustion. If excluded from the air surrounding a fire, the blaze would immediately be extinguished.

OXYGEN CLEANING PROCESS for cylinders of automobile engines. From report of Underwriters' Association of New York.

The apparatus consists of an ordinary commercial metal oxygen cylinder containing the gas at an original pressure of about 300 lbs. The outlet is piped to a reducing valve set at from 15 to 25 lbs. and at this pressure the gas flows into some 5 to 8 feet of rubber tubing terminating in a combination handle and controlling throttle by which the oxygen is fed through a small metal tube some 10 to 14 inches long, forming a nozzle. In some cases it would appear that the reducing valve is omitted and the pressure reduced by expansion only.

The practice seems to be to remove spark plugs from the automobile cylinders, and bring each piston successively to the top of its stroke as its own cylinder head is being treated, thus closing both ports of the cylinder. A burning match or taper or a small piece of kerosene-dipped waste or piece of paper is then dropped into the spark plug opening and the oxygen jet introduced. The combustion thereon becomes much more active, consumes the original kindling rapidly and continues at high temperature until all carbon deposits are also burned away. When the last of the carbon is consumed the flame ceases. The only outlet during this process is the spark plug opening, through which the oxygen is introduced and bits of incandescent carbon, varying in size according to the conditions, some as large as a medium-sized pea, are blown out with considerable velocity. Some precautions in the shape of asbestos sheets are usually taken to prevent these sparks from falling inside the engine hood or elsewhere where they might do harm. It seems to be the practice to keep an extinguisher or two at hand while the work is being done.

OXYGEN GAS CYLINDERS—The approved type have a safety outlet sealed with a fusible metal, which melting, allows the slow escape of the gas. Storage should be outside of building, if possible.

OXYOZON—Metal polish. Flash, 208 deg. F. Classed non-volatile.

OZOKERITE—A natural mineral wax. Melts at 140 deg. F.

OZONE—A colorless gas with a pungent odor like chlorine.

P

PACKING—The material placed in the stuffing box of shafting to prevent leaks. Also pipe-covering. Materials used in boxing merchandise.

PACKING BINS—All inflammable substances used in packing, such as straw, tow, moss, tissue paper, excelsior, should be in a standard packing bin. Wood boxes must be lined with lock-jointed sheets of tin, hiding the nails so they cannot come out, and prevent the oxygen reaching the wood. The cover of box of same material, arranged with fusible link to close automatically.

PACKING CASES—Yards where boxes are made or re-made usually locate in congested sections. They may be in high piles under windows of adjacent buildings and contain considerable rubbish. Sometimes classed as conflagration breeders.

New Packing Cases—Firms making them usually locate in old buildings. Ordinary woodworking hazards. If un-dressed lumber is used, planers are necessary. Soft woods are used exclusively. Not considered desirable insurance risks.

PAILS AND CASKS—Are liable to freeze in cold buildings. Non-freezing solutions should be put in them at the approach of winter. Calcium chloride can be used to good advantage. See Fire Pails.

PAINT REMOVERS may contain alcohol, wood alcohol, benzole, gelatine or naphtha. The flash points are usually high, but the wax content prevents evaporation to a certain extent and the fire hazard is reduced thereby.

PAINTERS AND DECORATORS—Busiest season, April to October. Stock consists of the usual paints, wall paper samples, scaffolds, ladders and may include inflammables, such as benzine and turpentines. Smoking on premises should be prohibited. Fires have resulted from spontaneous combustion of oily rags and overalls. In buildings where painters have been at work, care should be exercised to see that all refuse and waste material is removed at night before locking up. Gasoline torches for burning off paint have caused many fires, due mainly to the workman leaving the device unattended.

PAINTINGS—In writing insurance on paintings care should be used as to the wording of the policy form, and the moral hazard investigated. There are three general forms. First, one of agreed limit of value; second, "it is understood and agreed that this is its true value." Under this form, company must pay total loss in case of fire. Third, with abandonment feature, the company is required to accept surrender of paintings in case of loss. Co-insurance is quite necessary in writing paintings, to protect the interest of the company.

PAINTS—Composed of pigment and liquid. Pigments are inert substances, such as asphalt, clay, coal, barytes, coke, coal-tar, charcoal, chalk, feldspar, carbon, flint, granite, graphite, gypsumite, lamp-black, lime, magnesia, manganese, ochre, iron, pitch, quartz, resin, sand, silica, zincs and oxides.

Oils and Solvents—Bisulphide of carbon, carbon tetrachloride, benzine, cotton-seed oil, cod oil, poppy oil, resin oil, petroleum, turpentine, ammonia, linseed oil, alcohol, acetic acid, sulphuric acid, muriatic acid, glycerine, carbonic acid. The degree of inflammability depends wholly on the nature of the liquid ingredients. The quantity on hand for use should be kept to a minimum.

Acid-proof Paints may contain coal tar, pitch, minerals, cement, ochre, asbestos, slaked lime, dryers, litharge, saltpetre, sulphur, mica, zinc, acetone.

Fire and Waterproof Paints may contain coal tar oil, gypsum, japan, liquid rubber, nitric acid, silicate, slate dust, salsoda, potash, antimony, sodium, ochres, sulphur, caustic potash, mica, sulphate of zinc, acetone, soap, saltpetre.

PALM OIL—A semi-solid fat extracted from the fruit of several species of palm. Used in soap making.

PANAMA STRAW HATS are not damaged by clean

water and only need to be reblocked even though being in water for a considerable length of time. The best grade of Panama hats are woven by hand under water.

PANEL RAISERS—A wood-working machine similar to jointers. Make considerable refuse. Bad features, overheated bearings, ignition of greasy sawdust.

PANEL WALL—An exterior non-bearing wall in a skeleton structure, built between piers or columns and supported at each story.

PAPER BOXES are made principally from cardboard which is cut to size, grooved (scored), where the sides and ends are to be folded, and the edges fastened together by strips of paper. This latter process is called "stripping." At times cold paste may be used or the corners wired together. The method of glue heating is important. The premises are usually crowed and untidy. Rubbish and clippings may be found in concealed spaces and around steampipes. The class of help is generally of an inferior quality and the fire record of the class is very poor. Printing labels or boxes is an incidental hazard. See Folding Boxes.

PAPER-HANGING FACTORIES—See Wall Paper Factories.

PAPER MILLS—Raw materials, wood pulp, rags, straw, hemp, old paper, flax, jute, small amount of powdered gypsum, clay, sulphates of barium and calcium. Wood pulp is cut into small bits, ground and pulverized, pressed into sheets, baled, then sent to the factories.

Wood pulp is received at the mill in bales. The bales are split open and the pulp separated into layers of about 2 inches thick. These layers are placed on a movable belt which carries it to a cutting machine. It is then carried by a belt to the top of the building, where it is directed into one of four separate tanks.

There are two types of cutting machines in use. One used in winter and the other in summer. The type used in winter is similar to a metal drum with three 3-inch grooves cut on opposite sides, in which sharp steel plates are placed. These revolve at high speed and when the wood pulp is forced through the machine, it is cut into narrow strips about ¾-

inch wide and 4 inches long. The type of machine used in summer for cutting the wood pulp resembles a very coarse circular saw and there are many of them on one shaft and set about 2 inches apart. This cuts the pulp much finer and is used in summer because the pulp is then much softer and can more easily be cut. This process is called shredding.

The tanks used are about 25 feet in height and 18 feet in diameter, constructed of wood. These are filled to within three or four feet of the top with water. The water used is called chalk water, and is that which is squeezed out of the wood pulp in the final process of making the paper. About 28 of these bales are put into each tank and also a quantity of white clay resembling chalk, mixed to a milky consistency, and also a small amount of rosin. This is churned for about one or two hours. It is then sent to another mill a short distance away, where it is further churned, glue and alum is added, and the pulp is then sent through presses where it is squeezed and made into paper.

The clay is put into a tank and thoroughly mixed with water for about two hours and at the end of that time is put into another tank, where it is mixed again so that there is no possibility of any lumps or hard substances remaining in the mixture.

The hazards in this process are the collecting of wood-pulp dust around the bearings of the motors and cutting machines, which may become oil-soaked and are then liable to spontaneous combustion. It is also conceivable that foreign parts, such as metal, might enter the cutting machines and there cause a spark, starting a fire.

There are other processes, such as boiling in caustic soda, and sometimes lime, or in sulphuric acid, sulphate of lime or magnesium. Pulp is also boiled in sodium sulphate. In all these, a similar process reduces the mass to a pulp, then bleached in acids, the minerals added, colored, pressed into sheets of paper, sized. The sulphur burners should be in a detached fire-proof building. Dusters to remove dust from stock should have blower system. Rags and old paper are used in making cheap grade paper and spontaneous combustion has occurred in rooms where they are stored. Other hazards in this process are storage of sulphide pulp and lime, friction and hot bearings in high-speed cutters, high pressure steam cookers, sorting tables and uncleanliness.—S. T. Skirrow.

PAPER PATTERNS—Very susceptible. Stocks may be obsolete. Lines should be written with caution.

PAPER RULING—The machine consists of a flat wooden bed, in centre and between sets of wooden rollers located at either end. Cords are run over one set of rolls, through an ink trough or pad and rolled over the rollers at opposite end. The paper is ruled as it travels under these cords across the bed of the machine. For double ruling, springs are connected to a bar with tail-piece of cloth wet with ink. From this cloth, the ink runs down a series of needles set like a comb, and as the paper passes under the needles a ruled line is made.

PAPER SIZINGS composed of soda ash, resin, alkalis and colors. In manufacturing, the hazards are direct heat for rosin kettles, drying ovens, mixing tanks, recoopering and painting barrels used in shipping the material.

PAPER STOCK—Rags, old paper or other material used for making paper. (A K. O. class.)

PAPER TUBES—Mailing tubes, ribbon spools and the like. In manufacturing, raw stock is rolled paper, glue, pasteboard and labels. Processes are slitting, winding, cutting, glueing, and tube forming; all similar to paper-box making.

PAPIER MACHE—Produced by pressing the pulp of paper between dies or by pasting paper in sheets upon models. Porous paper is used, saturated with flour and glue. As each layer is made it is heated. The form is then varnished, dried, shellaced and again dried. Principal hazards are dry rooms, use of lamp-black varnish, heating of glue and untidy premises.

PARAFFINE—A solid wax obtained from petroleum. Melts at 125 to 135 deg. F.

PARAFFINE OIL—Heavy, non-volatile oil, high flash point.

PARANITRANILINE—A moist substance resembling yellow ochre, received in 50-gallon wood casks, claimed to be non-combustible and non-inflammable. Used in combination with iron filings, borings and muriatic acid.

PARAPET—The portion of a wall extending above the roof.

PARAPETS, while designed to prevent fires from spreading from one building to another over the roof boards, do not prevent a fire from spreading to a raised roof, monitor light or roof structure on another building if they extend above the parapet.

PARCHMENT PAPER—Paper treated with dilute sulphuric acid, washed in water, dipped in solution of either ammonia, sodium carbonate or zinc chloride.

PARIS GREEN is made of blue vitriol, sulphate of copper, arsenic and soda ash.

PARKS—See Amusement Enterprises.

PARQUET FLOOR MANUFACTURING—Hazards of woodworking with varnishing and shellacing, gluing, oiling, painting. Boards that are to be laid in damp locations have the underside coated with asphaltum. Stores engaged in this business sometimes have considerable lumber on hand, a generous supply of floor oil and wax, a circular saw and a machine for dressing floors.

PARTITIONS should be built of incombustible material. Wood is not recommended. In sprinklered risks, wood partitions should not be placed nearer than two feet from ceiling unless the upper two feet is thin glass in light wood frame. If partition is solid, it should extend midway between the sprinkler heads.

PARTY WALL—A wall used to support floor or roof members of adjoining buildings. Should be at least twelve inches thick to allow four-inch space between ends of beams.

PASSEMENTERIE—See Embroideries.

PASTE COLORS—Aniline dyes are dissolved in hot water in large wooden tanks and allowed to cool, then run into large wood vats, and the precipitate treated with hydrochloric acid, sulphuric acid and alum. This is filtered through a cloth and a pasty mass secured which is put in a steel mixer with lithographic varnish, then through slow-moving rolls, where most of the water is squeezed out, and dried in dry rooms. No benzine, turpentine or alcohol is used in the process. An unprofitable class to insure. See Aniline Dyes.

PASTE FILLERS are mixtures of ground quartz, pigments, oil and japan.

PATENT AND ENAMELED LEATHER—Consists of several applications of "daub" which is generally linseed oil and lamp-black or some other pigment. It is usually thinned with naphtha. The main hazards are boiling linseed oil over an open fire, the reducing of oil with naphtha, the mixing of lamp-black, preparation of the "daub," japanning the leather, and drying ovens. Solutions of nitro-cellulose also used. A hazardous process. See Leather.

PATTERN LATHES, for turning shoe lasts, etc., are made so that the scroll pieces to be turned at one time are rotated slowly and simultaneously with a pattern over which a blank pointer passes. By following the surface of the pattern, the pointer advances or withdraws by means of a parallel or pantograph motion, rapidly rotating cutters to and fro form the various pieces to be turned. Large amount of refuse, high speed, danger from overheating bearings.

PATTERNS—Underwriters seldom write patterns without having a share of the stock or machinery and usually limit the pattern item to not more than 10 per cent. of the amount of the policy. Patterns are easily damaged and difficult to replace without much labor. Should be stored in vaults. See Dress Patterns; also Records.

PAWNBROKERS' STOCK—Considered good insurance if mainly covering on silverware, jewelry and tools. Where the stock is largely wearing apparel, the risk is not as attractive. The stock belongs to the person pledging same, except the right and interest which the pawnbroker acquires by law when accepting same. See Right and Interest.

PEANUTS are rendered unfit for food if subjected to fire damage, and little salvage can be expected. An analysis of burned peanuts after a recent fire showed that the oils, fats, protein and ammonia contents were greatly reduced.

PEARLASH—See Carbonate of Potash.

PEARL BUTTONS—Snail, oyster and mother-of-pearl usually used. The snail is cheap, the mother-of-pearl expensive. A greater portion of all the shell is wasted in the cutting owing to the varying thicknesses. As the shell is worked the value increases. The mother-of-pearl veneers are the most expensive, as all the shell is ground from the back, leaving only the ornamental face. The thinner the veneer, the more expensive per pound. The thinnest cost $25 to $200 per pound.

Pearl is porous. As it is worked, it is kept soaked in water. Considerable water damage can result from a fire if the shell is left for any length of time in dirty or stained water, because it will become discolored. Even smoky water will lessen its value. The shell buttons are cleaned with pumice stone, emery dust and muriatic acid. Fire at a temperature of an ordinary baking oven will ruin shell if subjected to the heat for as much as ten minutes. The fire eats out the carbon, leaving only lime. Gas blow pipes and small furnaces are required for heating lead for buttons with lead backs.

PEAS, if wet and left in bags, will mildew and may be confiscated by health authorities.

PEAT MOSS—Used in stables in place of straw, is cleaner, less dusty and presents less fire hazard.

PEBBLE MILL—A tumbler revolving on an inclined axis. Used for grinding. The material to be ground is put in the mill with iron balls or round stones. These grind the material as the machine revolves.

PENCIL WORKS—May include steel and fountain pen making, involving wood, metal and rubber working and machine shops. Use linseed oil, benzine, alcohol, turpentine, varnish, lacquer, crude oil, graphite, white lead, dryers, amyl acetate and paraffine. Pencil rounding machines create considerable dust and fine shavings, and should be equipped with blowers.

Hazards of dry rooms, gluing, embossing presses, lacquering by dip process, color grinding and mixing, graphite and firing in retorts, kilns for baking pencil leads.

Gold and Silver Pencils—Hazards of goldsmiths and silversmiths, metal working, annealing, tempering and engraving.

Rubber Fountain Pen Holders—Hazards of rubber making, calendering, steam heated mixers, cutters and tube machines, sandpapering, vulcanizing, dry rooms, buffing, use of rubber cement.

Incidental hazards of printing and paper box making.

Copying Pencils and Ink Pencils are made of a concentrated solution of aniline violet added to graphite and china clay.

Colored Pencils are made of Prussian blue or chrome yellow mixed with white wax and tallow.

PENTANE—A clear colorless volatile liquid. Boils at 95 deg. F. or less. Flash point zero F. Highly inflammable. It is obtained from the more volatile portions of petroleum.

PENTINE—A benzine substitute, flash 102 deg. F. Classed non-volatile.

PENTONE—A hydro-carbon. See Gas Plants.

PENT HOUSE—The enclosure on the roof which is generally used for the elevator machinery or store room.

PER CAPITA FIRE LOSS—See Fire Loss per capita.

PER CENT. PROFIT INSURANCE—See Profit Insurance.

PERCHLORIDE OF POTASH—A white crystalline solid used as an oxidizing agent.

PER DIEM PROFIT INSURANCE—See Profit Insurance.

PERFORATED PIPES are not recommended, as they allow the water to flow throughout the entire floor instead of only directly to the seat of the fire, as in automatic sprinkler equipments. The large water damage incurred, even at small fires, offsets the salvage which might otherwise be expected.

PERFUMERS, making toilet preparations, mix, sift and grind dry powders. Use alcohol, essential oils, nitric, hydrochloric and oxalic acids, paraffine and herbs. Confectioners stoves usually used for heating salves. Always inspect before binding this class.

PERMANGANATE OF POTASH is subject to spontaneous combustion whenever brought into contact with organic matter. This may occur either from foreign matter leaking into the packages, or from small crystals of permanganate falling on the floor of a warehouse. Agitation, such as caused by trucking, will facilitate the process.

PERNASEL—A dipping fluid for coloring glass bulbs. Inflammable.

PEROLIN—Composed of sand, iron slag, sawdust, paraffine oil, is a disinfectant and an ordinary floor oil.

PEROXIDE OF BARIUM, if exposed to the air and sun, may cause spontaneous combustion.

PEROXIDE OF SODIUM is a yellowish white powder used as a bleaching agent. Chemically it is a combination of the elements sodium and oxygen in equal proportions. It is a powerful oxidizing agent, and has a strong affinity for water. In combination with the latter it forms caustic soda and hydrogen peroxide. As a fire hazard, this substance ranks among the most dangerous found in ordinary manufacturing plants. The danger lies in dropping the substance on tables or floors, where it is liable to get wet, or in leaving it in uncovered vessels where water may be dropped on it. In combination with water it may heat so rapidly as to set fire to surrounding material.—Gorham Dana.

PET-PRO-CO SPIRITS—Flashes at 108 deg. F. in open cup tester. Graded as non-volatile.

PETROLEUM OR CRUDE OIL—(Charles E. Jahne.) A natural rock oil composed of hydrocarbons. It is classed with natural gas and asphalt as bitumens—natural gas containing the more volatile members of the series, and asphalt the solid, while petroleum is composed chiefly of the liquid members, although it contains a small proportion of the solid and gaseous compounds. Other names of petroleum are rock oil, mineral oil and naphtha, the latter being employed especially in Europe for the Russian oils. In 1635 Pennsylvania settlers dug small wells and found it seeping in from surrounding rocks. Wells were driven to greater depths and the flow naturally increased. New fields continue to yield same, especially in Pennsylvania, Ohio, West Virginia, Kentucky, Texas and California. Of the foreign countries, Russia is the most serious competitor the United States has in the oil production. Petroleum is of various tints, but largely of green and black. The modern method of drilling for petroleum is similar to that used in sinking artesian wells. The most prominent feature of the oil drilling outfit being the derrick, which is a tall pyramid-like wooden frame about 75 feet high, 12 feet square at the base, and 3 feet at the top. A churn drill is used. A round rock core is drawn out and an iron pipe inserted. In many cases the oil does not flow when the oil rock is struck, and it is customary to explode a torpedo in the hole, whereupon the oil gushes out with force and continues to flow until well or vein is drained. The cheap and rapid transportation of crude oil from the wells to the refineries is one of great importance. At first the oil was transported on carts, then by barges or tank cars, but the modern method is by pipe lines. Pipes are four to eight inches in diameter laid underground with bends in them at regular intervals to allow for expansion and contraction. Stations with pumps and storage tanks are placed every 25 or 30 miles, the oil being received in tanks at one station and pumped from there to tanks at the next station. Since all petroleum contains more or less wax or paraffine, much trouble is often experienced in the clogging of the pipes, especially in cold weather, and to clean them out, an instrument known as a "go-devil" is sent through the pipes. This is so constructed that it is forced along by the moving current of oil and scrapes the paraffine coating off of the inside of the pipes. Pipe lines now run from the Appalachian region to New York, Jersey City, Philadelphia, Baltimore, Chicago, Cleveland. The refining process consists of the separation of the component hydrocarbons by a system of fractional distillation. This is usually carried out by the use of horizontal steel cylinder tanks of about 600 barrels capacity each, with a dome on top of it, and from this dome is a pipe which carries the vapor from the steam heated oil to a condenser, which is a series of pipes surrounded by cold water. When the oil is placed in the tank or still, and the steam is turned on, the various increases of temperature cause the vapors of the various products to escape to the condensers intended for them.

The first product is a light gas known as cymogen, for

medical purposes, escaping at 32 deg. F. The next is rhigolene, a petroleum ether sometimes called sherwood oil, at 65 deg. F. The next is naphtha at 80 to 120 deg. F. The next benzine at 120 to 150 deg. F. The gasoline product will vary from 190 to 200 deg. F., depending on oil's condition. Ligroine is a special grade solvent naphtha produced at a boiling point from 190 deg. F. to 250 deg. F. Then follow the illuminating oils of kerosene type. The residuum remaining in the still is then passed through a further process and produces paraffine wax and lubricating oils. The composite remaining at the ending is used for fuel oils.

Gasoline, naphtha or benzine, while lying absolutely motionless is not dangerous, but the slightest tremor will cause a vapor to rise, and this vapor coming in contact with gas or other flame will ignite, and a stream of fire will follow from the point of ignition to the body from whence comes the vapor and an explosion will follow. A lighted match was dropped into a barrel of benzine which was absolutely still and no explosion followed, but if that barrel had been disturbed a little and the vapor had arisen ever so lightly, an explosion would surely have resulted. These oils are classed as extremely volatile, and for that reason the insurance and fire departments are compelled to prescribe stringent laws for the storage and handling of them. See Gasoline.

Petroleum Ether—See Benzine; also Ether.

Petroleum Naphtha—See Benzine.

Petroleum Oil may include any oil derived from crude petroleum.

Petroleum Soap—Common soap made from resin and low grade tallow containing petroleum bodies mechanically held.

Petroleum Spirits—Highly inflammable. See Benzine.

PEWTER—An alloy of tin, lead and antimony.

PHENOL is, chemically speaking, hydroxy-benzine, and is prepared from the carbolic or middle oils by treatment with caustic soda, alkali and precipitation with sulphuric acid, followed by refining by distillation.—W. D. Grier.

PHONOGRAPHS—Dealers in this line may carry a large quantity of records equal to one-fourth to one-half of the value of the entire stock. They are kept in open pigeon-holed cabinets, and are very susceptible. Repairing and refinishing machines are incidental hazards.

Records are made of such materials as shellac, wax, silicates, rosin, and lamp-black for making composition records; copper and brass sheets; copper and nickel salts for plating. Processes are grinding, compounding, mixing and rolling stock for records; wax discs and cylinder making, buffing, polishing, plating, machine shop work and assembling.

PHOSPHATE OF AMMONIA—Sometimes used for fireproofing scenery.

PHOSPHORETTED HYDROGEN—When phosphorus combines with hydrogen it forms a gas having a strong odor resembling garlic. This gas takes fire of itself when mixed with air and burns with a bright yellow light. It is this gas, sometimes seen at night over marshy land, which causes the light to be called "Will o' the wisp."

PHOSPHORIC ACID—When phosphorus burns it forms a snow-like substance which dissolves very rapidly in water, forming phosphoric acid.

PHOSPHORUS—Generally sold in cylinders, is commonly obtained from bones in which it exists, combined with lime. It is white and has a waxy appearance. It has so strong an affinity for oxygen that it is kept in water. Exposed to the air, fumes arise from the surface. This results from its uniting with the oxygen of the air. It takes fire from so little heat that it is necessary to be very cautious in experimenting with it. It is so eager to unite with the oxygen of the air that a little friction produces heat enough to make it unite with it and so quickly as to burn. (Hooker.) It is used in most laboratories. In one of the colleges of Brooklyn a bottle containing phosphorus immersed in water was upset and immediately set fire to the surrounding woodwork. It gave off a luminous glow and had the appearance of a large fire.

PHOSPHORUS (red) amorphous, a reddish brown powder not subject to spontaneous combustion. Inflammable.

PHOSPHORUS (yellow)—A waxy solid. Will ignite at ordinary temperature if exposed to the air. Usually shipped under water. Besides being very poisonous, it is very inflammable.

PHOSPHORUS (white)—The same as yellow phosphorus.

PHOTO AND ADVERTISING MOUNTS—Cardboard used as mounts for photographs and the backs for signs. Similar hazards to paper box making with gluing and embossing.

PHOTO ENGRAVING—Half-tone work is the process which reproduces pictures or designs on metal plates by means of photography. The name half-tone is applied to this kind of work because in printing the picture or design on the plate, a glass with fine intersecting lines is placed between the plate and the negative. All that appears in the picture from these fine intersecting lines are numerous small dots, each of which results from the point of intersection of the above-mentioned lines. It is necessary to mention at this point that in half-tone work the wet plate process is used, and this necessitates the use of collodion in preparing the negative. Collodion is therefore one of the important hazards. This mixture is usually prepared on the premises, consequently open lights in the vicinity are dangerous. As it evaporates quickly, and is quite expensive, the bottles in which it is kept are seldom left uncorked. Electric lights are usually used in dark rooms. After completing the negative, it is printed in the usual way on a copper plate sensitized to receive the impression, and developed in chemical solutions, then gently heated over a gas flame. It is then placed in an iron solution which etches all the surface except the design or picture to be printed. The plate is then trimmed and cut out by power machines and is finally backed with a wooden block.

PHOTO-ENGRAVURE PLATES are steel faced copper plates. Hazards are plating, washing plates in whiting and nitric acid and coating with wax to prevent rusting. Method of wax heating is important.

PHOTOGRAPHERS' DRY PLATE (mfg.)—Sheet glass is sensitized (coated) with emulsion of gelatine and nitrate of silver, usually on a coating machine by cold process, the plate being passed through a trough of the solution and dropped on a felt belt passing through the machine. No heat; on the contrary, ice is put in tub under emulsion to keep it cool; dried in low temperature room. Chemicals used include nitric, acetic, euramic acids, ether, ethyl alcohol, nitrous phenol, chlorides. In making colored plates, the above process is also followed, anilines being used for coloring. Printing in some places is done by an electric printer operated by motor of light voltage and "lined" (blue lines put in) by violet rays with arc light under a hood. May use an autoclave for testing colors. Stock of plates is very delicate. They are stored in a dark room and are ruined if subjected to light as would be the case in a fire. They also would be spoiled by water. Hazards are indicated above and include photographing, developing and printing, dry rooms and gas heated developer.

PHOTOGRAPHERS' Developing Solution consists of distilled water, silver nitrate, citric, oxalic and other acids, and solutions of a non-hazardous character.

PHOTOGRAPHY—In wet plate work, collodion is generally used, and this is a hazardous process. In dry plate work only mild acids are used and the process is not hazardous. Dark rooms should have electric light rather than gas or kerosene oil.

PIANO MFG.—Lumber thoroughly dried in kiln is brought to the mill-run, sawed and planed into the proper sizes. Many parts are made of quarter-sawed pieces glued together. The wooden portions of a grand piano are referred to as consisting of cases and trimmings. The case includes the rims with the supporting beams or braces within, the legs and pedals. The rim is made of continuous pieces of wood (veneer) glued together. The outside finishing veneer is applied at the same time when forming is done. The processes consist of sandpapering, finishing (which includes staining, filling, varnishing, rubbing, flowing and polishing. The sounding board (or belly) is the most important part of a piano, and calls for a special kind of wood, thoroughly dried. The work on iron plate, wires and stringing, hammers, heads and actions presents very little fire hazards. The hazards are those of woodworking plants where varnishing is done. See Celluloid Piano Keys.

Sea grass is sometimes used instead of cloth for polishing cases. The rubbing varnish contains oil and turpentine. The sea grass is very light and evidently confines the heat more than cotton cloth or waste, as spontaneous combustion in waste cans is very frequent. It will heat up in a few hours sufficiently to warm the can.

PICKERS—See Cotton.

PICKLING—The term is used in connection with plating risks, where the metal is cleaned by dipping in nitric and sulphuric acid.

PICRATES should be kept away from mineral acids, carriers of oxygen, ozone, organic substances and sulphur. Obtained from carbolic acid or phenol by the action of nitric acid. Used as dye for woolens and leather, and making explosives. Highly explosive.

PICRIC ACID is highly explosive.

PICTURE FRAME DEALERS—Hazard is hand woodworking, usually only mitering of corners, varnishing, painting and gilding. Susceptible stock. Other classes of art goods may be included in the stock.

PICTURE FRAME MAKING—Woodworking hazards, paper back making, painting, bronzing, varnishing, glazing, embossing mouldings on gas-heated presses. A poor fire record class.

PIE BAKERIES—Hazards include mixing dough by machinery, preparing and cooking fruits and jellies on confectioners' stoves, lard and grease melting pots, baking. Usually greasy risks.

PIER—The support of two adjacent arches or the support of the lower part of the building. If bond and cap stones are in pier they should be insulated.

PIERS—Open piers are usually built of crib construction, i. e., wood piling (usually creosoted), then the heavy wood timbers and cross bracing, and finally the heavy plank flooring. The frame covered pier is similar to above, except that it is covered over with a frame shed or enclosure. The corrugated iron pier is the type usually found in local territory, with sides of corrugated iron on iron or angle iron on wood stud, the roof of corrugated iron on wood purlins on steel truss or wood frame. The fireproof pier is of non-combustible material throughout, although some piers having wooden piling have been termed fireproof. The strictly fire-proof pier should have incombustible piling (concrete) with a reinforced concrete flooring or base, the sides of pier structure either concrete, copper filled in with concrete or terra-cotta tile. All steel work, including roof trusses, should be protected with at least two inches of concrete or tile. Sky-lights should be thin glass in metal frame with standard screen above. Curtain boards should be extended from the roof to divide the roof area and thus prevent the rapid spread of fire along the ceiling. These should extend to the lower side of the roof trusses, or lower if possible. In lieu of curtain boards, the area can be divided into smaller sections by the use of fire walls, which should extend to below low water line and be parapetted and have standard doors. Partitions or walls enclosing the boiler, oil room, rigging and other storage rooms should be of fireproof material with labelled doors at the openings. The fire protection usually consists of an approved standpipe and hose system, a supply of water casks with pails, and a special fire signal. A few of the latest types are protected by an approved dry pipe sprinkler system and day and night watchman service. The occupancy is usually general merchandise with fibre in transit. At this writing war material, including small arm ammunition, may be included. Automobiles enter to unload or load freight. The fire record of the unsprinkled non-fireproof piers is far from good. Fires have been spread by burning objects floating under piers, therefore we recommend planking for enclosing sides and ends of piers to extend to low water mark. Hazards may include immigrant stations with lunch counters, gas or coal stoves in workmen's lounging rooms, baling waste paper from railroad cars and smoking. Pier fires are usually severe, owing to large areas. (C. C. Dominge, "Live Articles on Special Hazards," The Weekly Underwriter.) See Cotton; see Canals and Feeders.

PIGMENTS—The dry inert colors used in paint making.

PILASTER—A reinforcement of a wall by increased thickness at various points. Used mainly as an additional support for wide span roofs.

PILES—Large timbers driven into the ground for the purpose of making a secure foundation.

PINTLE—A contrivance of cast iron, consisting of two thick circular plates connected by a solid cylindrical supporter, placed between posts between the floors of stories. Used in mill constructed buildings.

PINTSCH GAS—Pintsch process. Petroleum oil subjected to high temperature, which converts oil into a vapor gas, and, after going through purifying process, is pumped into compression holders to a pressure of 75 pounds or more. By this pressure the gas is carried by underground pipes to car tanks. Oil is stored underground. Other apparatus consists of retorts, purifying cylinders and gasometer. The tar deposit is put in iron drums. The great danger is of escaping gas. See Oil Gas.

PINTSCH TAR OIL—Flash point above 100 deg. F. Classed as non-volatile.

PIPE LINES, if above ground and used to convey hazardous liquids such as gasoline or crude oil, are not looked upon as desirable by the inspector or underwriter. A short time ago the following was reported: "An overhead pipe line was used for conveying crude oil from Penn Horn creek on the Hackensack meadows to Bayonne for refining. It is believed the pipe was weakened by the shaking it received a month ago when the munitions plant at Kingsland was blown up. The oil seeped out until the surface under the pipe line was coated with it, and it is supposed a hot spark from a passing locomotive ignited it and a severe fire resulted. All pipe lines should be underground and securely bedded. See Petroleum. See Gasoline.

PIPING—Doubling the diameter of a pipe increases its carrying capacity four times. Suppose a 2-inch pipe is used; the cross section 2-inch pipe contains 4 square inches, which is the result of squaring the diameter (multiply the diameter by itself). A 4-inch pipe will have a cross section of 16 square inches, which is four times greater than a 2-inch pipe.

The orifice of a sprinkler is ⅝-inch diameter, or .39 square inches. See Water Mains.

PIPE OPENINGS—Ordinary Construction, Single Floors. Flooring to be closely fitted around all pipes, except steam pipes, and each pipe to be provided with a satisfactory floor plate. Steam pipes to be fitted with metal sleeves in accordance with requirements of the New York Board of Fire Underwriters.

Ordinary Construction, Double Floors, Mill Constructed Floors—Flooring to be closely fitted around all pipes except steam pipes, and each pipe to be provided with a satisfactory floor plate. Steam pipes to be fitted with metal sleeves in accordance with requirements of the New Board of Fire Underwriters. Space between pipe and sleeve to be filled in with non-combustible material (mineral wool, asbestos, etc.), securely held in place by satisisfactory ceiling and floor plates. Each pipe opening to be provided with substantial wood curbing extending 3 inches above floor. A water-tight joint to be effected between curbing and flooring by means of tar paper properly flashed around the curbing.

Fireproof Floors—Space between pipes (except those subject to unusual expansion, such as steam, hot water, etc.), and floor arches to be made water-tight by means of Portland cement mortar properly filled in.

Steam pipes, etc., to be provided with an approved water-tight metal sleeve cemented into floor as above, and extending 3 inches above finished floor surface. Portion of sleeve above floor surface to be protected from injury by a cast iron collar or by a curb of Portland cement mortar at least 3 inches thick. Space between pipe and sleeve to be filled with non-combustible material (mineral wool, asbestos, etc.), securely held in place by satisfactory ceiling and floor plates.

PIPES (smoking pipes)—Briar root received in crude form, cut, bored, sandpapered, varnished and buffed. Holes are filled with stick shellac heated over gas flame. Gas heat used for glue and oils. Woodworking machinery creates considerable fine shavings and dust, and should have blower attachments.

PIPE SHAFTS should be enclosed in standard shafts of concrete, terra cotta or brick, with standard fire doors at all openings and a thin glass skylight at the roof. Many fires, especially in fireproof office buildings, have started in these shafts, which contain electric cables and canvas wrapped pipes. There may also be waste paper and rubbish. Once on fire, they are hard to extinguish. It sometimes becomes necessary to chop away walls and floors to locate the seat of the fire.

PITCH KETTLE—Usually a direct-fire heated brick set furnace. Used in breweries to heat pitch for the lining of kegs. Room containing pitching apparatus should be cut off in a standard manner. Superheated steam is used to melt out the old pitch in the kegs.

PITCHED ROOF—A sloping roof.

PIT PITCH—Made of gas tar.

PLACERS—Persons employed by brokerage houses to place insurance with companies. One of the main requisites of the business is to be frank and honest in the statements made about the risk to the underwriter or counterman. One false statement or "fib" will forever remain in the mind of those accepting the placer's propositions, and they will always be suspicious for fear that the placer is trying to "put one over."

PLANERS—Rapidly rotating blades mounted upon horizontal shafts parallel to the latter, together with a feeding mechanism and table upon which the stock is laid in its passage through the machine. There are four kinds, surface, matchers, flooring machines and dimension planers. Great deal of refuse is made. Should have blower attachments.

PLANS—All plans on buildings about to be erected should be reviewed by an insurance expert before the work is started in order that the lowest insurance rate may be obtained when the structure is complete.

PLANT—The outfit of machinery, stock and fixtures necessary for carrying on any kind of business.

PLAN VIEW—The drawing of any one floor of a building looking down on it from a point above the drawing.

PLASTER—A mixture of plaster of paris, sand, wool or animal hair. Plaster is made by heating gypsum sufficient to drive off three-fourths of all the combined water which it contains, and grinding finely the hydrated residue.

PLASTER BLOCK—Plaster block, if solid and not less than 3 inches thick or cinder plaster block can be expected to give a very good account of itself (as a protection to iron work) in very severe fires, comparing very favorably, although not as reliable as common brick or good concrete. To prove this fact, attention is called to the excellent manner in which the plaster block stood up in the Mansard in the Equitable fire, although the intense heat melted brass in many cases.

Plaster Block, Laboratory Test of—A fire test at an average temperature of 1700 deg. F. on a 6-inch plaster block showed that the block calcined ½ inch after one-half hour's duration, increasing proportionately until at four hours' duration the calcination amounted to 2⅝ inches.

The building code for New York City will permit 3-inch solid plaster block as standard insulation for iron columns, 2-inch blocks for lower flanges of girders and 1½-inch blocks for lower flanges of beams.

For all shafts, whether stair, vent or elevator, blocks must be at least 4 inches thick.

PLASTER BOARDS are made of gypsum plaster with a binder such as wood pulp, wood fibre, excelsior. Made in sheets one-half to one inch thick, and used extensively as a fire retardant furring. The plaster is received in bags, mixed with water, pressed in roller machine where the fibre is added, cut into slabs with saw, air dried. Drying is usually done on the roof of the building or a lattice frame enclosure as a separate structure. Large amounts of excelsior or other fibre stored in premises is a menace. Construction of building usually light frame. Not very attractive fire risks.

PLASTER FIGURES—Made by moulding plaster, wire or excelsior used as a binder. They are sized with glue, dried in dry rooms, shellaced and coated with paint or bronzing liquid. Hazards are heating wax or glue by direct heat, dry rooms, excelsior storage, painting, untidy premises. Poor fire record.

PLASTER OF PARIS—Calcined and powdered gypsum.

PLATE GIRDER—A large steel girder used to span an arch or opening, as for instance, over the top of the proscenium in a theatre.

PLATE PRINTERS—See Engravers. See Etching.

PLATFORMS—Temporary overhead sidewalks are sometimes put up in front of buildings in course of construction so that pedestrians can traverse the street, and workmen can carry material into the building. Sometimes electrical apparatus for lighting and hoists are installed under these platforms. As all wiring, switchboards, etc., are for temporary use, they are usually very carelessly installed. In April, 1918, a severe fire occurred underneath such a platform at the Pennsylvania Hotel, and was evidently the result of defective electric installation at switchboard. The fire was severe enough to totally destroy that portion of the limestone front under the platform for a distance of over 150 feet and scorched buildings on the opposite side of the street. See Course of Construction; see Builder's Risk; see Spall.

PLATINUM—A metal used largely in the manufacture of chemical utensils, owing to its immunity to the effects of acids, heat, etc. Considered good insurance.

PLINTH—The square, lowest member of the base of a column or pier.

PLUMBAGO—A mineral lead used in crucible manufacturing. As this substance passes through intense heat during the manufacturing process, it suffers practically no fire damage, and is considered good insurance.

PLUMBERS—Usually carry only a small amount of insurance on stock, the value being mostly in tools and fixtures. May have gasoline torches or furnaces, charcoal furnaces, forge, light metal working, painting.

PLUMBERS' SUPPLIES MANUFACTURING—Hazards of wood and metal working, sandpapering, dip staining, painting, lacquering, varnishing. Not an attractive class as a rule.

PLUSH—Is of different grades and weaves. Cop yarn (cotton and worsted) is for warp and woof. The plush piling is silk, cotton and mohair woven together in one single strand. The cop yarn, which furnishes the top and bottom body fabric, is woven together with the plush piling by means of a weaving machine, and a knife attachment separates the top and bottom warps or fabrics. Cop yarns come in skeins. In this process very little lint or flox is produced. The "tigers" or rough combers of plush, however, produce considerable silk flox, which should be cleaned up daily. See Silk Plush.

POLE-PLATE—A longitudinal timber resting on the ends of the tie beams of roof.

POLICY—A personal contract between the assured and the company. When the property covered is sold or transferred to a new location, the policy does not cover new owner nor new address unless so endorsed.

POLISH AND POLISHING COMPOUNDS may contain such inflammable agents as will make the flash point of mixture 80 deg. F. or lower. May include an abrasive material, gasoline, chlorate of permanganate, nitrates, varnish, mineral and vegetable oils.

POLITICS—The truth of the statement that there is a fire hazard in politics, although but vaguely comprehended by the average citizen, comes oftentimes with distinct emphasis to those interested in maintaining municipal fire departments in a state of high efficiency. Politics may interfere directly by forcing fire chiefs to fill their ranks with men physically incapable and sometimes insubordinate, and also indirectly, by tampering with the building department in such manner as to allow the flagrant disregard of most needful precautions.

POOL ROOMS—Tables are usually bought from the manufacturer on the installment plan. "Ivories" must be warm for good playing, hence, unless the place is steam heated, large pot stoves are usually employed. Smoking hazard. Place may be used as a "hang-out."

POP-CORN MANUFACTURING—Raw stock is corn, molasses and glucose. Work consists of sugar coating and making pop-corn into balls and cakes. Hazards are coke and gas heated poppers, and confectioners' stoves. Portable ovens used by bakers, usually gas heated, should set on at least 4 inches of brick on sheet iron (with air space) and a safe distance from all woodwork, and be vented to a proper flue.

PORTLAND CEMENT—Composed chiefly of lime, alumina and silica.

POST-CARDS—Picture post-card making includes designing; embossing, lithographing, printing. Air brushes are used for coloring. A poor fire record stock.

POSTS—Square or round timbers set on ends; used for corner supports.

POT STOVES—Made of an unlined iron casting varying in thickness from ⅛ to ¼ inch and set on three legs. Many of the stoves are too small to properly heat the entire floor, and in consequence they are forced and the fire-pot kept red hot. This condition causes the casting to crack. After these cracks appear the pressure from the heat and fuel within spreads the opening, which soon becomes large enough to allow the burning fuel or sparks to fall out on the floor. Any stove having an unlined fire pot and standing on three legs should be prohibited. Cracked fire pots should be instantly repaired.

POTASH—Hydrate of potassium.

POTASSIUM—Obtained from potash, is very difficult to keep because it is continually uniting with the air, but the air may be shut out by placing the potassium under naphtha. It has a bluish white color and is quite soft. If potassium be left exposed to the air, it tarnishes at once, and in a short time is all turned to potash, the oxygen of the air uniting with it. If you throw a little piece of it upon water, it steals away the oxygen from the hydrogen of the water and flies about the surface burning with a beautiful violet flame. The flame is the hydrogen set free by the union of the potassium with the oxygen of the water.—Hooker's Chemistry.

POTASSIUM CHLORATE—In the dyeing of fabrics where potassium chlorate is used as the oxidizing agent, there is considerable danger of fire due to the rapid oxidation of the aniline dye and the chlorate. Not inflammable, but its presence increases the intensity of fire by the evolution of oxygen. See Barium Chlorate.

POTASSIUM CYANIDE—A heavy white solid; not hazardous.

POTASSIUM METALLIC—See Metallic Potassium.

POTASSIUM NITRATE—White crystalline salt, classed as non-inflammable and not dangerous, but its presence increases the intensity of fire by the evolution of oxygen.

POTASSIUM PERMANGANATE—A purplish crystalline salt rich in oxygen. May cause fire when mixed with combustible material.

POTASSIUM PEROXIDE—See Sodium Peroxide.

POTASSIUM PICRATE—Mixed with water, is used as substitute for yellow ink in coloring maps.

POTATO CHIPS—Use power machines for paring and slicing. Cook the slices in grease by direct or indirect fire. Greasy risks. A poor fire record class.

POTATO IVORY—Artificial ivory made from good potatoes, washed in dilute sulphuric acid and boiled in same solution. They become solid, then are washed and slowly dried.

POTATO SPIRITS—See Amyl Hydrate.

POWER HOUSES are generally F. P. construction with approved electrical equipment. Considered desirable insurance.

PREFERRED BUSINESS (so-called) is insurance on risks of minimum hazard or maximum protection, such as dwellings, fireproof buildings or sprinklered risks.

PREMIUMS—Companies must accumulate sufficient reserve from premiums collected each year to pay for large losses occurring from conflagrations which, as a rule, occur every few years. See Earned Premium.

PRESERVATION OF TIMBER—Several methods are used to artificially preserve timber from decay. The sap may be expelled by hydraulic pressure and replaced by chemical fluid, or the timber may be saturated with some chemical fluid which will combine or act upon the albumen and prevent decay. See Wood Preservatives.

PRESERVING AND FIREPROOFING Natural and Artificial Foliage. See Artificial Flowers and Feathers.

PRESSING IRONS (electric) should be made foolproof. The temperature of a flat iron for safe and satisfactory use is from 400 to 600 deg. F. This temperature is not dangerous, but when the irons as now designed are allowed to remain with the current on continuously, then the temperature rapidly increases to 1200 to 1400 degrees, or even 1800 degrees in some instances, and the iron may reach red heat. The hazard may be overcome by means of a new device called a thermostatic switch placed in the iron, and which automatically cuts off the current when the temperature exceeds a predetermined range, usually 400 to 600 degrees. See N. F. P. A. Bulletin for details.

PRESSING TABLES in tailor shops. The boards and bucks should be covered with metal. Also floors under and 2 feet at sides of tables. Many fires are caused by hot irons resting on woodwork.

PRESSURE—How to figure pressure on the top line of a sprinkler equipment. Take a building seven stories high, or 80 feet above the grade, with a pressure of 40 pounds at the main hydrant. Multiply .434, which is the pressure for each foot of elevation, times height (80 feet), which equals 34.7 pounds. Deduct 34.7 pounds from the pressure at the main (40 pounds) which leaves a working pressure of only 5.30 pounds on the top line of sprinklers. Note.—A column of water 12 inches high having an area of one square inch weighs .434 pounds. See Water Pressure.

Pressure—Assume a gravity tank is 12 feet high and elevated 20 feet above the roof and sprinkler heads are one foot below the roof. Take 12 feet plus 20 feet plus 1 foot equaling 33 feet x .434 equals 14.19 pounds pressure on highest line of sprinklers. Note.—The combined pressures of gravity tank and pressure tank cannot be added, for in case of fire, the water will first be used from the pressure tank until the pressure is below that from the gravity tank, then the water will flow from the gravity tank.

Assume, in the case of a pressure tank, that it is eight feet above the roof and sprinkler heads one foot below the roof.

Add 8 feet plus 1 foot equals 9 feet x .434 equals 3.9 pounds pressure, plus the pressure showing on gauge on pressure tanks, say 75 pounds, equals 78.9 pounds pressure on highest line.

PRESSURE TANKS of sprinkler systems, steel or wrought iron, are two-thirds full of water and one-third of air. A gauge to show height of water in tank is placed at end of tank. 75 pounds pressure is usually maintained. Pressure tanks operate prior to gravity tanks when the water flows through sprinkler pipes. The pressure of water in the pressure tank holds shut the check valve on riser to gravity tank, and when the water or pressure is released, the water from gravity tank starts to flow.

To ascertain if water is at proper level in pressure tank, first close pet cock at the bottom, then open valve at top of glass gauge, then open valve at lower end of glass gauge and the water will rise. After finding water level, close lower valve in glass gauge first, then close valve at top of glass gauge and open pet cock at the bottom. See Sprinklers.

PREST-O-LITE (acetylene gas)—A fire in one of these plants demonstrated that acetylene gas itself will explode if compressed with air. Excessive heat and high pressure will also cause explosion.

PREVAILING WIND record for 35 years shows N. Y. City to be on average W—N.W. See Wind.

PRIME—To put on the first coat of paint. In sash, door and blind factories benzine thinned paint is generally used.

PRINTING HAZARDS—Composing, ink mixing, press work, wrapping, benzine or a substitute for cleaning presses, oily waste, waste paper, oily floors. Job presses are used only for small work. In this type of press, the type bed and tympan (sheet holder) come together on a vertical plane. Metal should be placed under all presses to prevent floors from becoming oil soaked. The fire record is usually good. See Cylinder Press.

PRINTING INK is generally made of boiled linseed or nut oil, and mixed with lamp-black and soap. Write class with caution.

PRINTERS' ROLLERS are made of glue, glycerine and

molasses on a steel core. There are two kinds, one for summer and one for cold weather use. The former is made of a harder mixture to withstand heat.

PRISM LIGHTS—Used principally on extension skylights in order to lighten dark locations. In New York City they are classed as thin glass unless the part in the valley is one-half inch thick, or unless glasses are not more than four inches by four inches on metal frame, in which case glass must be one-half inch thick over all and one-fourth inch thick in valley. See Sun's Rays.

PRIVATE DWELLINGS—See Dwellings; also F. P. Dwellings.

PRIVATE FIRE PLANTS—A steam fire pump capable of furnishing at least two good fire streams, should be provided and connected directly to standpipe system, with gate and check valves in such connection, taking suction preferably from city main through a connection not less than 4 inches in diameter, or in the event or this supply not being available, the pump to take suction from a reservoir of say 20,000 gallons capacity, with a possibility of some variation according to the special case under treatment, such reservoir to be filled by connection to the city main, automatically controlled by float valve.

The pump and boilers should be cut off from the building by preferably a fire wall, in which case the sill at the doorway should be at least two feet above the basement level, or if this is not possible, a dwarf wall not less than two feet high should be provided, which would prevent flooding the pump and boiler room in the event of the water which finds its way into the basement reaching the depth indicated. A sufficient quantity of steam to run the pump should be kept up at all times and an engineer on duty night and day.

A signal system with a station on each floor with gong and indicator in the engine room for the purpose of notifying the engineer of the location of a fire and when the pump should be put in operation.

A watchman should patrol the building at night, and during the day, on Sundays and holidays, making hourly rounds, a record of the rounds being made on an approved watch clock, and stations connected therewith to be located on each floor and in such manner as to require the watchman to patrol practically all parts of the building.

PRIVATE WATER WORKS—See Water Works.

PRODUCER GAS PLANTS—The producer and all apparatus connected therewith should be safely set on a solid foundation, and all platforms used in connection with generators should be of incombustible material. For detailed description, see National Board Standards. Producer gas is made by partial or incomplete combustion of coal in the presence of an air supply which is regulated, and leaves no combustible residue.

PROFIT INSURANCE—Insurance on profits may be written under two or more forms, which may be principally described as "per diem" and "per cent." Per diem profit insurance is generally used where only a very small stock of merchandise is carried. Percentage profit insurance in this case is not acceptable to most companies as can be readily seen from the following example: A cafe has a $1,000 stock; 50 per cent. profit would be $500. If fire ensues with a total loss the companies must pay $500, whereas if policy was written under the "per diem" form with an amount of $500 at $20 a day profit it would be 25 days before the total amount of insurance would be used up and the chances are that the premises would be in working order before the 25-day period terminated.

Per cent. profit insurance is the most commonly used and should always follow the stock adjustment. Extreme care should be exercised in writing this class of insurance as many brokers' forms read "company shall be liable for a loss of profits equal to, say, 20 per cent. or 25 per cent. of the value of merchandise insured. With this form the stock may only suffer a 1 per cent. fire loss and yet the company would be obliged to pay a 20 per cent. or 25 per cent. profit loss. The form should read that the loss would be a certain per cent. of the value of the **damaged merchandise** (not the value of the merchandise insured); in other words, the profit loss should follow the stock adjustment. Only competent underwriters should accept profit insurance. The following will illustrate the reason why large concerns carry percentage profit insurance. A large woolen firm has stock of piece goods and are well stocked up, their fall stock being all in. A fire breaks out and they sustain a total loss. Their own mill cannot fill orders for three months, therefore they are obliged to go to other mills to supply them. In order to protect themselves against such a contingency, they carry percentage profit insurance so that they will receive their regular profit just as if nothing had happened.

PROFITS OF A LEASE—This is considered good insurance if the conditions of the proposed insurance are thoroughly understood by the underwriter. The amount of insurance is determined in the following manner. Assume that ten years ago, a very old building was leased for a term of years at $10,000 per year. The building is remodeled and the lease is now worth $20,000 a year. Should the building burn, the lessee may be forced to pay $20,000 a year for a similar lease in the vicinity. Therefore he secures a "profit of lease" policy for the difference for which he paid $10,000 and the present value, $20,000, to protect his interest for each year the lease has to run. Again he may have leased the building, and sublet the property for a much larger sum; in which event, the amount of difference between what he pays and what he receives is his profit.

PROHIBITED RISK—One of a class which has shown such an unprofitable loss ratio that a company will not write any insurance therein or thereon.

PROOF OF LOSS is the sworn statement of the insured to the insurer, setting forth the time fire occurred, the amount of loss and damage sustained, information concerning ownership, the cash value of property covered, the names of other companies interested, and the amount of their policies, the total amount of insurance carried and the occupancy of building at the time of fire. See Adjuster.

PROOF SPIRITS—See Grain Alcohol.

PROPRIETARY MEDICINES (liquid or tablet form)—Use stone and iron mills, chasers, pulverizers, dry rooms, presses for tablets. May use in the manufacture such things as nitroglycerine, carbon bisulphide, sulphuric ether, turpentine, essential oils, sulphur, phosphorus, camphor, nitric, hydrochloric and glacial acetic acids, lamp-black, powdered charcoal, denatured and grain alcohol. Sometimes use portable oil or gas stoves.

PRO RATA—Used when a policy is cancelled by other than the assured (unless rewritten), in which case the premium retained is figured in the proportion to the time the policy has been in force. See Short Rate.

PROTECTED RISKS—Risks under fire department protection. See Accessibility; also Topography.

PROVISION DEALERS—Work consists of meat washing and trimming, sausage meat grinding and stuffing, cooking, lard rendering and pressing, smokehouses, refrigerating, pickling, coopering. May have small carpenter and paint shop in large plants, also stable and garage. See Smoke Houses.

PRUSSIAN BLUE—Made of sulphate of iron and yellow prussiate of soda. Chlorate of potash is used for oxidizing. See Soluble Blue.

PRUSSIC ACID (hydrocyanic)—Composed of hydrogen, carbon and nitrogen. See Hydrocyanic Acid.

PUBLIC HALLS—See Halls.

PUDDLING FURNACE—Used to convert cast-iron into wrought-iron.

PUG MILL—A mixing machine used chiefly in clay and paint factories. Used for tempering brick clay in potteries.

PULLEYS (wood) in an elevator head may cause fire when the elevator becomes choked. Experiments prove that when a choke-up occurs, the friction of the wood pulley on a canvas or rubber belt will produce actual fire (not merely excessive heat or smoke) in from six and one-half to twenty minutes, depending principally on the kind of belt used, the size of the pulley, and the height of the elevator. Iron pulleys should always be used. See Strut Boards, also Elevators.

PUMICE STONE—A volcanic product. Used as an abrasive. Considered good insurance.

PUMPS—If a pump shows 43 lbs. of pressure it is the

equivalent to head of 100 feet, in other words, same as a gravity tank 100 feet elevation.

On the approach of cold weather, pumps should be tried to see if in proper working order. Examine the pump suction pipe to see if strainer is clear and free from refuse or otherwise obstructed. See Fire Pumps.

PURCHASE MONEY MORTGAGE—Where a party purchases a business and pays the former owner a certain amount each month. The former owner retains a mortgage until the full amount is liquidated. This transaction is considered O. K. by underwriters. The buyer is constituted the sole owner. Loss is usually made payable to the mortgagee. (Inspect and get trade report.)

PURLINS—The horizontal pieces placed on rafters for supporting the roof covering. See Piers.

PUTTING-OUT MACHINE (in leather works)—A machine which squeezes the water out of the skin.

PUTTY—Linseed oil and whiting. Mixed and heated in steam kettles with agitators. Rapid motion mills for grinding. Barrel painting, soldering irons for can tops, linseed oil storage and oily rags and floors are principal hazards. Glue putty is made from whiting and hot, melted glue.

PYRALIN—Celluloid.

PYRENE—A secret liquefied gas, said to consist of carbon tetra-chloride charged with carbonic acid gas to the point of saturation, with a small amount of ammonia gas and hydrochloric acid. Pyrene extinguishers are recommended for garages, car barns, chemical plants, calcium carbide fires, paints, oils and varnishes but not for general factories' purposes, department stores, etc. It vaporizes and forms a gas blanket excluding the oxygen from the fire.

PYRIDINE—Used for denaturing alcohol.

PYRITES—Or natural disulphide of iron. A dense, hard mineral of crystalline structure and pale yellow color. There is some doubt as to whether they are subject to spontaneous combustion, although several cases are on record of fires starting in the holds of ships where only this cargo was stored. The pyrites used in manufacturing sulphuric acid usually contain about 48 per cent. of sulphur, 40 per cent.

of iron and the balance silica, copper and arsenic. It is burned in a kiln which is kept supplied with fresh quantities of ore.

PYRO—A prefix signifying fire. Also abbreviation for Pyrogallic Acid.

PYROBAR PARTITION BLOCKS—Hollow; are made of gypsum (plaster of paris) and wood fibre. Approved for partitions when 3 inches thick.

PYRODENE—A so-called fireproof paint.

PYROGRAPHIC OUTFIT—Consists of a bottle of benzine, a rubber tube connecting to a needle and a small bulb which is squeezed by hand the same as an atomizer. The needle is first heated, and then the benzine vapor pumped to the needle to keep it hot while burning the wood. Flemish white wood is mostly used.

PYROLIGENEOUS ACID—The crude acid obtained by the destructive distillation of wood. Has smoky odor, not inflammable.

PYROMANIAC—A fiend who sets buildings on fire, usually only to see them burn, or watch the fire engines run to the fire. See Incendiarism.

PYRONONE—A high explosive.

PYROPHORES—Substances glowing and igniting spontaneously.

PYROXYLIN—Solutions of pyroxylin, nitrocellulose, or soluble cotton dissolved in amyl acetate or other solvents. See Celluloid.

Q

QUARRIES (slate)—Hazards of large frame areas and dry kilns. Moral hazard is most important. The natural supply of slate may be exhausted and render the plant useless, or slate may be of poor quality which would cause a great depreciation in the value of the quarry. Cost of transportation to markets may be so high that the plant cannot operate at a profit.

QUEBRACHO—An extract from wood bark, used in tanning. Will melt, but will not burn.

QUEEN POST OR QUEEN ROD—See King Post.

QUICK LIME—See Lime.

QUICKSILVER—Commercial name for mercury.

QUILL TOOTH PICKS—Work consists of sterilizing and repacking natural and artificial quills or straws and covers for same. Use motor-driven machines for making covers, and gas or steam for heating water.

QUINOLENE—An oily inflammable liquid.

QUOIN STONES—Stones placed along the vertical angles of a building.

R

RABBET OR RABBITT—A groove along the edge of a board or a door frame, as for instance, fire doors of swinging type must be rabbetted.

RACING STABLES have a poor fire record. Belmont Park, Long Island, burned twice in one month in 1917. See Stables.

RACKING OFF (in breweries)—This means drawing the beer into kegs. A filling machine and liquid gas tank are used for pressure. See Breweries.

RADIANT METAL POLISH—Flash point 200 deg. F. Classed non-volatile.

RAFFIA—A grass fibre.

RAFTERS—Those timbers which form the inclined sides of a roof and carry a roof covering. Joists to which roof boards are nailed.

RAGOSINE OIL—A mineral oil. Flash, 380 deg. F.

RAG STOCKS—This business has a very poor fire record, especially where sorting or baling is done. Open gas jets over sorting tables, smoking and coal stove heat are poor features. Generally occupy basement with poor class of help. See Clippings.

RAILROAD CAR HOUSES—A standard Railway Car Storage House should be so constructed and protected that it may not contribute in any manner toward the spread of fire therein, and contribute only, in case of fire, not to exceed sectional losses of the structure. One single division should not exceed dimensions to expose to any one fire a greater number of cars therein than would represent a valuation of $200,000 of combustible rolling stock, or a total interior trackage of not more than 1,800 feet.

Floors—To be of brick, concrete, stone, cinders or earth.

Pits—To have brick, stone or concrete retaining walls or piers; brick or concrete floors; steps of stone, concrete or iron; the rails to be supported on brick, concrete, stone or wood stringers exposed on one side only, and to have not more than four-track sections communicating.

Tracks—To run clear from building, without break or transfer table. To be terminated by suitable bumpers, so that there will be a clear space of not less than three feet between bumpers and wall of building. Special track work in front of building to be provided with guard rails, where necessary.

Track Doors—Track doors to be in pairs, to be arranged so that whether open or closed any door of one pair will not interfere with the operation of any other pair. When within 10 feet of cut-off walls, to be constructed and hung as for a standard swinging fire door. Approved metal roller doors may also be used.

Hazards—All electrical, heating, power and occupancy hazards to be installed and maintained, and where necessary to be cut off, to be in accordance with the rules and requirements of the National Board of Fire Underwriters.

RAILROADS—Protection along railroads to prevent brush or forest fires. Along railroads, fire safety strips are employed. A strip about 25 feet on each side of the track is cleared of all material. Back of this there is a strip of woods from 50 to 60 feet wide, on which the timber is left but from which all the underbrush on the ground is removed. Beyond this wooded strip is a ditch from 5 to 6 feet wide and a foot or more deep. The dirt from the ditch is thrown back toward the railroad and forms a small embankment. Cross ditches are dug through the wooded strip about 100 yards apart. After the material on the ground is cleared each year there is nothing else to be done and it is seldom that a fire escapes. By this device, and by strict enforcement of laws governing the use of spark arresters, etc., the number of fires started by railroads is kept down to a surprisingly small total. See Forest Fires.

RAILROAD TERMINALS—Usually large area of frame

construction. Should have plenty of fire pails and extinguishers and a good standpipe system. In unheated portions, the water in standpipes is apt to freeze. Oftentimes the standpipes are drained at the beginning of winter and supply must then be turned on in engine-room or pumping-station, when there is a fire. In transporting perishable freight, such as potatoes, in box cars during cold weather, there is grave danger of freezing. Instances are known where the burlap and straw covering was deemed insufficient and a coal fire built in the car, with the result that the car and the freight were destroyed. A poor fire record class.

RAINES LAW HOTELS—Hotels only in the eye of the law as the furnished rooms above the saloon are seldom, if ever, used. Always inspect this class.

RAIN-LOOP—A loop made in electric wiring just before it enters the wall of a building, to prevent rain from following in.

RAISING PLATE—See Wall Plate.

RAMIE—A fibre from an oriental plant of the nettle family, used instead of cotton for braids, trimmings, napery, etc. Similar in appearance to thrown silk and woven the same as straw braid in a straw hat factory, on a "ramie" machine, then sized with glue or starch, dried over steam coils and smoothed in steam or gas-heated roller.

RANDOM STONES—Stones thrown into the water to form a foundation or retainer wall.

RANGES (large) should have a hood to confine, and ventilating duct to carry off grease-laden vapors or smoke. A fan draws the vapors to a stack or flue. These hoods and vents become coated on the inside with grease, which takes fire from the stove. Steam jets are sometimes installed under hood so that if grease is ignited a valve on steam pipe can be turned on to smother the fire. See Gas Ranges.

RANGES (Small)—Should be set on one course of brick on sheet-iron. Large ranges should be set on fireproof floors. If the floors are combustible, ranges must be set on a foundation consisting of two courses of four-inch terra cotta or three courses of brick, top course pigeon-holed, on metal. Foundation to extend 12 inches in front (except if solid fuel is used, in which case 24 inches are required), also 12 inches sides and rear. If ranges have four-inch legs, only one course of terra cotta needed. If 18-inch clear space metal shield only is required. See Gas Ranges.

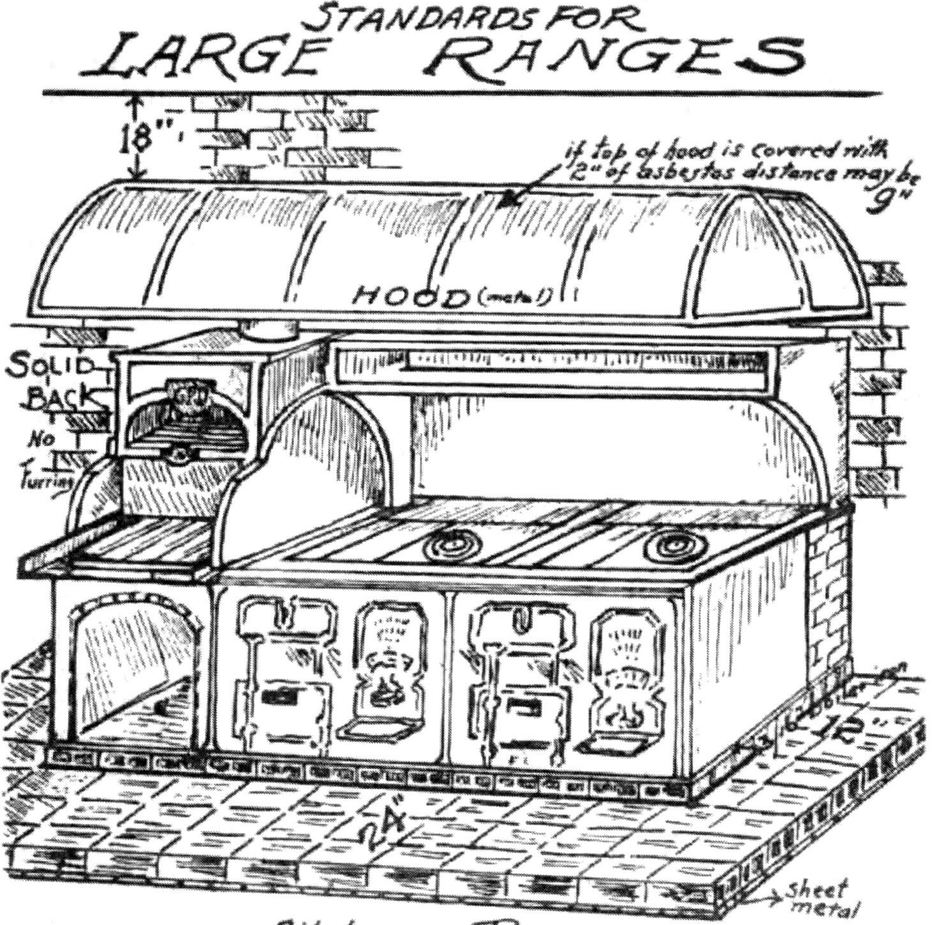

All Large Ranges should be set only on fireproof floors. If floors are Combustible, ranges must be set on a foundation consisting of two courses of terra cotta (each 4" blocks) well laid in cement on sheet metal and 3/16" boiler iron on top of the first course of brick (if common brick is used require 3 courses, top course to be laid on edge so as to produce ventilating air space. One course of brick to extend beyond range as shown, the other merely sets under. (If GAS extend brick only 12")

If ranges have 4" legs only one course of terra cotta required

If ranges have 18" clearance metal shield only is required

RAPE OIL—An oil resembling olive oil, pressed from rape seed. Flash, 440 to 580 deg. F. Used at altars.

RATES—The object sought in fixing fire insurance rates in New York City.—By W. O. Robb.

1. To provide such a premium income from the aggregate of fire underwriting operations in the metropolitan district as will in average years be sufficient to pay the losses incurred in that district plus the specific expense and a pro rata share of the general expense of doing business, and yet leave margin enough both to pay a fair profit on the capital and surplus invested and to provide for the accumulation of a reserve against extraordinary or conflagration losses not occurring in average years and not to be treated as exclusively a metropolitan district contingency.

2. To so apportion this levy, or insurance tax, among the various classes of risks as to make each class come as near as possible to the payment of its own losses and the contribution of its proper proportion toward the expense, profit and reserve accounts.

3. So to distinguish among individual risks of the same class that proper credit will be given or proper charge made for all variations above or below the standard of the average risk of the class, according to best judgment of underwriters and the fire protection experts; that every property owner can be made to see just what it is that operates, and how far it operates, to make his insurance cost more or less than his neighbor's in the same business, so that the suspicion as well as the actual practice of unfair discrimination may be removed, and that every proper kind of pressure and inducement may be brought to bear in the direction of the improvement of the fire hazard and the reduction of the fire waste. See Schedules.

RATS, FIRES CAUSED BY—The following is quoted from a bulletin of the United States Biological Survey:

It is generally believed that rats and mice cause fires by igniting matches with their teeth. The testimony of chiefs of fire departments and adjusters of fire insurance claims confirms this belief, and many specific instances have been given of fires caused in this way. A fire, which resulted in the partial destruction of the Sultan's place at Scutari, Asia Minor, in 1856, had such an origin. During 1907 the fire department of Washington, D. C., gave a similar explanation of a fire which seriously damaged a large store and its contents.

Manufacturers of matches often dip them in paraffine to protect the phosphorus. The paraffine is attractive to rats and mice, and the matches are often carried under floors and behind partitions, where they are subsequently gnawed. Paper and other combustible materials collected by the animals add to the danger of fires. Moreover, since the heads of phosphorus matches contain from 14 to 17 per cent. of phosphorus, it does not require actual gnawing by rats to ignite them. Hot weather, excessive heat from furnaces, or friction of any kind may effect the same result as the teeth of rats, when the matches have been carried into a nest made of combustibles.

Fires in mills and warehouses have been traced to the spontaneous ignition of oily and fatty rags or waste carried under floors by rats or mice. Cotton mills are said to be peculiarly subject to fires from this cause.

Phillip's Warehouse, Church Street, London, was twice set on fire and damaged by reason of gas leaks. In both instances the lead gas pipe leading to the meter had been eaten through by rats, and the escaping gas was accidentally set on fire by workmen who were searching for a leak. In a similar instance of gas leak caused by rats in a London private residence, no fire resulted, but a sleeping family of four persons narrowly escaped death by asphyxiation. An inspector in the employ of the Washington Gas Light Company recounts a similar instance in that city where pipes were gnawed by rats, but fortunately it occurred when the inmates were awake.

The most common way in which rats cause fire is by gnawing away the insulating covering from wires used in electric lighting, where the wires pass under floors or inside of partitions. The insulating materials are used for nests, which rats often build of combustibles placed in contact with the naked wires. Insurance companies, a few years ago, estimated the fire loss of the United States due to defective insulation of wires at $15,000,000, yearly; and since rats and mice are the chief agents in impairing the insulation after the wires are in place, a large part of the above sum must be charged to these animals.

RAW RUBBER—See Crude Rubber.

RAZOR STROPS—After being tanned and dressed, they may be oiled with tallow or neatsfoot oil dressing, and then embossed. Wooden handles may also be made on the premises. See Leather.

REAR YARDS which are untidy with rubbish, old boxes, etc., have been the cause of many fires. Should be kept clean. See Vacant Lots.

RECEIVING STATIONS are depots where customers' goods are received to be sent away to factories, such as goods to be dyed, laundered, etc. Usually good risks if only minor repairs are made.

RECIPROCATING MOTION—The opposite of revolving motion.

RECORDS—On wooden racks, tier upon tier, offer no resistance to fire and the dried-out bindings and paper conduce to the rapid spread of a fire. Government archives with records of surveys, and similar records of private firms are irreplaceable, when once destroyed. Heads of institutions show a marked lack of thoroughness in leaving such records exposed to the fire fiend. See Patterns.

RECTIFYING—A cold process by which the "proof" of the liquor (percentage of alcohol contained therein), is either raised or lowered. Water is used to reduce, and additional alcohol to raise the proof. Commercial alcohol is about 90 proof. Aside from the handling of alcohol, there is no hazard to this process. See Concentration by Fractional Distillation; see Liquors and Distilleries.

RED LEAD—An oxide of lead. In its making, special furnaces are required. The cuppellation furnace converts metallic lead into litharge. The reverberatory furnace or oven reduces metallic lead into litharge.

RED OIL is oleic acid. When impure, said to ignite spontaneously.

RED-SANDERS WOOD—An East Indian wood used in dyeing.

REDUCTION—A process carried on by treating the compound to be reduced with powdered metal, the purpose being to abstract a certain amount of oxygen by forcing it into combination with the reducing element.

REDWOOD—Although a soft wood offers considerable resistance to fire; is very slow to ignite and will not burn except under the most favorable condition. Used for outside walls of frame buildings in the western part of the United States.

REED AND RATTAN—See Artificial Flowers and Feathers. See Willow.

REFINERS AND SMELTERS OF METALS—Furnaces, kettles, pits, etc., should be carefully inspected as to setting and clearance. Usually occupy ramshackle properties. See Sweep Smelters.

REFRIGERATION—There are two systems of producing artificial refrigeration in common use at the present time, in both of which the use of volatile liquids is necessary. They are commercially known as the "compression" and "absorption" systems, named in order of their popularity. In the compression system, ammonia and carbon dioxide are commonly used, the former being the more dangerous from nearly all points of view.

The **compression system** is divided into three parts, namely the compressor, the condenser and the expansion sections. The compressor draws the expanded or heated gas from the expansion coils, compresses and forces it under pressure through the condenser coils (coils of pipe cooled by running water), where the gas is again reduced to a liquid and conducted to the expansion coils which it enters through an expansion valve (usually a needle valve). The expansion coils are iron pipes in which the volatile boils or vaporizes. Volatiles in use require a great deal of heat to vaporize. This heat is taken from the surroundings of the expansion coils. As the gas becomes heated it is again withdrawn by the compressor and forced through the same cycle of operation as before.

The **absorption system** is not as hazardous as the compression system inasmuch as no mechanical energy is necessary except a small pump used in forcing the solutions from one part of the system to another Volatile gases will not condense at the temperature produced by the running water at the condenser unless they are under pressure. In the compression system, the pressure is maintained by the compressor. In the absorption system, the pressure is maintained by boiling. A solution of aqua ammonia is placed in a boiler (usually steam-heated). The ammonia having much the lower boiling point is promptly vaporized at a pressure sufficient for condensation and is conducted through various sections (purifying and separating), until it reaches the condensers, where it returns to liquid form and is conducted to the expansion coils (refrigerator) as in the compression system.

After the gas has done its frigorific work, it is conducted to a chamber in which it is mixed with and finally absorbed by water, the mixture returning to the boiler or generator where it undergoes the process of distillation as before. The expansion coils are sometimes used in direct refrigeration, i. e., the volatile is allowed to expand in coils of pipes in the refrigerator, usually located at the sides or top. Where high temperatures are desired, however, the expansion coils are immersed in tanks containing a rich brine, which is cooled by the expansion of the volatile, and forced through pipes in the refrigerator.

Hazards—Boiler and engine-room hazards usually exist in connection with refrigeration plants, and the inherent hazards should be properly guarded. In addition there are severe incidental refrigeration hazards, especially where ammonia is used. Ammonia forms explosive mixtures with lubricating oils in the compressor. In order that this hazard be confined to the least possible space, oil traps are placed in the pipe line between the compressor and condenser, designed to remove the oil from the gas. No open lights should be allowed in engine room. No ammonia cylinders (filled) should be kept on the premises except in room at low temperature.

Fire Department Connections are now required in New York City for plants above a certain tonnage capacity. A connection is made between by-pass connected with safety valve and sewer. The connection is provided so that water may be injected to absorb and cool ammonia, and neutralize the inflammable gas, if any be present.—W. J. Tallamy. See Bunker Rooms; see Cold Storage.

REFRIGERATION (iceless) in the home. The refrigerator is made on the principle of the "ammonia absorption" system. The machine has a combined absorber, generator or still, condenser and receiver. Into the generator (which is heated by artificial means), is placed a mixture of ammonia and water. The heat distills the ammonia, which passes through a water jacket pipe to the condenser and cooler, and passes on in the form of anhydrous ammonia to the receiver. The ammonia vapor in the receiver takes up considerable latent heat, and the receiver becomes intensely cold, cooling the surroundings. The process is repeated automatically by cooling of the generator by means of a water jacket, which creates a vacuum in the generator, and the vaporized ammonia rushes from the receiver back to the generator. A small apparatus.

REFRIGERATING PLANT FIRE—Fire was caused by ignition of waste paper, etc., and generated an intense heat which melted the lead joints in the condenser, releasing the ammonia gas. This gas (probably foul gas), composed largely of hydrogen, due to the disassociation of ammonia gases under heat from pressure, ignited and burned like huge blow-torches under heavy pressure. After the inflammable foul gases had been expelled from the piping, pure ammonia vapor undoubtedly issued and probably aided in smothering the fire. It is recommended that all rooms containing refrigerating apparatus be cut off from the balance of plant by fireproof partition, with approved automatic fire doors at the openings.

REGULATING RHEOSTATS are boxes containing resistance coils. They are attached to the motor generators and can be adjusted to give any resistance desired. The speed of machines can be thus varied at will and their voltage thus controlled.

RE-INSURANCE—Oftentimes a company will write a larger policy on a risk than the "line sheet" calls for, to accommodate a broker or an assured, who desires policies for large amounts. To reduce its net liability, the company then places part of its line in another company. A re-insuring company may require "a retainer clause" to be put on its policy, especially on poor risks, which, in brief, states that the company holding the original policy and reinsuring agrees to retain as much liability as it is reinsuring. See Liability; see Placer.

RE-LYT—A water-proofing compound used in shoe factories for softening leather. Made of oils and greases. Flash about 350 deg. F. Classed non-inflammable, non-hazardous. No thinner required.

REMOTE RISKS should be written with extreme care. The one fact of being in territory not readily accessible for inspection is enough to satisfy the company that low liability should be assumed. See Accessibility.

RENDERING FATS AND GREASE—Unprofitable as a class. The entire interior is usually grease-soaked and burns rapidly. The tankage, or solid matter left after rendering, is pressed into blocks and used as fertilizer. See Fat Rendering.

RENEWAL—A policy continued in force at the expiration of the original contract by the issuance of a "renewal receipt" or by issuing a new policy under the same conditions as the original, to take effect as the old policy expires.

RENT INSURANCE is written mainly on apartment houses to cover loss of rents in case of fire. Two forms are used, occupied or occupied and vacant. Better than building insurance. While the fire loss may be 50 per cent., the rent insurance may be one-third or less, figured on the length of time it takes to repair the building. Only competent underwriters should accept "rent" insurance.

RENTS AND LEASEHOLDS—Sums derivable from real property, which are lost by the assured if a fire interrupts the continuous enjoyment of the property. As to the tenant under lease, a fire means the destruction or impairment of the property right for which he has paid or is obligated to pay.

REPELLO—Waterproof compound used in shoe factories, not volatile or inflammable. Can be used inside of building.

RESERVE of an insurance company is based upon the amount of unearned premiums of policies in force. States require a definite percentage of all premiums to be set aside by the company ranging from 40 to 100 per cent. It is for the protection of outstanding policy holders.

RESIDENCE SECTIONS—Usually deteriorate when changing from one class of people to another less desirable class. Values depreciate especially near the border of a growing "colony" section. Very important to watch the growth and changes in all sections of a large city.

RESIDENT BUYER—One who buys from manufacturers or wholesalers for other concerns. They receive goods for examination and act as a buying agent. Stock therefore is only on trust, belonging to the manufacturer who ships same, or to the consignee.

RESIN can be obtained by distilling the exudations of the fir tree, oil of turpentine passing over, and resin remaining. Inflammable. See Rosin.

RESINATE (precipitated) of zinc. If moist may ignite spontaneously. The New York Board of Underwriters excludes this from listed storage stores.

RESINIFICATION—See Gumming.

RESIN OIL—Distilled from resin.

RESISTO—A water-proofing compound for sole leather. Used in shoe factories. No thinner required. Flash 400 deg. F. Not inflammable.

RESPONSIBILITY FOR FIRES—Under the Code Napoleon in France, a man is held responsible for fire damage to his neighbor. Each fire is investigated and the owner or tenant of any premises must show he is not responsible for a fire starting in any premises occupied or owned by him. In France a tenant usually insures by one policy the following items. (1) His own property; (2) The risk of responsibility for damage to the building; (3) The risk of responsibility for damage to his neighbors. A landlord insures in one policy the following items: (1) His own property; (2) His responsibility for damage to the property of tenants; (3) His responsibility for damage to the property of neighbors.

RESTAURANTS—Kitchens in hands of careless people are apt to become very greasy. Bread is frequently dried in a wood box on shelf over range, under hood. See Ranges, also Hotels and Chinese Restaurants.

RETAIL BUSINESS has been said to embrace everything good, bad and indifferent. It is this class which requires careful scrutinizing both by inspectors and underwriters.

RETAIL STOCKS—Considerable value is under counters and subject to water damage in case of fires. Those in wardrobes are better protected if top is watertight to prevent staining or streaking of goods from water. See Second-hand Stocks.

RETAINING WALL—A wall which retains adjoining earth or other material producing lateral thrust.

RETENE—Highly inflammable hydrocarbon.

REVETMENT—A retaining wall.

RHEA—A species of nettle, the stalks of which contain fibre.

RHEOSTAT—An electrical device for introducing and cutting out resistance. See Regulating Rheostat.

RHEXITE—A sort of dynamite.

RHIGOLENE OR SHERWOOD OIL—See Petroleum.

RIBBONS—Usually rolled in paper strips on a pasteboard centre. This method gives considerable protection from water, smoke and dirt. If dried quickly, the salvage should be large. If this stock is laid sidewise on racks instead of on ends, the salvage will be greater.

RIBBONS (manufacturing)—Consists of weaving, braiding, tubing, singeing, yarn preparing, curling, gilling (combing and straightening).

RICE, if wet and left in bags will mildew and be unfit for food.

RICE MILLS—Classed as a cereal mill but with less hazard. Process is cleaning, separating, removing outer shell (shelling), hulling, separating bran, "pearling" or scouring, drying bran, grinding in iron attrition machine at high speed, and polishing. Hazards are overheated bearings, steam dry-rooms, friction and dust at attrition mills and polishing. Elevator legs, spouts and hoppers set through floors conduce to rapid spread of fire.

RIDGE OF A ROOF—Its peak or sharp edge along its very top.

RIDGE POLE (ridge piece or ridge plate)—The highest horizontal timber in a roof extending across the tops of the rafters of the truss.

RIDGE ROLL—The roll along the ridge of the roof and on the peaks of dormer windows.

RIDING ACADEMIES—See Stables.

RIGHT AND INTEREST OF PAWNBROKER—Companies only insure money pawnbroker advances on goods pledged or pawned together with the interest accrued. The form covering right and interest of the assured in the articles and stock of merchandise in fireproof safes is considered good insurance. See Pawnbroker.

RING ICE FORMATION—A condition sometimes found in sprinklered refrigeration plants. It is the formation of ice inside of the pipes due to condensation of moisture in the compressed air. See Ice Formation.

RIP-RAP—See Random Stones.

RIP-SAW—A kind of circular saw.

RISERS—See Dead Risers; also Live Risers.

RISK—In insurance literature the term "risk" is a term applied to any piece or kind of property which an insurance policy may cover. A "risk," therefore, is any article or commodity or building which is liable to be damaged or destroyed by fire, which liability or danger the insurance company assumes for a stated price, called "the premium." (Fire Facts, issued by Washington Surveying and Rating Bureau.) See Occupancy; also Hazard.

RISKS declined by other companies should only be accepted after careful survey and trade reports. Usually the other company had a very good reason for declining. See Full Risk; also Prohibited Risk.

ROAD HOUSES—Usually conduct a season business. Most of them are of light frame construction and located in open country subjected to high winds. They may be left unguarded part of the year. Moral hazard should be investigated. Fire record of this class is poor.

ROASTING is accomplished in high temperature kilns or ovens, see Kilning.

ROCK OIL—See Petroleum. A mineral naphtha.

ROCK SHAFT—One that rocks or only makes part of a revolution each way.

ROD PIN AND DOWELL MACHINE—Small machine resembling a lathe. Ordinarily consists of a cutter-head and chuck mounted in line with the pulley driving them, the stock passing through the axis of both. Considerable refuse is made.

ROENTGEN RAYS—See X-Rays.

ROLLING STOCK—The cars, locomotives and all other equipment on wheels of a railway. See Railroads.

ROOF LATHS—Narrow strips, laid on rafter to which the shingles are nailed.

ROOF SPACES—The space between the top floor ceiling and roof. They are usually accessible from the scuttle opening leading to the roof and may be used for storage purposes. The openings leading from scuttle to roof space should be closed in with one-inch boards or trapped at ceiling. In frame rows, roof spaces between buildings must be cut off by incombustible partitions. Usually, unless the party walls are brick filled to the lower part of the roof boards, plaster boards are nailed each side of the studs, the joints filled with cement plaster. Many disastrous fires have spread through these concealed spaces, and firemen experience difficulty getting at the seat of the fire. See Attics; see Frame Rows.

ROOFING—A five-ply composition roof properly laid is considered the equal of a metal roof by some rating bureaus.

ROOFING CEMENT—Consists of pitch, tar or asphalt with inflammable solvents.

ROOFING MOPS—Those dipped in asphaltum or coal tar and left to dry or drain may ignite spontaneously. Used in making tar and gravel roofs. Should be removed from the building when not in use.

ROPE MANUFACTURING—The fibres used are hemp, jute and coir. Machinery consists of tearing machines

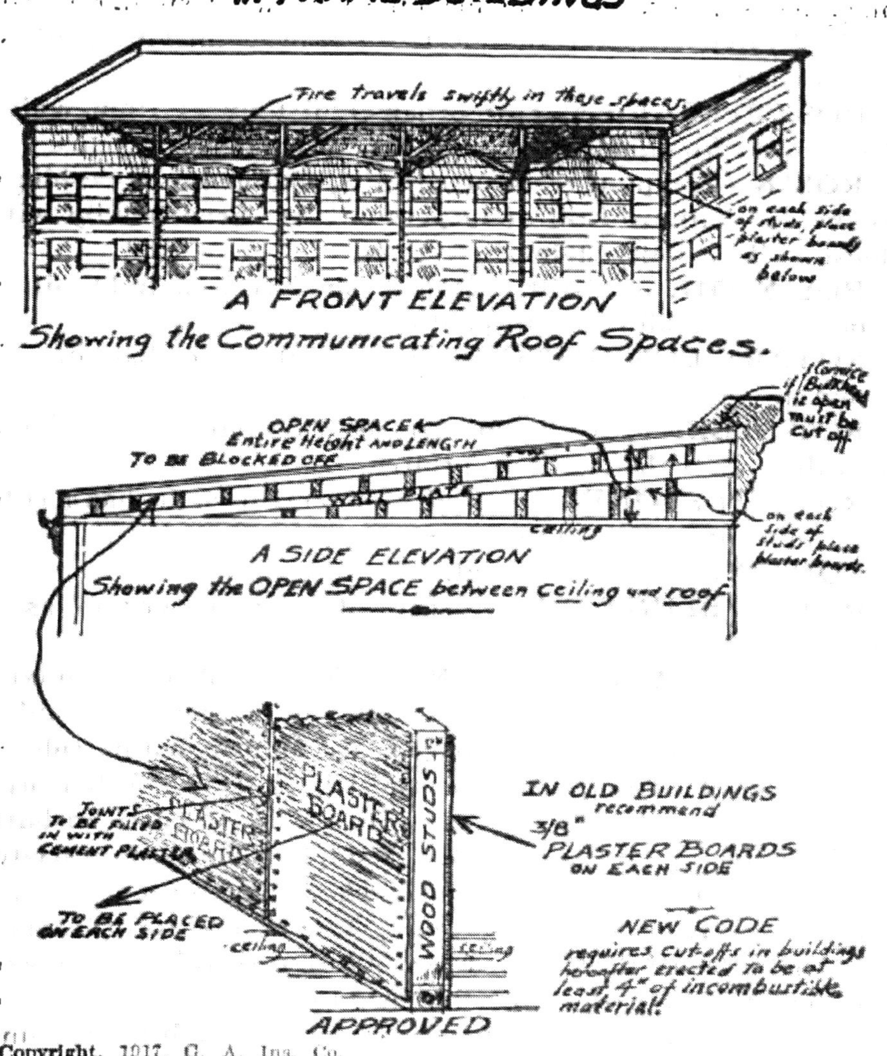

(devils) which break up the long tow ready for treatment in the breakers, finishers and carding machines; the hemp softening machines, which reduce the harshness of the fibre by the crushing action of the fluted surface of the rolls; the spreading or preparing machines, called "chain drawer" which dress the hemp fibres, parallelizing them and forming them into "sliver." At the back end of this machine there is a tank containing an emulsion of oil and water used as a lubricant for the fibre under treatment. The drawing-frame machine is a fibre dressing machine somewhat similar to the chain drawer, but used for the more refined finishing process of dressing.

ROSETTES—Circular or ornamental fixtures from which drop cords for electrical lamps are suspended.

ROSIN—Common resin or rosin is obtained as a residium in the distillation of oil of turpentine. It burns rapidly with dense yellow sooty flame.

ROSIN OIL is distilled from rosin. It is a light oil of same inflammability as turpentine.

ROTARY CONVERTOR—An apparatus for changing alternating currents into direct currents.

ROT-STEEP—An alkaline lye used to remove the sizing on calico cloth before it is printed.

ROTTEN-STONE—An earthy mineral used in hand rubbing and finishing furniture.

ROUTING is grooving out.

ROYAL SPIRITS—Not approved by underwriters as a benzine substitute.

RUBBER BALLOONS AND TOYS—Rubber is mixed with naphtha in power mixers and put in open dip tanks. Wood forms, previously shellaced, are dipped in this rubber solution until coated, and then dried by hot air. When dry the thin rubber skin is stripped from the form, cured in bath of bisulphide of carbon, chloride of sulphur and alcanin paste, powdered with soap stone and packed. Water colors and lamp-black are used for coloring. A poor fire record class.

RUBBER CEMENT—A heavy solution of rubber in gasoline, naphtha or carbon bisulphide. Inflammable. In factories underwriters permit only two quarts for each floor, same to be kept in safety pots and thinned with carbon tetra-chloride. If a greater quantity is required, the excess must be stored outside of building.

RUBBER-COATED CLOTH—Rubber grinding machines wash and remove the impurities. It is then mixed with mineral powders such as paris white, pyrites, etc., and dried by air. A machine with two steel rolls grinds the mineral matter into the rubber. It is then churned in gasoline. The dissolved rubber is spread upon sheets of cloth in a spreading machine which coats the cloth, after which it is either coated with potato starch and printed or the printing is done with a solution containing carbon tetra-chloride as a solvent. All machines should be grounded especially at the knives of spreaders to remove any static electricity. The rubber is vulcanized by being draped on racks in steam heated room at about 250 deg. F. or cured by passing the goods over a roll partly submerged in a trough of carbon-bisulphide, carbon tetra-chloride and chloride of sulphur.

RUBBER, Crude—Considered desirable insurance, as it has practically no fire hazard. It is apt to deteriorate from heat if piled closely, therefore it should be piled loosely in a cool place such as a basement. It is received in this country in large chunks called "biscuits."

Raw Rubber shrinks greatly in transit, and the loss is made up by covering the rubber with sulphur, rosin and turpentine after it reaches the warehouse. The rubber absorbs this mixture and the loss is made up in a few weeks. There is some danger of rubber igniting when treated in this manner.

RUBBER (imitation)—As used for parts of electrical apparatus, telephone receivers and transmitters and for insulating. Made of crude shellac, ground mica, terra elba (or infusorial earth) ground asbestos and tar oil. These are all placed in a steam heated mixer and reduced to a pliable pulp, then rolled into sheet or block form, or placed in hydraulic presses containing steel moulds. From presses they are cooled by natural air, then passed to cutting, trimming and buffing machines. No benzine or cement. Hazards, mixing, rolling, pressing, buffing, packing, trimming. The material is worked on machines for ordinary use.

RUBBER (old)—Rubber or old metals are considered desirable insurance by themselves; but in connection with rag or paper stock are poor risks.

RUBBER FOR MECHANICAL PURPOSES—Process similar to manufacturing other forms of rubber. The rubber is made into strips or sheets from the crude stock.

RUBBER LINED CLOTH is made by inserting a sheet of rubber between two thicknesses of cloth and drawing them through steam heated calender. The cloth is coated with talcum to prevent adhering when it is rolled up.

A fire occurred in a coating machine when in operation, probably from static electricity. The coating mixture was being poured into a tank which communicated with trough in "dope" (mixture) machine by pipe. The difference between "dope" machine and the spreader is that the dope machine runs over roller which revolves in mixture in trough, while the spreader mixture runs directly on the upper surface of stretched cloth and is spread out by the cloth passing under knife edges.

RUBBER RECLAIMING—Old shoes, rubber boots, hose and the like are used. Much foreign matter, such as nails, tacks, fabric are extracted by hand. The stock is then cut up by hand and broken in small pieces in a "cracker," then placed in a lead lined wooden tank of sulphuric acid, which eats out the remaining foreign matter. It is then washed, ground, calendered, dried, mixed with coal tar residium and vulcanized.

RUBBER SHODDY—Regenerated or reclaimed rubber consists of old rubber which has been subjected to chemical treatment to prepare it for further use in the rubber industry. Liable to ignite spontaneously. Called "springs."

RUBBER TIRES for automobiles. Crude rubber is washed, cut, dried by air or vacuum, made into sheets. Fabric is impregnated with rubber in calender rolls, cut into bias strips (a cotton cloth being placed between strips to prevent adhering). Tire is built up in successive layers and cemented together with rubber cement, then worked on core or form.

The rubber cover is applied and the mass pressed under hydraulic power, vulcanized, painted with chalk on inside, inspected and packed.

Some makes, when received from the factory, are wrapped in a waterproof paper, lined on the inside with a waterproofing solution containing black asphaltum. When this paper is thoroughly wet, the black sticks to the tires, and unless it can be readily cleaned off with benzine, the tires must be sold as seconds. All tire stocks should be skidded.

RUBBING OIL—That used by furniture dealers usually has a crude oil base. Rags saturated with this are subject to spontaneous combustion.

RUBBISH of most any sort is a breeding place for fires.

RUBBLE—Masonry of rough undressed stone.

RUINS—See Fire Ruins.

S

SACCHARINE—Similar to sugar, the saccharine matter of the cane juice. It is artificially prepared from toluene, the substance found in the light distillate of coal tar. Used in making candy.

SACKETT BOARD—Made of four layers of wool felt and three layers of gypsum plaster, the outer surface being felt. Made in thicknesses of 1/4 inch, 3/8 inch and 1/2 inch. Fire retardant and a non-conductor of heat and sound.

SADDENING—In the mordanting of cotton, iron or copper sulphates are used for saddening or darkening.

SAFES are rendered fireproof by the moisture held in the intermolecular spaces of the fireproof composition. When the safe gets hot this moisture is driven by the exterior heat into the interior of the safe in the form of steam, thus keeping the interior or temperature of the safe below the point of ignition or charring. This is proved after the safe has passed through a hot fire and is opened. Everything inside the safe is protected, owing to the condensation of the steam. Inspectors should measure thickness of all walls and doors. See Vaults.

SAFETY-VALVE—A valve on a boiler which automatically opens at a predetermined pressure, and above which pressure it would not be safe to force the boiler. It lessens the danger of explosions.

SAGAX WOOD—Made of ground straw and cement binder.

SALAMANDER—A paper used between floors. It is waterproof and fire-resisting.

SALAMANDER—An open top, portable, cylindrical stove on legs. Used in buildings in course of construction, stone yards, sheds and foundries for heating purposes. Coal and coke are commonly used as fuel.

SALIENT—An angle or corner projecting outward.

SALOL—A modern drug made by treating phosphorus with chlorine and carbonic acid gas. The product is mixed with salicylic acid in powdered form and carbolic acid in a heated glass retort.

SALOONS—The bar fixtures and advertising signs are usually owned by the brewery supplying the beer. Ordinarily only the stock is owned by the saloonkeeper. They are considered good fire risks, and the loss ratio is very good. Saloons situated along water fronts and in "dive" localities catering to a low element are not considered good risks, but when profitable to the owners, can be written with caution. Prohibition legislation, police activities, etc., have forced liquor stores out of business. Many fires in this class are caused by men of a nationality naturally hot tempered and quarrelsome, who may upset a stove or lamp in a saloon brawl. Usually have gas stove on wood with rubber tube connection behind lunch counter and an unsafe swinging gas bracket in basement at ice box.

SALT, if placed with kerosene or other hydrocarbon oil, will arrest hydrogen and prevent an explosion.

SALT DEALERS—The incidental hazards are mixing, milling and packing salt. Power belt conveyors should be given special attention by inspectors. Salt in bins is rendered inedible if wet with dirty water.

SALT HAY is recommended for packing material in glassware and other risks where large quantities are used. It burns very much slower than ordinary hay. See Packing Bins.

SALT HIDES—See Hides.

SALTPETRE—(Extracting saltpetre from nitre and chloride of potash.) A saturated solution of water and nitre is made in flat, iron, open-top steam-heated tanks, to which is added chloride of potash. The mixture is boiled for about 24 hours, pumped to cylindrical steam-heated kettles where it is concentrated by re-boiling. Both the water and the residue are drawn off to open-top iron tanks where they are allowed to settle and evaporate. The mixture at this point consists of saltpetre with impurities, dirt and sodium carbonate. The salt settles at the bottom of the tanks containing the water of solution, and after the water is drained off, the salt is shoveled out. The mixture when evaporated, is placed in other tanks where it is boiled and washed, then crystalized in wooden tanks. The crystals are carried in a worm conveyor, and are dried while passing through a dryer which is usually frame, steam and hot-air heated. The crystals are sifted and ground in burr mills. About 100 pounds each of nitre and potash will make 116 pounds of saltpetre and 60 pounds of salt. The nitre while in bags absorbs moisture from the air and is always damp. When empty, the potash and nitre bags are boiled to reclaim the remaining substances. The floors are soaked and dripping with saltpetre when the plant is in operation. If the plant were shut down, there might be some danger from spontaneous combustion in wood floors when very dry, as they might ignite spontaneously, as do dry nitre bags. Brick drying ovens are sometimes used for the higher grades of crystals. See Potassium Nitrate.

SALTPETRE OR POTASSIUM NITRATE is found principally in the warm sections of India where rain rarely falls. It is produced by the decay of nitrogenous substances in the presence of air, moisture and alkaline earths. It is used in the manufacture of high explosives, gunpowder and fireworks, as a preservative and for medicinal purposes.

SALTPETRE AND NITRE, storage and handling.—Like the chlorate, it gives up its oxygen very readily and has many similar characteristics. In contact with any combustible matter it decomposes rapidly, five-sixths of its oxygen being available for the oxidation of combustible matter. Its capacity for supporting combustion will be appreciated when it is known that one volume of nitre represents 3,000 volumes of air in its power for supporting combustion. Fires in the empty bags in which the nitre has been kept are therefore imminent and burn fiercely. In fact, in the presence of carbon (as in wood) nitre burns stubbornly in all cases. When in contact with hot coals occasioned by an external fire or by a fire resulting spontaneously it deflagrates violently. It oxidizes sulphur with unusual ease.—Hooker's Chemistry.

SALTS—This term ordinarily used by chemists, means

substances which are neither acid nor alkaline and yet contain the main ingredients of both acids and alkalis, like sulphate of potash.

SALVAGE (buildings)—When a large fire is reported most insurance companies immediately send an inspector to give a rough estimate of the amount of loss, so that they may know their approximate losses each day. In a six story and basement brick building of ordinary construction, the brick walls can be figured at 40 per cent. of value and 8.5 per cent. for each floor and roof. See Valuation of Building.

SALVAGE CORPS—The New York Salvage Corps is maintained by the New York Board of Fire Underwriters for the purpose of salvaging goods when a fire occurs. Tarpaulins are thrown over the merchandise, water is pumped out of basements, temporary roofs are put on buildings, to prevent further water damage. A patrolman is stationed on the premises to prevent removal of goods by trespassers. The corps is financed by the company members of the Board of Underwriters by a system of taxation according to the amount of premiums received by each company in the territory covered by the Salvage Corps. A number of wagons are employed which race to the fire when an alarm is sounded.

SALVAGING STOCK—The New York Salvage Corps now employ a gasoline-driven pump which will pull 1,800 gallons of water a minute out of any flooded basement. Care must be taken where the "forced out" water is thrown or there is a likelihood of choked sewers and more trouble.

SANDPAPER MACHINE, for smoothing stock. There are five types—belt, drum, disc, spindle, and slip-and-slap. Belt sanders consist of carrying sanders or other belts covered with sandpaper operating over two pulleys some distance apart. Drum sanders are cylindrical in shape, resemble planers. Disc sanders consist of discs covered with canvas and at the end of shaft, revolving rapidly. Spindle sanders are small in diameter and either vertical or horizontal. Slip-and-slap sanders consist of strips of sandpaper fastened to hub-radials. All these machines create a great deal of dust and should have blower systems attached.

SANDPAPER MANUFACTURING—See Emery.

SANDSTONE, used for building fronts, withstands the action of fire better than any other stone front. The fire and water will in time flake off the stone.

SANGAJO—Flash point 139 deg. F. Classed non-volatile.

SANITAS—A disinfecting and preservative solution made by forcing a current of air through vessels containing hot water and turpentine.

SAPONIFICATION—Decomposing fats into fatty acids and glycerine, as in soap manufacturing.

SAPON-WOOD—A dye wood.

SARDINE FACTORIES—The fish are dumped into a conveyor and carried to the cutting room, where in the case of large fish, the heads and tails are removed by knives and the entrails cleaned out. They are then washed automatically and scales are removed by attrition during the conveying and washing. The fish are then deposited in pickling bins. An endless belt with cups scoops up the washed fish, elevates them to the packing room and deposits them on a flaking machine with a carrier belt which receives fish from the conveyor and deposits same side by side and passes them between large hollow belt-covered squeeze rolls to remove the excess water. The fish are then deposited on metal trays or "flakes," and as the trays are filled they are removed to the drying process or the cooking ovens. The hazards of cooking, drying, oil filling, bathing and testing require special attention.

SASH—The framework which holds the squares of glass in a window.

SASH FRAME—The frame which receives the sash.

SATOLITE—A substitute for celluloid made from soya beans. Claimed by the manufacturers to be non-inflammable.

SAUSAGE CASINGS—The casings are packed in salt in barrels, pounded down to make them compact, and water is added to fill the barrel. Clean water will not have any bad effect on this stock, but dirty water will have a very bad effect, especially to the stock at the top of the barrel. Excessive heat will injure the quality of the casings.

SAV-ON SPIRITS—A benzine substitute classed as non-volatile.

SAWDUST mixed with bicarbonate of soda has been found efficacious in extinguishing oil and grease fires. Sawdust in a finely divided state excludes the oxygen from the fire, without which it must die out. It is used by storekeepers; in factory spittoons, and at gas engines and motors. No sawdust is permitted on the floor (except in meat and fish markets). Sand should be substituted in place of sawdust for these purposes.

SAW-TOOTH ROOFS are generally used by textile mills and machine shops because they slope like a mound and offer better lighting facilities than the flat skylight. They are sometimes called "Northern Lights."

SAXON BLUE—A mixture of indigo, sulphuric acid, potash and water.

SCANTLING—A timber less than five inches square at the end.

SCENIC STUDIOS (painting scenery) not in connection with theatres. The main part of the studio building is a very high one-story, tower-like structure which permits the stretching and painting of very large canvases. Use coal or gas stoves for heating glue for sizing, and water. May also use benzine thinned paint. Considered poor insurance risks.

SCHEDULE, as used by rating bureaus, is the make-up of the insurance rate, as, for example, Metal Workers, whose base rate is 75 cents plus five cents for skylights, plus 10 cents for floor openings, less 10 cents for water pails, etc.

SCHEDULE is a general form used in writing insurance on plants consisting of several buildings instead of writing a separate policy on each building or contents thereof. The total amounts of each item are arranged in order, and the insurance companies write a certain percentage of the entire schedule. This also simplifies matters for the assured and reduces danger of non-current forms. See Blanket Policy.

SCHEDULE EXPERT is primarily an inspector of merit who is thoroughly conversant with the many schedules in use. He must be well versed in construction, hazards, salvage of various merchandises, heating apparatus, chemistry, etc. His mission is to reduce the rate of insurance to its lowest figure by installing fire protection and other devices.

SCHOOL HAZARDS—Manual training rooms, with oily rags, rubbish, shavings, glue-pots and domestic science rooms with gas stoves; janitors' rooms with floor oil, paints for use about building, janitors' supplies; small repair shop, and storage rooms for old fixtures and desks; floor mops, chemical laboratory. Where plumbing is taught small plumbers' shop hazard.

Inspectors should be very careful to note the termination of the air ducts in schools built a decade ago, whether they terminate at the floor of the attic or are carried through roof. Unless through roof, a fire can be sucked through the duct to the attic and burn off the roof.

SCOURING SOAP POWDER, usually made of caustic soda, soda ash and silax. Scouring soap same as above with cocoanut oil added.

SCRATCH COAT of plaster; the coat applied directly to the lath, then scratched with a trowel to form a key for the finishing coat of plaster.

SCREED—A wooden strip or a strip of mortar laid on a wall to gauge the thickness of the plastering to be applied.

SCULPTORS' STUDIOS—Work consists of composition, plaster, clay, bronze, and stone-work and sometimes wood-working of frames.

SCUPPERS—Holes or tubes to allow the floors to be drained of water in case of fire. If standard scuppers are installed they usually have a bearing on the insurance rate; generally used in warehouses and fireproof or mill constructed factories.

SCUTCHING (in bleach works), the process of opening the cloth after it has been washed.

SCUTTLE—The small opening leading to a roof.

SEA GRASS—Used for upholstering and polishing furniture. See Piano Manufacturing.

SEASHORE HOTELS—Usually large area frame, subject to sweeping winds, undermining by high tides, etc. Few companies write them. Season occupancy. In case of bad season by reason of epidemics, unseasonable weather or similar circumstances, a severe moral hazard creeps in. See Hotels.

SEAMEN'S OUTFITTERS—The stock consists of men's furnishings, hats, caps, ready-made overcoats and clothing, notions, novelties, toilet soaps, perfumes, overalls, oil suits, rubber boots, shoes, cheap jewelry, musical instruments and similar articles used by sailors on board ship. See Ship Chandlers.

SEARCHLIGHT ENGINES are used by the New York Fire Department in cases where the lighting system of the building or street have been put out of commission on account of fire.

SEBASTIN—A high explosive.

SECOND-HAND STOCKS should always be avoided. Sometimes when a line covers new stock, together with second-hand stock, a clause is added, "It is understood and agreed that this company shall not be liable for a loss or damage to any of the above-described property for an amount in excess of the actual cost price to the assured."

SECRETAGE—A process of crisping hair to make it into felt by means of mercury and nitric acid.

SECRET PROCESSES should not be written, even though the inspector is told "nothing of a dangerous character is used," because the fire record shows that in many instances this statement has been untrue or misleading.

SECURITE—An explosive compound.

SEEDS IN BINS on storage will not burn readily, but when wet will sprout and be rendered useless. The swelling of wet seeds and hops in large quantities in compact masses has been known to push out the walls of brick buildings.

SEGMENTAL ARCH—A curved arch, forming the segment of a circle.

SEIDLITZ POWDERS contain bicarbonate of soda, rochelle salts and tartaric acid. The hazards are grinding, mixing and sifting.

SELF-CLOSING DOOR—One ordinarily closed and which closes automatically after being opened.

SELF-REDUCING CLAUSE—Used in connection with leasehold insurance. See Profits of a Lease.

SELF-RELEASING BEAMS—See Bevelled.

SERPENTINE PAPER—Colored; used for decorating narrow papers.

SETTING—Term used in boiler or furnace installations to denote the enclosing walls.

SEVIN OIL—Same as olive oil. Shale oil and petroleum. Each liquid yields on fractional distillation a heavy volatile and inflammable gasoline.

SEWERS FROM GARAGES—These are used for draining off surface of cleaning floors, the water from which contains oils and grease and gasoline. The sewers are always warmer than the air above the streets. In many cases they are made warm from the escape of steam or hot water from factories. With volatile oils in the sewer, we therefore have the conditions for their ready conversion into vapor. The gasoline vapors rise and mix with the air, while the heavy oils find their way into the river, or when the mouth of the sewer is closed they gather at the water level within the sewer at some distance from the river, to be discharged only at low tide. The law forbids the throwing of gasoline into the sewer, hence oil separators are required in garages. See Oil Separators.

SEWING TABLES—Where a double row of tables is used a continuous trough should be built between the rows in which to place the work as it is made, thus preventing it from falling in between the rows of machines. See Cutting Tables.

SHAFTINGS AND BEARINGS of all sorts may be dangerous on account of heating, especially if connected to rapidly moving machinery, due to poor alignment, binding, or insufficient oil. They are likely to become oily, and to accumulate dust and inflammable "fly" or lint, and also saturate nearby woodwork with flying oil.

SHAPERS OR FRIEZING (spindles) consist of two vertical projections through a table and rotating rapidly in opposite directions. Make considerable refuse and bearings become overheated. Classed as heavy woodworking machines.

SHAFTS—Open shafts are the quickest and most natural means for a fire to travel through a building, aiding the quick destruction of the building and endangering the lives of the occupants. See Dumbwaiter Doors.

SHARP SAND—Sand, the particles of which have facets with sharp edges.

SHAVING SOAP—Principally tallow, stearic acid, palm oil, barium chloride, peroxide of hydrogen, oil of euchrelytu: A steam process, using kettles, filters, stills, rolling and moulding presses. Also use solution of lye, ammonium sulphate and glycerine.

SHAVING VAULTS should be constructed of brick or concrete walls not less than 12 inches thick and parapetted at least 3 feet above roof and situated outside of building, with no communication. Vault should be used only for the storage of shavings and dust. No machinery, shafting or belts should be operated within or pass through the same. The roof to be of fireproof material with proper vent. The floor, of concrete, with an incline from the rear to the front. There should be only one opening, three feet from floor (not over 9 square feet) for the removal of the shavings to the boiler room, and this opening should be protected by a ¼-inch boiler iron drop door, operated automatically in vault channels, which should be bolted through the wall. The boiler iron vault door opening just mentioned should be at right angles to the firing door of the boiler and not nearer than 6 feet from same. Steam jets or automatic sprinklers are sometimes placed inside of the vaults. Feed-pipes which empty their shavings directly into the boilers are not recommended. See Direct Feed.—(See Illustration on page 398.)

SHEATHING—Matched or unmatched boards on the exterior of a building; covering a surface with wood boards, metal, etc.

SHEAVE—A grooved pulley with block and bearings, and sheave brackets over which cables or ropes are run.

SHEEP DIP sometimes contains inflammable liquids. A liquid into which sheep are dipped to remove vermin.

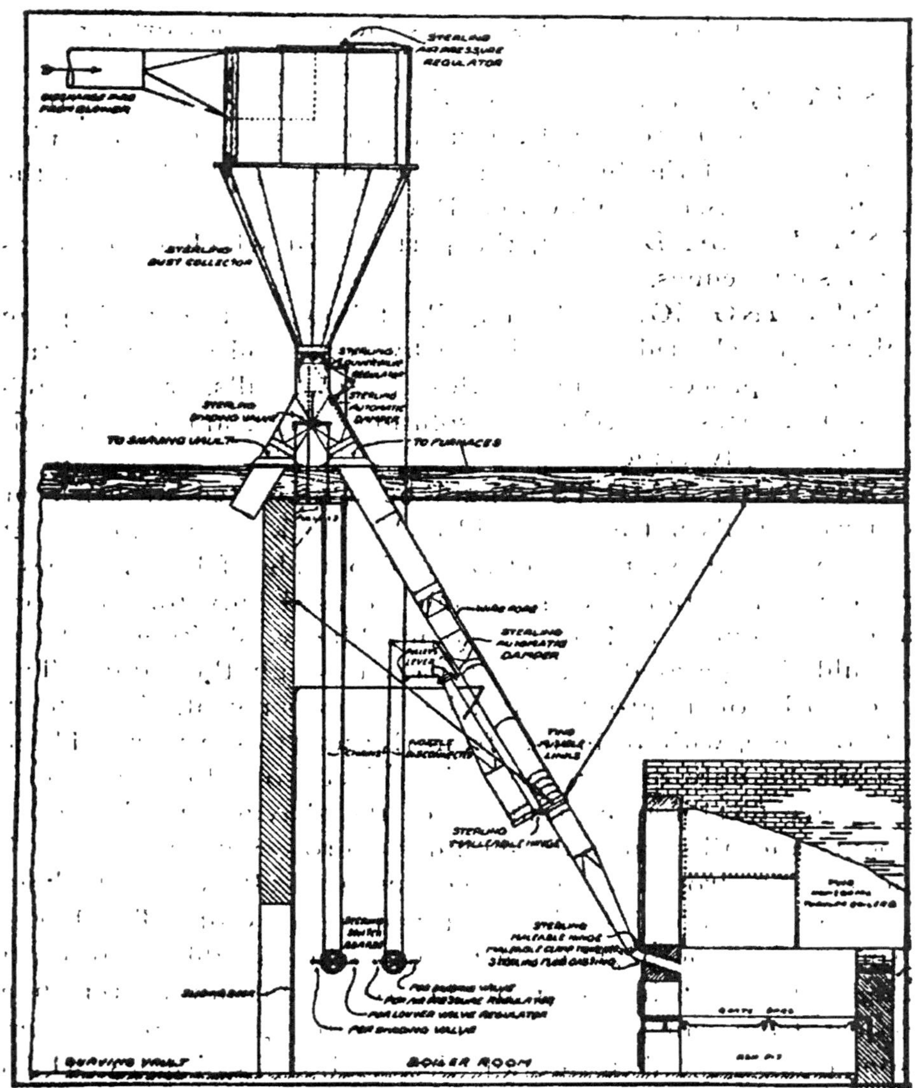

(Copyrighted. Patent applied for.)

Sterling Automatic Improved Furnace Feeder, Showing Method of "Direct Feed to Boiler from Blower System
(Side Elevation)

SHEEPSKIN—Dyers and dressers use sumac, logwood, quebracho, sulphuric acid, ammonia and alcohol, anilines, potash. Splitters, staining with air brush, embossing presses for fancy articles, greasing, fur dyeing and dressing, are principal hazards. See Hides.

SHEETING—See Lagging.

SHEET TIN—See Tin.

SHELLAC—A resinous exudation produced by the puncture of a species of insect which congregate in large numbers on the tender branches of various East Indian trees. The insects become surrounded by the resinous exudation which gradually hardens, and in which the larvae of the female remain. Dissolves in alcohol, muriatic acid, acetic acid.

SHELLAC VARNISH—Gum shellac, partly dissolved.

SHINGLE ROOFS of wood should not be permitted. The fire record shows many fires from this type of construction. If a building has a wood shingle roof, the chimney should be provided with a spark-arrester. See Spark-arrester.

A patented fireproof shingle is now being made of felt saturated with asphaltum, in which ground rock is imbedded, coated with asphalt and finished with ground slate.

SHIPBUILDERS' YARDS usually have many low frame buildings with power wood-working and metal-working; foundries, blacksmith shop, welding with compressed gases, and painting. Not a profitable class with most companies.

SHIP-BUILDING (Hazards of)—In Wood Ship-building yards, woodworking, large woodworking machinery, large quantities of sawdust, shavings and chips; recommend shavings vault and blower system; accumulation of waste wood and chips under hulls in shipways. This space should be constantly kept cleaned up and refuse removed. Lumber in yard, clear space rules should be strictly adhered to. Storage of oakum should be kept in detached building a safe distance from ways and other buildings. Spinning of oakum should be done in a separate building from main oakum storage building, this latter building to be properly ventilated at eaves and ground level and screened with fine wire mesh. Heating of pitch and creosote important; steam only should be used. This work should not be done on the ships. Oils and paints, etc., should be stored in a separate and preferably fireproof building. Burning of waste material for fuel, special care should be taken to see that stacks are provided with approved spark arresters. Glue heaters in joiner's shop should be according to underwriters' rules. Locomotives and Gantry cranes should be inspected for fuel used. Storage of fuel-oil and supply stations should be underground. (J. H. Ryan.)

SHIP CHANDLERS—Stock consists of those things which are required by seamen on board ship, such as oiled clothing, clothing, parts of machinery, lanterns, oils, heavy hardware, ship's tackle. A hard burning stock, not easy to extinguish. See Seamen's Outfitters.

SHIP FIRE PREVENTION—It is recommended that vessels be required to be equipped with spark-arresters and that their funnels, or smokestacks, be covered with an efficient metal spark-arrester (the wire mesh, which shall not be less than four to the inch) when crossing the pierhead line in approaching any grain elevator or any pier. The owners of such vessels should be required to protect all hatch combings, so that cargoes of cotton or naval stores shall not come in contact with the combings; also the vessels should be required, while loading or discharging cargoes, to couple their firehose and keep the same ready for use at all times. See Fires at Sea.

SHIP YARDS (Steel)—Machine-shop hazards. Fuel-oil used for heating furnaces, also portable rivet furnaces on board ships. Fuel-oil should be underground, as per rules. Wood framing, staging and shoring used during construction are bad features. Space under keels should be kept free of inflammable material. (J. H. Ryan.)

SHIRTWAIST MANUFACTURING — See Garment Manufacturing.

SHODDY is picked rags, shredded and torn apart by pickers. It may be wool or part cotton. If all-wool shoddy is desired, the stock is "carbonized" by removing the cotton in vats of dilute sulphuric acid and chloride of aluminum. The wool is then washed in alkalis, dried in high-temperature dryers, "picked," and baled.

SHODDY AND MUNGO REFUSE is used in manufacturing artificial guano. After being dried and pulverized, it is used by wall-paper manufacturers as "flock."

SHODDY MILLS—Picking and carding rooms are the most hazardous. The shoddy is usually conveyed from the pickers to the baling room by suction ducts. Only steam heat and electric lights should be used. Few companies write this class.

SHOE FACTORIES—The upper leathers and linings are cut either by hand or power die-presses. These are stitched or cemented together and attached to the inner sole. The center of the sole is "filled" or waterproofed, and the outer sole put on and trimmed smoothly. In the finishing department, the sole and heel are sandpapered, stained, waxed and polished and the uppers cleaned and polished. Considerable rubber cement is used. Safety pots only should be used for rubber cement and the supply of cement and naphtha kept outside of main buildings. Cement with a binder of ground cork is usually used for a filler for soles (between the inner and middle sole). Edge-setter machines, which sew the soles with waxed threads, have a pot of wax through which the thread runs. The pot is usually heated by steam or gas, steam preferred. Buff wheels for polishing, sandpapering machines, and heel-trimmers should have blowers. In the lasting department, where the workers hand-sew the uppers to the soles of turn-shoes, gas or electric stoves are used for heating the hand-tools. In the finishing department, benzine may be used for removing spots. A very important hazard is the cutting-board scrapings. The cutting boards, where leather is cut either by hand or power, are dressed with a dressing composed mainly of glycerine, linseed oil and carbolic acid. They are dressed (scraped to remove ridges) by hand. The boards are of hardwood, the scrapings are in a finely divided state, and when mixed with the dressing are peculiarly subject to spontaneous combustion. These scrapings will ignite in a few hours and are considered by some manufacturers to be more hazardous than the use of rubber cement and benzine.

Box Toes are stiffened with dextrine and glue. Celluloid is also used for box toes, heel coverings and counters. The celluloid is usually found in the "lasting" department. Alcohol and acetone are used to soften the celluloid. Heels are covered with celluloid, for ladies' shoes, the celluloid being softened and applied by presses, trimmed, cemented and buffed.

Shoe Tips, after being perforated, are singed over a gas flame to give the leather a clean edge, after which they are dipped in dye (sometimes naphtha dye) for the desired color.

Waterproof Compounds for Shoes—Trade names are Viscol, Resisto, Repello, Anti-hude, Soleoil, Relyt and others. They are oily substances and some are thinned with naphtha.

Dip Black is made of lamp-black and naphtha.

Oilproof—Made of gelatine and carbolic acid dissolved in naphtha. It is put on the inner part of outer soles to prevent the natural oil of uppers from staining the lower part.

Boot Dressing for uppers is made of lamp-black, gum tragacanth or soap. The leather is soaked in water, covered with blacking to lay the nap, dressed, and oiled with neat's-foot oil.

SHOEMAKERS' FINDINGS—Miscellaneous findings consist of leather, buttons, nails, polishes, brushes, rubber cement, stains. If mercantile rating is good, stock can be written at a profit.

SHOE POLISH may contain shellac, nigrosine, caustic soda, potash, aniline colors, salicylic acid, japan, beeswax, oil of mirbane, alcohol, ammonia, lamp-black, glue, benzine, gum tragacanth, canauber and candellia waxes and borax. Hazards of direct fire heat for kettles, oily floors, storage of raw materials. A poor fire record class. A quick burner.

SHOES, RETAIL—Considered very desirable insurance. Stocks usually give a salvage. Inspectors should note if any work is being done on premises.

SHOOKS—Sets of boards in knock-down shape, used in crate or box-making.

SHOOTING GALLERIES usually occupy grade floors or basements. Some are located in poor sections and cater to low element. Temporary occupancy with makeshift heating apparatus, smoking, oily rags for wiping guns, gas lights in rows under targets, and untidiness constitute the hazards.

SHORING—Bracing by means of props.

SHORT CIRCUIT—A contact between electrical conductors of different potentiality without the intervention of resistance, so that for an instant a theoretically unlimited current flows through the conductors and the contact point. See Electrical Terms.

SHORT-RATE TABLE—Used in writing insurance for a term less than one year. Also applied to contracts for any term when the assured desires cancellation of a policy. See Pro Rata.

SHRAPNEL, in ammunition manufacture, is composed of three major parts, the cartridge, the projectile and the fuse.

SHUTTERS—All windows should be protected either by standard lock-joined shutters (similar to firedoor construction), or iron shutters having angle-iron frames. The old style "flat bar" iron shutters are not recommended because they buckle under intense heat. Most engineers advise wire glass windows in "labeled" hollow metal frames instead of shutters, because they are sure to be in place when a fire starts. Many a risk protected by shutters suffered severe damage because they were open and could not be closed in time. See Window Protection.

SIAMESE CONNECTION—Called fire department connections. An intake pipe located outside of a building, with two hose coupling connections. In sprinkler systems they are connected with header system or at base of live riser. In standpipe systems, connect with riser. In both instances have flap-check valve. Connection should point horizontally and be at least 18 inches above the sidewalk in order that the fire department can make a quick hose connection to steamer or hydrant. Many siamese connections point downward and are only several inches above the sidewalk, making it almost a physical impossibility to connect the hose. See Standpipes.

SIDE CONSTRUCTION in fireproof arches, the terra-cotta blocks are placed on the sides.

SIDEWALK STANDS may have gasoline torches for light, electric wires on nails, swingng gas brackets, unsafe stove for heating or cooking.

SIGN PAINTING—Light painting hazard. All colors ar in small lots but use considerable turpentine, and som times benzine for cleaning brushes. Usually located in "ru down" properties. Not a very desirable class on accou of cheapness of work, smoking, oily rags, crowded conditions and making wood frames.

SIGNS (on a roof) especially if of wood, are great handicaps to the firemen. All signs should be built of incombustible material and be so located that firemen may get under them so as to gain access to the roof.

SILESITE—An explosive compound.

SILICA—An oxygen compound, or oxide of a substance called silicon.

SILICATE OF SODA consists of 31 parts sand, freed from iron, and 53 parts of dry carbonate of soda melted together. It is used as a sizing to render fabrics, paper, wood, etc., fireproof, also used as a mordant for aniline colors. Sometimes called soluble glass.—Harris.

SILICATES—See Silicic Acid.

SILICIC ACID—Sometimes called Silica. Silicic acid unites with potash and soda and lime-forming bodies called silicates.

SILICON—Not a metal, but a very hard substance resembling carbon in appearance.

SILLS for fire doors (usually concrete or iron frames) should be raised at least 1½ inches above the floor and set entirely under the fire-doors. These sills prevent water running from one section to another.

SILK (ARTIFICIAL) is cellulose fibre artificially prepared from suitable solutions of cellulose by forcing the liquid through fine orifices and coagulating the cellulose as it emerges in the form of a delicate thread. Artificial silk resembles true silk very closely, in general appearance possessing even a higher lustre than the latter. It is not as strong or durable as true silk and its strength is greatly lessened when wet with water. One variety is made from wood-pulp.

SILK (BROAD) is woven piece silk. It is wound, reeled, woven and "quilled." Weavers use benzine for removing spots.

SILK CONDITIONING—Practically the same as wool finishing.

SILK DYEING—Use acetic, sulphuric, muriatic and tannic acids, bicarbonate of soda and bicarbonate of potash. Nitrate of iron is used in black dyes. Where goods are sold by weight, gambia is usually used.

SILK FINISHING—Process consists of cutting, rolling, calendering, singeing, rubbing, straightening, steaming, cleaning, spraying, stretching.

SILK FINISHING COMPOUND—A secret mixture, said to contain potato flour, glycerine, glue and soap. Silk is bleached with sulphide of soda.

SILK FLOSS—A vegetable fibre from the Kapoc trees of the Dutch Indies, used in mattresses, etc.

SILK-GUT—Derived from the silk worm; similar to catgut; used on ends of fish hooks.

SILK NECKTIES are sometimes cut on boards similar to cutting boards in shoe factories with same hazard, also singeing with gas flame.

SILK NOILS—The short fibres or waste silk from mills.

SILK PLUSH—The top yarn as used in this territory is received in skeins from the mills making same, and is woven by the local mills into the various materials. In silk and plush works, it forms the strands for the warp and filling for the backing of plush goods. The plush or piling is made of silk, cotton and mohair threads woven into a single strand.

Plush is made on a weaving loom similar to a silk loom with the exception that two backings are used between which is woven the silk piling for the plush. As the woven piece leaves the loom a rapidly moving knife cuts the piling which leaves two pieces of plush. See Plush.

"Striking out" machines, "tigers," "brushes" are then used. These are smilar in design with the exception that the wires forming the comb are heavier for the first process. The machine consists of a wooden roller spiked with wire combs over which the goods pass. They are employed to remove any loose piling and to whip it up. The "tigers" tear out most of the loose stuff, which is found on the floor. As this is silk the hazard is light. Very little lint is made.

The "Nellies" is next employed. This machine is a four-sided wooden frame in upright position. At the bottom, a wooden roller with light wire comb; at top a similar roller with bristles. The plush is wound on a centre roller, the upper roller turned by hand. As it turns an employee "batters" the plush to open up the piling. It then enters a dry room as the plush is put on the "Nellies" wet.

At the "striking out" machine, the plush is attached to a strip of cambric which is first drawn over the rollers and brushes so that as soon as the machine is started the end of the plush will be combed. At this machine the material is first steamed to soften the texture.

The cambric cloths are dried in a dryer similar to laundry drier.

Silk is woven on a single loom.

Winders and spoolers are similar to those in knitting mills. Dyeing is a wet process; aniline colors, muriatic acid, bichromate of potash and nitrate of soda being used.

SILK (RAW)—Silk as it comes from the cocoon. It is spun into threads, skeined, wrapped in bundles called "books," in colored or white tissue paper (tissue should be white, as colored paper will streak the silk if wet), baled and wrapped in matting for shipment. It is tested for elasticity, strength of thread, quantity of natural gum, weave and twist. Moisture causes mildew. Water and smoke do not seriously affect its quality unless the smoke contains chemical agents which will eat the fibre. Mildew and discoloration by smoke or water can be removed by boiling, as in any event, it must be boiled in water to remove the natural gum before it can be dyed. The loss would be practically the cost of labor for re-boiling, drying and re-reeling. A salvage of about 75 per cent. may be expected in smoke or water damage. It does not support combustion. It smolders, but burns only upon the application of fire. Considered good insurance.

Silks are "loaded" or "weighted" with tin, sugar and other materials. It is claimed to make the silk firmer and cheaper without lowering the quality. Silks are sometimes 40 to 60 per cent. tin. The raw silk is first boiled to remove the natural gum of the silk worm. About 4 ounces in weight is lost in every 16 ounces boiled. It is "dyed to a certain weight," according to the purpose for which the silk is to be used. If silk is dyed to 14 ounces it means that 2 ounces of the lost weight is made up in loading and 14 ounces returned to the dealer in place of the original 16. The tin, in very minute particles, is added during the dyeing process. "Weighting"—This process adds on an average of seven-tenths of a pound to 100 pounds of dyed goods.

Silks of cheap texture may contain considerable cotton, and if wet, every color is liable to run.

SILK SIZING—Fires have occurred in naphtha sizing machines from static electricity generated at the glass rods or guides over which the silk passes.

SILK, SPUN or "SCHAPPE" SILK is the silk yarn spun from cocoon waste (fibres from pierced cocoons) or from waste made by throwsters. Carded and spun the same as cotton yarn.

SILK (THROWN)—Raw or dyed silk that has been thrown or doubled ready for the weaver. It has more than one strand.

SILK VELVET generally suffers very little from water damage if immediately salvaged.

SILK (WASTE) is prepared for the weavers and spinners as follows: It is put through "lappers," fillers or combers," "dressing frames," "spreaders," "cards," "pomers," "flossing machines." The poor pieces of silk are picked out by hand by means of strong electric lights under glass top tables. Slow-speed machinery is used but lint covered journals result. Steam jets are used to keep down the lint and prevent a dusty atmosphere in the work rooms. See Noils.

SILK (WATERPROOFING)—The silk is first sponged with dilute mixture of sulphate of alumina, then with a solution of soap made of light-colored resin and crystalized carbonate of soda and water. The soap thus formed is separated by adding common salt. The soap is dissolved in boiling water and the silk rinsed in same.

SILK (WILD) is divided commercially into three classes: true silk, wild silk and artificial silk. Wild silk is the fibre obtained from numerous wild varieties of silk-producing moths.

SILK YARN AND FLOSS DYERS—Use sulphuric, nitric and acetic acids, caustic soda. Hazards of dry rooms, silk pickers, centrifugal extractors.

SILVERING—See Mirror Backing.

SILVER-PLATED WARE—Hazards are heavy and light machine shop work, with drop hammers, rollers, hydraulic presses, plating, buffing, pitch-heating, forging, soldering, burnishing, engraving, lacquering, making lead, copper and plaster moulds.

SILVERSMITHS—For cementing handles on sticks, use canauba wax or a mixture of yellow ochre and resin, or a mixture of resin, pitch and lime. Direct fire heat used. Plating—See Goldsmiths.

SISAL—See Fibres.

SKATE—A term used in the insurance business when speaking of a very undesirable risk.—Eugene Eagles.

SKATING RINKS—If built of frame or ordinary brick constructon, are avoided by most insurance companies. Heating and refrigerating apparatus should be in cut-off section. They are "season" occupancies, the moral hazard is an important consideration.

SKELETON CONSTRUCTION—A term applying to a simple framewoork of columns and beams whose efficiency is dependent largely on the existence of exterior walls and partitions which brace the building and hold the framework in position, just as the utility of the human skeleton is dependent on the covering of sinews and muscles that hold the component parts together. On the other hand, the light framework of an ordinary wire cage bound into one compact unit is suggestive of an inherent strength and elastic persistence that renders any covering an incident rather than a necessity. (J. F. Kendall.) See Cage Construction.

SKEWBACK—The inclined stone from which an arch springs. The protecting tile at the web to the lower flange of a beam or girder.

SKIDS—Stock of a susceptible nature should be raised at least six inches from the floor so as to prevent water damage.

SKINS are obtained from calves, sheep, goats, etc. See Hides.

SKIRTING—Narrow boards nailed along a wall.

SKIVING—Removing thin shavings from the flesh side of skins. See Hides.

SLAG—The dross left in the process of refining metals. Also a compound of silica with metals, lime and clay.

SLAG ROOF—A covering of slag spread over tar or a composition.

SLATE (ARTIFICIAL) is formed of clay which has been hardened under pressure and heat.

SLATE ROOFS are a source of danger in case of fire on account of pieces dropping on the firemen.

SLEEPER—A strip embedded in arches of fireproof construction to which the top flooring is nailed.

SLEEVE—See Thimble.

SLIP—The water lost in the delivery of pump due to leakage past piston, and too much clearance between piston and cylinder.

SLIPPERS (carpet and cloth) are usually made from small pieces or "tag ends" of carpet or cloth. The inner sole is pasted and the outer sole tacked on the upper. Cold paste or glue is used. Shops employ cheap labor and are usually untidy. A class avoided by most underwriters.

SLIPPER TRIMMINGS—Skived leather, laces, buckram and felt tops, metal ornaments, embroidery. Concerns usually give the sewing to "home workers," who do it as piecework. Shopwork consists of making lead buttons, metal working, enameling metal parts, cementing linings with rubber cement, sewing, embroidering, skiving leather.

SLOW BURNING—See Mill Construction.

SMALT—A powdered blue glass, colored with cobalt. Used by sign painters.

SMELTERS—See Refiners.

SMOKE-HOUSES should be built of incombustible material with a vent to the outer air. The doors should be at least three-sixteenths inch iron, with angle-iron reinforcements to prevent the doors from buckling. The hanging racks and grating over the fire should be of iron. The meat is suspended from racks, and the lower grate is to prevent the meat from falling into the fire. Sills should be raised six inches. If possible smoke-houses should be in a detached structure. Steam jets are sometimes used to extinguish fires in these compartments. The fires used for smoking may be of sawdust, beech shavings, hickory wood, charcoal. These fires are either built directly on the floor or are placed in earthenware pots. The entire interior of the smoke compartments becomes in time thickly coated with a black, greasy covering from the grease-laden fumes from meats or fish. See Provisions.

SMOKELESS POWDER consists of nitro-lignum, purified, and mixed with nitrates other than nitrate of lead.

SMOKEPIPES must not be nearer than 18 inches to any lath-and-plaster or board partition, ceiling or any woodwork, nor shall they pass through any wood floor, partition, or roof. Smokepipes of furnaces, laundry stoves, large cooking ranges, etc., shall be not less than 18 inches from woodwork unless guarded by shields; then not less than 9 inches.

SMOKING.—The National Board records for 1916 state that careless smokers caused a total loss of $4,505,963 in the United States. In Philadelphia, 413 fires are credited to smokers. It should be made a penal offense to throw away a burning cigar, cigarette in or about any building, structure, car, or where it may ignite any inflammable material. In New York City, a specific charge of five cents per $100 per annum is applied to sprinkler risks, and is removable upon the proper posting of "No Smoking" signs. In garment manufacturing establishments a charge of 25 cents is made, at present, removable only after a series of unannounced inspections covering a period of six months. Because of the class of labor employed in this kind of business, this requirement becomes necessary to absolutely assure the bureau that all smoking has been stopped. In garages a charge of 25 cents is applied, which is added upon the recommendation of the New York Board of Fire Underwriters, and is removable upon the installation of proper signs. For theatres, 10 cents is added if smoking, by other than the actors during the play, is allowed. (S. T. Skirrow, "Live Articles on Special Hazards," The Weekly Underwriter.) See Matches.

SNAP FASTENERS.—A machine-shop hazard. Machinery consists of die presses, drills, lathes, emery wheels, milling machines, blowpipes and annealers, in addition to cleaning with acid and japanning.

SNOWFALLS (fire danger of)—In Northern climates, heavy snowfalls which remain on the roofs of houses are apt to cause the roof to sag and the consequent cracking of the chimney. Snow should be cleaned off roofs.

SNUFF MANUFACTURING—The lower leaves of the tobacco plant come to the factory in hogsheads. After ageing in the factory warehouse for a few years the leaf is coarsely cut up, "ordered," and reprised back in the hogsheads to sweat or ferment. It is then ready for dessication and pulverizing. It is toasted in a furnace dryer or toaster (which is an iron cylinder revolving in a breeching of brick, in which are heating fires), or shaken in a series of trays in a room heated by steam to a high temperature. The toasted flake is ground or pulverized in machines termed "mulls" and the snuff cleaned in a bolting reel and packed. The principal hazards are toasting, grinding and cleaning. Also kettles for heating water, salt and licorice; labeling and lacquering the inside of boxes; dry-rooms.—Ira G. Hoagland.

SOAP FACTORIES—The hazards of the usual modern soap factory are not very bad, as the entire process is by steam heat. The rendering of fats is usually carried on in a special plant for this purpose. There may be glycerine evaporators (steam-heated), stearic acid making, refrigerating machinery for cold-storage rooms. The oils used are palm, olive, fish, whale, rape, cottonseed, cocoanut and corn. The alkalis, soda, bicarbonate of soda, soda ash, carbonate of potash, caustic soda. Soap making is mainly a boiling process. "Crutching" is mixing the soap in an agitator kettle with coloring matter, perfumes, etc. When soap rises to the surface of the kettle, it is skimmed off and run into "frames" to cool. A "frame" is a rectangular metal box on wheels, with detachable sides and ends. When the soap cools, the sides and ends of the frames are removed. The slab of soap is cut by vertical wires protruding through a flat bed on which is placed the soap. See Shaving Soap.

SOAP POWDER and Dressings for Textile Workers—

Manufacturers use lactic acid, corn-syrup, gluten, tallow, gelatine, sugar, boric acid, formic acid, carbon tetra-chloride, aqua ammonia, chalk. Hazard that of soap factory, including chemical laboratory with usual chemicals, such as ether, ethyl alcohol, tin-chloride, nitrate of soda, and caustic soda in small bottles. Other soap powders are generally made from absolutely dry chip soaps, ground into a fine powder.

SODA—The general term applied to compounds of sodium. Sodium is metalic in nature. Usually found in areas resembling frozen lakes that consist of carbonate of soda in powder or crystals. Has an affinity for oxygen and should be kept in air and water-tight receptacles, because the least moisture may start a blaze. Soda is oxide of sodium. See Sodium.

SODA ASH—See Sodic Carbonate.

SODA WATER SIPHONS are sometimes charged up to 160 pounds pressure and have been known to explode with great violence.

SODIUM is made from soda. It is not inflammable, but its presence increases the intensity of a fire by the evolution of oxygen. When wet, it is combustible.

SODIUM BISULPHIDE—A chemical not dangerous in itself, but if allowed to come in contact with chlorate of sodium will cause a fire. Should be stored outside of main building in same manner as chlorates or other oxygen agents.

SODIUM CARBONATE—Called soda-ash and is used for bleaching cotton goods, scouring wool, and in the manufacture of soap.

SODIUM CHLORATE—Dangerous on account of its capacity for liberating oxygen.

SODIUM CHLORIDE—Common salt.

SODIUM HYDRATE—Called caustic soda, and is used in soap making.

SODIUM NITRATE—A yellowish white salt, and a great oxidizer. When mixed with organic matter will ignite.

SODIUM NITRATE CRYSTALS (in litharge manufacturing) are dried in a wooden, rotary, cylindrical dryer, having open ends, driven by gearing and cogwheels, and heated by hot air. Fires have started at the greasy driving-gears due to friction. See Litharge.

SODIUM PEROXIDE—A white or yellow powder. A strong oxidizer. When in contact with organic matter will cause fire.

SODIUM SULPHIDE—Used in tanning leather.

SODIUM TUNGSTATE—See Fire-Resistive Solutions.

SOFFIT—The lower or underneath surface of an arch.

SOFT WOODS are those from coniferous or needle-leaved trees, such as pine, spruce and cedar. See Coniferous Woods. See Hard Woods.

SOLDER—Usually composed of lead and zinc.

SOLE TENANT RISK—One having but one tenant. An allowance is usually given in the rate for this feature.

SOLIDIFIED ALCOHOL consists of wood alcohol which has been colloided to a soft semi-transparent mass; made by colloiding with nitro-cellulose or soap. Gives off inflammable vapors at about 50 deg. F. See Alcohol.

SOLUBLE BLUE—Apt to cause fires in color works through friction and spontaneous combustion. See Chromes.

SOLUBLE COTTON—See Nitrocellulose.

SOLUBLE GLASS—Silicate of soda.

SOLVENTINE—Used as a varnish. Has a low flash and fire test. Composed of low-grade varnish, linseed oil, benzine or its equivalent. Cotton waste, saturated with it, will ignite spontaneously.

SOLVENTS are likely to include inflammable liquids containing such substances as acetone, ether or naphtha.

SOOT—Mostly carbon. It is made up of little particles which are thrown off from the burning wood and lodge on the chimney sides.

SOUND VALUE—The actual value at the time of fire after depreciation has been deducted. The terms "market value," "cost price," etc., as sometimes used, are misleading.

SOURCE OF SUPPLY—See Water Mains.

SPALL—To chip or flake off. Stone or brick, or other masonry walls spall after being heated and subjected to hose streams. See Platforms.

SPAN—The space between the iron beams, as for instance, the terra-cotta arches are spanned 5 feet on centers.

SPANISH BLACK or cork black is made from the combustion gases of burning cork.

SPANISH MOSS—Used in upholstering; will ignite spontaneously,

SPANISH WHITE—Same as whiting.

SPARK ARRESTER—Used on foundry cupolas, chimneys, to catch sparks and prevent them from flying and igniting shingle roofs. Made of wire netting and built like a cage over the top of the stack.

SPECIAL BUILDING SIGNAL is a manual device requiring some one to pull the lever which sends in the alarm. See Manual Alarm. See Alarm.

SPECIAL FORMS OF INSURANCE—See Use and occupancy; also Leases and Profit Insurance, Improvements.

SPECIAL HAZARDS are the fire dangers incident to manufacturing plants in their process of work. See Hazard; also Risk.

SPECIFIC GRAVITY OR DENSITY plays an important part in the engineering end of fire insurance, in that it points out the connection between weight and bulk. In other words, the specific gravity of the liquid is its weight in proportion to the same bulk of water. Example: A bottle which holds 1000 grains of water will only hold 830 grains of spirits of wine, which shows the comparison of weight under the same bulk. The density of the liquids containing alcohol is used by the excise to determine the amount of alcohol they contain.—W. D. Grier.

SPECIFIC RATES—Those properties subject to a special rate by a central rating board or bureau by reason of an occupancy more hazardous than called for under a minimum rating. See Rates.

SPECIFIC WEIGHTS—See Specific Gravity.

SPERMACETI—A solid wax taken from the mixture of solid and liquid matter which occurs in the head of the sperm whale. Melts 110 to 120 deg. F.

SPHINCTER HOSE—Rubber or other hose wound with

wire. Prevents wear and tear and gives added strength to hose.

SPICE MILLS—The principal hazard is grinding. If the spices are ground wet, the hazard is mild. If they are ground dry, the grinder should be in a separate fireproof room and be equipped with magnets. Burr mills are often used. Additional hazards are found at the sifters, bolters, and dryers where considerable dust abounds. Considered by most companies as an unprofitable class of insurance.

SPINDLE CARVER—A small cutter rotated at the end of a horizontal spindle.

SPIRITS OF HARTSHORN—See Ammonia.

SPIRITS OF NITROUS ETHER—See Ethyl Nitric.

SPIRITS OF TURPENTINE—See Turpentine.

SPONGES—The best are grown in salt water where no sandy bottom abounds as the sand smothers the growing sponge. Sponges, when brought to the surface are black and slimy and filled with water and animal matter called "gurry." Several days are required for the gurry to run off when the sponges are dead. They are squeezed out with the hands and strung on lengths of coarse twine. Sponges, contrary to general belief, suffer a very severe water damage, and insurance should be written carefully.

SPONTANEOUS COMBUSTION—When a house is being redecorated, the painters frequently use a wood polish containing raw linseed oil and turpentine. In one instance, a piece of waste with this oil was found smoldering in a workman's pocket and he did not know it until his attention was called to it. Polishing cloths about the home should not be placed in drawers of cupboards, but hung where air can circulate around them. Oily floors left when soap manufacturers, furriers and machine shops vacate buildings have caused spontaneous combustion when a new tenant has laid new floor over the oily one. Sawdust in ice houses and cold storage plants has been known to ignite spontaneously when moist. Soft coal piled in bulk and dampened will ignite spontaneously. See Vegetable Oils. Oily Waste Cans.—(See illustration on page 416.)

SPONTANEOUS COMBUSTION POINT—The point or

temperature at which gases, vapors or solids will take fire of their own accord without being brought into contact with burning or incandescent substances. See Flash Point.

SPORTING GOODS—Hazards of repair shops with varnishing, hand woodworking, stock of gun-powder and cartridges, rubber cement, calcium carbide, automobile specialties, photo supplies.

SPREADING—A spreader machine is a skeleton table-like structure made up with steam coils or steam-heated plates. At the feed end of the spreader is located a roll, above which and parallel to it, is set a knife-like piece of metal, fitted with proper adjustment device so that it may be set a greater or less distance from the roll. There is also provision for a roll of fabric at the feed end and a reeling up device at the other end of the machine. See Static Electricity.

SPRINGER—The lowest stone of an arch.

SPRINGS—A name given by manufacturers to rubber shoddy.

SPRINKLER EQUIPMENT (AUTOMATIC)—Briefly speaking, consists of iron piping filled with water or air,

Photo by Paul Thompson.

Distribution of Water by Automatic Sprinkler.

securely supported immediately beneath the floors, i.e. the ceilings. At intervals of eight to ten feet are attached fusible plugs called sprinkler-heads having deflectors designed to spray water over the area desired. In the ordinary sprinkler a solder having a melting point of about 160 deg. F. is employed (solder of bismuth, tin, lead and cadmium). The melting of this solder releases the disc from the valve-seat and the water is forced out under pressure through the orifice formerly closed by the valve-seat. The deflector causes the water to spray in all directions like rain thus effectually wetting anything within the area which the sprinklers are designed to cover.

Among the important questions to be considered after the design and probable occupancy has been considered is that of heating. It should be definitely determined that all portions of the building will be heated to about 40 deg. F. during the winter. Unfortunately water will freeze at 32 deg. F. even when in pipes, a condition that some of those planning equipments must realize if a wet-pipe system of sprinklers is under consideration.

The latter system is preferable for the following reasons: It costs less to install and to maintain and results in a slightly greater reduction in insurance rates. By way of illustration: A complete wet-pipe system of 1,000 sprinklers including tanks and alarm service will cost about $5,000, maintenance cost about $300 per annum, insurance reduction approximately 60 to 75 per cent., depending upon the grading of the equipment. The same equipment, but dry-pipe system, including tanks and alarm service, will cost approximately $16,000, maintenance cost about $450 per annum, insurance reduction approximately 50 to 60 per cent., depending upon grading of the equipment. It may also be said that the dry-pipe system, being under the control of one or more automatic valves under constantly maintained air pressure of forty pounds in the pipe system, is somewhat complicated and with its auxilary attachments calls for much more care than the wet system. —E. P. Boone. Author's Note: The figures given above are pre-war figures. See Alarm, Central Station, Coal Shortage, Curtain Boards, Dry Pipe Sprinklers, Dead Riser, Gate Valve, Gravity Supply, Hoops, Live Riser, Open Sprinklers, Pressure, Sprinkler and Heating System, Sypho-chemical Sprinklers, Tables, Valves, Staggered, Tell-tales.

SPRINKLERS are made to fuse as follows:
Without color except that of its composition, 160 deg. F.
Black-corro-proof to prevent corrosion, 160 deg. F.
White color, 212 deg. F. Blue, 286 deg. F. Red, 360 deg. F.

SPRINKLERS, QUESTIONABLE OCCUPANCIES—Automatic sprinklers in the following occupancies may not be expected to control a fire if it has a good start owing to the construction, processes involved, and the hazardous materials: Celluloid workers, cereal mills, cooperage plants, cork factories, cotton warehouses, grain elevators, flour mills, furniture factories, match factories, oilcloth works, rubber works, saw mills, starch factories, varnish works, window-shade factories, rough woodworking and sugar refineries,

Automatic Sprinkler Head in Operation.

aluminum powder factories, chemical risks using substances which might explode or ignite from the application of water, such as sodium. It can be readily seen that fires of a flash nature which might be expected in many of the above lines, or those where dust explosions are imminent, could spread a fire throughout an entire floor before sufficient heat would be confined in one place to operate a sprinkler head, or which might disrupt the sprinkler system.

SPRINKLERED RISKS IN ZERO WEATHER.—Where sprinkler equipment has been drained or is known to be frozen, the following precautions should be exercised in placing the equipment in commission in order to avoid water damage and prolonged interruption of protection.

In order to prevent unnecessary annoyance and delay, it is suggested the making of repairs be left with the company that installed the equipment.

Have equipment examined by competent party, pipe system including filling and steam pipes for tanks tested for ice and leaks, and repairs effected where necessary.

Open all drain valves and remove plugs at low points to insure the pipe system being properly drained.

Close all controlling valves and fill tanks slowly one at a time.

Turn water slowly into system one floor at a time, after having closed all drain valves and replaced plugs at low points.

The following day if no leaks develop, place air on pressure tanks and notify central station company where such service obtains to restore alarm service.

Note.—The above precautions apply to both wet and dry pipe sprinkler systems.

Where sprinklers are in a pendant position it may be necessary to remove each sprinkler so located in order to test for ice, and in doing this extra care must be exercised not to injure the sprinklers. Those injured must be replaced with new sprinklers before placing equipment in commission. (N. Y. Fire Ins. Exchange.)

Upon the approach of winter, test all post indicator valves for proper drainage to prevent freezing. Open all valves that should be opened and ascertain if all pipes are free from sediment and ready for instant use. Box in and pack all exposed piping, both water and steam, the latter so that there will be sufficient heat for building and for tank coils. Have extra sprinkler heads on hand for emergency.

Sprinklers (Dry-Pipe) should be controlled all year on approved dry-pipe valves rather than being "wet system" for eight months and "dry system" for four months. In changing from a dry system to a wet system there is an increased amount of sediment deposited in the pipes. The pipes are not always drained when cold weather sets in, and the dry valve is not always properly adjusted. All pipes should be pitched to properly drain so that water could not collect in them and freeze.

Cold Weather Lines, i. e., branch lines in driveways, hallways, elevator shafts, coal holes and other unheated portions which are shut off during winter should be thoroughly examined in the spring to detect frozen or bursted pipes and imperfect valves. Upon the approach of warm weather the valves should be kept open.

SPRINKLER EQUIPMENT ON VESSELS—Statistics furnished by shipowners show that approximately 20 per cent. of the ocean travel hazard is caused by fire or explosion. A large percentage of these losses could be overcome by the installation of an adequate automatic fire-fighting system. See Fires at Sea; also Ship Fire Prevention.

SPRINKLER FAILURES are due to allowing steam pressure to run down below minimum pressure over Sundays and holidays, inadequate electric power to drive fire pumps, shutting off water and then delaying repair work. Notify the insurance company when it is necessary to shut off water. When extensive repairs are necessary, provide additional fire pails, hose and watchmen. Put red tag (as used by Factory Mutuals) on closed valves.

Fires quite often occur in unsprinklered portions, even those parts where it seems impossible for a fire to originate, or just after the equipment has been shut off or before its installation is complete.

SPRINKLER LEAKAGE is protection against loss or damage due to accidental discharge of water from the sprinkler system or tanks supplying same (including accident caused by freezing). Does not protect against loss due to discharge of water when fire occurs nor for collapse of building unless the latter is caused by accidental leakage of water from automatic sprinkler system or the tanks supplying it. Penalties are imposed in rating for absence of floor control valves, lack of proper watchman service and (or) alarm service, wood tanks on wood trestle, tanks with flat hoops, concealed spaces and furring.

Sprinkler leakage. "It is claimed from experience that about 50 per cent. of the losses are caused by the sprinkler head itself, 30 per cent. of the losses being attributed to piping, including freeze-ups, and the remaining 20 per cent. arise from the occasional, but very severe losses which occur in connection with the collapse of the tanks or the eruption of a header or equivalent full volume of water supply. The main thing is "what device have they on system to notify those in charge in case of a break in order to shut off the supply?" (N. F. P. A. Vol. 10, 1916.)

Sprinkler Leakage—Some of the causes of tank collapse, preciptations and leakage for which the inspector should constantly look, are as follows:

1. Freezing; excessive pressure, settlement of tanks on risers, belts unguarded, near pipes; wearing out of packing on valves; defective castings; overloading floors; light castings and heavy pressure; neglect to drain and put on dry pipe valves; alternating systems in exposed places during winter months, which, if undiscovered, would result in the bursting of pipes.

2. Sun's rays through skylight; pendant heads on dry systems in extremely cold climates from condensation of moisture; extraordinary heat and low-degree heads; belts unguarded near heads; chemical action on pipes and heads; disintegration of fusing material on old heads; carelessness of employees handling stock, hanging or leaning things on or against pipes; leaving open in cold weather windows, doors, ventilators, hatchways, monitors and other openings, which, if undiscovered, would result in the discharge of heads.

3. Use of timber, which, if exposed, is unduly subject to rot; filling tanks before concrete or masonry is thoroughly dried to the core; neglect of tanks and supports, resulting in rot, rust, corrosion and decay; defects in casting or rolling of metal supports; constant vibration or jarring of building; inadequate supports; inadequate size of bearing plates under tank supports; crumbling of cement or mortar; flat hoops;

faulty construction; heating water in tanks to too high temperature; using old buildings without consulting architects as to carrying strength and builders as to condition of building; overloading floors, which if undiscovered would result in the collapse of tanks.

4. Carelessness in maintenance of system (uninstructed employees, especially new ones; alarms out of order; no alarms on system); watchman not visiting all parts of plant; concealed spaces in which sprinklers are located not known or indicated in some manner, which, if undiscovered, would result in excessive losses.—Thos. M. Donaldson in "Weekly Underwriter."

SPRINKLER AND HEATING (COMBINATION) SYSTEMS—The most interesting feature of this system is the method used for preventing the operation of the sprinkler heads from the heat of the water. The hot water has an average temperature of 180-200 deg. F. The maximum temperature used being about 245 deg. F. The melting point of ordinary sprinklers is 160 deg. F. In order to prevent the overheating of the sprinklers, they are placed on short offsets in which the water does not circulate. At first straight off-sets were used, but at present a curved pipe ¾-inch diameter and 18 to 20 inches long is used.—Gorham Dana.

SPRINKLERS, OPEN TYPE—These are used to protect the windows facing serious exposures and are not automatic in action (having no seal at the valve outlet). They depend upon human hands to operate a valve at the base of the riser through which water is conveyed to the sprinkler heads. They are also used at eaves and cornices and are sometimes called eave and cornice-sprinklers.

SPRINKLER RULES OF THE N. F. P. A.—Clear Space Below Sprinklers—Full effective action of sprinklers requires about 24 inches wholly clear space below the sprinklers, so that they may form an unbroken spray blanket from sprinkler to sprinkler and sides of room. Any stock piles, racks or other obstructions interfering with such action are not permissible. Sprinkler piping should not be used for the support of stock, clothing, etc.

Position of Sprinkler—Shall be located in an upright position. When construction or occupancy of a room or enclosure makes it preferable, permission may be given, except on dry-pipe systems, to locate sprinklers in a pendant position.

Position of Deflectors—Sprinkler deflectors shall be parallel to ceilings, roofs or the incline of stairs, but when installed in the peak of a pitched roof they shall be horizontal. Distance of deflectors from ceilings of mill or other smooth construction, or bottom of joists of open joist construction, shall be not less than 3 inches nor more than 10 inches; 6 to 8 inches is the best distance with average pressure and present types of sprinklers. Note particularly that the rule for distance refers to the deflector of the sprinkler.

In the case of fire-resistive buildings, the distance between deflectors and ceilings may be increased where conditions warrant; i. e., under panel ceilings. In semi-mill or other unusual construction, consult the inspection department having jurisdiction.

Detailed Locations—Sprinklers shall be placed throughout premises, including basement and lofts, under stairs, inside elevator wells, in belt, cable, pipe, gear and pulley boxes inside small enclosures such as drying and heating boxes, tenter and dry-room enclosures, chutes, conveyor trunks and all cupboards and closets unless they have tops entirely open, and are so located that sprinklers can properly spray therein. Sprinklers are not to be omitted in any room merely because it is damp wet or of fire-resistive construction.

Spacing of Automatic Sprinklers—Distance from Walls—The distance from wall or partition to first sprinkler shall not exceed one half the allowable distance between sprinklers in the same direction. Additional sprinklers may also be required in the narrow pockets formed by bay timbers or beams and wall.

Partitions—A line of sprinklers should be run on each side of partition. Cutting holes through a partition to allow sprinklers on one side thereof to distribute water to the other side is not effectual. This rule applies to both solid and slatted partitions.

Where no inflammable material is stored close to the ceiling; the inspection department having jurisdiction may waive the requirement for providing extra sprinklers in narrow pockets formed by beams and partitions where the construction is entirely fire-resistive, including the partitions.

MILL CONSTRUCTION—Under mill ceiling (smooth solid plank and timber construction, 5 to 12-foot bays) one line of sprinklers should be placed in center of each bay and distance between the sprinklers on each line should not exceed the following:

8 feet in 12 foot bays.
9 feet in 11 foot bays.
10 feet in 10 foot bays.
11 feet in 9 foot bays
12 feet in 5 to 8 foot bays.

Measurements should be taken from center to center of timbers.

Ceilings of modified mill construction having bays less than three feet should be treated as open joist construction and sprinkler heads spaced accordingly.

Bay timbers spaced three feet or more on centers but less than five feet on centers, will require special ruling by the inspection department having jurisdiction.

JOISTED CONSTRUCTION—Under open finish joisted construction, ceilings, floors, decks and roofs, the lines shall be run at right angles to the joists and the sprinklers "staggered spaced," so that heads will be opposite a point half way between sprinklers on adjacent lines and the distance between sprinklers not exceeding 8 feet at right angles to the joists or 10 feet parallel with joists; the end heads on alternate lines being not more than 2 feet from wall or partition.

Exception—An exception may be made to this rule if the conditions warrant, viz., special permission may be given to install but one line of sprinklers in bays 10 to 11½ feet wide from center to center of the timbers which support the joists. In all cases where such bays are over 11½ feet wide, two or more lines of sprinklers should be installed in each bay as required by the rules for spacing. Where permission is given, the sprinklers should be placed closer together on a line so that in no case will the area covered by a single sprinkler exceed 80 square feet.

Smooth Finish, Sheathed or Plastered Ceilings—Under smooth finish, sheathed or plastered ceilings, in bays 6 to 12 feet wide (measurement to be taken from center to center of timber girder or other projection or support forming the bay), one line of sprinklers shall be placed in center of each bay, and distance between the sprinklers on each line should not exceed the following: 8 feet in 12 foot bays; 9 feet in 11 foot bays; 10 feet in 6 to 10 foot bays. Bays in excess of 12 feet in width and less than 23 feet in width should contain at least two lines of sprinklers; bays 23 feet in width or over should have the lines therein not over 10 feet apart. In bays in excess of 12 feet in width not more than 100 square feet ceiling area should be alloted to any one sprinkler.

Pitched Roofs—Under a pitched roof sloping more steeply than 1 foot in 3, sprinklers shall be located in peak of roof, and those on either side of peak spaced according to above requirements. Distance between sprinklers should be measured on a line parallel with roof. Where the roof meets the floor line, sprinklers should be placed not over 3½ feet from where roof timbers meet floor.

Sprinklers not more than 2½ feet distant each way from peak of roof, measured on a line with the roof, may be used in lieu of sprinklers located in peak of roof as above.

In sawtooth roof the end sprinklers on the branch line shall not be over 2½ feet from the peak of the sawtooth.

FIRE-RESISTIVE CONSTRUCTION—The rules for slow-burning construction should apply as far as practicable. The rule may be modified, however, the intent being to arrange the spacing of sprinklers to protect the contents rather than the ceilings; but in no case shall the distance of a sprinkler on a line exceed 12 feet to a sprinkler on an adjoining line.

PIPE SIZES—**General Schedule**—In no case should the number of sprinklers on a given size pipe on one floor of one fire section exceed the following;

Size of Pipe.	Maximum No. of Sprinklers Allowed.
¾-inch	1 sprinkler
1 "	2 sprinklers
1¼ "	3 "
1½ "	5 "
2 "	10 "
2½ "	20 "
3 "	36 "
3½ "	55 "
4 "	80 "
5 "	140 "
6 "	200 "

Where practicable, it is desirable to arrange the piping so that the number of sprinklers on a branch line will not exceed eight.

FEED MAINS AND RISERS—**Location of Risers**—"Center central" or "side central" feed to sprinklers is recommended. The former is preferred, especially where there are over six sprinklers on a branch line. In high buildings, allowance must be made for frictional loss and sizes of risers increased accordingly. Risers should not be located close to windows, and should be properly protected from mechanical injury or a possible freezing.

Pressure Gauges—A standard make, 4½-inch dial, spring pressure gauge shall be connected with the discharge pipe from each water supply, including each connecting pipe from public waterworks, and also as follows:

In each sprinkler system above and below the alarm check or dry-pipe valve.

At the air pump supplying the pressure tank.

In each independent pipe from air supply to dry-pipe systems.

Use of High Degree or Hard Sprinklers—High degree sprinklers should be used only when absolutely necessary and Inspection Department having jursdiction should be consulted in each instance. When used, the following table should be referred to:

For ceiling temperature exceeding 100 degrees but not 150 degrees, install 212 degree heads.

For ceiling temperatures exceeding 150 degrees but not 225 degrees, install 286 degree heads.

For ceiling temperatures in excess of 225 degrees, install 360 degree heads.

SPRINKLER FIRE TABLES

	Watchman.		Sprinkler Alarm.		Thermostat.		Supervisory.		Total.
	Satis-fact'y.	Fail-ure.	Satis-fact'y	Fail-ure.	Satis-fact'y.	Fail-ure.	Satis-fact'y.	Fail-ure.	
Watchman & Sp'kler Al'm	77	81*	139	19	..	..	..	..	158
Watchman & Thermostats.	6	1*	..	..	6	1	..	..	7
Sprinkler Alarm & Thermo.	..	..	31	5	27	9	..	..	36
Watchman, Sprinkler Alarm & Thermostats	1	2*	3	..	3	..	..	..	3
Spr'kler Alarm & Sup'vis'y	..	..	31	3	..	..	34	..	34
Watchman & Supervisory.	2	..	..	..	..	..	2	..	2
Watchman, Sprinkler Alarm & Supervisory	8	9*	16	1	..	..	17	..	17
Sprinkler Alarm, Thermostats & Supervisory.......	..	..	5	1	5	1	6	..	6

Efficiency of Alarm Service, 1897-1916, Inclusive.

	Satisfactory.		Failure.		Total.
	No. of Fires.	Per Cent.	No. of Fires.	Per Cent.	
Watchman alone	1383	89.5	162	10.5	1545
Sprinkler alarm alone	1460	93.6	100	6.4	1560
Thermostats alone	170	78.7	46	21.8	216

	Watchman.		Sprinkler Alarm.		Thermostat.		Supervisory.		Total.
	Satis-fact'y.	Fail-ure.	Satis-fact'y	Fail-ure.	Satis-fact'y.	Fail-ure.	Satis-fact'y.	Fail-ure.	
Watchman & Sp'kler Al'm.	1008	631*	1439	200	..	..	..	..	1639
Watchman & Thermostats	19	6*	..	..	23	2	..	..	25
Sprinkler Alarm & Therm.	..	..	439	35	361	113	..	..	474
Watchman, Sprinkler Alarm & Thermostats	35	55*	83	7	70	20	..	..	90
Watchman & Supervisory.	4	4*	..	..	..	..	8	..	8
Spr'kler Alarm & Sup'vis'y	..	..	147	7	..	..	150	4	154
Watchman, Sprinkler Alarm & Supervisory	47	54*	100	1	..	..	100	1	101
Sprinkler Alarm, Thermostats & Supervisory......	..	..	26	1	22	5	27	..	27

*These include fires where sprinkler alarm or thermostats notified the watchman.

Note.—These tables do not include fires where alarm service does or does not operate promptly if fire is at once discovered by employee, the alarm service having no bearing on such fires one way or the other.

Table No. 4

Number of Sprinklers Operating.

No. of Sprinklers Operating	No. of Fires 1915-1916	No. of Fires 1897-1916 Inc.	Per Cent of Whole 1915-1916	Per Cent of Whole 1897-1916 Inc.
1	450	5314	34.6	31.1
2	226	2797	17.4	16.4
3	149	1761	11.5	10.3
4	86	1262	6.6	7.4
5	57	815	4.4	4.8
6	49	695	3.8	4.1
7	26	445	2.0	2.6
8	30	440	2.3	2.6
9	20	294	1.5	1.7
10	9	260	.7	1.5
11	12	226	.9	1.3
12	16	245	1.2	1.4
13	7	140	.5	.8
14	15	170	1.2	1.0
15	8	132	.6	.8
16 to 20......	29	460	2.3	2.7
21 to 25......	28	306	2.2	1.8
26 to 30......	12	210	.9	1.2
31 to 35......	15	133	1.2	.8
36 to 40......	8	104	.6	.6
41 to 50......	12	155	.9	.9
51 to 75......	17	212	1.3	1.2
76 to 100.....	10	104	.8	.6
Over 100	8	413	.6	2.4
Total, with data given.	1299	17093		
Water shut off sprinklers	19	178		
No data	22	262		
Total....	1340	17533		

Table No. 5

Number of Sprinklers Operating.

No. of Sprinklers	No. of Fires 1897-1916 Inc.	Per Cent of Whole 1897-1916 Inc.
1	5314	31.1
2 or less	8111	47.5
3 or less	9872	57.8
4 or less	11134	65.2
5 or less	11949	70.0
6 or less	12644	74.1
7 or less	13089	76.7
8 or less	13529	79.3
9 or less	13823	81.0
10 or less	14083	82.5
11 or less	14309	83.8
12 or less	14554	85.2
13 or less	14694	86.0
14 or less	14864	87.0
15 or less	14996	87.8
20 or less	15456	90.5
25 or less	15762	92.3
30 or less	15972	93.5
35 or less	16105	94.3
40 or less	16209	94.9
50 or less	16364	95.8
75 or less	16576	97.0
100 or less	16680	97.6
Over 100	413	2.4
Total with data given........	17093	
Water shut off sprinklers.....	178	
No data	262	
Total	17533	

Table No. 6

Sprinklers Opened on Wet or Dry Systems.

	No. of Fires 1915-1916	No. of Fires 1897-1916, Inc.	Per Cent of No. with Data Given 1915-1916	Per Cent of No. with Data Given 1897-1916 Inc.
Wet system	1046	12236	79.3	80.2
Dry system	272	3016	20.7	19.8
Total with data given	1318	15252		
Water shut off system	19	178		
No data	3	279		
Total	1340	15709		

Table No. 7

Primary Water Supplies to Sprinklers Opened.

	No. of Fires 1915-1916	No. of Fires 1897-1916, Inc.	Per Cent of No. with Data Given 1915-1916	Per Cent of No. with Data Given 1897-1916, Inc.
Waterworks	707	7809	53.8	51.5
Gravity Tank	270	4196	20.5	27.5
Pressure Tank ..	252	2353	19.2	15.4
Auto. Steam Pump	85	867	6.5	5.55
Auto. Elec. Pump	0	4	..	.029
Steamer Connection	0	3	..	.021
Total with data given	1314	15232		
Water shut off system	19	178		
No data	7	309		
Total	1340	15719		

Table No. 8

Effect of Sprinklers.

	No. of Fires 1915-1916	No. of Fires 1897-1916, Inc.	Per Cent. of No. with Data Given 1915-1916	Per Cent. of No. with Data Given 1897-1916, Inc.
Practically or entirely extinguished fire .	984	11310	73.43	64.51
Held fire in check..	305	5410	22.76	30.84
Total successful	1289	16720	96.19	95.35
Unsatisfactory	51	813	3.81	4.65
Total	1340	17533		

Table No. 9

Showing Effect of Sprinklers by Class of Occupancy.

	Extinguished Fire.		Held Fire in Check.		Total Satis-factory.		Unsatis-factory.		Total No. of Fires
	No.	%	No.	%	No.	%	No.	%	
Agricultural Implements	42	59.2	26	36.6	68	95.8	3	4.2	71
Auto. & Bicycle Fact's	53	59.5	31	34.9	84	94.4	5	5.6	89
Awning Factories	5	100.0	..	...	5	100.0	..	..	5
Bag Factories	4	57.2	3	42.8	7	100.0	..	..	7
Bakeries	27	67.5	11	27.5	38	95.0	2	5.0	40
Basket Factories	7	100.0	..	...	7	100.0	..	...	7
B't, N't & Screw Wks.	11	73.3	4	26.7	15	100.0	..	..	15
Boot and Shoe Shops..	371	74.7	107	21.5	478	96.2	19	3.8	497
Bottling Works	4	100.0	..	...	4	100.0	..	..	4
Braiding Mills	4	80.0	1	20.0	5	100.0	..	..	5
Breweries	5	83.4	1	16.6	6	100.0	..	..	6
Broom Factories	8	61.5	3	23.1	11	84.6	2	15.4	13
Brush Factories	8	80.0	2	20.0	10	100.0	..	..	10
Button Manufactories .	15	88.3	2	11.7	17	100.0	..	..	17
Candle Factories	4	66.7	2	33.3	6	100.0	..	..	6
Candy Factories	49	74.3	16	24.3	65	98.6	1	1.4	66
Canning Works	7	70.0	2	20.0	9	90.0	1	10.0	10
Car Houses	19	47.5	16	40.0	35	87.5	5	12.5	40
Car Works	52	65.8	25	31.7	77	97.5	2	2.5	79
Carpet Mills	102	57.7	66	37.3	168	95.0	9	5.0	177
Carriage Factories	81	66.4	34	27.9	115	94.3	7	5.7	122
Cel'u'd (PyroxylinPl's'c,	77	66.3	23	19.8	100	86.1	16	13.9	116
Cement & Plaster Wks.	2	66.7	..	...	2	66.7	1	33.3	3
Cereal Mills	25	67.6	8	21.6	33	89.2	4	10.8	37
Chemical & W'te Lead.	32	56.1	21	36.9	51	93.0	4	7.0	57
Clothing Factories	344	78.8	85	19.5	429	98.3	7	1.7	436

Coffee and Spice Mills.	34	72.3	18	27.7	47	100.0	..	..	47
Coffin Factories	32	80.0	7	17.5	39	97.5	1	2.5	40
Cold Storage Plants....	3	50.0	3	50.0	6	100.0	..	..	6
Cooperage Plants	41	55.4	25	33.8	66	89.2	8	10.8	74
Cordage Works	173	66.3	79	30.3	252	96.6	9	3.4	261
Cork Factories	6	50.0	4	33.3	10	83.3	2	16.7	12
Corset Factories	4	57.2	2	28.6	6	85.8	1	14.2	7
Cotton Ginnery	10	66.7	5	33.3	15	100.0	..	..	15
Cotton Mills	2808	60.7	1763	38.2	4571	98.9	52	1.1	4623
Cotton Warehouses ...	86	43.2	92	46.2	178	89.4	21	10.6	199
Cotton Seed Oil Mills..	36	53.8	21	31.3	57	85.1	10	14.9	67
Cutlery and Hardware.	7	53.8	5	38.5	12	92.3	1	7.7	13
Department Stores	256	79.6	55	17.0	311	96.6	11	3.4	322

SPRINKLER SUPERVISORY SYSTEM—"Weekly Underwriter." 1. No gate valve in the sprinkler system can be closed, wholly or in part, without immediate notice to the outside central office.

2. The presence of water leakage equal to the discharge of one or more sprinkler heads is instantly recorded at the Central Station and from there, if necessary, to the fire department.

3. Thus the operation of a sprinkler head, or the pulling of a manual fire alarm box, that is included in this equipment, assures at the earliest possible moment notice to the fire department of the presence of a fire and brings immediately the most important auxiliaries to the aid of the sprinklers.

4. Not more than six inches of water can drop in any of the sprinkler tanks without immediate notice to central office.

5. The water in any exposed tank can neither freeze nor become dangerously warm without instant signal to the central station.

6. There cannot be a drop of more than five pounds of pressure in either the pressure tanks or fire pumps without immediate notice to Central Office.

In short, no defect or disorder in the sprinkler system can occur without due notice to the district office.

SPRINKLER VALVES (Closed) have resulted in total losses even in risks with 100 per cent. equipments. A closed valve prevents water from reaching the seat of fire. Frequent causes of closed valves are repair work to system and then forgetting to turn water on, cutting off mains or supplies which are subject to freezing. If it is necessary to

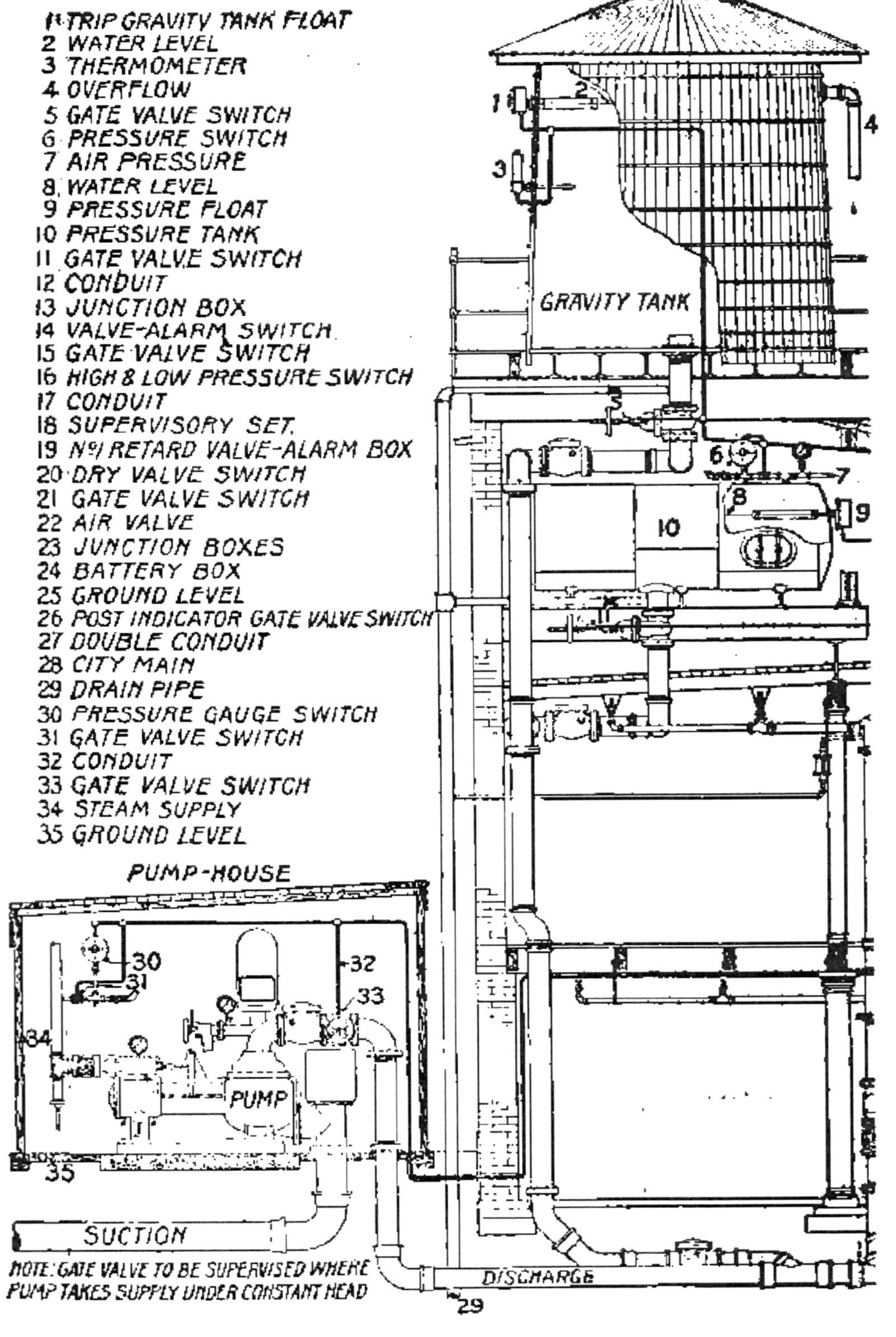
1 TRIP GRAVITY TANK FLOAT
2 WATER LEVEL
3 THERMOMETER
4 OVERFLOW
5 GATE VALVE SWITCH
6 PRESSURE SWITCH
7 AIR PRESSURE
8 WATER LEVEL
9 PRESSURE FLOAT
10 PRESSURE TANK
11 GATE VALVE SWITCH
12 CONDUIT
13 JUNCTION BOX
14 VALVE-ALARM SWITCH
15 GATE VALVE SWITCH
16 HIGH & LOW PRESSURE SWITCH
17 CONDUIT
18 SUPERVISORY SET.
19 Nº1 RETARD VALVE-ALARM BOX
20 DRY VALVE SWITCH
21 GATE VALVE SWITCH
22 AIR VALVE
23 JUNCTION BOXES
24 BATTERY BOX
25 GROUND LEVEL
26 POST INDICATOR GATE VALVE SWITCH
27 DOUBLE CONDUIT
28 CITY MAIN
29 DRAIN PIPE
30 PRESSURE GAUGE SWITCH
31 GATE VALVE SWITCH
32 CONDUIT
33 GATE VALVE SWITCH
34 STEAM SUPPLY
35 GROUND LEVEL
GRAVITY TANK
PUMP-HOUSE
PUMP
SUCTION
DISCHARGE
NOTE: GATE VALVE TO BE SUPERVISED WHERE PUMP TAKES SUPPLY UNDER CONSTANT HEAD

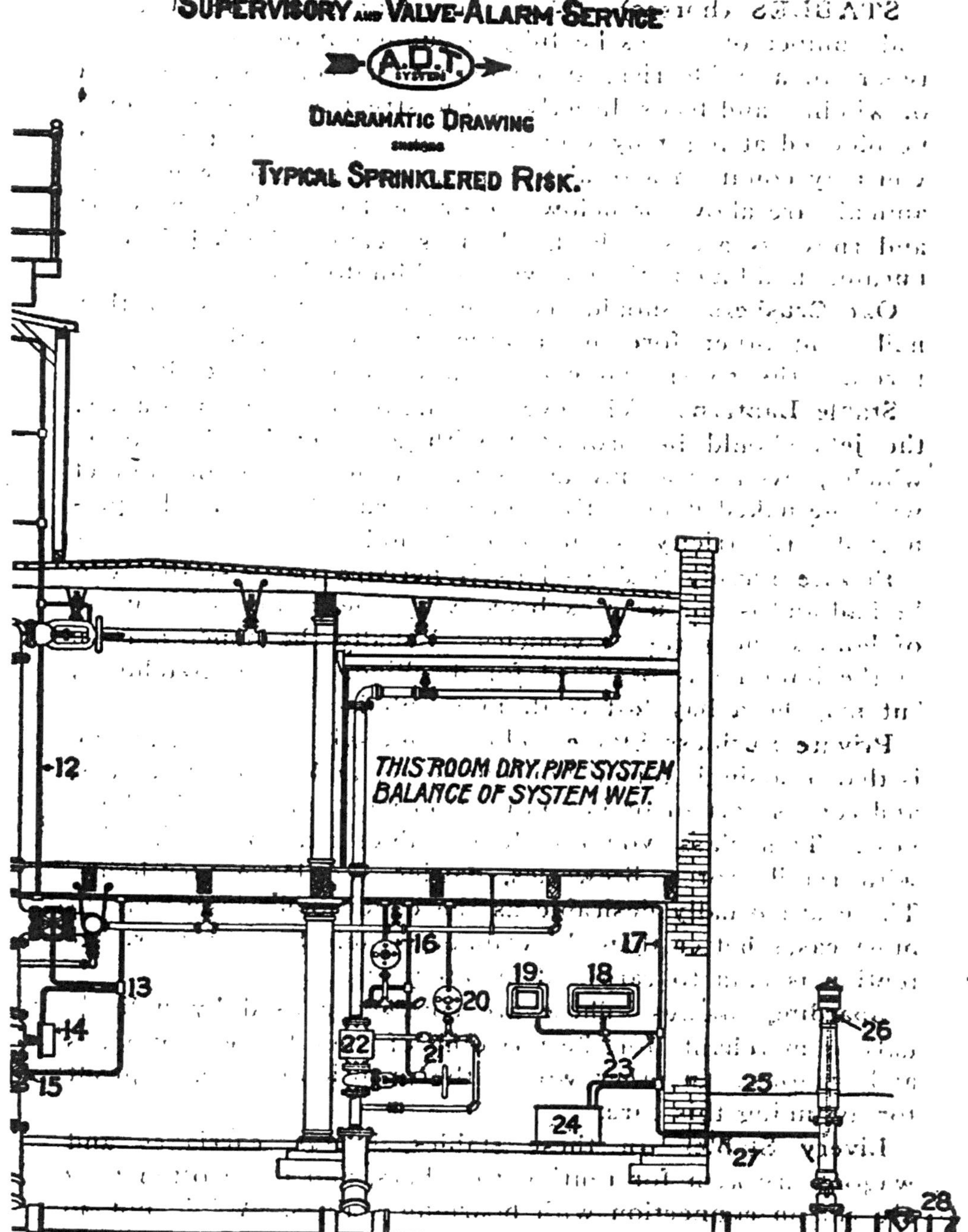

SUPERVISORY AND VALVE-ALARM SERVICE
A.D.T. SYSTEM
DIAGRAMATIC DRAWING
SHOWING
TYPICAL SPRINKLERED RISK.
THIS ROOM DRY PIPE SYSTEM
BALANCE OF SYSTEM WET.
12
13
14
15
16
17
18
19
20
21
22
23
24
25
26
27
28

close a valve, station a man at the valve to turn it on in case of fire.

STABLES (horses)—It is important that the location and number of horses be fully brought out in an inspection report of a stable risk, also whether the runway is straight or winding and leads directly to the street or whether it may be blocked at night by wagons. The fire record proves that you may count on a total loss in almost all cases where the animals are above or below the grade floor, unless the exits and runways are standard. A horse cannot be led from a burning building until his eyes are blindfolded.

Oat Crushers—Should have magnet attachments so that nails and other foreign metallic substances will not pass through the roller and cause sparks to ignite the dust.

Stable Lanterns—Whenever gas lights are used in stables, the jets should be protected with glass enclosed lanterns which prevents the hay and straw from coming in contact with the naked flame. Kerosene lanterns should not be permitted. Electricity is the best method of lighting.

Private Family Stable—This is perhaps the best that can be had and is one used exclusively by one family for housing of horses and pleasure vehicles. Usually the upper portion of the building is occupied for dwellings by the coachmen, but may be a hay loft containing rubbish.

Private Business Stable—This is one where the occupancy is that of a single tenant housing horses and business vehicles and run as part of or in conjunction with some regular business. This class would include stables run in conjunction with retail stores, breweries, dairies and large merchants. These are usually desirable as the conditions present are in most cases better than the ordinary stable because more attention is paid to care and maintenance.

Boarding Stables—These are commonly used by individuals or merchants for the boarding of their horses, carriages and wagons. In other words, the proprietor reaps a profit for assuming this care.

Livery Stables—In these stables, horses, carriages and wagons are kept for renting to others, and quite often they are run in connection with boarding stables. While not so desirable as a private business stable, they are good as second choice.

Riding Academy—This is usually an adjunct to a livery stable and consists of a large covered addition with tan-bark floor for indoor riding. It can be placed in the same class as a livery stable.

Express and Trucking Stables—While similar to a private business stable, attention should be given to the kinds of merchandise apt to be stored on the premises overnight.

Contractors' Stables—Private, business in nature, but usually filled with wooden forms and moulds, tools, machinery, etc.

Sales Stables—At these stables, usually only horses are kept and they are held for private sales or auctions. This is one of the most carelessly kept classes, mainly because the help employed is not of the best. The sporting trade and representatives of buyers frequent these stables smoking, etc. As a rule, there is not much interest in keeping these stables clean, because the horses are kept for a short time only. They are not so good as would be in a private business or family stable.

Veterinary Stables—In these stables, horses are doctored and treated for wounds, lameness, etc. The class can be likened to hospitals, for in case of fire, many of the horses will perish because some cannot be moved except with great difficulty. In some cases it will be found that horses are suspended from the ceiling by braces.—S. T. Skirrow in "The Weekly Underwriter."

STACK—The brick chimney of a boiler or furnace.

STAGGERED—A term used in connection with spacing of sprinkler heads; also casks of water on piers or foundry roofs. Say casks of water on one side of pier are placed every 100 feet. The next row should be placed so that the casks will be opposite a point half-way between casks on the opposite side.

STAGING the temporary flooring of scaffolds or platforms. In fireproof buildings, especially theatres and churches, this constitutes an extra hazard while the building is in course of construction because of the large amount of light wood framing used in the interior.

STAIN REMOVERS—Sometimes contain inflammable liquids.

STAIR—A boxed stairway is one that is enclosed without a hallway, the enclosing material being fastened against the under side of the stairs and boxing in the sides. If there is a self-closing door at the top of each stair-landing, it is much better than a wood enclosed hallway.

A wood enclosed stairway is one with a continuous shaft including the hallway. Fire in this class of shaft could travel from the lower floor to the top of the building. Boxing is better.

STAIRCASES of wood may be rendered practically fire-resisting, if the spaces underneath the treads and risers and between stringers, and also under the lower joists of landings are closed solid with mortar or other incombustible material. See Shafts.

STAIR PADS—Usually made in mattress factories, and the hazards are practically the same. A cheap grade of stock is generally used. Some manufacturers buy up old cotton-stuffed settees and upholstered furniture and use the stuffing for the stair pads. Jute, moss and other fibres are used. Hazards of pickers, "garnet" machines, lappers, untidy premises, dust-laden atmospheres. A. K. O. class.

STAMP COLLECTIONS—Many single stamps are quite valuable, and a small collection of rare stamps reaches a large sum. An expert is needed to determine values as minor defects or flaws render an otherwise valuable stamp nearly worthless. A class of insurance not usually solicited.

STAMPING—See Embroideries.

STANDPIPE—A water tower or a vertical water pipe with hose connections for fire purposes. Those installed in new buildings should always be given a fire test. A recent test in New York City showed many risers to be badly clogged. A fire chief in New York City declared that carelessness and lazy workmen frequently throw bricks, dirt and cement into the open riser rather than take the trouble of carting them downstairs. The hose should be inspected occasionally, as they have been found badly rotting close to the nozzle and couplings. This is caused by the porters cleaning the brass-work with polishing acids, and the seepage of water. Siamese or fire department connections on the street become clogged unless properly capped. They should be carefully examined periodically as caps become rusted at the threads or are stolen. On piers, or other similar places where many outsiders have access, it is quite customary to remove the brass nozzles so that they will not be stolen, or substitute iron ones. As a ruse, some owners paint brass nozzles black to resemble iron. See Siamese Connection.

STANFOIL is tinfoil made of pure tin.

STARCH is composed of carbon, hydrogen and oxygen, made from wheat, potatoes, corn, rice, etc.

All machinery such as pulverizers, grinders, attrition machines should be grounded to carry off static electricity generated by rapidly-moving machinery. All conveyor pipes and ducts, elevator legs, should have dust collectors to prevent dust explosions. Explosion boxes to vent and reduce the force of explosion are necessary on legs and conveyors. Fires occur in pressing and drying rooms where the drying and pressing oil from "germ" (ground corn) takes place. The germ left in dryer tank decomposes from the heat given off, generating a gas which ignites.

Starch (as made from potatoes)—The potatoes are washed in water in revolving tube and grated. The grater is a cylindrical tube of iron, encased in wood, having perforated iron bands and rough side which, in revolving grates the potatoes. The pulp passes over a moving screen upon which water is played from hose streams. This forces the pulp through the screen, the waste matter being shaken off. The pulp travels through troughs to precipitating tanks, where, after settling, the water is drawn off and the starch placed in agitator vats. The mass is then dried by atmosphere on slatted wood floor and barrelled.

STARCH BUCK—A wood enclosed automatic machine with an inner screen working back and forth, and a hopper at one end for candy, and at the opposite end an opening for the starch. This machine automatically separates the

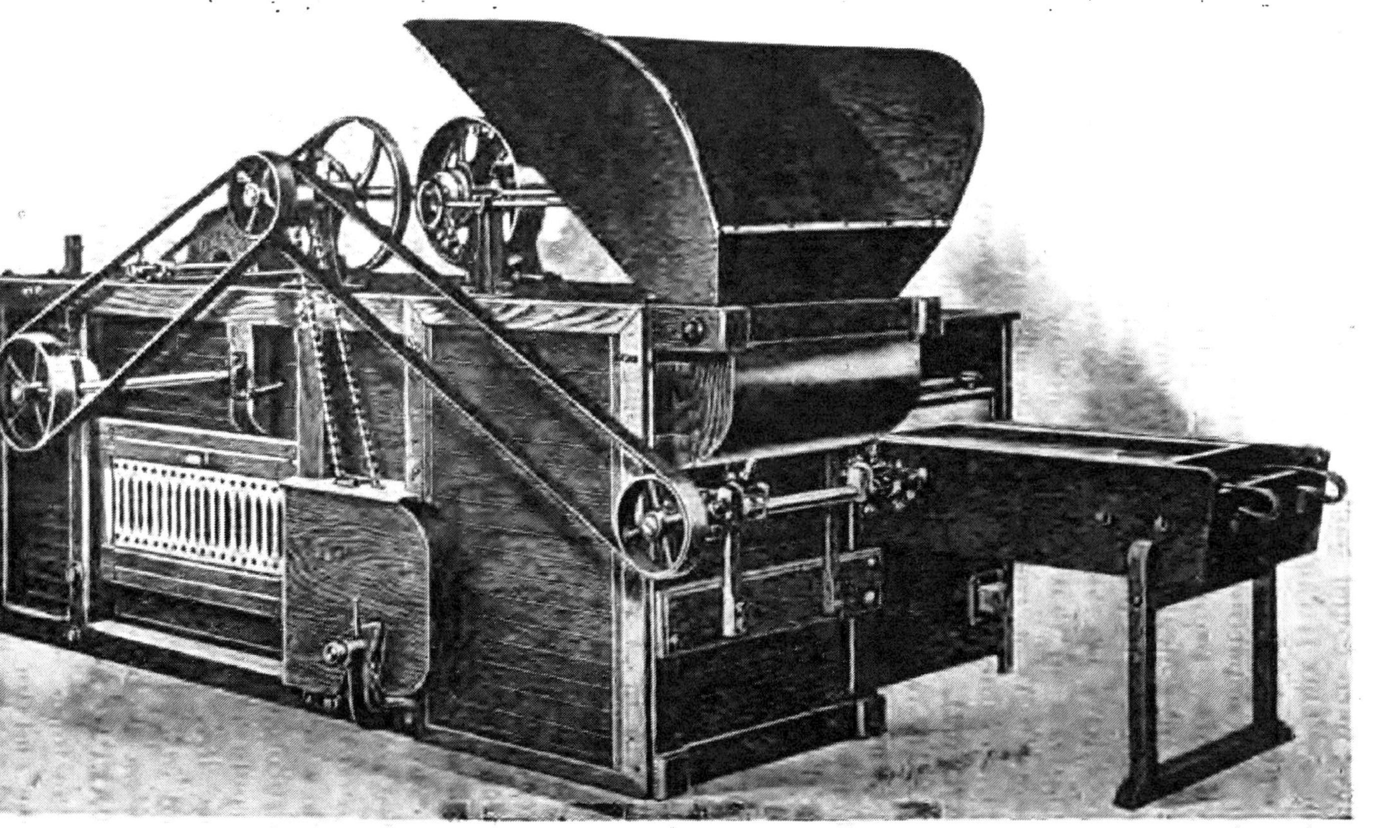

"Simplex" Starch Buck.

starch from the candy, cleans and delivers candy, refills and delivers trays with a minimum amount of dust, and is therefore recommended for factories making candies. See Candy Factories. See Illustration.

STARTING BOX—A rheostat used for starting and controlling motors.

STATIC OR FRICTIONAL ELECTRICITY is more liable to be generated when the atmosphere is clear and dry than when it is moist. It is generated by the rubbing together of substances that in themselves are non-conductors of electricity (or one conductor and a non-conductor); such as, dry wood or rubber. It may be generated by friction between a non-conductor and a conductor; such as, gasoline and a metal pipe; although in the latter, the intensity is much diminished. During the process of filling an automobile there should be a good metallic disc connection between the storage tank and the tank of the motor vehicle, so that all electricity generated may readily pass off to the ground as fast as generated. (Automobile Topics.) In filling tanks of automobiles or can with gasoline strained through chamois from metal cans, the can should rest on metal to afford a good ground. See Lightning.

STATIC PRESSURE is pressure created by the weight of water while at rest.

STATIONERS' SUPPLIES—Consist of various wood, metal and paper articles and novelties, school supplies, toys. Celluloid goods are sometimes included.

STATIONERY STORES (together with penny candy trade) should be written only as an accommodation risk, after a survey has been made and a trade report examined. Failures and fires are quite frequently reported in this class.

STATUARY (bronze)—Those of large size are made from miniatures, or replicas of wax which are covered with a plaster form or a covering applied by hand. The wax is melted out in a furnace and the hollow space remaining is filled with molten bronze. The wax used is a mixture of glycerine, gelatine, canauber wax and bees-wax. The foundry work is extensive. Here we find built-up brick kilns, core ovens, wooden flasks, furnaces. Dilute sulphuric and nitric acids are used for cleaning bronze parts. The waxes used are usually heated by direct fire. This work is found in most of the departments. Large stocks of models constitute considerable proportion of the value of the contents and should be considered the same as patterns. Usually frame risks of foundry type. See Sculptors.

STAYS—Generally applied to props, struts and ties for keeping timbers in place.

STEAM—Water converted into an elastic vapor by the application of heat. Low pressure steam has a pressure below 15 pounds to the square inch.

High pressure steam according to the rules of the Exchange has a pressure above 15 pounds to the square inch. They will treat boilers as low pressure if the safety valve is set at 15 pounds. If boiler room is cut off with 12-inch brick or concrete side walls with standard doors at openings and 8-inch concrete or brick ceiling on steel beams, no extra charge is made in rate.

STEAM JETS—The efficiency of steam jets for fire extinguishment lies in the confinement of the steam and its smothering effect on the fire, depriving it of its life-giving oxygen.

STEAM PIPES must be at least 2 inches from all unprotected woodwork. If protected by a metal collar, the distance may be 1 inch. There is much less damage likely from low pressure than from steam at high pressure.

Steam pipes, if in contact with wood, have been known to cause occasional fires. It is claimed that any steam pipe in contact with wood no matter how low the pressure, will in time produce charcoal, and as charcoal is unquestionably subject to spontaneous combustion, the recommendation to remove woodwork from all steam pipes is well founded.

Before heat is turned on, all dust and refuse around pipes should be removed. See Pipe Openings.

STEAM TANKS or kettles (set through flooring) where high temperatures are needed, should be 2 inches from wood flooring.

STEARIC ACID—Usually prepared from beef tallow by

saponification with sulphuric acid, distilling and hot pressing. Used in soap and candle manufacturing.

STEARINE—Similar to paraffine-wax. Non-volatile.

STEEL—A kind of iron or rather a compound of iron and

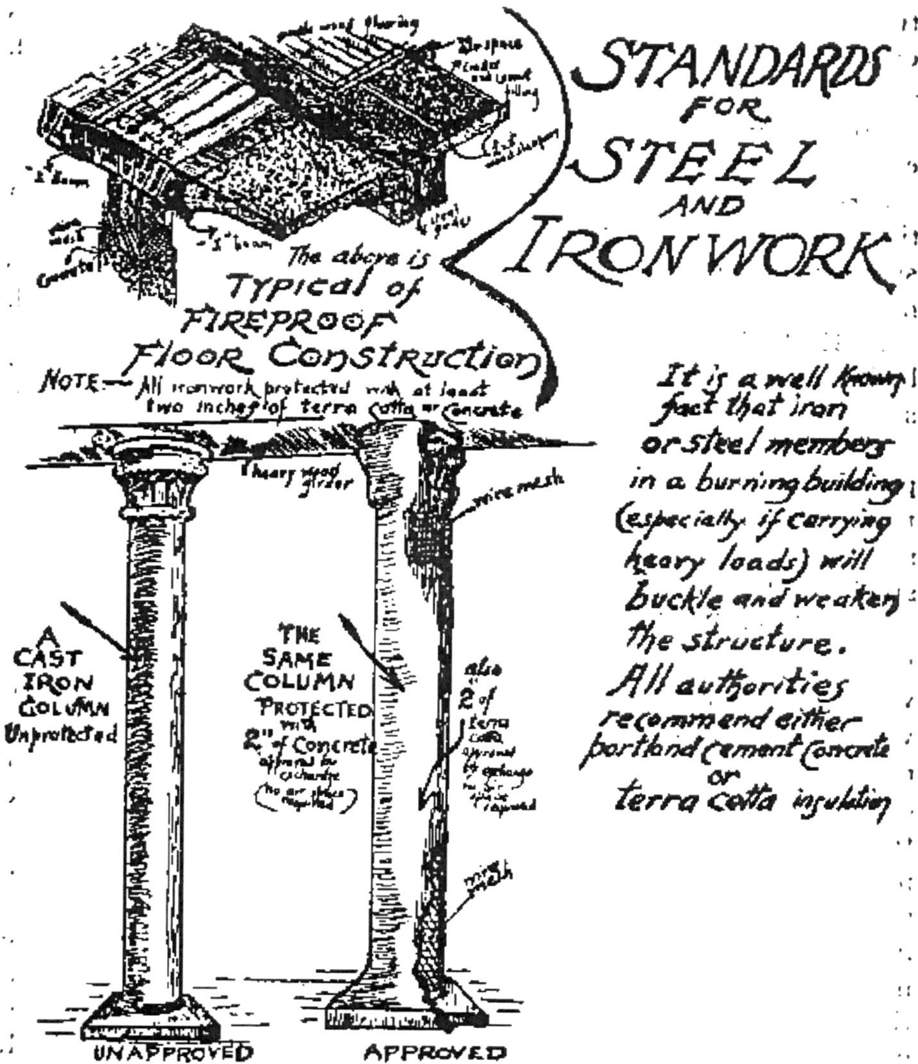

carbon. In every 100 lbs. of steel there are from 2 to 2½ lbs. of carbon. Steel is made from either cast or wrought-iron. There are two kinds of steel, one is brittle, the other is just the opposite, i. e., very flexible. If steel is heated then suddenly cooled, it will be hard and brittle. If it be cooled slowly it will be soft, and can be readily hammered out like wrought-iron.

Steel begins to lose its supporting strength at a temperature of about 900 deg. F, after which its loss of strength is extremely rapid until at 1600 deg. F. it is practically nil. —Hooker's Chemistry.

Steel (shear)—Hammered steel of fine texture and tougher than ordinary steel.

Steel (soft)—Naturally a gray color, is turned to a bluish tint by heating. A long, narrow metal frame is used with small perforations at top. Gas flames at the perforations heat the steel when it is placed on top. See Structural Steel.

STEELITE—A new metal composed of 75 per cent. cobalt and the remainder chromium. Used for tools; will cut steel on a lathe; impervious to rust or acids.

STEEL WOOL—The shavings from steel wire. It is practically useless if wet. Steel wire rusts readily and in that condition cannot be used until the rust has been removed. Spontaneous ignition is apt to occur in piles of steel wool, if oily.

STEREOTYPING—This necessitates the formation of the type in a cylinder or roller form, while the metal which provides the backing must also be in the same form. To provide this cylindrical form is the next step. The form is removed to a table and a sheet of specially prepared paper called the matrix is moistened and laid over the face of the type and is either beaten with a large brush so that an impression of the type is fully made or it is run through a power roller press to accomplish the same result. After the impression has been satisfactorily made the form with the matrix is placed on a steam table to dry, and when removed the matrix is still flexible enough to shape in the desired manner. The matrix is now put into a casting box which when closed forms a mould in the shape of a crescent on one side of which the matrix is placed. Molten lead is poured into the remaining space from the top and when filled the metal soon hardens sufficiently to be removed. The form has now been reproduced on a solid piece of metal which after being trimmed and grooved is ready to be placed in the press for printing the paper.

STICKERS—Woodworking machines similar to matching-planers but smaller. They have cutters for each of four sides of stock and make considerable refuse. Should have blowers.

STICK LAC—Lac in its natural state, encrusting leaves.

STILES—The flat vertical pieces between and at the sides of panel doors or windows.

STIPULATED WAREHOUSE—See Warehouses.

STOCKS should not be placed against the walls and should be on skids at least 6 inches from the floor. Aisles of 2 feet should be maintained and stock not piled nearer than 2 feet to the ceiling.

Stocks on grade floors of frame buildings are considered nearly as good as similar stocks in brick buildings. They are just as accessible to fire department. The hazards are the same, and salvage is as great. Furthermore, frame building being smaller in area and height than the usual brick structure, if collapsing, will precipitate less weight on grade floor stock.

Stocks in poorer sections of the city may not be attractive in appearance, but where the stock is suitable for the neighborhood, the business established for a length of time, and the other conditions incident to the business are satisfactory, they are sometimes preferable to more pretentious stores in better sections.

STOCK VALUATIONS are usually based on the assured's inventories. If these are destroyed by fire, the inventories of similar plants of like size and character are used to get at an approximate value. See Lines; see Retail Stocks; also Upper Floor Contents.

STONE under the action of severe heat will crack, shell or calcine. It should be used most cautiously in fireproof construction.

STONE YARDS—Usually enclosed in a high roofed over, light constructed frame shed. Many have a traveling, motor-power crane on track and trestle. Granite and polished stone subject to severe damage by fire and water.

STORAGE AND REPAIR CLAUSE should be placed on all policies where goods are likely to be left on storage.

STORAGE LINES—Companies prefer to write short term insurance on contents instead of yearly insurance on the buildings themselves, as a greater premium income is thus derived because "short rates" are charged. For knowledge of hazardous commodities see books, "The Handling of Dangerous Goods," by Joshua Phillips, and "Fire and Explosion Risks," by Von Schwartz.—D. Van Nostrand Co., publishers.

STORAGE STORES, FREE AND BONDED—The difference between these stores is—in the "Free Store" the duty or revenue is paid to the government before the goods go in storage; while in a bonded store it is paid when the goods are removed.

To remove goods from a "Bonded Store" it is necessary to pay the duty or revenue on the amount that is desired to be taken out of storage. When the duty (amount demanded by Government) is received by the Custom House, they issue an order to their representative at the storage store showing that the duty has been paid and he permits goods to be removed.

NOTE—Each bonded store has a Custom House officer on the premises at all times. His duty is to see that no goods are removed unless an order is shown that the duty has been paid.

The object is so that the owner need not pay the duty or revenue until the goods are actually sold and removed from the warehouse.—Richardson. See Warehouses.

STORAGE STORES LISTED must be occupied, and be under the exclusive control of the warehouseman. In New York City, in order to have a store listed, the Board of Underwriters issue certain requirements as to lighting, construction and occupancy. No volatiles or chemicals are permitted.

STORAX—An imported resinous gum used by perfume manufacturers.

STORE FIXTURES—Manufacturing hazards are those of woodworkers, including painting and varnishing. The fire record is not good.

STOVE-PIPE WORKS—Mainly sheet metal working. Elbows are dipped in a mixture of three parts naphtha to one part of machine oil for "varnishing." An unprofitable class for insurance companies.

STOVE POLISH may contain a large percentage of benzine. Test for flash point.

STOVES—Should be on iron stands or legs, with metal under and 12 inches in front of stove, and 3 feet from combustible partitions; if partitions or woodwork are shielded with metal, the distance may be 18 inches.

STOVES (kitchen)—There is a type of kitchen range being used, from which it is unnecessary to remove the ashes by means of the ordinary pan. A funnel is provided underneath the grate of the range. This funnel or pipe extends through the floor to a receptacle in the basement. The pipe or funnel should be insulated by a protecting sleeve so as to provide air space where passing through the floor. There is danger of clogging the funnel from neglect in emptying the container in the basement. This method of dropping hot ashes out of sight does not appeal to most underwriters unless they drop into a substantial brick enclosed ashpit having a heavy iron door.

STOVES (pot stoves)—Used extensively in lofts as they give out large volumes of heat. The fire pot which consists of an unlined iron casting one-fourth to one-half inch thick expands or contract from excessive heat, and sudden cooling when the fire goes out. This causes cracks. The cracks enlarge and allow hot coals to fall on the floor.

STRAIN—When a solid body is subjected to a stress of any kind an alteration is produced in the volume or shape of the body and the alteration is called the strain. Strain, is therefore, the result of a stress or stresses (Kidder).

STRAINER—Used on sprinkler suction lines where water is likely to contain weeds, refuse, etc., or where intake is from a pond. See Foot Valve.

STRAW GOODS stock will give a very poor account of itself in a fire because the strands are usually glued together and sized.

STREETS (Unpaved)—Should always be indicated on inspection reports. In bad weather fire departments experience difficulty in traversing unpaved, muddy roads, hence a delay in reaching a fire.

STRENGTH OF MATERIAL—See Stress, Compression and Tension.

STRESS—A stress is an internal resistance which balances an external force. By placing a weighty object on another object of similar character there is a downward pressure (weight) or external force which is met by the internal resistance (stress) of the under object, preserving the same in equilibrium, otherwise the lower object would be crushed.

STRETCHER—A brick or block of masonry laid lengthwise to the wall.

STRIKES—Firms which are constantly at logger-heads with their help, should not be considered desirable insurance as fires may be caused by dissatisfied or discharged employees.

STRINGER—Any longitudinal timber or beam.

STRIPPING in paper box factories is the glueing together of the ends and sides of boxes. The "stripper" has a glue pot at one end which is heated by steam or gas. If the latter, the glue pot should be "jacketed" and a "baffle-plate" placed under the burners to catch the hot carbon. An operator sits at one end of the machine and draws a strip of paper (from a roll) through the glue pot.

STRONTIA—Called strontium nitrate; heavy, white, crystaline salt; a strong oxydizing agent.

STRUCTURAL STEEL should be protected with fire resistive insulation such as terra-cotta, concrete or brick sufficiently thick to withstand a powerful stream of water without being destroyed thereby exposing the steel work.

STRUT—A prop, the piece that sustains compression.

STRUT BEAMS—Struts that are also subject to transverse strain.

STRUT BOARD—A board located under the pulley at top of an elevator (lofter) leg and forming part of the enclosure. Should be slanting to prevent grain or dust from banking up and clogging the mechanism, thereby generating sparks which would ignite the dust or grain. See Breweries.

STUCCO—Its composition varies. The following may be used, plaster of Paris, glue, cement, silica, sand or marble dust, sea sand, lime, water.

STUCCO BUILDINGS are classed as frame.

STUCCO CONSTRUCTION—The older method is to stucco over metal lath taking the place of clapboards or weatherboards. The newer method, no sheathing is required, the stucco and metal lath takes the place of sheating or clapboards. The sheathing should be diagonal to the studding to make a firmer brace and prevent cracking, and covered with waterproof paper well lapped, providing the stucco is placed over the sheathing. The waterproof paper prevents the wood from absorbing the moisture from the cement (stucco) which would otherwise prevent proper setting. Wood or metal furring strips fastened 12 to 16 inches over the paper-covered sheathing will fur out the wall and metal lath and allow a proper key for the stucco. Stuccoed walls are a better protection against exposure fires than frame, because sparks cannot find lodgement between crevices and it will resist heat longer. Dense smoke will color stucco, and cleaning is more difficult than painting a frame building.

STUDIOS—Hangings in studios such as tapestries, portierres, portable scenery, pictures on easels, spread fire rapidly.

STUDS—The small size (usually 2 x 4 inches) intermediate posts in walls or partitions.

STUFFING BOX—The small boxing at the end of a steam cylinder and surrounding the piston like a collar. This box is usually filled with flax or other packing.

SUBERINE—Organic thickening material used in calico bleaching.

SUBLIMATE—To bring by heat into a state of vapor, which on condensing or cooling returns to a solid state.

SUBROGATION is the substitution of another person in the place of a creditor, so that the person in whose favor it is exercised succeeds to the rights of the creditor in relation to the debt. More broadly, it is the substitution of one person in the place of another whether as creditor or as the possessor of any rightful claim. The Court of Appeals of

New York State defines "subrogation" as the "mode which equity adopts to compel the ultimate payment of a debt by one who in justice, equity and good conscience ought to pay it." In the fire insurance business, the operation of subrogation is used in payment of fire claims to mortgagees.

SUGAR in nature is composed of carbon, hydrogen and oxygen although it cannot be made by mixing these ingredients together.

SUGAR MANUFACTURING—In obtaining sugar from the cane, the juice is first pressed out between heavy iron rollers. This juice is then cleaned of most of its impurities, and is boiled down to such a degree that the sugar will crystallize as it cools. While this crystallization is going on, a syrup trickles from the sugar and this is molasses. The sugar crystallizes in grains, forming the common brown sugar. To make it white it requires additional purifying processes.

SUGAR REFINING—Requires the continuous movements of the sugar in either liquid or solid form through the various conveyors, boiling pans, filters, chutes and driers. The process consists of mixing, filtering, open boiling, purifying through bone black, vacuum boiling, molding, open-air drying and rotary driers, cutting, grinding and packing. The nature of the processes make necessary many large openings through the floor which cannot be cut off. The charhouse where the bone black is prepared should be in separate cut-off building. Sugar and filter bags should be dried outside of the building. The drying process should always be carefully noticed by the inspector. The grinding produces a dust hazard. Only competent underwriters should accept this business.

Sugar Refinery (Pan-house)—Sugar pumped from charhouse in semi-liquid state to receiving tanks, filtered, boiled in vacuum pans and steam kettles, impregnated with sulphur fumes, then to mixers and to centrifugal extractors where liquid is extracted and then to storage bins, and next to separators and granulators (heated by hot air), screened, bagged or barrelled or sent to cube presses where it is pressed into cube form, dried by steam or hot air and boxed. Sugar is also pulverized or powdered. Fires, due to dust and friction of machinery at pulverizers and powdering machines are frequent. As these machines have suction blower system, fires may be spread from floor to floor. Dust hazard also present at granulators and conveyors. The nature of the business requires numerous ducts, pipe openings, hoppers and machinery set through floors which cause fires to spread rapidly. Sulphur storage should be in separate fireproof compartment. Fires cause considerable loss from dirt, etc., to sugar in bins, open pans or evaporators.

Sugar refinery fire, N. Y. Board report, May 25, 1911.

The fire shows clearly the hazard attending the pulverization of sugar and the need for conducting this process in a separate building or the process should be conducted in a section cut off by 12-inch fire walls without direct openings to the other buildings. The outer unexposed wall preferably to be of light material such as plaster on wire lath or terra-cotta blocks, so that the force of any explosion may be vented outward. No dust room should be used. Dust from granulators and pulverizers should be settled by spraying in an enclosed chamber of incombustible material thus eliminating the hazard of dust rooms and dust tubes. All pulverizing mills should be equipped with magnets. Sugar bins should be of incombustible material.

SUINT—The natural grease of wool.

SULFONAL is unsafe in a chlorate mixture.

SULPHATE—Sulphuric acid compound.

SULPHATE OF AMMONIA—Made by neutralizing diluted sulphuric acid with carbonate of ammonia.

SULPHATE OF COPPER—Composed of sulphur, oxygen and copper. Used in dry batteries, etc. Made from copper (usually scrap) sulphuric acid and water. Process is steam as a rule.

Sulphuric acid is emptied into a lead-lined wood tank from which it is pumped to a wood tank lined with vitrified brick and called a pump tank. Into this tank, copper is dumped where a water spray forms a mixture of copper, water and acid. This mixture is then pumped to the oxidizing tank in order to obtain the proper strength, then passed over to the crystallizing tanks (which resemble plating tanks with copper strands at intervals) where the sulphate of copper crystals form and adhere to the copper strands. The crystals are then taken from the copper strands and placed on top of an open dryer with perforated top and air blast below. The finished product is then barrelled and shipped. The process is usually classed non-hazardous.

SULPHATE OF LIME—Lime and sulphuric acid.

SULPHATE OF MAGNESIA—Magnesia and sulphuric acid.

SULPHATE OF SODA—Soda in sulphuric acid.

SULPHATE OF ZINC—Is white vitriol.

SULPHATING—Changing chlorides into sulphates.

SULPHIDE—Compound of sulphur with a metal.

SULPHONIC ACID—Used in aniline color works by treating aniline oil or naphthalene with sulphuric acid in closed, steam or gas-heated kettles, diluted, washed and filtered. May nitrate same with sodium nitrate and sulphuric acid or nitration mixture. Can be converted into sublime-beta-naphthol, an intermediate product.

SULPHUR—Ignites at about 500 deg. F. When mixed with oxidizing agents, such as potassium or sodium chlorates or nitrates, becomes explosive. Is highly inflammable; when well ignited burns fiercely, but is not subject to spontaneous combustion except when mixed with other chemicals. Explosions occur in grinding operations due to friction of machinery and dust. Difficult fires to fight owing to sulphur fumes. Firemen must wear masks in fighting these fires. See Sulphur Extracting Factories.

SULPHUR BLACK—A dye used in the hosiery trade. It is prepared as follows: A liquid called monochlor-benzol is made by passing chlorine gas through benzol. This is then converted by nitrition into di-nitrochlor-benzol.

SULPHUR BLEACHING—See Bleaching Rooms.

SULPHUR DIOXIDE—Formed by burning sulphur or iron pyrities in air. Non-inflammable.

SULPHUR AND IRON PYRITES are burned in what are known as sulphur burners (brick-set furnaces with iron doors) until the fumes go to the Glovers tower (which is a lead tank lined with an acid brick) to cool. The fumes then go to the sulphuric acid chambers which are lead tanks with outside frame crating, where they are converted into sulphuric acid.

SULPHUR EXTRACTING FACTORIES are filled with huge boilers (usually oil fuel), which heat water to nearly 335 deg. F. This is pumped down into the ground through pipes at a pressure of 125 lbs. It melts the sulphur beds which forces the sulphur to the surface by compressed air.

SULPHURETTED HYDROGEN contains sulphur and hydrogen.

SULPHURIC ACID MANUFACTURING—Plants usually consist of three connecting buildings, known as burner room, tower building, and chamber building with an adjoining shed used for the storage of pyrites.

SULPHURIC ETHER—Very inflammable.

SUMAC—The powdered leaves and bark of an Indian tree. Used in tanning. See Tanneries.

SUMMER—A large piece of timber supported by piers or posts; when it supports a wall it is called a brest-summer or bressummer.

SUMMER PIECE—The wood or sheet covering placed in front of and covering a fireplace opening. Often times, rubbish or paper will be found back of it.

SUMP OR SUMPT—A low enclosure or pit to catch waste water.

SUN'S RAYS focused through imperfect prism or bull's-eye glass such as in skylights have ignited celluloid goods, clothing, etc.

SUPERHEATER—Used at pitch kettle in breweries for superheating steam coils to melt out all old pitch from kegs. See Breweries.

SUPERIOR CONSTRUCTION—See Fireproof.

SURBASE—The inside horizontal moulding on wall near floor.

SURGEONS' LIGATURES—Made of catgut, treated with chloroform and hermetically sealed with wax in glass tubes. Blow-pipes are used for heating the sealing wax. As the heat is applied near the mouth of the tube, a certain amount of chlorine gas is generated by reason of vaporizing the chloroform. This is drawn off by suction pipes. Culture incubators, cuemol dryers, sterilizers, alcohol stills, and dry box for catgut are gas-heated.

SURGICAL INSTRUMENT MANUFACTURING—Hazards of metal working, annealing, blow-pipes, forges, tempering, nickle-plating, cleaning metal parts with benzine, buff-wheels, making wood handles. At times, have an extensive laboratory for making exhaustive tests. Stock is liable to severe water or moisture damage unless wrapped moisture proof. See Instruments.

SURGICAL SUPPLIES—See Surgeons' Ligatures.

SURVEY—The detail report of a risk made by an inspector.

SURVEYOR—A title applied to insurance inspectors. See Inspectors.

SWARF—A trade term for borings from iron or steel.

SWEATING HAY—See Hay.

SWEAT-BAND MANUFACTURING—They are made of leather. Use cutting machines, perforators, embossing presses, rubber cement. Poor fire record class.

SWEAT SHOPS—A name given to the clothing manufacturing class doing contract work, i. e., making up the garments from goods belonging to dealers and sent them already cut to size, and employing piece-workers. Cheap labor is employed and the shops are usually untidy. Smoking, individual motors at machines, cracked pot stoves are the main hazards. See Clothing Manufacturers; see Smoking; also "Goods in Hands of."

SWEEP SMELTERS—Trade name for smelters who buy up the sweepings of gold and silversmiths, and refine it to reclaim the precious metal. The setting of furnaces and kettles should be according to standard rules.

SWING SAW—A woodworking machine with the saw in the centre of a flat table or stand, operated by swinging back and forth.

SWITCHBOARDS in telephone exchanges form considerable of the value and should always be brought out in the inspector's report.

SWITCHBOARD MANUFACTURING—Hazards are power-cutting and drilling machines for marble and slate slabs. Machine shops, plating, lacquering, enameling, buffing, testing with high voltage electric current and packing material.

SYNAGOGUES—Same hazards as schools and churches. Scrolls, vestments, parchments, etc., while susceptible, offer good insurance as all efforts are made to recover them in case of fire. Many of the scrolls are priceless and cannot be duplicated. Smoking and candles at altars constitute the principal hazards. See Churches.

SYNTHETIC PERFUMES—Those derived from coal tar instead of essential oils.

SYPHO-CHEMICAL SPRINKLER SYSTEM—Manufactured by the Sypho-Chemical Corporation. Protection from this system consists of a series of sprinkler pipes and heads covering every portion of the building's interior just like a regular sprinkler system. These pipes are filled with calcium chloride, a non-freezing solution, which also has fire extinguishing qualities. The supply tank will usually be placed in the basement though it may be set elsewhere if that location is not suitable. This supply tank is filled with bicarbonate of soda solution. Attached to it is a syphon chamber containing charges of sulphuric acid. At the top of the riser pipe which extends above the roof is an expansion chamber which, like the pipes, is filled with calcium chloride.

Method of Operation—When a sprinkler head is opened by heat the first discharge is the calcium chloride which is always in the pipes. The fall of this liquid in the expansion chamber causes a suction which is transmitted to the acid syphons, causing a discharge of sulphuric acid into the bicarbonate of soda solution. Chemical force then sends the extinguishing fluid through the pipes as through the discharge hose and nozzle of a soda and acid fire extinguisher. The entire operation is completed in a few seconds. The system is also equipped to turn in fire alarms and warning signals when tampered with. It is claimed for this system that it will make practical the sprinklering of smaller buildings and manufacturing plants. Special emphasis is placed on the efficient fire extinguishing qualities of a soda and acid solution. One sprinkler company has announced that it does not sell the system, but sells the service of its protection in consideration of an annual charge based upon the area to be protected.

TABLES—To find the circumference of a circle, multiply the diameter by 3.1416.

To find diameter of a circle multiply circumference by .31831.

To find area of a circle multiply square of diameter by .7854.

To ascertain the capacity of a cylindrical tank—Example: Tank is eight feet high, ten feet diameter at base, eight feet diameter at top. Take mean diameter which is nine feet. Square the diameter (9 times 9) times .7854 equals the square feet of diameter times eight feet (height) which equals the cubic feet times 7.48 (gallons in cubic foot of water); the total is capacity of tank in gallons.

Table Showing Dimensions and Capacity of Standard Water Tank:

Diameter	Height	Capacity
6 feet 0 inches	5 feet 11 inches	1000 gals.
8 " 6 "	5 " 11 "	2000 "
10 " 3 "	5 " 11 "	3000 "
11 " 9 "	5 " 11 "	4000 "
13 " 3 "	5 " 11 "	5000 "
8 " 3 "	7 " 11 "	2500 "
10 " 3 "	7 " 11 "	4000 "
12 " 5 "	7 " 11 "	6000 "
10 " 4 "	9 " 11 "	5000 "
12 " 5 "	9 " 11 "	7500 "
11 " 10 "	11 " 10 "	8000 "
13 " 3 "	11 " 10 "	10000 "
16 " 0 "	11 " 10 "	15000 "
18 " 3 "	11 " 10 "	20000 "
20 " 2 "	11 " 10 "	25000 "
28 " 6 "	11 " 10 "	50000 "

Cylindrical Tank with Round Bottom—To find the capacity in gallons of the hemispherical portion of a steel cylindrical tank, cube the diameter of the tank (11 x 11 x 11) and multiply by 1.96.

Rectangular Tank—The capacity of a rectangular tank in gallons is found by multiplying its inside length, breadth and height together (to find cubic contents), and dividing this result, if in inches, by 231, or multiplying it, if in feet, by 7.4805. Example: Tank eight feet by eight feet by eight feet. Ascertain cubic feet by multiplying eight times eight times eight, equals 512 cubic feet, times 7.48 (gallons in cubic foot of water), equals capacity of tank in gallons.

Amount of water necessary for gravity and pressure tanks in sprinklered risks—Example: A six-story and basement building; add the number of heads required for each floor and divide by seven, (number of floors including basement) to get the average number which we will say is 150 heads. Allow 100 gallons of water for each head, i. e., 150 times 100 equals 15000 gallons for gravity tanks and one-half that amount or 7500 gallons for pressure tank. Pressure tanks should be two-thirds full of water and one-third full of air under pressure. Another way to figure, producing the same result would be to average the number of heads per floor (150) and take one-quarter (the number which might be expected to operate at one fire) which equals 37.5 heads. Allow 20 gallons of water a minute for each head (20 times 37.5) which equals 750 gallons per minute. For a fire of twenty minutes duration (length of time of average small fire) multiply 750 by 20 which equals 15,000 gallons for gravity tank and one-half that amount for pressure tank.

Communicating Buildings—Two buildings may communicate in a standard manner, i. e., with approved fire doors at each side of each opening. One building may have a floor area of 5,000 square feet, and the other 10,000 square feet. The size of tanks in such a case would be that required for the largest cut-off section (10,000 square feet) which will be considered by most rating bureaus sufficiently large enough to supply both sections. See Pressure.

T

TAILORS' TRIMMINGS—Consist of buttons, piece goods, ornaments for cloaks and suits, braids. Usually kept in tills or pasteboard boxes.

TALLOW—A solid fat extracted from the suet of beef or sheep. Melting point 115 to 121 deg. F.

TANKAGE (dried blood)—The waste material from rendering plants. Used in fertilizer plants. Non-hazardous, non-inflammable. See Extracting Plants.

TANK FIRES—If the contents of a tank is on fire, it can usually be extinguished if the cover is quickly put on as this shuts off the supply of oxygen, providing the cover is tight-fitting. See Oil Tanks.

TANNERIES—Process consists of tanning, coloring, stuffing, oiling, drying, finishing, embossing. Some plants extract grease from wool by naphtha process. Fires are apt to take place in any of these processes. Lime and tan pits, storage of hides and pickled skins should not be in main building. All storehouses should be detached. Dry rooms are usually heated by hot air blown from steam coils. If fans are used in dry rooms they should be self-oiling to prevent overheated bearings. In oiling and stuffing, grease is used which should be heated by steam. Floors become very oily from dripping hides hung up after oiling. Lime should be slacked outside of building. Fleshings and scrapings are subject to spontaneous combustion. Buff wheels should have blowers. Hair and wool should be dried in iron textile dryers. Lamp-black should be stored outside of main building free from dampness. Bark mill (grinding bark) should be detached. In writing use and occupancy it is well to remember that tanning is a continuous process. Small fires may stop entire process. Tanning liquors are spoiled by water (which would happen if a fire occurred) in the leach house, and a fresh supply of liquor is not always available. See Hides; see Tanning; also Skins.

TANNERS—Some use a compound of paint containing pyroxilin or gun-cotton dissolved in amyl acetate.

TANNERS' OIL—A by-product of the operation of the tannery.

TANNIN occurs very vividly in nature as a constituent of many barks, leaves and wood. Used for tanning purposes.

TANNING—Is done in three different ways: (1) With tan bark extracts and other vegetable substances containing tannin. (2) With alum or bichromate of potash and other mineral salts. (3) By impregnating or "shamoying" the raw skin and oil. See Tanneries.

TANQUA NUTS—A product of South America; are used for making vegetable ivory buttons.

TAR is obtained as a residue from wood distillation. Fires in this material can be readily extinguished by covering with sand. Water will scatter the flames.

TARCOLINE—A benzine substitute classed as non-volatile.

TAR PAPER while cooling after being made, sometimes takes fire spontaneously due to chemical changes. Fires in this stock burn fiercely.

TAR PAPER MANUFACTURING—Coating is a heavy coal tar oil containing impure carbolic acid, anthracene and naphtha. The liquid will not flash at ordinary temperature, but the vapor given off during coating process is inflammable. The "saturating" machine consists of a steam-heated tank containing the coating material through which is passed the felt paper. A rack, supported by an iron frame, forces the paper into the coating material. A coated and an uncoated roll of paper are then pressed together. Fires have occurred from static electricity igniting the fumes at the machine. **Susceptible stocks** in the neighborhood of these plants are likely to suffer a severe loss on account of pungent odors from burning tar. See Tobacco.

TARPAULIN—A waterproof canvas used for covering

merchandise. It is usually coated with linseed oil. Those used by the fire patrol to cover stocks in case of fire are made of brown twill and given two coats of a preparation composed of linseed oil mixed with lithia. It takes 120 days to dry.

TAR POTS, boiling over, have caused frequent fires in buildings in course of construction. When on fire, should be smothered with sand. Water will scatter the burning tar.

TARTARIC ACID—Made from crude argol or tartar, or from the mass remaining after wine is removed from the casks. The mass is pressed and dried and used as a basis for making cream of tartar.

TAXIDERMISTS—Stock consists of stuffed birds and animals and is very susceptible to fire, smoke or water. Use glue, cement, excelsior and hair, wood for frames and shellac. For museum work on large animals the skin is placed on a model of plaster of paris reinforced with iron and wood strips. The clay is put on about an inch thick, then shellaced and the skin glued on. Glass or celluloid eyes are inserted and nose and mouth retouched with wax. Hand carpenter shop, glue and wax heating, shellacing and stuffing material are main hazards.

TAX LIEN INTEREST (Double the Regular Fire Rate)—The form should read as follows:

On the tax-lien interest of the assured in the building situate No................

It is especially understood and agreed that it is the intention of this insurance to cover the assured's tax-lien interest in the above-mentioned property, the nature of such interest being transfer of a tax by virtue of the assignment from the City of New York to collect taxes, assessments and water taxes.

It is mutually understood and agreed that if the above described building is totally destroyed by fire or damaged to such an extent that it must be demolished in order to comply with any law or ordinance of the city, or the owner and or the mortgagees elect not to repair, then this company shall pay the assured the full sum hereby insured, or such a sum as would be sufficient to reimburse the assured for whatever actual loss he may have sustained by reason of such total or partial destruction, this sum in case of disagreement to be determined by appraisement in the manner provided for in the conditions of the policy.

It is further understood and agreed that whenever this company shall pay the assured any sum, this company shall to the extent of such payment, be thereupon legally subrogated to all the rights of the assured under such a tax-lien assignment (or at its option, in the event of the full sum hereby insured being paid to the assured, receive an assignment and transfer of such tax-lien) to the extent of the payment made by this company.

TAXPAYERS—A term sometimes applied to a row of one or two-story buildings erected for store purposes and built to derive enough rent to pay for taxes until such time as a higher building is erected or the property is sold.

TAWING—Leather treated with alum and salt.

TEA—Almost as susceptible to smoke or water damage as tobacco.

TEAK—A very durable wood for all work that is exposed to the weather. It contains a resinous oil.

TEA RISKS—The main hazard is cleaning. A motor blower "blender and dust remover" is used which should have an enclosed fan with suction to draw off the dust to outer air.

TEAR-OFFS are the portions of the hide or skin which are torn off when they are being stretched. Classed as remnants. Used for horse collars and corners for suit cases.

TEASING MACHINE OR "DEVIL"—Used to break up long tow or fibre to prepare it for the cards.

TEEL OIL—Used to adulterate olive oil. Non-hazardous.

TELEGRAPH OFFICES—Practically an office occupancy with telegraph instruments. Fires caused by messenger boys smoking and short circuits.

TELEPHONE STATIONS—See Power Houses; see Switchboards.

TELL-TALES—On sprinkler equipments should be sealed shut. It is an electrical mechanism by means of which an alarm is sounded when water in gravity or pressure tanks gets below the prescribed level.

TEMPER—If cast iron or other metals are relieved of some of their carbon by heating to "red heat" with an oxidising agent, it is called tempering.

TEMPERATURE—This question is of vast importance to the fire underwriter. The ignition temperature varies greatly with different materials and with the same materials under varying conditions of pressure, moisture, fineness of division, etc. It does not require the actual contact of a flame or spark to cause a fire. Radiated heat alone from a burning building, if intense enough may ignite nearby property. See Chemistry of a Candle. See Illustration.

From observations, temperatures in very large fires average slightly over 2000 deg. F.

TEMPERING STEEL TOOLS—The tools are heated to white heat in furnaces, plunged into cold water, then reheated and plunged into fish oil.

TEMPLATE—An iron plate inserted in a wall on which the floor beams rest to distribute the load over a wider area.

TEMPLET—The outline of a moulding cut out of wood or sheet iron.

TEMPORARY KEROSENE OIL BURNERS (in fire boxes of coal stoves)—See Kerosene Burners.

TENEMENTS—Buildings classed as tenements are occupied by three or more families. The New York City law states that in rooming houses or other buildings occupied by more than two families there shall be no cooking unless the buildings are classed as tenements. This is to offset the number of fires due to "light housekeeping" in theatrical or other rooming houses. See Apartments.

TENON—A projecting tongue fitting into a corresponding cavity called a mortise.

TENONING MACHINES—Woodworking machines; produce considerable refuse.

TENSILE STRESSES tend to pull fibres of **materials** apart.

TENSION—See Compression.

TERCERA—A roofing compound made of chalk, tar and sand.

TERPENES—Volatile oils of coniferous resins.

TERRA COTTA—A fine quality of clay. The highly ornamental terra-cotta fronts of buildings are easily damaged by fire. Porous terra-cotta tile, used in building construction, is porous as compared to hard or dense tile. Sawdust is used in its manufacture which burns out leaving pores. Under intense heat the faces of terra-cotta tile blocks crack badly and fall away. See Tile Works.

TERRORALL (a recent discovery)—High explosive, more violent than T. N. T.

TESSELATED FLOOR—One formed of small blocks of wood or mosaic work.

TEXACO SPIRITS—A benzine substitute, classed as non-volatile.

TEXAS—A large frame roof structure or room, smaller in area than the roof itself, having one or more stories in it. Sometimes called a lantern.

TEXENE—A benzine substitute, class non-volatile.

THATCH ROOFS—Consist of bundles of wheat straw. Used for decorative purposes on summer cottages.

THEATERS (Stage Building)—Usually a high one-story building equal to 6 stories, with a deep basement; walls should be of brick or concrete at least 16 inches thick, parapetted and coped. The roof should have a steel truss with steel beams and with either brick or terra-cotta arches, spanned about 5 feet. The roof topping should be tile or plastic slate, the cornice brick or tile, and the windows of wired glass in hollow metal sash and frames; shutters, if any, to be standard lock-jointed. The stage floor in wings each side of stage to be of brick, tile or concrete arch, supported by protected iron columns or brick walls. Wood flooring is permitted only on the working part of the stage (center). The fly galleries, which are located at the sides and over the stage, should be constructed of steel beams and fireproof arches. These are used to handle the drops, etc., and are at quite an elevation above the stage floor. The painters' bridge is always located against the rear wall of the stage, connecting the fly galleries. This should be of steel slats laid about 2 inches apart. Above the fly galleries, about 5 feet under the roof is the gridiron (sometimes called rigging loft), built entirely across the stage.

Proscenium Wall—This separates the real hazard of a

Model Theater, Showing Fire Prevention Methods.

theater from the auditorium section. The proscenium wall (between the stage and auditorium) should be built of brick walls, thickness the same as the outside walls, never less than 12 inches, with 4-inch pilasters, and should extend the entire width of building. It must start at the ground, and extend at least 4 feet above the auditorium roof. If stage building is the highest, wall should extend 4 feet above the same. The steel girder over the proscenium opening must be protected with at least 2 inches of portland cement concrete. There must be a relieving arch in the proscenium wall over the girder. This is compulsory as it relieves the weight of the wall resting on said girder. The proscenium wall under the stage should extend to the under part of the stage flooring level, or flooring should be cut away the width of the curtain and filled in with concrete. This would form a complete separation of the stage floor from the apron. The only openings allowed in the proscenium wall should be the curtain opening and not more than two others, to be located either below the stage level, or one on either side of the stage on first floor; no opening of any kind should be permitted above the first floor. Openings are not to exceed 21 square feet, each with 3-inch standard double lock-jointed, tin-clad fire door on each side of the wall. Only one standard automatic fire door is required at openings to musicians' pit. The proscenium frame should be of non-combustible material, i. e., wire lath or plaster, stucco or concrete.

Skylights over stage—Thin glass on metal frame skylight, at least one-eighth the stage area should be installed. To be fitted with rolling sash and glazed, glass ⅛ inch thick and no one to exceed 300 square inches. Rolling sash should be fitted with brass wheels not less than 2½ inches in diameter; the latter should roll on brass plate on iron frame extending entire length of sash. The skylight must be set on curb so that the lowest portion of the tracks will be not less than 12 inches above the roof. The angle of the skylight frame to be on basis of 1 inch rise to 1 foot length. The skylights to be constructed as to open instantly on the cutting or burning of a hempen cord which should be arranged to hold the skylight closed. The said ropes should come together at the first fly gallery by iron triangle and then by single rope directly under skylight to stage floor. Skylight frames to close under metal hood at top, sides and bottom with metal aprons lapping 4 inches downward to prevent the elements lodging on same. See Asbestos Theatre Curtains.—Dominge "Weekly Underwriter."

THEATRICAL TENANTS—Usually not attractive unless well known and at the top in their profession. See Actors; see Furnished Room Houses.

THERMIT—Pulverized aluminum for welding; inflammable. See Gas Evolution.

THERMOSTAT—A self-acting apparatus for regulating temperatures by the unequal expansion of different metals by heat. See Automatic Alarm.

THIMBLE (sometimes called a "sleeve")—Perforated or plain, single or double pipe. It is used for fire protection when placed about a smoke pipe which passes through a partition or roof. Should be eighteen to thirty-six inches larger in diameter than the pipe enclosed.

THORIUM—A powder, metallic in nature, obtained by smelting process from a mineral known as monozite. Reclaiming thorium from discarded mantles or clippings from new mantles. They are very brittle and are received from concerns who make a business of collecting them. The mantle dust is washed and filtered in water in stone tubs, then boiled in thin solution of sulphuric acid and water, then treated with pickling solution of anhydrous ammonia, sulphuric, acetic or nitric acid. Ammonia is added to crystallize the sediment. Product is then in crystal form, put in porcelain cups and dried over gas burner. Gas heat is used for boiling and drying cups. Storage of acids important.

THREAD WORKS—The thread is spun at spinning mills and skeined. It is received in this form at the ordinary thread mill where it is wound on spools. The spools are either wood or "tubes" made of cardboard. Cotton thread is "silk finished" on a "dressing-machine." The thread is on reels on a frame, drawn through a sizing tank, then over a hair-covered, steam-heated iron drum which dries and polishes the thread, which is respooled. The sizing is made of gelatine or glue, borax, dextrine, starch, water, cocoanut or other similar oil. The sizing kettle should be steam-heated. The steam pipes at machine are apt to become covered with fine dust or "fly" from the thread and should be cleaned often.

THROWSTER—One who throws, twists or winds silk.

TIE-BEAMS—Ties that are also subjected to a transverse strain.

TIGERS—See Plush.

TILE WORKS—In brick and tile works, driers about 6 feet high, 8 feet wide and 100 feet long are used, built of brick and iron frame, heated by furnace at one end and below level of flooring or by heat passing off from kilns. Tile or brick is put on boards, called "pallets," placed on racks on cars, and run slowly through this tunnel. Fires are caused here by racks becoming very dry; alternating moisture and heat, and the rapid absorption causes the wood to ignite spontaneously. The lowest pallet becomes heated very rapidly.

TILLS as applied to stocks refer to wooden drawers or bins.

TIMBER—Heavy timber resists fire better than small iron columns. When superficially charred, the coating does not necessarily weaken the timber.

TIN—Recovering tin from used cans. An air-tight masonry room is filled with cans, and warm chlorine gas forced into the room, which unites with tin and forms tin chloride (highly volatile). The gaseous mixture, (free chlorine, air and vapor of tin chloride) passes through a condenser where the tin chloride is separated from the other gases, and by a chemical means, pure tin is precipitated.

I. C. Tin—This term is used to denote the covering to lock-jointed fire doors. I, C. tin is charcoal iron, i. e., iron with the charcoal removed.

In sheets, tin will sustain considerable water damage unless each sheet is thoroughly dried immediately after becoming wet.

TIN-CLAD FIRE DOORS—See Standard Fire Doors.

TINCTURE OF IRON and diluted aqua regia, sometimes mixed as a tonic, gives off an explosive gas which has been known to shatter the bottle.

TINFOIL—Melted pig lead, antimony, and block tin. The alloy is cast in slabs, and rolled out in plates or sheets. The machinery consists of furnaces, heavy and light rolling-machines and cutters, presses for coloring and printing.

TIN PLATE consists of iron or steel rolled into very thin sheets, coated with a composition of tin and lead.

TINSMITHS have caused fires in buildings by leaving gasoline torches unattended when lighted. In shops, may use gas-heated soldering mufflers, gasoline torches, sheet-metal cutters; paint.

TITAN POWDER—A form of dynamite.

TOBACCO—As a general rule tobacco is very susceptible to smoke and water. Some tobaccos offer practically no salvage as in the case of Sumatra leaf. Havanna filler is tougher and offers more salvage than most other leaves. The damaged leaves, however, have some little value as fertilizer.

At a recent fire, in a burlap bag risk adjoining a tobacco warehouse, tons of water were poured to drown the fire. The moisture penetrated the walls of the warehouse and a large loss was paid on tobacco. Tobacco should not be stored in basements against the walls of the building. See Cigarette Factories; see Tar Paper Manufacturing.

TOILET ARTICLES AND PREPARATIONS—Work consists of making cosmetics, face creams, pomades, nail buffers, nail polish, wood, celluloid or metal articles and packing powders. Use cologne spirits, alcohol, glycerine, Russian white oil, vaseline, petrolatum, vegetable oils, and waxes and clay. Hazards of woodworking, metal working, celluloid working, powder grinders, sifters and mixers; stoves for wax and oil heating, benzine for cleaning metal parts, painting and varnishing wooden parts.

TOLUENE—Coal tar distillate, boils at 230 deg. F. Vapor very inflammable, smells like benzine, but not as dangerous to handle. Solvent for fats, rubber and resins.

TOLUOL—Is a chemical substance. It is the basis of the explosive called tri-nitrotoluol, more familiarly known as T. N. T. The Ordnance Department of the United States Army says that this is the best explosive for our use in the war, as it is manufactured and transported with comparative safety and is a very effective destructive agent.

The chief source of toluol are the retorts of the gas companies throughout the country.

So great is the demand that steps are being taken to begin

the recovery of toluol from every gas plant in the United States.

What that means is vital. Toluol to-day is what gunpowder was yesterday. See Toluene.

TOOLS AND INSTRUMENTS of all kinds, if polished, are easily damaged by water. Their value, as far as sale is concerned, is thereby lessened. See Hardware; see Cutlery.

TOPOGRAPHY OF LAND—Very important to the Underwriter in considering surburban or "out of town" properties. All hilly or inaccessible sections should be noted with advices as to whether fire apparatus can reach the risk and fire hydrants adequate, also kind and condition of roads.

TOW—After such fibres as hemp, jute and the like, are put through the cleaning process, the residues left are known as tow, a ligneous product used by upholsterers. Tow is dangerous inasmuch as it will glimmer at about 257 deg. F. and, therefore one of the most easily kindled of fibres. This material in large piles is apt to give off certain gases during storage, which gases when mixed with dust and ignited by contact with a flame produce a violent explosion.

TOY CAPS consist of small portions of a mixture of antimony, sulphide, red phosphorous and postassium chlorate between two layers of paper. They do not ignite spontaneously.

TOY TORPEDOES—Contain red phosphorus and chlorates.

TOYS, (metal)—Manufacturing machine shop hazard with numerous heavy and light stamping presses, cheap paints, soldering, lacquering and japanning. See Celluloid.

TRACK TORPEDOES—Consist of hollow discs filled with a mixture of sulphur, potassium chlorate and sand or gravel.

TRADE NAMES often hide the identity of the owners who may have bad fire record or poor financial record.

TRADE REPORTS—These reports usually assist the Underwriter or Examiner to intelligently pass or reject a line. They usually give a brief outline of an assured's business career including failures, antecedents, fires, standing in the trade and credit. See Blank Rating; also Branch Stores and Mercantile Reports.

TRAIL—The pipe from the reservoir to the intake of pump; should not be over 25 feet long.

TRANSEPT—One of the lateral members or projections between the nave and the choir of a church.

TRANSFORMER—A device acting by induction to lower or raise the voltage of an electric circuit.

TRANSIT CLAUSE—This clause covers the goods being brought to or from lower floors of a fireproof building to those occupied by the assured. When writing insurance covering contents of a fireproof building (unless sole tenant), underwriters require the floors on which the merchandise is located to be stipulated in the policy.

TRANSLUCENT FABRIC—Is a wire gauge cloth covered by a layer of solidified linseed oil which penetrates between the meshes. Used for skylights. Process consists of dipping the wire fabric several times into linseed oil until covered to the required thickness.

TRANSOM—A beam over the opening for a door. Transom light is the glass window above.

TRANSPARENT LEATHER—Ordinary skins are shaved, cleaned, stretched on frames and rubbed with glycerine, salicylic, picric and boric acids.

TRANSPARENT SOAP—Ordinary soap mixed in hot alcohol.

TRANSVERSE SECTION—A drawing showing a section across the object.

TRAPPED—A floor opening is trapped when it has a door which can be raised or lowered so as to completely close the opening. Automatic traps are those held open by rope and fusible link.

TRAP-ROCK—On account of its strength and its fire-resisting properties, is considered the best of the stones for use as aggregate in concrete making.

TREATY COMPANIES—Re-insurance companies who by agreement accept a percentage of lines taken by a company on any and all kinds of risks.

TRESTLE—A braced framework for supporting sprinkler or water tanks, stringers of bridges, etc.

TRIATOMIC ALCOHOL—Glycerine.

TRIM—Woodwork used for wood finish. It is now being replaced by metal-covered or kalameined-covered wood. Wood trim, in fireproof office buildings tends to cause a fire to spread.

TRIMMER—A short cross timber framed into two joists to sustain the ends of intermediate joints. Example—trimmer in arch so as to prevent joists from entering the chimney breast.

TRIMMINGS—Most stocks may contain bright colors which run when wet or the goods may be drawn entirely out of shape. Very susceptible.

TRI-NITRATING is a very hazardous process.

TRINITRO BENZOL, compound, when dry is a high explosive. When wet with not less than 20 per cent. water and in water-proof containers, may be shipped as inflammable solid.

TRINITROPHENOL (or picric acid)—A very powerful explosive used in military work under the name of Melinite, Lyddite or Shimmse. (See Nitro Benzole.)

TRINITROTOLUOL (T. N. T.)—A pale, yellowish finely crystallized substance somewhat resembling brick dust or powdered rosin, made by treating toluol, one of the lightest distillates of coal tar with strong nitric acid in three successive operations. It takes fire and burns at about 480 deg. F. When heated by a fire it may explode with tremendous violence. (W. D. Grier.)

TRIPOLI—Buffing wax, composed of decomposed silica, iron oxide, paraffine, mineral colors, rosin, lamp-black, Vienna lime. This lime is unslaked lime with 40 per cent. magnesia, and is not dangerous.

TROCHAS SHELLS are imported from Fiji Islands; used for making buttons.

TROTTER OIL—Made by boiling sheep feet, called hair oil.

TRUNKS AND BAGS, (manufacturing)—Use wood, leather, imitation leather, fibreboard or fibre for covering.

Woodworking hazard, glue heating, cabinet work, caul boxes, dry-rooms, veneering; enamelling, japanning, painting, varnishing, using benzine as thinner; metal working, soldering. Celluloid articles for trunk accessories. Shops are crowded, as a rule. Fire record of class is poor.

TRUSS—Timbers assembled for supporting purposes.

TUMBLER (for polishing metal or other wear) is usually a barrel in a horizontal position on an axis with sawdust, carborundum or sand inside.

TUNG OIL—See Chinese Oil.

TUNGSTATES of sodium, potassium and molybdenum are used for fireproofing inflammable material.

TUNGSTEN—A heavy steel-gray metallic element. Used extensively in making incandescent lamps. It is a deposit in rock formation. It is blended with steel for use in armorplate and projectiles; as a mordant in dyeing; calico printing; fireproofing vegetable fibres; as an alloy with aluminum, copper, nickel, titanium or zirconium; as filaments for electric lamps.

TURKISH AND OTHER BATHS—The setting of boiler, which is usually high pressure, is important, also clearance of all woodwork around pipes. Majority of buildings are converted dwellings or of similar construction, divided into many small rooms. Hazards are swinging gas brackets, portable gas radiators, smoking by patrons; dormitories.

TURNOVER—A business term applying to the value of the produce sold.

TURPENTINE—Distilled from crude resin, the sap of fir or pine trees. Flashes at 103 or 104 deg. F. When brought in contact with a mixture of muriatic or nitric and sulphuric acids it TAKES FIRE. Adulterated with crude petroleum and benzine.

An odorless turpentine has been produced from sulphate turpentine, a product in the manufacture of sulphate pulp. Substitute turpentines are usually petroleum distillates with a flash point below 80 deg. F.

TURPENTINE (Mineral)—The spirit or most volatile part of the native rock oils, or from artificial paraffine prepared from coal and shales. Very volatile.

TURPENTINE OIL—Obtained from the resinous exudations from the wood, bark or leaves of pine or fir trees. It is volatile, giving off inflammable vapors at about 95 deg. F. Burns with a smoky flame because it contains considerable carbon.

TURPENTINE TANKS—Several fires have occurred where tanks were being filled with turpentine which was being poured through a brass wire strainer, probably from static electricity. See Static Electricity; see Oil Tanks.

TURPENTOLE—Distilled from paraffine; highly inflammable spirit.

TURPINO SPIRITS—Flash 112 deg. F.; an acceptable benzine substitute.

TURPO SPIRITS—Flashes at 98½ deg. F. by open cup test. Classed as volatile and inflammable.

TURPOZINE—A substitute for turpentine; has a high flash point. Classed as non-volatile.

TURPSITINE—Flash 105 deg. F. Classed as non-volatile.

TUXY—The thin ribbon which contains the cordage fibre is known as the tuxy.

TWIN-BEAMS—Two beams of same dimensions laid side by side on edge.

TWIN-GIRDER—Same as twin-beam, but larger.

TWO-WAY HYDRANT OR FIREPLUG—One which has two hose connections. See Siamese.

TYPE-CLEANING COMPOUNDS—None but approved makes should be used. Many contain naphtha.

TYPEWRITER INKS, CARBON PAPER AND RIBBON—Ink factory hazard. Grinding mills for ink, steam kettles, laboratory testing, mills, mixers. Use lard oil, cottonseed oil, alcohol, benzine, sulphuric and nitric acids, etc. Ribbon-winding wheels and eyeletting machines, ribbon inkers (cold), knitting, looms for weaving, steam baths, drying machines (gas heat), singeing machines (gas blow-pipe arrangement), extractor, steam-heated rolling-machines. See Carbon Paper.

U

UMBRELLA MANUFACTURING—Work consists of making sticks or handles, wire ribs, cementing handles on sticks and covering the frame with fabric. Handle and stick-making involves wood and metal-working and silversmith work. The handles are cemented on sticks with canauba wax, varnished, and the metal parts plated and buffed. The fabric is sewed by hand or power-machines. Sometimes use benzine for removing spots from fabric. Write this class cautiously.

UNBROKEN AREA—An area with no subdivision walls or fire-resistive partitions, and where fire could have a full sweep. See Area of a Building.

UNDERGROUND WORK—See Contractors.

UNDERMINE—To excavate beneath anything. This work is going on continually in subway-building.

UNDER-PIN—Add to the height of a wall already constructed by excavating and building beneath. Also to introduce additional support of any kind beneath anything already completed. See Builder's Risk.

UNDERTAKERS—Good risks, if well established. Inspectors should report on casket-lining, stuffing, embalming and varnishing. They use a small amount of muriatic, acetic and sulphuric acids, alcohol, and formaldehyde in embalming work.

UNDERWRITER—One who authorizes the lines the company will accept, and passes on the business taken by the countermen. Should be thoroughly acquainted with construction, hazards and losses. See Map Clerk.

UNDERWRITERS' LABORATORIES—Tests are made to establish the relative fire strength of materials and devices for insurance purposes. It is an institution supported by stock fire insurance companies of the United States. Inspection is also made at the shops of manufacturers and labels issued by the Underwriters' Laboratories as evidence of compliance with standards are affixed to the appliances.

UNDERWRITING—Increase of lines and resulting premium, rather than indiscriminate cancellations, is what pays. An ideal risk is scarce, and with proper regard of hazard and line, the best underwriter is one who uses good judgment in selection rather than wholesale declinations. Look at the risk from the average of its class.

Successful underwriting requires knowledge of hazards and construction from personal inspection, familiarity with local conditions, fire and loss costs of various classes of risks, the adequacy of rates, trade conditions, and common sense.

Conditions and hazards in all manufacturing processes change, usually for the better, as years advance and a more intimate knowledge is had, and a more minute study of processes is made, to reduce producing costs. Probably the best example of this is in the shoe industry. Only a short time ago this class was tabooed by most underwriters on account of the fire record of the class. The manufacturers were charged very high rates and only small lines were written by individual companies. With increased knowledge as to hazards, such as the handling of rubber cement and benzine, cutting-board scrapings, etc., the hazards and also the fire loss and rates were greatly reduced. Breweries and woodworkers were in the same class. They now show a profit in underwriting. See Upper Floor Contents; also Accommodation Line; see Authorizations; also Average Risk.

UNDISCLOSED INTERESTS, such as "for account of whom it may concern," etc., should always be investigated before line is passed. See Enemy Alien.

UNEARNED PREMIUM—That portion of the premium which is returned to the insured in case of cancellation of the policy. It represents the premium for interim between the date of cancellation and date of expiration of the policy.

UNIT SYSTEM of construction is making each building and each floor of each building a separate fire risk.

UNIVERSAL MACHINE—A woodworking machine of patented type capable of performing different kinds of work.

In general, they are a combination of jointers and borers with mandrels for saws. Produce considerable refuse and should have blower attachments.

UNOCCUPIED OR VACANT BUILDINGS. Such buildings rapidly depreciate in value. Those without caretakers, especially if located outside of protection, are not considered favorably by most companies. Tramps or mischievous boys may gain access and set fire to the building. See Vacancy.

UNPROTECTED IRON—See Steel (for protection).

UPPER FLOOR CONTENTS—Those above the reach of fire departments should be written cautiously. Hose streams can hardly be expected to be effective above the sixth floor, consequently firemen usually rely on the standpipe system in the building for upper floor fires. See Stocks.

USNIC ACID—A yellow dye material.

USE AND OCCUPANCY INSURANCE is usually intended to protect the assured against the loss of the use of premises, also to cover net annual profits, general maintenance cost to the extent of taxes, heating and lighting, and legal liability for royalties and salaries or wages which may not be discontinued by reason of an interruption of business by fire. This class of business is intended for manufacturing concerns; mercantile establishments usually carry profit insurance. Use and occupancy insurance is somewhat difficult to understand unless you make a specialty of this form of coverage. It is desirable that the words "not exceeding" appear before the amount per day to be agreed upon so that the form will not be a "valued" one; also that the words "if the property mentioned is destroyed by fire" instead of "if the firm is destroyed by fire." The reason for the above being to cover only the property mentioned in the policy, as the firm may have a fire in another location which would in turn affect their use and occupancy. Should the assured, while their building is untenantable as the result of fire, conduct their business at another location the loss to the insurance company would be correspondingly less, because the profits made by the assured at their temporary quarters could be deducted when final adjustment is made, and this feature should be incorporated in policy forms.

It is well to avoid risks that are not well established and managed or those manufacturing "fads" or catering to a temporary trade. Summer resort hotels, concessions at summer parks, seasonable business, hotels located on roads which are becoming less popular with motorists or situated in localities which have lost their prestige are poor for use and occupancy insurance. In the case of seasonable trades, the fire may occur during a dull season and the fire damage be entirely repaired before the busy season has resumed. If the concern carries use and occupancy insurance, the companies might be obliged to pay the claim even though no actual loss through use and occupancy had resulted. In seasonable risks, some forms specify a larger amount for busy months and only a nominal amount for dull months. The following would be a good use and occupancy proposition: A clock factory of good mill construction, modern machinery, raw materials being mainly brass goods, and easily obtainable; duplicate power system; boilers in fireproof section cutoff by approved fire doors. A line of $24,000 insurance offered would be divided by 300 working days which equals $80 per day. On account of the good construction and splendid arrangement of the factory with duplicate power plant, cutoff boiler room, and raw materials easily obtainable, this plant would probably be in operation again inside of 30 days.

In some cases the building and contents of a plant may not be desirable as a fire risk and yet may be a good use and occupancy risk; as for instance, a large one-story frame planing mill would not appeal to most underwriters as a fire risk on account of probably suffering a total loss and yet the use and occupancy might only suffer a 20 per cent. loss. The building could be erected and all machinery, being modern and purchasable near the risk, be set up inside of two months. The following are examples of poor use and occupancy propositions: $200 a day on use and occupancy of a hotel having 150 rooms at $2 per room, decline unless the amount is $300 a day, i. e., 150 times $2.00 for each room. Another case of note was the recent fire in a lace paper factory in Brooklyn where a small fire put the boiler and engine room and a few of the imported dies out of commission, with the result that the manufacturing was stopped for about two months. The loss on the building and contents did not amount to over $1,000, while the use and occupancy loss amounted to eight times that figure. Use and occupancy insurance is written very cautionsly during war times on account of shortage of labor and inability to receive raw materials and machinery except after considerable delay.

The principal features to be considered are construction; whether sprinklered or not, nature of occupancy; average daily output, idle periods, market favorable for steady operation, future outlook, would assured hasten to resume operations, arrangement for any other plant to produce output, special processes, processes in duplicate, specially made or foreign machinery or dies, source of raw materials, power plant in duplicate, would a small fire cripple entire plant or could part of the work continue, length of time it would take to replace any portion of plant.

Only competent underwriters should accept Use and Occupancy business.

William H. Gartside of the National Fire in a recent address to the Examiners' Club of Chicago—"When we cover the use and occupancy of a manufacturing plant," said Mr. Gartside, "we are covering a more or less intangible something, the characteristics and features of which are not as plain to the underwriters as are the physical aspects of the risk. The value of a building, machinery and stock may be fairly judged from an inspection, but who can tell what the value of the plant is as a producer?

"Two plants with physical values approximately the same may vary widely from the standpoint of productivity or profit, and in a large degree it is necessary to rely on the owner's figures as to the use and occupancy value.

"That is one reason why some companies restrict their lines to well-established firms and individuals of good financial standing who have demonstrated their ability to conduct their business profitably."

Increases the Moral Hazard—He thinks that use and occupancy insurance is more apt to increase than decrease the moral hazard. It is human nature to lose the sense of responsibility as the penalty for failure to exercise that sense lessens, and the man who is so completely insured that he cannot lose by any fire is likely to be less vigilant than the man who will have a material loss regardless of the amount of insurance collected.

V

VACANCY—A building is vacant when all movable property has been removed except that belonging to the building proper. It is unoccupied when no one is living in it (in case of a dwelling), even if some of the furniture remains or building is in hands of a caretaker. Vacant buildings should always be inspected to see if they are clean and in charge of a watchman. When located outside of protection, they are not considered attractive fire risks. A burglar hazard is present when no watchman is employed. Thieves remove lead pipe and fittings, brass, etc., and sometimes rig up a melting furnace by connecting to the gas supply pipe with a rubber tube. See Unoccupied or Vacant Buildings.

VACANT LOTS (not enclosed) are not a serious menace to surrounding property if kept clean. Those enclosed or partly enclosed by fences are usually "hangouts" for boys and men who are apt to commit acts of depredation, such as building bon-fires, etc. Where lots adjoin tenements, they are apt to become the depository of rubbish thrown by tenants. Fires communicate to cellars of risks through areaway windows or doors. See Wagons; also Rear Yards.

VACUUM OIL—See Hydrocarbon.

VALERIANIC ACID—A colorless, oily liquid, not inflammable.

VALLEY—The space between two inclined sides of a roof.

VALUATION OF BUILDINGS—Thumb rule for finding the approximate valuation of buildings in normal times. The following figures should be increased approximately 30 per cent. at the present time.

Frame, 10 to 15 cents per cubic foot.

Brick, 18 to 25 cents per cubic foot (stores and dwellings, 6 stories or under).

Brick, 18 to 20 cents per cubic foot (lofts).

Fireproof, 25 to 30 cents per cubic foot (lofts).

Fireproof, 30 to 40 cents per cubic foot (theaters).

Fireproof, 35 to 50 cents per cubic foot (apartment houses, hotels, office buildings).

Example: A brick store and dwelling. Front, 36 feet multiplied by 85 feet (depth) equals 3060 square feet, times height, 60 feet (10 feet to a story including basement of 5-story building), equals 18360 cubic feet. At 18 cents per cubic foot, the cost would be $33,048. Note—In New York City, "New Law" tenements may occupy not over 85 per cent of area of building lot, which is usually 100 feet deep; hence 85 feet depth as above. See Depreciation; also Salvage.

VALUE OF A LEASE—See Leasehold Insurance.

VALUED POLICY—A contract where no co-insurance is required and the company accepts the amount of insurance as the value of the property. Horses and paintings are usually written under a valued form. See Profits.

VALUES—One of the important features to be ascertained before the underwriter assumes liability on a risk.

VALUES OF BUILDINGS—When prices of building materials rise and thereby increase the cost of replacing same in case of fire, the value of buildings increase and the insurance should be increased proportionately to maintain the ratio to co-insurance. See Depreciation; see Salvage.

VALVES—Various devices for permitting or stopping at pleasure the flow of water, steam, gas, etc.

Valve, O. S. & Y. (meaning outside screw and yoke)—The approved gate valve for sprinkler equipments. The distance the stem projects indicates at a glance exactly the distance it is open. See Sprinklers; see Gate Valve.

Valves (control)—On a sprinkler equipment should be kept open with a leather strap, with ends sealed so that the valve cannot be closed without breaking the seal. They are placed on feed lines on each floor or each section of a risk, so that water can be shut off from small areas in case of accident.

VANADIUM STEEL is steel that has been treated with vanadium—a semi-rare mineral, which washes the molten steel of its impurities, bringing the molecules closer together, giving them greater adhesiveness and making the resultant product infinitely tougher and stronger.

VAPOR-PROOF GLOBES—See Open Arc-lights.

VARIABLE PRESSURE ALARM VALVE (working of) When the water flows just slightly, the check valve partly rises and some of the water flows through a small pipe connected to a long receptable known as a "niggerhead" chamber. If this is only a temporary flow the water will only go about one-half or one-quarter way up this chamber and will find its way out of the chamber by means of a disk valve; but should the check valve completely open (as in case of fire) the water will immediately fill the chamber and travel up to the "niggerhead" at top and bend the diaphragm, causing an electrical circuit, thereby sending in an alarm to headquarters or allowing water to ring the water motor alarm and at the same time the diaphragm will close the drip valve. See Sprinkler Equipment.

VARIETY STORES—Stock is very susceptible. Considerable packing material is used. Financial standing of firms is important, as they cannot buy to advantage in the open market in competition with large firms. See Five and Ten-Cent Stores.

VARNISH is composed of three essential ingredients: Gum to give hardness and lustre, oil to impart elasticity, a solvent or thinner to keep it in a liquid state and dryer usually composed of lead and manganese. It is invariably added to the oil before the varnish is made and varies according to the kind necessary to produce required results. Fossil gums are used for the best varnishes; and are the hardened sap of trees that lived thousands of years ago. The gum known as kauri is the chief and most widely used. The oils for varnish are made chiefly of linseed and china oils, specially prepared and well aged. The solvent is chiefly turpentine. **In the manufacture of varnish,** the varnish-maker first melts the gum over a coke fire in a copper kettle. When the gum is properly melted, the oil which is hot having been separately heated, is added. After adding the oil, the gum and oil are heated together until the two are uniformly combined, when the kettle is withdrawn from the fire. The kettle is next taken to the thinning room where the mixture is allowed to cool to a certain temperature and the thinner (benzine or turpentine) or solvent added (called reducing). After thinning, the varnish is pumped through a pipe to a vat or cooler where, in addition to cooling, it settles and becomes clearer. From the cooler the varnish is passed through a filter press, which removes all the dirt and foreign matter. The varnish is next pumped to the ageing tanks where it is allowed to thoroughly ripen. This ageing makes the varnish bright and clear. Filter cloths are cleaned with caustic soda, but sometimes with benzine. Filter cloths in piles, unless clean, might ignite spontaneously.—Pratt and Lambert.

Some varnishes have a flash point below 80 deg. F.

Spirit Varnish is made by dissolving resin in methyllated spirit or other volatile solvent.

VARNISH AND PAINT REMOVERS—Consist of a wax dissolved in benzol and gelatinized by an alcoholic or ketonic body, usually wood alcohol. Flash point same as gasoline, but on account of wax used (to prevent evaporation) the flash point is not considered as dangerous except when in use by workmen.

VARNISH WORKS—If a fire occurs in the boiling house, the doors opposite the fires should be opened. This will create a draft, which will suck the flames up the brick stacks and prevent the fire spreading to the balance of the plant. If the thinning and boiling buildings are detached, without communication, the class ought to be profitable.

VARNOLENE—A benzine substitute approved by Underwriters.

VAULT—A compartment of brick, concrete or similar material used for storage of records, paints, etc. See Bank Vaults.

VAULT LIGHTS—Usually small, heavy bull's-eye glass in heavy iron frames.

VAULTS FOR SHAVINGS or other refuse should be of fireproof construction and located outside of main building with communicating openings as small as possible. Doors to same should be standard, tight-fitting and automatically arranged. See Shaving Vault; also Direct Feed.

VEGETABLE ALBUMEN, if wet will form a jelly like the white of an egg. Unless immediately dried will be total loss. Used chiefly in medicine.

VEGETABLE IVORY—Made from Tanqua nuts. Used mainly for making buttons.

VEGETABLE OILS are extracted by hydraulic pressure after cooking, or by what is known as the bisulphide of carbon or mineral naphtha process. Naphtha is put in a steam-heated receptacle with the material which has been previously crushed. This digester is sealed up, allowed to remain for a while, the liquid is drawn off and the naphtha vapor passed out through a condenser. Electric lights and steam-heat should be used because in case of accident, the naphtha vapors may escape into the room and be ignited if any open flame is present. They are more hazardous than mineral oils as they have an affinity for oxygen and dry quicker by the absorption of the oxygen. Animal oil, unless rancid, is not apt to cause spontaneous combustion, but all oil-soaked substances should be treated as hazardous. See Mineral Oil.

Vegetable Waxes such as those extracted from candelila plant are being widely used. Candelila wax is used in making candles, phonograph records, wood and leather polishes, floor wax, varnish, linoleum, rubber compounds and celluloid, also for electrical insulating compounds.

VELLUM—Parchment made of suckling calves' hides.

VELOCITY—The rate of motion or the degree of quickness with which an object moves.

VELOCITY OF EXPLOSION—See Explosion and Explosive.

The heat and gas evolved are the two principal factors which govern the power of an explosive, i. e., the amount of work it can do in the way of displacing objects. But the time taken by the explosion is also a matter of great importance. The rate of explosion is measured by making a column of the explosive, confining it if necessary in a metal tube, and measuring the time that the explosive wave takes to travel a known distance. In black powder and similar nitrate mixtures the velocity of explosion is only a few hundred metres a second but with modern high explosives the velocity of detonation is from two to seven thousand metres a second. This naturally makes them much more violent and destructive. Explosives of the gunpowder type are used when earth or soft rock is to be blasted or when the material must not be broken up too much.—A. Marshall.

VELVET BEANS—A product of Florida, used as a forage crop and for fertilizer. A growing industry is that of converting the beans into meal. They are dried and ground in machines similar to a disc cottonseed huller, and also in a velvet bean "beater." The former cracks the pods and the latter cut them up. The meal is collected in hoppers, sacked and shipped. The machines used should have magnets to catch metallic substances. The beans do not burn readily and are only remotely subject to spontaneous combustion, whether whole or ground.

VELVETEENS are easily damaged by water.

VENEER—Made by sawing lumber into thin slices, or by turning off the veneer from short lengths of logs which have been previously soaked or steamed in vats. The lathes used in the latter process are of heavy type with automatic features for turning the log slowly and at the same time advancing the cutting blade against the log. Other processes may include gluing and pressing the veneer upon a backing, drying and filling, varnishing. The hazards are those of woodworking. Stocking susceptible to fire and water damage, as these elements will destroy or cause the veneer to warp.

VENTILATING SHAFTS—Should be enclosed in a standard manner, and have thin glass skylights. Those opening to toilets should have standard louvres. See Pipe Shafts; see Illustration on page 486.

VENTURES—See New Ventures.

VERANDAS—Enclosed porches if continuous along rows of buildings, act as communications.

VERMILLION—A red pigment consisting of powdered cinnabar, or red sulphate of mercury.

VIBRATION OF BUILDINGS—Buildings, large or small,

vibrate like a tuning fork whenever a heavy train passes by or a storm beats against the structure. Accidents from vibration are rare as it is well understood and guarded against. The most violent are felt in the low buildings rather than the

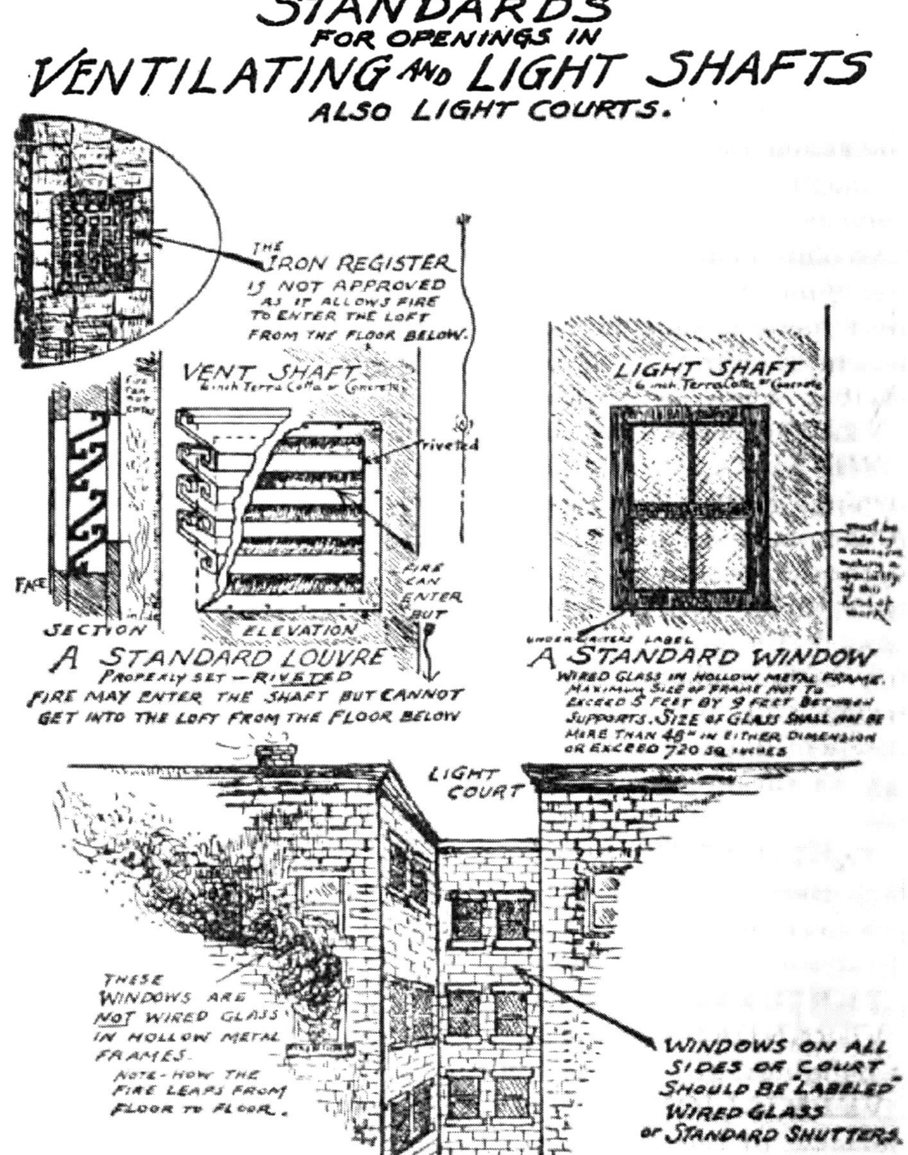

high ones, and, as a rule, those of solid construction with masonry walls and foundations. The pulsations are registered and recorded on a delicate instrument such as records earthquakes, a movement of 1-100 of an inch being noticeable.

VINEGAR (cider or apple)—The product made by the alcoholic and subsequent acetous fermentation of the juice of apples. Wine or grape vinegar, same as above, only made from the juice of grapes. Imitation vinegar consists of a diluted solution of acetic acid.

VINEGAR AND YEAST WORKS—They are usually combined processes. Yeast is made from grain, beet pulp, malt sprouts, corn sugar, beet meal and similar ingredients. They are milled, mashed, cooked, fermented, germinated, filtered, dried, pressed into cakes. Vinegar is fermented from spirits and beech shavings and such other ingredients as the manufacture may add. Hazards are in some respects similar to breweries, including malt milling. Twenty per cent. proof spirits are usually distilled from grain for use in the process. Incidental hazards of barrel painting and re-coopering. The alcohol stills require good ventilation to the outer air.

VISCOL—Used in shoe factories as rubber substitute. A water proof dressing for dressing leather. Thinned with petroleum oil or benzine. In liquid form classed as benzine hazard. Dipping should be done in detached building.

VISCOLOID—A trade name for celluloid.

VOLATILE ESSENTAL OILS—Are oils of turpentine, camphor and the like. See Essential Oils.

VOLATILE OILS—If in doubt as to whether an oil is volatile or not, place a small amount on the finger or hand. If it dries very quickly, consider it volatile. See Benzine or Gasoline.

VOLATILE SOLVENTS—Ether, carbon bisulphide, gasoline, acetone, benzol, flavoring or fruit ethers, ethyl chloride, naphtha, benzine.

The hazard depends largely on the flash point or temperature at which the volatile solvents begin to give off inflammable vapors. All the above named are highly inflammable and evolve inflammable vapors at temperatures from below freezing point up to 80 deg. F.

The less hazardous solvents amyl alcohol, fusel oil, wood-alcohol, grain alcohol, amyl acetate, turpentine and kerosene are all inflammable, and some of them have low flash points and are capable of generating inflammable vapors at temperatures of from 60 to 120 deg. F.—W. D. Grier.

VOLATILITY—A property of bodies by which they are disposed to assume the state of vapor and dissipate on the application of heat, whether natural or artificial.

VOLT—The electrical unit of pressure. See Amperes; also Electrical Terms.

VOMITORIES are short, intermediate exit passages connecting to the larger or main exitway. Used in theaters between main aisles of balconies to facilitate exit and for convenience.

VULCANIZERS—The same rule applies as to the setting of gas stoves. Gas heat is penalized, no matter how safely arranged, because gas heat at an appliance where rubber cement is used is considered dangerous. Steam heat is approved.

VULCANIZING—Cementing two or more pieces of rubber together to form a compact mass. High temperature steam or gas-heated machines of various designs are used.

W

WAFERS AND CONES (ice cream cones)—The hazards are gas-heated bakers, mixers, automatic wafer and cone-baking machines. The cones are made up in winter for summer trade. The largest stock is on hand in March. The busiest season January to March, but the plants start active production in October. The machines are of several types; flat-rotating, pan-revolving (operated by hand) sheet wafer, and large automatic cone bakers. The gas heat is directed on the moulds from inside burners. The dough is poured on the moulds, and baked in one revolution of the baker. An operator at each machine scrapes off the charred baked dough from the edges of the wafer or cone and the charred parts fall to the floor. In low setting bakers, the scraps accumulate under the baker and are frequently blazing piles. All baking machines should set on at least six inches of concrete. Baffle plates, although advocated by most rating bureaus, under machines, tend to bank up the burning scraps and should be omitted. Over the large bakers, there should be a metal ventilated hood, the same as over a range, to carry the heated air to the outside. Paper box making, machine shop for repairs, printing labels and pasting labels are incidental hazards. This class has a bad fire record.

WAFERS (cocoanut)—Hazards are similar to ordinary bakery. Glucose is heated in kettle with cocoanut, cooled on marble slab, toasted in gas or coal ovens. Note the kind of heat used for kettles and ovens.

WAGONS in open yards are good insurance if the yard is fenced in, and the neighborhood is free from rowdies. Open trucks are preferable to closed wagons because they offer no concealment to trespassers. See Vacant Lots.

WAINSCOT—A wood facing to walls in rooms, extending from floor.

WALLS—Several important considerations enter into the construction of walls. The first is the nature of occupancy of the structure bearing in mind that at some future time the occupancy may radically change. The wall must be sufficiently thick to safely carry a maximum live or dead load, to stand upright to resist wind pressure and vibration and form a solid fire wall especially where there is an adjoining building. See Fire Wall.

Walls—For the warehouse class of buildings should be common brick as follows: Twelve inches if not over 40 feet high. If over 40 feet high require 16 inches for first 40 feet, and 12 inches above up to a height of not exceeding 60 feet. If over 60 feet, 20 inches for 25 feet and 16 inches the balance up to 75 feet. If over 75 feet, 24 inches for 40 feet, then 20 inches for 35 feet, and 16 inches the balance up to 100 feet. If over 100 feet, 28 inches for 40 feet, then 24 inches for 35 feet, then 20 inches for 25 feet and 16 inches balance up to 125 feet. If over 125 feet, 32 inches for 30 feet, then 24 inches for 35 feet, then 20 inches for 35 feet and balance 16 inches to 150 feet high. See Bearing Wall.

WALL CHIMNEY—A chimney built into and forming part of a wall. See Bracket Chimney; also Corbel.

WALL COVERINGS—Some are made of oxidized linseed oil, Swedish clay, wood flour, chrome and earth colors, paraffine, lithopone, or similar materials. Mixed dry, passed through calender, spread over and pasted to paper backing. Surface is polished with linseed oil and turpentine.

WALL-HYDRANT or fire plug. One set against or close to a wall, connected with a supply pipe through or under the wall.

WALL PAPER DEALERS AND HANGERS—Busiest months, July to October. Unless stock is turned over annually, there is apt to be considerable shop-worn stock, and out-of-date patterns on hand.

WALL PAPER—Finishing Process—Paper is varnished in "varnishing and printing" machine by passing the paper over a rubber-covered drum, coated with benzine or turpentine-thinned varnish, which deposits a thin coat of varnish on the paper. Paper then passes by means of a traveling belt over steam pipes to dry, and carried in festoons a long distance, being thoroughly dried before being removed at far end. A ventilator, with a suction fan is located over the steam pipes, which sucks the benzine or turpentine vapors to the outer air. Static electricity is often produced in this process if paper is passed too close to the metal ventilator. The hazards consist of color-mixing, using clay, glue, lard and oil; drying and embossing. Inspectors should note color room, glue heaters, machine shop, sample book making, care of waste and storage of oils. Fires in this class are usually very severe.

WALL PLATE—Timber laid along the tops of walls for the roof trusses or rafters to rest upon so as to distribute their weight more equally upon the wall. See Template.

WALL SIZING—Consists of caustic soda, soda ash, tapioca flour, cornstarch, dextrine, neutral salts, gum arabic and dry soap powder. Grinding, mixing, sifting and packing are the important hazards.

WALNUTS—See Nuts.

"WAR CONDITIONS"—Constitute the great outstanding cause for the high loss record. These conditions must be classified as due to—

(a) Malice, to inflict damage from hostile motives or to cripple war supplies. This has been a very serious factor, affecting particularly grain depots, waterfront properties, lumber, tobacco, factory and warehouse risks.

(b) Fires occasioned by the high pressure under which the work of production and distribution has been rushed and which has been the direct cause of large factory and pier fires, including many sprinklered risks of large values. With this should be included the menace of employment of masses of untrained, inefficient help on technical processes.

(c) Fires and explosions resulting as an inevitable consequence of the handling of vast quantities of explosive and inflammable materials of which the Kingsland, N. J., and the Halifax explosions and conflagrations are typical instances. —(Frank Lock.) See Guards.

WAR RISK INSURANCE can be written under two forms, limited and broad. The limited form covers losses caused by war, invasion, insurrection, riot, civil war, civil commotion, including strikes, military or usurped power, bombardment and for explosion directly caused by any of the hazards mentioned. The broad forms affords protection against all of the hazards covered by explosion and war risk policies.

WAREHOUSE, PRIVATE—One where the contents are owned by an individual or a corporation who agrees to certain specifications laid down by local rating bureaus.

WAREHOUSES—Bonded warehouse is one where the goods are stored under government bond or control and from which goods cannot be removed until certain government requirements have been complied with. See Storage Warehouses. See Alphabetical List; see Fibre Warehouses; also Wharf Clause.

Listed Storage Stores are divided into two classes: fibre and non-fibre, a distinction made to denote those which store cotton and other vegetable fibres and those which do not. In turn, non-fibre warehouses are divided into stipulated and non-stipulated and chemical warehouses.

Stipulated Warehouse will not accept certain merchandise and chemicals. For instance, ammonia, benzine, chlorates, etc., must be stored in a non-stipulated store.

Non-stipulated warehouse will accept, in addition to what is allowed to be stored in a listed store, such chemicals and merchandise which is not allowed in a stipulated warehouse. Warehousemen sign an agreement stipulating that they will not store any fibre (in case of non-fibre warehouse) and to exclude from their premises explosives and all drugs of a poisonous or nauseous character. Non-stipulated warehouses may store any kind of goods except fibre. See Chemical Warehouses.

WARP in weaving is the threads which are extended lengthwise in the loom and crossed by the woof.

WASHING POWDERS usually contain soap powder, soda ash and fine sand.

WASH-TUBS—Usually made from soapstone, called Alberene (taken from the name of the town from which the stone is quarried).

WASTE (cotton) if clean, is not subject to spontaneous combustion. See Oily Waste.

WASTE CANS (for oily waste or rags) provide a metal can well riveted and with legs or rims holding bottom off the floor, and the cover with a short spring or bar to keep the lid off center so as to keep the can normally closed. For rubbish or ashes, provide a metal can with metal rim at bottom, so as to keep the base off the floor, and a metal cover.

WASTE-PAPER STOCKS are prolific fire breeders. A K. O. class with most insurance companies.

WATCHMAN AND CLOCK—Rounds are made hourly nights from 6 P. M. to 6 A. M. and during the day on Sundays, holidays, and all idle periods. The clock must be approved by the underwriters. Central station supervision preferred.

WATCH OIL—Obtained from the dolphin, walrus, blackfish, snuffer, or shark.

WATER—The total amount of water used in large fires is not as great as frequently thought. A fire, for example, requiring ten streams for five hours would use 750,000 gallons. However, the rate of draft for fire fighting is frequently high in comparison with the ordinary consumption. Three standard fire streams discharging 750 gallons per minute use water at a rate of a little more than a million gallons a day, and ten streams means a rate of flow of about three and one-half million gallons per twenty-four hours. Pipe sizes must, of course, be proportioned for the maximum rate of demand which any fire is likely to cause.—French. See Tables.

WATER CURTAINS—See Open Sprinklers.

WATER GAS—A process in which the main volume of gas, consisting of hydrogen, is taken out of the water. The process, in brief, is: Steam is passed through retorts filled with anthracite coal raised to a white heat by the air blast. In its passage it is decomposed and the gas coming from the pipes at the top consists of a mixture of hydrogen and carbon dioxide. This serves as the carrier for the true illuminating agents which are a comparatively small percentage of the entire volume, and these are combined by mingling with naphtha vapor. This mixture has now about the same composition as ordinary coal gas, but must be fixed—that is, made a staple compound by subjecting it to the effect of heat and cold. This is accomplished by conducting it through two series of pipes, surrounded in one case by cold running water and the other by steam. It is then purified in the same manner as mentioned. By passing it through a water-tower loosely filled with material such as charcoal, down through which water trickles as the gaseous vapor ascends, the ammonia is dissolved; then, passing it through thin layers of lime, the other main impurity, sulphureted hydrogen, is removed. It is then ready for distribution through the city.

WATER-HAMMER in water pipes may best be overcome by introducing devices which compel the slow opening and closing of cocks and valves.

WATER HEATERS—See Heaters.

WATER JACKET—A device to prevent combustibles from flowing on a naked flame. See Jacketed.

WATER PUTS OUT FIRE (HOW)—In order to understand this, we must first know what fire is and what keeps it burning.

Fire is a form of chemical combustion in which flames make their appearance. There may be combustion or burning without flame, although not without heat. When a body becomes heated from any cause and wastes away, turning into something else (as smoke or ashes), it is said to undergo combustion.

In the process of combustion or burning there must always be at least two things. First, there must be the combustible, and second, some supporter of combustion. When wood burns in the open air, the wood is the combustible and the air the supporter of combustion. The wood could not continue to burn if it were not surrounded by air. The air supplies the gas (oxygen) which is essential to the act of combustion.

Water in small quantities is of no use because the elements of water themselves are combustible (consisting of oxygen and hydrogen), but when poured in from large streams and falling in a deluge upon the flames, the heat of the latter is insufficient in quantity to rapidly turn the water into steam and then disassociate the oxygen and the hydrogen. Water has a very high specific heat, i. e., it takes a great amount of heat to change water from the cold liquid to the hot vaporous form which we call steam. The heat of the fire is swiftly devoured, so to speak, by the water falling upon it and absorbing it. The constant streams of water pouring in and the clouds of steam arising serve as a blanket (not itself combustible), which shuts off the air from the flames and thus prevents them from obtaining oxygen from the surrounding atmosphere as fuel as they did before. (Extracted from lecture by Prof. Garret P. Serviss.) See Water Pressure.

WATER MAINS should be laid in complete circuit and be of sufficient size, not less than 6 inches, to provide volume under such head or pressure as will insure the delivery of full streams at each outlet in the service with a loss of head of not over 10 to 12 pounds below normal pressure. Exposed water pipes in dwellings can be prevented from freezing by covering them an inch thick with a paste made of boiled starch and sawdust, using a hemp twine or similar cord as a binder, and then coating with tar. See Water Systems; see Dead Ends.

WATER PRESSURE—A cubic foot of sea water weighs 64 pounds. Each cubic foot may be regarded as standing on a base of one square foot. Therefore, the pressure at the base of a cubic foot of sea water is 64 pounds per square foot. A cubic foot of water having a base of one square foot must be one foot high. The pressure at its base (64 pounds per square foot) is, therefore, the same as the pressure which would be encountered at one foot below sea level.

One hundred and forty-four square inches make one square foot. A vertical column of water having a sectional area of 1 square inch would therefore weigh 1-144 as much as a column equally high, but having a section area of one square foot. Since the pressure per square foot is 64 pounds, the pressure per square inch is 1-144 of 64 = 64-144 = 4-9 = 0.44 pounds per square inch. At two feet below sea level, or double the depth, double the height and weight of water stands on each square inch, therefore the pressure is double, or 2 × 0.44 = 0.88 per square inch.

Each extra foot of depth adds an extra pressure of 0.44 pounds per square inch. To find the pressure at any depth, multiply the depth in feet by 0.44 pounds per square inch. —The Steamship. See Pressure.

How to determine the number of gallons of water discharged at a fire—Let us assume that a gravity tank is elevated 20 feet above the roof and the height of the tank is 12 feet and the building is six stories high.

The fire takes place on the second floor. Example:

	Feet.
Height of tank, full........................	12
Distance above roof........................	20
Height of sixth floor........................	12
Height of fifth floor........................	12
Height of fourth floor........................	11
Height of third flour........................	11
Height of second floor.... (at sprinkler head)	2
	80
To get the pressure at second floor, multiply elevation by........................	.434 *
Which equals........................	34.720 lbs.

Say pressure is 35 pounds. With Grinnel type "A" head 21 gallons of water per minute would be discharged. (Always find out type of head, as amount of discharge differs.) If 21 gallons of water per minute from each head, for two heads it would be 42 gallons, and if heads operated for ten minutes' duration there would be approximately 420 gallons of water discharged. See Water Puts Out Fire.

WATERPROOFING CARDBOARD OR PASTEBOARD—Paper is treated in nitric acid solution, then piled in sheets and placed in hydraulic press.

* See Pressure.

WATERPROOFING CONCRETE BUILDINGS—This subject has received great attention from architects and builders owing to the natural tendency of concrete to absorb moisture. One method, and perhaps the oldest, is the tar and asphalt method of coating either with or without a paper or fabric binding or reinforcement. This method is useful in most cases but could not be used to advantage on the outside surface of a sea wall or under similar conditions. On the outside surface of a building, or on a floor where acids or alkali liquids are used, the integral method might be employed. In substance, this method is the introduction of a waterproofing compound into the cement or concrete which does not hasten or retard the setting of the concrete but which tends to close up all pores or voids and thus render the concrete work a solid moisture resisting body. There are other methods employed by builders, and many patented compounds on the market; but all of them rely on the principle that there must be a continuous bond between the aggregates of the concrete of sufficient strength and durability to withstand the elements of time and weather.

WATERPROOFING PAPER—Paper is coated with a resinous soap, given bath of zinc chloride, pressed in rollers, washed, dried, coated with paraffine, then run through a calender.

WATER SUPPLIES—See Tables for Capacity of Tanks. Also Private Fire Plants.

WATER SYSTEMS—The first duty of an inspector is to find out the merit of the water supply available in case of fire, and if inadequate, lay out a private water supply to properly protect the property. See Water Mains.

WATER TABLE—A slight projection of the lower masonry or brickwork on the outside of a wall and reaching to a few feet above the ground surface.

WATER-TIGHT FLOORS should be required in all plants where a heavy water loss is possible to the lower floors. The use of scuppers for carrying off the water is recommended.

WATER TOWERS should be constructed so as to send a horizontal stream into a building at a height of 80 feet.

Sometimes they throw streams almost vertical, which are of no use.

WATER-TUBE BOILER—A boiler in which the water circulates in tubes, around which the heat and gases of combustion pass.

WATER VARNISHES—Gum lac dissolved in hot water and mixed with ammonia and borax.

WATT—See Electrical Terms; also Kilowatt.

WAX KETTLES should be steam-heated. If gas-heated, the kettle should be provided with a suitable water jacket.

WAX POLISH may be beeswax and turpentine.

WEATHER BOARDS—The boards nailed to vertical or inclined timbers at the sides of a building.

WEAVE—To unite, as threads of any kind, in such a manner as to form a texture; to entwine or interlace into a fabric.

WELD—To join two pieces of metal together by first softening them under the action of heat and then hammering them in contact with each other. See Oxy-acetylene Welding.

WELL HOLE—A larger opening than an ordinary light or ventilating shaft, piercing a series of floors for purposes of light and ventilation. Are dangerous features. Their large area makes all floors practically gallery floors, and fires quickly spread from floor to floor. See Shafts.

WHARF CLAUSE is attached to insurance policies when lines are to cover in storage, so that the assured is covered for ten days while the goods are on the wharf waiting assignment to a warehouse. See Piers.

WHEELWRIGHT—The hazards are those of small woodworkers and machine shops with painting.

WHITE LEAD is a compound consisting of carbonate of lead and hydrate of lead in chemical solution.

The Carter Process—Metallic lead is melted, and while molten is riven into fine particles, like flour, by a jet of high-pressure superheated steam. This amorphous powder, of a steel gray or dark blue color, is charged into a revolving cylinder 5 to 7 feet in diameter, by 8 x 12 feet long. One end of the cylinder is connected to an exhaust fan, and the other to a flue leading from a furnace where carbonic acid gas is generated from burning charcoal. Generally the products from combustion from a coke fire under a steam boiler of the plant are used for the corroding gas, the furnace gases having been washed and purified to free them from the sulphur present. The temperature of the revolving cylinder and the charge of powdered lead is kept at 140 deg. F. Diluted acetic acid and hot water is sprayed into the chamber at different times during the corroding process. The agitation is constant, as is also the heat. Balance of treatment, such as grinding, is the same as Dutch process. "Rustless Coatings; Corrosion and Electrolysis of Iron and Steel."—John Wiley & Sons, Inc., publishers.

Dutch Process—In this process thin perforated sheets of lead are exposed in gall pots containing a weak solution of acetic acid (water 2½ parts of strong acid) or common cider vinegar. The pots are placed in long tiers, each tier being loosely covered with boards and stacked in large numbers. The bed of pots is then imbedded in tan bark, sawdust, stable litter, etc., that ferments and soon raises the temperature of the mass to 140 to 165 deg. F. A quantity of vinegar containing 50 lbs. of strong acid converts two tons of lead into the carbonate of lead in about 100 days. The only attention the beds require during the process of corrosion is to control the temperature of the mass by regulating the admission of air to the interior of the bed by opening or closing the apertures left for that purpose. The corrosion is practically completed at the end of sixty days; but the lead is of light specific gravity, so it is the practice to allow the beds to remain 30 to 40 days longer, in which time the lead acquires a proper density. If the lead is allowed to remain in the bed too long, say 5 or 6 months, it is liable to become crystalline and transparent, and will be of poor covering power. Care is necessary in the use of stable litter to change the white carbonate of lead as it forms, into a dark sulphide of lead from the sulphurous hydrogen evolved during the process of decomposition of the manure.

At the time of stacking, the air in the beds contains 20 parts oxygen; after two weeks it contains only 17 parts; in five or six weeks 7 to 15 parts, while the carbonic acid element will have increased from 5/8 to 23 or 27 per cent. during the process of corrosion. (Note. I believe there is not enough oxygen and too much carbonic acid gas to support combustion. W. O. L.)

From 30 to 40 per cent of the lead remains unchanged, which is separated from the carbonate by passing contents of the pots through a series of rolls, beaters and screens. The corroded lead is then mixed with water and ground in burr stones to a powder. Generally this part of the process is omitted (by the quick process lead manufacturers) because of the fine state of division necessary to reduce the metal lead for these processes. The uncorroded particles are so intimately associated with the carbonate that they are indifferently eliminated in the separator and if run over the water stones, will cover the face of the stones with a coating of metallic lead that soon impairs the grinding power and imparts a dark color to the product.

After grinding, the mixed carbonate and water is mechanically floated to remove any coarse particles, then pumped to large settling tanks where it is double washed with pure soft water and bicarbonate of soda to remove any trace of acetic acid. When settled pumped to large copper drying pans and water evaporated. Drying requires 6 to 8 days, the temperature of the dry rooms being 140 to 165 deg. F. Then pulverized and marketed as dry white lead or ground in burr stones with linseed oil for a paste or paint.

A modification of the Dutch process, known as pulp lead, consists of taking the pulp lead from the settling tanks and placing same in a tank of linseed oil and subjecting the moisture to a high speed mechanical stirring for a number of hours. Some of the water rises to the top and is drawn off but a great part is whipped into the emulsion or forced into combination with the lead. Pulp lead is inferior.

All processes are detrimental to the health of the men owing to the gases evolved during the process. "Rustless Coatings; Corrosion and Electrolysis of Iron and Steel."—John Wiley & Sons, Inc., publishers.

WHITE LEAD, IMITATION—Made of lithopone, barytes, zinc oxide, linseed oil, fish oil, corn oil, tallow, water, whiting.

WHITE VITRIOL—Also known as zinc sulphate and is soluble in water.

WHITEWASH—Merely pure lime mixed with water and perhaps a little salt.

WHITING—Made from chalk which is ground in a chaser, settled in vats, cooked in water, dried and ground. Dry room hazard.

WIND—That the direction of the prevailing wind should be a factor in the underwriting of a fire insurance risk on account of the exposures is a fact not apt to be taken in consideration by the inexperienced. A building to windward of another, which is peculiarly liable to take fire, will be penalized less than one in the lee of the dangerous building.

WIND MILLS—The old style types are subject to a serious fire hazard due to the ignition of the wooden shafts, by reason of over-heated gearing caused by racing in a heavy wind.

WINDOW DECORATIONS have caused numerous fires, especially where gas lights are used. Highly inflammable material, such as tissue paper streamers, cotton wadding wrapped around strings, should not be permitted in windows, where gas is used. A draft of air may blow the material into the gas flame. Such materials should never be wrapped around electric light globes. Celluloid articles can be set on fire by heat radiated from lamps and sun's rays.

WINDOW PROTECTION—In the Alwyn Court apartment house fire, March 4, 1910, the fire burst through the windows at tenth floor and by means of thin glass windows at court gained access to floors above. Being out of reach of fire department hose streams, it was hard to combat. In fireproof buildings, the intense heat of burning material is projected through windows, and as smoke and flames curl upward from the top of the window it thus spreads to upper floors. Wired glass window protection is recommended. See Wired Glass.

WINDOWS—The different parts are sill, horizontal muntins, vertical muntins, transom bars, stop stile, upper rail, jamb, head and walling-in flange.

WINDOW SASH WEIGHTS are made from old tin cans which are placed in rotary furnaces and come out as molten metal; then cast into window sash weights. Foundry hazard. An unattractive class.

WINDOW SHADES—Factories are usually one long frame building without lights, and heated by steam from a boiler in a detached structure. The sheets of cotton or muslin are fastened to large swinging wood frames. The first day, the cloth is sized with thin glue. The following day, it is coated with paint reduced about two-thirds with benzine. Usually a nuisance to neighborhood. A bad fire record class.

WINE contains about 8 to 25 per cent. of alcohol. No explosive vapors generated in manufacturing or handling. Manufacturing is not hazardous. See Distilleries.

WIRE is covered with cotton thread by drawing the wire over a roller revolving in a trough of glue then thread twisted on, dried by passing over steam plate, and wound on reels. An automatic machine.

WIRE FABRIC—Fine wire fabric of copper or brass is made into mesh by spinning, weaving and carding, similar to the process of making yarn. Other hazards are plating, annealing, tempering and light metal working.

WIRE LATH—A fabric or mesh of wires used in furring in place of wood lath.

WIRE SPIRAL COLUMNS—Consist of a continuous spiral of wire held upright and spaced equidistant by vertical reinforcing and spacing bars. Used as concrete reinforcement.

WIRE TEMPERING—The wire is drawn through the flame of a coke furnace. As it emerges, it passes through a sand pit and is reeled up slowly for gradual cooling. It then passes through a lead bath and is reeled. The lead pot is coke-heated. This method is called lead tempering.

WIRE WORKS—Hazards are drawing, spinning, annealing and tempering, metal working and machine shops. Considered good insurance risks.

WIRED GLASS—Its value lies in the fact that when broken, the pieces do not fall apart. Should not be less than one-fourth inch thick with wire fabric not larger than seven-eighths inch and wire not smaller than 24 B. and S. gauge. Plate glass is better than thin glass. See Shutters.

WIRED GLASS WINDOWS (efficiency of)—As a fire retardant wired glass has two defects: First, it will not stand as high a temperature as is known to occur in some fires and under some conditions; and second, it radiates heat to such an extent that combustible material at a distance of six feet may be ignited on the side away from the fire, even when the glass remains intact. Fusing point of glass is about 2200 deg. F. See Window Protection.

WIRELESS TELEGRAPHY outfits require extreme care in wiring and grounding.

WOAD—A plant used in blue dye manufacturing.

WOMEN'S NAMES—See Names. See Moral Hazard.

WOOD (spontaneous combustion of)—When wood is exposed to the long continued action of heat, it undergoes progressive changes nearly akin to those which have taken place during the conversion of vegetation into coal. If the wood remains in contact with the heated surface for a considerable length of time, a temperature of a few degrees above the boiling point of water is enough to produce a semi-carbonized film. The wood will start smoldering at a very low temperature. The heat from an oil lamp or gas flame some distance away is sufficient to start the smoldering combustion. Even the temperature of a steam pipe has been found sufficient to cause ignition.—Frank R. Fairweather, in "Insurance Engineering."

WOOD ALCOHOL—Clear, colorless, obtained by dry distillation of wood. Flash, 45 deg. F. Classed as inflammable. See Alcohol.

WOOD DOORS TIN LINED—See Fire Doors.

WOOD-ENCLOSED STAIRS—See Stairs.

WOOD ENGRAVERS—Light woodworking hazard.

WOOD FENCE HAZARD—Boys with bonfires occasionally ignite fences, which in turn set fire to nearby property.

WOOD FINISH AND TRIM IN FIREPROOF BUILDINGS—Ex-Chief Croker of New York at the meeting of the International Municipal Congress, said: "If I had my way about it, I would not permit a piece of wood even the size of a lead pencil to be used in the construction of finish of any building in the United States exceeding a ground area of 25 by 50 feet, or three stories in height. If there was still an absolute necessity for its use, if we could find nothing to replace it, it would then be well to attempt to conceive of something better. I am opposed to the use of wood in any form in fireproof buildings, and the law ought not to permit its use. Wooden floors, wooden window frames, doors and casings burn, and trim and bases burn, everything that is made of wood burns and helps the fire to spread. Eliminate wood—remove the cause, and you have precluded the possibility of fires."

WOOD (fireproofing of)—Lumber is run into large steam cylinders and vacuum is used to draw out the air; then it is run into a solution of ammonia salts or alum, then to dry kiln. Inspect this class and write cautiously.

WOOD FIBRE—Called wood pulp. Shavings boiled in caustic soda then chloride of lime.

WOOD FLOORS—In fireproof buildings should be laid without air space, i. e., "cement and cinder fill" should be laid around the sleepers to the underpart of the floor boards.

WOOD FLOUR—Wood reduced to fine powder. Not hazardous and will not ignite spontaneously.

WOOD GAS—Obtained by the distillation of wood. Very inflammable.

WOOD HEEL MANUFACTURING—Process consists of woodworking, nailing, trimming, sandpapering and covering with leather or celluloid. Glue heating. Celluloid is worked in acetone. A poor fire record class.

WOOD NAPHTHA—See Wood Alcohol.

WOOD OIL—A drying oil similar to linseed oil, derived from the nut of the Chinese tree; sometimes called Tung Oil. Likely to cause spontaneous combustion.

WOOD PRESERVATIVES—In preserving wood, the following materials are generally used. Coal-tar creosote, hardwood tar, wood creosote, copperized oil, sodium silicate, biproduct zinc sulphate, zinc chloride, zinc sulphate, cresol calcium, sodium flouride; heavy coal-tar oils mixed with small percentage of linseed oil, and a trace of turpentine, then chlorinated; i. e., treated with chlorine. Oil preparations increase the inflammability of the wood. Inspect class. See Preservation of Timber.

WOOD PULLEYS IN ELEVATOR HEADS—See Pulleys. See Strut Boards.

WOOD PULP—Commonly called wood flour when in finely divided state.

WOOD SPIRITS—See Wood Alcohol.

WOODWORKING—See Cabinet Factories.

WOOL (green)—Wool which has been shipped promptly after shearing, instead of lying in storage, as is usually the case. It is slightly heavier and contains more moisture than that which has been allowed to take the customary course through the warehouse.

WOOL NOILS are the short fibres combed out of the long wool.

WOOL PULLERIES—The principal hazards are the dryers which should be of standard construction; dusters which should have blowers, and the sweat room. Fair insurance risks.

WOOLEN CLIPPINGS, if clean, are considered fairly good insurance risks.

WOOLEN PREPARATION MILLS—Wool is "scoured" (washed) to remove dirt, natural oil and grease in steam-heated vats with water and soap, then dried. Dryers are usually heated by air blown from steam coils. The wool is placed on a continuous wire belting which travels through the dry room. See Worsted Mills.

WOOLENS—If of good texture and of dark color, they are not readily damaged by fire and smoke. Clean water causes little damage if dried immediately. If in bolts (piece goods), considered good insurance.

WOOLEYS SOLVENT—A cleaning fluid, classed as kerosene.

WORKMEN'S OVERALLS—See Lockers.

WORK TABLES—See Cutting Tables.

WORSTED MILLS—Raw stock is green wool. Processes in the main consist of wool sorting, wool scouring,

Y

YARN—Woolen or other thread spun and prepared for weaving.

YEAST is a living plant used for the purpose of causing fermentation. The yeast we use in baking is artificial, composed of a dough made of flour and starch and a little common yeast made into small cakes and dried. It is necessary to add water to start the fermentation.

YEAST FACTORIES—The process consists of receiving, elevating, cleaning, malting, grinding, conveying, mashing, cooking and fermenting the grain. The scum (yeast) from the tops of fermenting tanks is removed, mixed with water and starch, filtered and then pressed into cakes. The hazards are those of breweries. See Vinegar Works.

YELLOW METAL—A kind of brass.

YELLOW WOOD—A hard wood of the dyers' mulberry tree. Used as a yellow dye in consequence of the large amount of tannic acid it contains.

YUCCA GRANCA—A wild grass of the Southwest, is now being used in paper-making.

Z

ZACATON—See Yucca Granca.

Z BAR—An iron or steel rail, shaped at end or cross-section like the letter "Z," except that angles are 45 degrees.

ZANTE—Used as yellow dye.

ZAPON LACQUER—Used for varnishing metal. It is a solution of gun cotton.

ZEA FIBRE—May be used in paper or cordage manufacturing.

ZERO—In Fahrenheit's scale, 32 degrees below freezing point of water. In Centigrade and Reaumur's scales, zero is the freezing point of water.

ZERO WEATHER—Always brings numerous claims for fires caused by overheating stoves or furnaces. See Coal Shortage.

ZINC—A bluish-white metal; is brittle when cold, but can be rolled into sheets when heated to a certain degree. Explosions in chemical risks are known to have been caused where zinc is dissolved in hydrochloric acid.

ZINC (resinate of)—Not permitted in listed storage stores on account of the fine state of division of the resin in the compound. It may be expected to heat and ignite spontaneously, if moist; similar to zinc dust.

ZINC CHLORIDE—The salt obtained by heating zinc in chlorine gas; a powerful dehydrant.

ZINC DROSS—A material skimmed from zinc; a by-product of galvanizing iron.

ZINC DUST—Consists chiefly of finely-divided metallic zinc. Subject to spontaneous combustion when wet. Classed as inflammable. Not permitted in stipulated stores.

ZINC ETCHING, up to a certain point, is quite similar to half-tone work, and is usually employed to reproduce pen sketches or designs which are photographed, as in half-tone process. In printing on the zinc plates from the negatives, however, no screen is used as in making half-tones. After the sensitized zinc plate has been printed from the negative it is "rolled up" or inked. The ink is then removed from all parts of the plate except those affected by the light. On these parts it remains and then the plate is rubbed with dragon's blood, which adheres to the ink portions only. The application of dragon's blood is frequently necessary to protect the parts of the plate which are not to be etched. After sufficient number of etchings, or "bites" as they are called, the plate is passed to the router.

ZINC ETHYL ignites in air of ordinary temperature.

ZINC FLUE DUST is sometimes similar to zinc dust.

ZINC METHYL is very volatile and takes fire in contact with air.

ZINC OXIDES—Prepared by burning zinc in atmosphere, air or by heating the carbonate to redness. To prepare zinc on a large scale, metallic zinc is volatilized in large earthen mufflers whence the zinc vapor passes into a small receiver where it comes in contact with a current of air and is oxidized. The zinc oxide thus formed passes immediately into a condensing chamber, divided into compartments with cloths. Then filtered, pressed, dried, ground and pulverized. Attrition mills, burr mills and ball mills are used for grinding. Considerable dust is generated in the process.

ZINC SMELTERS—Hazards similar to foundries. Furnaces resemble those used in glass works.

ZINC SULPHATE—See White Vitrol.

ZINKENITE—A mineral containing sulphur, lead, antimony and copper.

ZUMIC ACID—An acid discovered in vegetable substances which have fermented.

ZYMONE—The residue of the gluten of wheat after it has been treated with alcohol.

Finis.

MEMORANDA

$8.[illegible]

8.00 net

CPSIA information can be obtained at www.ICGtesting.com
Printed in the USA
BVOW07s0853100214

344472BV00013B/732/P